Demonic Spirits Destroying America

Can America Be Saved?

Dr. Ricky Roberts, PhD

Unless otherwise noted, the Scripture quotations are from The King James Version of the Bible.

Name: Dr. Ricky Roberts, PhD

Title: Demonic Spirits Destroying America/ By Dr. Ricky Roberts, PhD

Identifiers: Library of Congress Control Number: 2025925929

ISBN: Paperback   978-1-966382-54-6

     Hardcover 978-1-966382-58-4

     Ebook 978-1-966382-55-3

Subjects: 1. Religion/General

2. Religion/Christianity/Personal Growth

3. Religion/Christianity/General

Published by EA Books Publishing, a division of Living Parables of Central Florida, Inc. a 501c3

EABooksPublishing.com

τοῦ γνῶναι αὐτὸν

(Philippians 3:10)

ACKNOWLEDGMENTS

We acknowledge all those who have helped us in this endeavor, and we acknowledge all those who have prayed for me while I have researched the resources and material that are in the domain of this work. And we also thank those who helped in the proofreading of this manuscript.

CONTENTS

PREFACE

It has been some time since I wrote a new book. I last wrote a complete book for myself in AD 2005. I decided not to write a book again until I could well come against and conquer some obstacles that gravely beset me. The obstacles were great and mighty and could not be gone around or bypassed. I was utterly at a standstill from AD 2005 to AD 2017. Was it me? Was it the resources that I had access to that were failing me? What should I do? Should I just lay down and surrender? Or should I go through these obstacles, fighting step-by-step, and never surrender?

What were the obstacles? The obstacles can be a question of resources at best or a lack of resources at worst. I kept on facing difficulties in how the ancient church, the schoolmen, the reformers, the revivalists, like John Wesley and Peter Cartwright, and the early scholars could arrive at their conclusions in specific interpretations when I could not find evidence such findings were correct. The saints of old, the ancient church, and the reformers, who had God working through them, had something I did not have. Something was amiss in my life of study. Until I could figure out what was lacking, I would not write another book.

I continued to write sermons, write blogs, and study extensively. However, the obstacles preventing me from writing another book were those 300-pound gorillas in the room that I did not want to discuss. And the 300-pound gorillas made their presence known by pushing doubts upon me.

Still, I preached the gospel and never denied or rejected any of the fundamental doctrines of Christianity. While 50 percent of ministers reject, for example, the virgin birth, I held with a death grip unto the faith that bought me. Some doctrines were held on only by one string of hair. Doubts flooded my mind because of these obstacles that Satan had set before me. I have also learned that obstacles like these cannot be bypassed but must be pushed through and conquered. Honestly, these obstacles were brick walls I must go through somehow!

I was not a newbie to the study of ancient languages. I studied every Hebrew and Greek grammar of worth. I translated the Hebrew Old Testament, the Greek Old Testament, the Greek New Testament, the Vulgate, the writings of the Greek fathers, the writings of the Latin fathers, and the Greek and Latin authors.

I knew the grammar; the problem was not the grammar. As I finally saw, the Hebrew and Greek grammar taught in the AD 1500s, AD 1600s, AD 1700s, AD 1800s, AD 1900s, and AD 2000s were very little different in principle. How? I went after the older grammars and compared the older grammars to the more modern grammars.

(Sometimes, the search for knowledge will destroy you; for example, seeking after occultic powers. Other times, the lack of resources will ruin you. Sometimes, the more you know, the more dangerous it becomes; other times, the lack of resources becomes dangerous).

The great crisis became apparent in AD 2012 when I could not take hold of the correct meaning of two Hebrew verbs (everything terrible had to happen in AD 2012).

Something had to be done about this. For my sake, I know what early scholars have written about these two verbs. Still, the Hebrew lexicons of today rejected their conclusions. My conclusion was the following and was based on the resources that I had at hand:

> Consequently, after having continually read, re-read, and studied both Hebrew verbs and their use as having been established by modern Hebrew lexicons, I could come to no other outcome than that they are almost entirely synonymous (though the former is to us the stronger of the two) and that because they are mostly interchanged. (See Genesis 1:21, 25, 26–27).

Something seemed wrong with this conclusion. Something was amiss and just not right. And every book, author, scholar, and commentary following that type of conclusion followed the same wrong path I was following. Consequently, this conclusion only changed when a new light came onto the scene. And this new light came in when I read some of the older resources I possessed and their reference to older lexicons. I could find evidence to support my conclusions based on older lexicons. The finding of older lexicons was my V−8 moment! These lexicons were written during the Reformation, soon afterward, or written mainly before the turning of the AD 1800s.

This light shone into the darkness, and the darkness faded. From that time forward, I sought every resource that I could find. I researched the history of Hebrew and Greek lexicons and the history of the editions of the Hebrew Old Testament, the Greek Old Testament, and the Greek New Testament. I uncovered several ancient Hebrew and Greek lexicons. I was provided access to them, whether digitally, reprints, or original copies. I uncovered several ancient Hebrew and Greek grammars, whether digitally, reprints, or original copies.

Besides these two Hebrew verbs, there appeared other words that I could not grasp the correct meaning of, such as two Hebrew nouns, one Greek adjective, and one Greek noun. Like the two Hebrew verbs, these words were not well expounded in modern lexicons.

Somehow, modern Hebrew lexicons have changed the true significance of these two Hebrew verbs by weakening them so that both seem to mean the same thing. Further, I noticed, in many ways, that what was taught years ago had changed for some reason or another. I saw an undertow beneath the studies, works, and writings beginning in the AD 1800s. I discerned that what was taken as clear, indisputable interpretations were being changed, and the Hebrew and Greek words were being changed in meaning to suit these new interpretations.

Nowadays, it is easily seen that modern Hebrew and Greek scholars reject and deny the scholarship of other Hebrew and Greek scholars of past years. If we must choose, let us choose those scholars of yesterday!

It is also easily seen where Hebrew and Greek grammar seemed to be changed, or at least the perception and what both mean. What ancient scholars understood by grammar, now new scholars see the very opposite. This difference is more profound in Hebrew than in

Greek. Remember, it is the same grammar and the exact text. According to some, the grammar has changed overnight. Impossible! If ancient Hebrew scholars saw that grammar could allow an interpretation and, in numerous respects, demand that same interpretation, then what would happen? Some would demand that grammar be changed. Again, this is impossible!

We must remember that we can have the correct grammar but the wrong information. We can have the right information, but we have incorrect grammar. All interpretations may be grammatically correct, but they cannot be all informationally correct. A deficient knowledge of Hebrew and Greek is probably the most critical factor leading to a wrong misunderstanding of the Bible. This problem has continued to play a significant role even in our own time.

The last part of this preface will expound these words as they were expounded by the ancient lexicons, comparing them with modern ones. It is something that six words can almost shipwreck your pursuits in understanding the Word of God.

This undertow that I kept noticing was present and yet not present. It would appear and disappear as a cloud or mist amid my studies. It was difficult to nail it down. But this undertow was there all the same, especially in the late AD 1700s and AD 1800s.

This undertow had three sources (foundations): Higher Criticism, Unitarianism, and Gnosticism. One form of Gnosticism that appeared and reappears is Adoptionism.

What came forth from all this research was a new principle of research that I have followed to this day:

> To believe no man's mere claim or opinion; to depend on original authorities or copies of those original authorities; to look at every passage with my own eyes as possibly can be done and read it regarding its context; to pick out the simple fact noticed from the chaos of theories, and to accept as exact only what I can reason myself from the authorities and see to be the apparent meaning of the observation, absolutely undisturbed how each random theory might be affected or the firm authority of such or such a scholar stand or fall.

Higher Criticism

It is Liberal Theology that despises the spirituality of Scripture. It denounces such doctrines as those that deal with the origin of evil and sin, the fall of Satan, and many other fundamental doctrines of the Bible. This scheme of interpretation has, at its heart, a prejudice against the Word of God.

One of the highest forms of Liberal Theology is Higher Criticism. Higher Criticism is humanism disguised in theological or religious terms, which has, more than anything, weakened and almost destroyed the high view of the Bible previously held throughout the centuries.

Higher Criticism transformed into a rationalistic and anti-Christian crusade. Its aim and purpose, above all, were to eliminate God from the Bible and to destroy the doctrine of Christ's deity. Today, no one is left free from its influence. The universities are its chief seminaries; the pulpit has become its platform; the pulpit has significantly become dishonored by it, and the pulpit has tried to become of little worth and no genuine esteem. It has dramatically affected and corrupted a considerable portion of modern scholarship. There is minimal scholarship, which this system has not touched.

Indeed, Higher Criticism is a system that deceitfully inquiries into the nature, origin, and dates of the books of the Bible, as well as into the historical value and credibility of the statements they contain, with a bias against each book's authenticity. It is a system that proposes to disprove the Bible at all costs.

The term "Higher Criticism," as defined here, was first coined as such by Eichhorn, who lived from AD 1752 to AD 1827.

The time of the "age of reason" is best summed up by Charles Dickens in his work entitled *A Tale of Two Cities*: "It was the best of times, it was the worst of times...It was the season of light, it was the season of darkness, it was the spring of hope, it was the winter of despair."

The "age of reason" was, in essence, a revival of Satanic rationalism. Satanic Rationalism is the same thing as humanism. Both mean a system of belief and philosophy whereby man is considered the beginning, center, and end of all things. Man becomes a god. On the other hand, genuine Rationalism, as understood, means the power and ability to reason things out with God, which is not suggested by the "age of reason." The "age of reason" had no place for the God of the Bible nor any place for miracles.

Further, Higher Criticism dismissed the Old Testament as a storehouse of the crimes and obscenities in which God connived with the chosen people.

The indestructible sword, known as prophecy from the beginning of criticism against the Bible, had been used and had defeated all foes. Still, it was now ridiculed and knocked out of the Bible and the church.

In this "age of reason," no longer was there any reason for a man to serve faith, obey authority, and spend his life in preparation for the next world.

The thinkers of the "age of reason" believed in happiness and fulfillment in this world. This concept became the belief in a "Utopia" in this world. The thinkers of the "age of reason" regarded the mind and knowledge rather than grace and faith as the best source of guidance and were suspicious of emotion, myth, and supernaturalism.

The "age of reason" initiated the modern manifestations of the rebellion against God in such philosophies as Higher Criticism, Liberalism, Cults in every fashion imaginable, Atheism, Secularism, Modernism, and a host of other ills and Isms.

A summary of the beliefs, motives, and results of Higher Criticism

1. The leaders of Higher Criticism based their theories on their own personal and biased conclusions.

2. The German leaders of this movement were the greatest fancies of personal, biased, and subjective conjectures that one could conceive.

3. These men framed all of this into a supposed scientific, grammatical, and literary attack against the Bible.

4. The dominant men of the movement were men with a substantial prejudice against the supernatural.

5. They denounced all miracles, the existence of angels and demons, and prophecy.

6. They had no faith in the God of the Bible.

7. They have not investigated the Scriptures to confirm their faith and help believers understand the Bible.

8. They denied the reality of revelation as believed universally by the ancient church.

9. They based all their theories on the assumption that the Scriptures are false.

10. They denied the inspiration of the Bible.

11. They were humanists dressed up in a Christian dress.

12. Their philosophy was paganism in Christian terminology.

13. They were men of compromise.

14. They denounced systematic theology.

15. They rejected a final authority for faith, life, and practice.

16. They deified reason.

17. They accepted the theory of evolution against the Bible.

18. Likewise, they applied the theory of evolution to literature and religion.

19. They saw the Bible only as a natural book and not a supernatural work written upon the very inspiration of God.

20. Not only that, but they rejected the historic faith of Christianity and claimed victory after victory.

21. They attempted at every point to disprove everything about the Bible and throw doubts on it all.

22. They rejected any system that would promote belief.

23. Likewise, they undermined men's faith without denying it themselves openly.

24. It is these men and others who opposed and fought against God and tried to destroy that which God stands for that are the ruin and utter downfall of all nations and countries.

25. They stated that the Old Testament Canon was not completed until about 100 BC.

26. They stated the books were written from 900 to 450 BC.

Keys to Recognizing Higher Criticism in Studies

1. Study how 1 Timothy 3:16 is translated.

2. Study how Isaiah 7:14 is translated.

3. Study how 1 John 5:7 is handled.

4. Study how the writer, author, or scholar deals with Genesis and Daniel.

5. Study how the writer, author, or scholar deals with the inspiration and authenticity of the Bible.

6. Study how the writer, author, or scholar deals with the fundamental doctrines of Christianity.

7. Study how the writer, author, or scholar deals with the overall editions of the Hebrew Old Testament, Greek New Testament, and the Greek Old Testament.

Higher Criticism and all its theories failed. Why?

1. The theories were born in an age of ignorance regarding ancient civilizations.

2. The critics attempted a literary analysis when they knew nothing of early writing methods.

3. The majority assumed that writing was not in use in the days of the patriarchs or before when the opposite had so quickly proven otherwise.

4. The Higher Critics built theories not upon real source documents but upon documents of their imaginations or mythical documents

and mythical writers who were not eyewitnesses to the events of the Bible. All this is in the minds and imaginations of the Higher Critics.

5.   The concept demanded to be accepted by Higher Criticism takes more faith to believe in than to believe in God and that the Bible is the inspired Word of God.

6.   The system of Higher Criticism hates the supernatural and the concept of miracles. Yet, the very idea theorized by the Higher Critics demands a miracle to be the truth.

7.   The advent of archaeology has blown all their theories to dust.

8.   The advent of science in recent years has, in connection with archaeology, blown all their theories to dust.

9.   The whole reasoning process is flawed.

Bishop Ridley said it the best:

> Whosoever loves their country in truth (that is to say, in God), they will always judge if at any time the laws of God and man be then contrary to the other, that a man ought rather to obey God than man (Acts 4). And they that think otherwise, and pretend a love to their country forasmuch as they make their country to fight as it were against God, in whom consisteth the only stay of their country, surely I do think that such are to be judged more deadly enemies and traitors of their countries. For they that fight against God, which is the safety of their country, what do they else but go about to bring upon their country a present ruin and destruction.[1]

Gnosticism

In the ancient church, a wave of heathenism spread throughout Christendom, known as Gnosticism. From the very beginning of Christianity, there was an antitype of Christianity present. The antitype of Christianity, which was and is a heresy, was and is known as Gnosticism.

The best definition of Gnosticism is that it is a belief and religious system that exalts knowledge and revelation over grace and faith as the key to one's salvation and incorporates numerous philosophies into itself, especially heathenism, exalting heathenism above all. Gnosticism consists of Oriental mysticism, Greek philosophy, Alexander, Platonist, Kabbalistic Judaism, and other heathen philosophies combined with a perverted Christian thought. Gnosticism also taught that it was impossible to grasp knowledge about God through the mind, understanding, and reason and that proper knowledge can only come through the spirit (or spiritual means).

This belief system destroys the need for the Bible and makes each person his own god (as it can be said), for the final authority becomes each person rather than the Scriptures themselves. Undeniably, the Gnostics had several schemes of redemption, having day-by-day new spiritual revelations that contradicted the Word of God and a knowledge thought of as perfect redemption. The hatred of Gnostics to that of anything of matter or anything of the senses leads them to deny that genuine divine knowledge could come through physical means and be in a written form. To them, the Word of God is nothing more than whatever they make it to be.

Gnosticism is another form of heathenism and is connected to all other forms of philosophies that are anti-god and Antichrist. For all of them come from the same source—Satan.

Today, Gnosticism has become the norm in Christian circles regarding morality. Its influence is present in our studies, teaching, Christian colleges, and texts. Its influence touches our view about God, angels, demons, whether Christians can be demon possessed, can light and darkness indwell the same person, our prayers, our understanding of faith, many of our fundamental doctrines, and finally, our understanding of what being saved means (the Gnostics ultimately denied that we can truly be saved).

Further, Gnosticism touches our view of sexuality, homosexuality, and all other sexual perversions and our view as a Christian upon such subjects.

It is wise for anyone who wants to study the Word of God to search the history and beliefs of Gnosticism and other heresies and see how these ancient heresies come back and forth from time to time and infect the Christian body.

Unitarianism

Unitarianism is a modern revival of the ancient heresy known as Arianism.

Unitarianism, like Arianism, denies the full deity of Jesus Christ and makes the claim that Jesus Christ is simply a created being and not God Himself. Unitarianism is a system that completely denies the biblical doctrine of the Trinity.

By the middle of AD 1700s and the early AD 1800s, Unitarianism infected numerous universities, churches, societies, and denominations. For example, by AD 1831, the British and Foreign Bible Society was inflicted with Unitarianism. That same year, an attempt was made to adopt a Trinitarian policy "to ensure that Unitarians denying the Deity of the Lord Jesus Christ could not be admitted to membership or hold office in the Society."[2] After a debate, the motion was rejected by a large majority of them. Because of this, the Trinitarian Bible Society was formed on December 7, AD 1831. The men who formed this society were concerned about doctrinal purity. There cannot be any doubt that Unitarianism gained much acceptance in the early part of the nineteenth century. The old heresies of the church are recycled with new names.

As time continued in the nineteenth century, many Unitarians in England were seen to accept many other heretical doctrines. Many rejected the infallible inspiration of Scripture; they further denied the fallen nature of man and continued trying, step-by-step, to destroy the fundamental doctrines of Christianity.

For Unitarians to attempt to destroy the infallible inspiration of Scripture, they had to lead or head up some societies or teams working on the Bible, its manuscripts, its translations, its editions, and its lexicons. Unitarianism, therefore, became a foundational influence on modern textual criticism in the AD 1800s and AD 1900s.

Many of the prominent early textual critics were Unitarians, including Johann Wettstein (AD 1693–1754), Alexander Geddes (AD 1737–1802), Edward Harwood (AD 1729–1794), George Vance Smith

(AD 1816–1902), Ezra Abbot (AD 1819–1884), Joseph Henry Thayer (AD 1828–1901), and Caspar Rene Gregory (AD 1846–1917). Others, such as Johann Griesbach, though not Unitarian, were modernists who denied the deity of Christ.

Many Unitarians loved the critical editions of the Greek New Testament. This general view of favoring the critical editions of the Greek New Testament began in the days of German modernist Johann Griesbach onward.

Johann Griesbach made textual changes that Bible believers roundly condemned. Griesbach was long and severely attacked by Trinitarian writers as being opposed to the doctrine of Christ's deity, primarily because he rejected 1 John 5:7[3] and for his rejection of the Greek noun θέος (God) in 1 Timothy 3:16.[4] He purposed to try his best to deprive proof texts showing the deity of Jesus Christ. There cannot be any doubt about this since I have read his notes in his books.

Bible believers of that day understood that these textual changes were severe doctrinal issues. Today, evangelicals and fundamentalists are expected to claim that such textual changes are inconsequential and have no doctrinal significance.

Another example, Wettstein was a textual scholar who collated manuscripts and published *Greek New Testaments* in AD 1730 and AD 1751–52.

Wettstein identified over 200 manuscripts, classifying them as uncial, minuscules, and lectionaries. His system of identifying manuscripts, designating uncial by capital letters and minuscules by Arabic numerals, held sway until Caspar Gregory modified it into its modern form.

In his massive work on the Greek New Testament, Wettstein retained the Receive Text. Still, his notes were heretical in various respects. In specific passages, he firmly denied the full deity of Jesus Christ. This is seen in his notes on 1 Timothy 3:16 and 1 John 5:7.[5] By doing this, it was proven that he had been holding heretical views for years.

His great work on the Greek New Testament supported heretical views and tried to weaken the doctrine of Christ's deity. Some have even said that he re-introduced doctrinal errors or mistakes made by heretics in the third and fourth centuries.

Even the Hebrew and Greek lexicons were affected by Unitarianism in the AD 1800s. For instance, Baker Book House put a warning about *Thayer's Lexicon*, which was a translation of Wilibald Grimm's *Clavis Novi Testamenti*:

> A word of caution is necessary. Thayer was a Unitarian, and the errors of this sect occasionally come through... The reader should be alert for both subtle and blatant denials of such doctrines as the Trinity (Thayer regarded Christ as a mere man and the Holy Spirit as an impersonal force)...and Biblical inerrancy.[6]

Both Crimm and Thayer are responsible for what is said in the quotation that I am about to give. Crimm is accountable for the overall words, but Thayer is responsible for what was inserted in square brackets. We should take notice of what is said about Christ under the Greek noun θέος (God):

> Whether Christ is called God must be determined from Jn. i. 1; xx. 28 ; I Jn. v. 20; Ro. ix. 5; Tit. ii. 13; Heb. i. 8 sq., etc.; the matter is still in dispute among theologians; cf. Grimm, Institutio theologiae dogmaticae, ed. 2, p. 228 sqq. [and the discussion (on Ro. ix. 5) by Professors Dwight and Abbot in Journ. Soc. Bib. Lit. etc. u. s., esp. pp. 42 sqq. 113 sqq.][7]

Behind the editions of the critical Greek text, like Westcott and Hort, and others, stands Unitarian's influence and the influence of Gnosticism, that of Adoptionism. The deletion of the Greek noun θέος (God) in 1 Timothy 3:16 and the deletion of 1 John 5:7 are clear examples. More than 90% of the evidence points to the necessity of keeping the Greek word θέος (God) in 1 Timothy 3:16. And the deletion of 1 John 5:7 altogether destroys Greek grammar there. And if John did not know his grammar, this was the only place.

These men were set up to develop editions of the Greek New Testament, with a few manuscripts, less than seventy, while rejecting most of the manuscripts. Another thing, they forgot that all editions of the Greek New Testament should be formed by studying the Greek manuscripts, the ancient translations, the writings of the church fathers, and finally, the lectionaries–these are Psalms and other readings pulled from Holy Scripture and authorized for public worship.

And as concerning the omission of the Johannine Comma, "ἐν τῷ οὐρανῷ, ὁ πατήρ, ὁ λόγος, καὶ τὸ Ἅγιον Πνεῦμα· καὶ οὗτοι οἱ τρεῖς ἕν εἰσιν" (in the heaven, the Father, the Word, and the Holy Ghost: and these three are one), Greek grammar is undone or destroyed. It is horrible Greek grammar. The words "Spirit," "Water," and "Blood" are all neuters, yet they are treated as masculine in verse 8. This interpretation of Greek grammar makes no sense if the Johannine Comma is omitted. But it makes perfect sense if the Johannine Comma is retained.

The masculine nouns "Father" and "Word" in verse 7 control the gender in the succeeding verse because of attraction. It is striking that although Spirit, water, and blood are all neuter nouns in Greek, they are introduced by a clause expressed in the masculine plural. The words 'that one' in verse 8 have no antecedent if verse 7 is omitted.

Modern textual critics have treated the grammatical argument lightly. Still, Gregory Nazianzus, the fourth century father of the church, understood its importance.[8]

Indeed, Theodore Beza, in his editions, defended the reading, "God was manifest in the flesh" in 1 Timothy 3:16. He said, "Vetus interpres pro θεός legit ὅ, ut qui conuererit quod manifestatum est in carne...Verum repugnat perpetuo consensu omnes Greci condices et (ut mox dicemus) res ipsa poslutat ut de ipsa Christi persona hoc accipiamus (The old interpreter, Erasmus, reads ὅ instead of θεός, so that he may modify the text as *who was manifest in the flesh*.... In truth, this modification is perpetually incompatible with the consensus of all the Greek codices, and (as we may soon say) this matter itself, among the Greek codices, demands that we must receive their conclusion about the very person of Christ).[9] Concerning 1 John 5:7, Beza said, "Hic versiculus omnino mihil retinendus videtur, (This verse, it seems to me, must entirely be preserved).[10]

Therefore, in my humble opinion, it is highly sacrilege to reject 1 John 5:7. It must be kept!

1 John 5:7 has thousands of witnesses in Old Latin preserved from as early as AD 157. It is cited by Tertullian [AD 200], Cyprian [AD 250], Priscillian [AD 350], Athanasius [AD 350], Council of Carthage [AD 415]; plus it is found in the following MSS and codices: Speculum [AD 550], Wianburgensis [AD 750], Greek minuscule MS. 88 [AD 1150], Waldensian Bibles [AD 1200–1400] and Greek MS. 61 [AD 1500].

Further, the editions of the Greek New Testament, beginning in the later part of the AD 1700s and the AD 1800s, attempt to divide or separate Jesus from Christ or Christ from Jesus. There is a slight reduction or weakening of the deity of Christ in these modern editions of the Greek New Testament.

Again, we should notice just how slight the differences are between the modern editions of the Greek New Testament and the ancient editions of the Greek New Testament. Almost all the modern English translations of the New Testament are based upon editions of the Greek New Testament, which Unitarianism and Gnosticism have influenced. For example, the Greek noun Χρίστος (Christ) is found only 427 times in Westcott and Hort's Edition of the Greek New Testament; in the Edition of Robert Stephanus, the Greek noun Χρίστος (Christ) is found 462 in AD 1550 Edition of the Greek New Testament. Why the change?

1 John 4:3 should read something like the *King James Version* has it, "And every spirit that confesseth not that Jesus Christ is come in the flesh is not of God: and this is that spirit of Antichrist, whereof ye have heard that it should come; and even now already is it in the world."

The King James Version's translation of this verse was based upon the *AD 1550 Edition of the Greek New Testament* by Robert Stephanus, as found in the *AD 1589* and *AD 1598 Editions of the Greek New Testament* by Theodore Beza.

The AD 1550 Edition of the Greek New Testament by Robert Stepehnus reads, "καὶ πᾶν πνεῦμα ὃ μὴ ὁμολογεῖ τὸν Ἰησοῦν Χριστὸν ἐν σαρκὶ ἐληλυθότα ἐκ τοῦ θεοῦ οὐκ ἔστιν· καὶ τοῦτό ἐστιν τὸ τοῦ ἀντιχρίστου ὃ ἀκηκόατε ὅτι ἔρχεται καὶ νῦν ἐν τῷ κόσμῳ ἐστὶν ἤδη" (1 John 4:3).

Many other editions, even some of the modern editions, have followed suit in following this reading.

The AD 1550 Edition of the Greek New Testament became the standard text. Walton, the publisher and printer of the AD 1657 Walton's Polyglot, held that the common readings must be retained at all possible in the editions of the *Greek New Testament*. He wrote,

> Though we grant, that variant Readings may be sometimes gathered out of Translations, yet we do not infer, nor doth it presently follow, that the present Reading is corrupt or false or must forthwith be corrected by the Translation. For though there were some difference in the Copies, yet it may be, the reading of present copies is the better, and therefore is not to be altered. Nay it is acknowledged and asserted in the Prolegomena, that the present reading being in possession of its authority ought not to be altered, though other Copies have formerly read otherwise, unless it can be evidently and clearly that some fault is crept into the present reading, and that we ought not to depart from the usual Reading upon mere conjectures, unless evident necessity require.[11]

Further, he wrote:

> By all that it appears, that the Prolegomena do not equal the Translation with the Text, or make this one end of Translation, thereby to correct the Text, or as is invidiously, to correct the Text—to correct the Word of God. For though it be affirmed, that in some cases various Readings may be gathered out of Translation, yet there is more to be considered, before any change may be made of the present reading, for it must first be proved that the present reading contains something false absurd, and cannot possibly stand, and then which other things are to be considered, besides the bare reading of a Translation, antecedents and consequents, the analogy of faith, collections of like places, the Commentaries of ancient Writers of the church, comparing of other Copies, wherein also respect to be had to, the antiquity, multitude and goodness of the copies in the care and exactness of the Scribe, as appears by the rules given about various readings' Proleg 6 Sect..6....That it is not for ever private man to alter anything in the received reading,

though he seem to have never so strong reasons, but the public authority of the Church, either express or implicit is necessary...that in correcting the original, we must take the consent of the guides of the Church, how truly let any man judge by what we have said......What is known and consent to be the Word of God, it must be madness and impiety in any to go about to correct it. . . .[12]

Notice the difference between the *AD 1550 Edition of the Greek New Testament* by Robert Stephanus and some modern editions of the *Greek New Testament* beginning after the AD 1750s and coming to its fulfillment in AD 1881 and after that, about 1 John 4:3:

Griesbach's edition of the Greek New Testament (AD 1806) reads, Καὶ πᾶν πνεῦμα ὃ μὴ ὁμολογεῖ τὸν Ἰησοῦν, ἐκ τοῦ θεοῦ οὐκ ἔστι· καὶ τοῦτό ἐστι τὸ τοῦ ἀντιχρίστου, ὃ ἀκηκόατε ὅτι ἔρχεται, καὶ νῦν ἐν τῷ κόσμῳ ἐστὶν ἤδη.

Tregelles' Edition of the Greek New Testament (AD 1857) reads, Καὶ πᾶν πνεῦμα ὃ μὴ ὁμολογεῖ τὸν Ἰησοῦν, ἐκ τοῦ θεοῦ οὐκ ἔστι· καὶ τοῦτό ἐστι τὸ τοῦ ἀντιχρίστου, ὃ ἀκηκόατε ὅτι ἔρχεται, καὶ νῦν ἐν τῷ κόσμῳ ἐστὶν ἤδη.

Tischendorf's Seventh (AD 1859) and *Eighth* (AD 1869) Editions read, καὶ πᾶν πνεῦμα ὃ μὴ ὁμολογεῖ τὸν Ἰησοῦν ἐκ τοῦ θεοῦ οὐκ ἔστιν· καὶ τοῦτό ἐστιν τὸ τοῦ ἀντιχρίστου, ὃ ἀκηκόατε ὅτι ἔρχεται, καὶ νῦν ἐν τῷ κόσμῳ ἐστὶν ἤδη.

Westcott and Hort's Edition of the Greek New Testament (AD 1881) reads, καὶ πᾶν πνεῦμα ὃ μὴ ὁμολογεῖ τὸν Ἰησοῦν ἐκ τοῦ θεοῦ οὐκ ἔστιν· καὶ τοῦτό ἐστι τὸ τοῦ ἀντιχρίστου ὃ ἀκηκόατε ὅτι ἔρχεται καὶ νῦν ἐν τῷ κόσμῳ ἐστὶν ἤδη.

The Nestle-Aland Editions (AD 1993 and AD 2012) of the *Greek New Testament* read, καὶ πᾶν πνεῦμα ὃ μὴ ὁμολογεῖ τὸν Ἰησοῦν ἐκ τοῦ θεοῦ οὐκ ἔστιν· καὶ τοῦτό ἐστιν τὸ τοῦ ἀντιχρίστου, ὃ ἀκηκόατε ὅτι ἔρχεται, καὶ νῦν ἐν τῷ κόσμῳ ἐστὶν ἤδη.

This is a slight attempt to weaken the deity of Christ and another effort to divide Jesus from the Christ and show that Jesus is not the

Christ. How? They believe Jesus became the Christ by having the Christ consciousness fall upon Him. If Jesus took upon Himself the Christ consciousness, then it is possible, in this way of thinking, for all of us to become gods. Christ never became a god; He was and is from age to age God!

While scholars and others have no fear in touching the living Word of God, I remember pretty well these words, "For I testify unto every man that heareth the words of the prophecy of this book, If any man shall add unto these things, God shall add unto him the plagues that are written in this book: And if any man shall take away from the words of the book of this prophecy, God shall take away his part out of the book of life, and out of the Holy City, and from the things which are written in this book" (Revelation 22:21). This prophecy is placed as a curse on anyone, adding or removing the words from the Book of Revelation. Also, it must be placed as curses over anyone, adding to or removing words from the Bible. As said before, I agree with Walton. We should follow the common reading of the Bible as closely as possible, particularly those readings in the Hebrew Old Testament, Greek New Testament, and Greek Old Testament.

The Edition of the Greek New Testament by B.F. Westcott and F.J.A. Hort in AD 1881 may be the criminal in this web of deception and the foundation of numerous scholars and believers rejecting the Divine Inspiration of the New Testament.

B.F. Westcott and F.J.A. Hort were determined to replace the *Received Greek Text* (Textus Receptus) with a new version of the Greek New Testament, based almost wholly under the Alexandrian family of manuscripts, only depending upon less than seventy manuscripts out of over 5,000. Further, they called the *Textus Receptus* (the Received Text) "the Vile Textus Receptus."[13] According to their own words, they were practicing occultists.[14] That they practiced necromancing cannot be denied.

Hort rejected absolute infallibility in the autographs of the New Testament.[15] He held an ancient heresy known as Universalism and denied everlasting punishment in the Lake of Fire.[16] He also spoke of Christ's Atonement like this, "Certainly nothing can be more unscriptural than the modern limiting of Christ's bearing our sins and sufferings to His death; but indeed that is only one aspect of an almost universal heresy."[17] Here is utter heresy!

And Hort was a believer in the doctrine of purgatory, "I agree with you in thinking it a pity that Maurice verbally repudiates purgatory, but I fully and unwaveringly agree with him in the three cardinal points of the controversy: (1) that eternity is independent of duration; (2) that the power of repentance is not limited to this life; (3) that it is not revealed whether or not all will ultimately repent. The modern denial of the second has, I suppose, had more to do with the despiritualizing of theology then almost anything that could be named."[18] Hort said, "Evangelicals seem to me perverted rather than untrue. There are, I fear, still more serious differences between us on the subject of authority, especially the authority of the Bible."[19]

Both men leaned toward Catholicism rather than the spirit of the Reformation.[20]

Westcott wrote about the first three chapters of Genesis, "No one now, I suppose, holds that the first three chapters of Genesis, for example, give a literal history-I could never understand how any one reading them with open eyes could think they did-yet they disclose to us a Gospel."[21] He said, "I reject the word infallibility of Holy Scriptures overwhelmingly."[22] In his *Greek Text with Introduction and Notes*, he speaks of Christians becoming the Christs, which is the belief in occultism.[23]

As pertaining to the deity of Christ, I have read many of Westcott's works; he speaks the speech about the orthodox view of Jesus Christ in most places, but writing the right view does not mean that a person believes it. I have noticed that he sometimes uses "divinity" rather than deity. Divinity, now, does not mean the same thing as a deity; it makes Jesus less than God, an exalted creature, or a demi-god, but not God who has no beginning or ending. Hence, there is a hint here and there about what he thinks about Christ. For example, Westcott wrote about Christ, "He never speaks of Himself directly as God, but His revelation aimed to lead men to see God in Him."[24] And he wrote, "(John) does not expressly affirm the identification of the Word with Jesus Christ."[25] In his same work, he questions the pre-existence of Jesus Christ, denies that God the Father and Jesus Christ are equal in power as pertaining to deity, and sees Jesus Christ as in absolute union with God only rather than being God Himself.[26]

Westcott and Hort follow the orthodox view in some statements while others follow a heretic view. In some cases, they are downright vague in their conclusions; in other places, their heretical views are seen. That they both sought to communicate with spirits by practicing necromancing shows their spiritual state more than anything else. We should run from such people rather than honor them!

The Life and Letters of Westcott and Hort reveal the mindset and malice of these two Anglican men who despised the doctrine of the divine inspiration of Scripture. Such hatred is seen for the Word of God in their readings! However, there is no evidence of an attempt to corrupt the Scriptures on the part of Erasmus, Stephanus, Beza, and the Elzivir Brothers, for instance.

From the *Received Text of the Greek New Testament* came many other translations of the Bible: The Swiss Version (AD 1529), LeFevre's (French) Bible (AD 1534), the Olivetan (French) Bible (AD 1558), de Reyna's (Spanish) Bible (AD 1569), the Czech Version (AD 1602), and Diodati's (Italian) Bible (AD 1607). English Bibles translated from the Greek Text of Erasmus, Robert Stephanus, and Theodore Beza include the Tyndale Bible (AD 1534), the Coverdale Bible (AD 1535), the Matthew's Bible (AD 1537), the Great Bible (AD 1539), the Geneva Bible (AD 1560), the Bishop's Bible (AD 1568), and the King James Version. By AD 1550, English Bibles were using the AD 1550 Edition of the Greek New Testament by Robert Stephanus.

The Hebrew and Greek Words

I cannot help but begin this section with the Song of Solomon 2:15. We read, "Take us the foxes, the little foxes, that spoil the vines: for our vines have tender grapes." This simple verse teaches us that the little foxes (little things) can often ruin or destroy the big and important things in life. It is not necessarily the big things but the small, little things that begin us on a downward spiral into destruction.

I accept Hebrew and Greek scholarships. How can I not? I have studied languages for over thirty years. But I can now discard or dispose of the little foxes, which have found their way in both Hebrew and Greek scholarship. We must identify these little foxes. The little foxes are not so much the people or persons that I am speaking about, but they are deception and error. Deception and error never come complete, but they come step-by-step and piece by piece.

When dealing with deception and error, I cannot but be reminded of what Irenaeus, second century and third century father, warned various years ago in his work on heresies. He wrote in his preface what all should be concerned about and what all should know about deception and error:

Ἐπεὶ τὴν ἀλήθειαν παραπεμπόμενοί τινες, ἐπεισάγουσι λόγους ψευδεῖς καὶ γενεαλογίας ματαίας, αἵτινες ζητήσεις μᾶλλον παρέχουσι, καθὼς ὁ Ἀπόστολός φησιν, ἢ οἰκοδομὴν Θεοῦ τὴν ἐν πίστει· καὶ διὰ τῆς πανούργως συγκεκροτημένης πιθανότητος παράγουσι τὸν νοῦν τῶν ἀπειροτέρων, καὶ αἰχμαλωτίζουσιν αὐτούς, ῥᾳδιουργοῦντες τὰ λόγια Κυρίου, ἐξηγηταὶ κακοὶ τῶν καλῶς εἰρημένων γινόμενοι· καὶ πολλοὺς ἀνατρέπουσιν, ἀπάγοντες αὐτοὺς προφάσει γνώσεως ἀπὸ τοῦ τόδε τὸ πᾶν συστησαμένου καὶ κεκοσμηκότος, ὡς ὑψηλότερόν τι καὶ μεῖζον ἔχοντες ἐπιδεῖξαι τοῦ τὸν οὐρανὸν, καὶ τὴν γῆν, καὶ πάντα τὰ ἐν αὐτοῖς πεποιηκότος Θεοῦ· πιθανῶς μὲν ἐπαγόμενοι διὰ λόγων τέχνης τοὺς ἀκεραίους εἰς τὸν τοῦ ζητεῖν τρόπον, ἀπιθάνως δὲ ἀπολλύντες αὐτοὺς ἐν τῷ βλάσφημον καὶ ἀσεβῆ τὴν γνώμην αἰτῶν κατασκευάζειν εἰς τὸν Δημιουργὸν, μηδὲ ἐν τῷ διακρίνειν δυναμένων τὸ ψεῦδος ἀπὸ τοῦ ἀληθοῦς· ἡ γὰρ πλάνη καθ᾽ αὐτὴν μὲν οὐκ ἐπιδείκνυται, ἵνα μὴ γυμνωθεῖσα γένηται κατάφωρος· πιθανῷ δὲ περιβλήματι πανούργως κοσμουμένη, καὶ αὐτῆς τῆς ἀληθείας ἀληθεστέραν ἑαυτὴν παρέχειν [l. παρέχει] φαίνεσθαι διὰ τῆς ἔξωθεν φαντασίας τοῖς ἀπειροτέροις· καθὼς ὑπὸ τοῦ κρείττονος ἡμῶν εἴρηται ἐπὶ τῶν τοιούτων, ὅτι λίθον τὸν τίμιον σμάραγδον ὄντα, καὶ πολυτίμητόν τισιν, ὕαλος ἐνυβρίζει διὰ τέχνης παρομοιουμένη, ὁπόταν μὴ παρῇ ὁ σθένων δοκιμάσαι, καὶ τέχνῃ [Int. τέχνην] διελέγξαι τὴν πανούργως γενομένην· ὅταν δὲ ἐπιμιγῇ ὁ χαλκὸς εἰς τὸν ἄργυρον, τίς εὐκόλως δυνήσεται τοῦτον ἀκεραίως [Int. ἀκέραιος ὤν] δοκιμάσαι; ἵνα οὖν μὴ παρὰ τὴν ἡμετέραν αἰτίαν συναρπάζωνταί τινες, ὡς πρόβατα ὑπὸ λύκων, ἀγνοοῦντες αὐτοὺς διὰ τὴν ἔξωθεν τῆς προβατείου δορᾶς ἐπιβουλήν, οὓς φυλάσσειν παρήγγελκεν ἡμῖν Κύριος, ὅμοια μὲν λαλοῦντας, ἀνόμοια δὲ φρονοῦντας, ἀναγκαῖον ἡγησάμην, ἐντυχὼν τοῖς ὑπομνήμασι τῶν, ὡς αὐτοὶ λέγουσιν, Οὐαλεντίνου μαθητῶν, ἐνίοις δ' αὐτῶν καὶ συμβαλὼν, καὶ καταλαβόμενος τὴν γνώμην αὐτῶν, μηνύσαι σοι, ἀγαπητέ, τὰ τερατώδη καὶ βαθέα μυστήρια, ἃ οὐ πάντες χωροῦσιν, ἐπεὶ μὴ πάντες τὸν ἐγκέφαλον ἐξεπτύκασιν, ὅπως καὶ σὺ μαθὼν αὐτὰ, πᾶσι τοῖς μετά σου φανερὰ ποιήσῃς, καὶ παραινέσῃς αὐτοῖς φυλάξασθαι τὸν βυθὸν τῆς ἀνοίας, καὶ τῆς εἰς Χριστὸν [Int. Θεὸν] βλασφημίας. Καὶ, καθὼς δύναμις ἡμῖν, τήν τε γνώμην αὐτῶν τῶν νῦν παραδιδασκόντων (Whereas certain persons are giving up the truth and are introducing lying words and "endless genealogies which," as the apostle says, "furnish matter for disputes rather than the edification of God, which is in faith" 1 Timothy 1:4), and by means of their cleverly hammered together persuasiveness, they lead away the minds of the simple-persons and take them captive. These men tamper with the oracles of the Lord, and become wicked interpreters of those words, which had been proclaimed very well. And they overturn the faith of many by means of leading them away from that faith, under a pretext of superior knowledge, from Him who framed and set in order this whole universe; just as if they had something more excellent and more extraordinary to show convincingly than God, who created out of nothing the heaven and the earth, and all things that are in them. Persuasively, through words of devilish cunning, they draw the simple-minded persons to investigate into the manner of their religious system; in addition, they crudely destroy them by making their own blasphemous and godless opinion regarding the Demiurge (creator), and these simple-minded persons do not have the ability to determine the falsehood from the truth in any matter.

2. For error is never displayed as itself, lest it being stripped naked, it might become instantly detected. But it being cunningly dressed out as in an elegant dress so that it would appear by its outside pomp to the more simple-minded persons truer than the truth itself. As it has been said of such persons by a much superior man than we are, that the

precious stone being the emerald, and that stone, which is most highly esteemed by some persons, is insulted by imitation in glass through skillful handiwork whenever the man who has the ability to prove and detect the skillful handiwork so deceitfully manufactured may not be present to show it as a counterfeit. Now, again, whenever brass may be intermixed into silver, what simple person shall easily be able to scrutinize it? So that, therefore, not through my own blame, should some be seized by force, as sheep are by wolves, while they not knowing them through the outside scheme of sheep's clothing (against whom the Lord has sent orders to us to be on our guard), and because their languages are like ours, but their minds are unlike ours. I have considered it my own obligation, after reading some of their commentaries, as these persons call them, of the disciples of Valentinus, and after considering and understanding their collection of doctrine to reveal unto you, my beloved friend, these threatening and deep−satanic mysteries, which things do not penetrate all persons intellectively because all persons are not fools to follow such perverted mysteries. In such manner as this, I do, so that after learning about their collection of doctrine, you may make them known unto all those in affiliation with you and advise them to flee from such an abyss of extreme madness and of blasphemy against Christ. And I speak to you such as my ability allows and refers now unto their collection of doctrine whose teachings are heresies).[27]

I never knew that when I stopped writing and started researching resources, it would open a sort of Pandora's box. I uncovered a lot. But not everything was corrupted in the modern lexicons. Again, there was an error here and there, which could only be corrected by antiquarian lexicons, the older translations of the Bible itself, the ancient church fathers, and others.

Through my research, I understood why so many have fallen from the faith of Christianity. All it takes is a little error here or there to destroy much.

Comparing the ancient lexicons with the modern lexicons, I uncovered that:

1. The definitions of the common and rare words are generally in agreement. Therefore, as some suppose, there is no need to throw out the modern lexicons or, worse, have a book burning. Further, all the modern lexicons cannot be traced to one modern source; all the modern lexicons go back to the ancient sources. If that were not the case, the modern lexicons would completely disagree with ancient ones.

2. I have been able to backtrack and locate the sources of the modern lexicons. These sources go back to the AD 1500s, AD 1600s, and AD 1700s.

3. The authors of the ancient lexicons, particularly in Greek, searched all texts that could be found—the Greek New Testament, the Greek Old Testament, the writings of the Greek fathers, the writings of the Greek moralists, Greek historians, and philosophers in order to arrive at a consensus of how each word was used in these texts. And godly scholars found nothing wrong with researching these resources.

4. Deletions, additions, or changes in the modern lexicons, whether in common or rare words, alter how a person can translate a text. And some of these deletions, additions, or changes are the little foxes (little errors). For example, I was translating the Greek text of a church father, and not one modern Greek lexicon had a definition that could fit only in the context of the text. However, the ancient lexicons did and pointed out that text as an example. My translation would have significantly been off if it had not been for the ancient lexicons.

5. Modern lexicons reduce some words to one definition while the ancient lexicons have more. Again, I was translating several Greek texts, including those of the Greek fathers and Greek moralists and historians. Each case had the same Greek word here that meant something, which was and is not defined as in modern lexicons. Again, the ancient lexicons had the answer.

6. Modern lexicons expand some words to more than one definition, while the ancient lexicons have less. English words define modern lexicons, while most ancient lexicons are defined by Latin words. One word in Latin can be translated into several words in English. So I see no problem here.

7. In some cases, modern lexicons reduce the scope of a word—the fullness of its meaning and leave the word only a shell of its former worth. As I shall show, the two Greek words that caused me problems are reduced in their meaning in modern times. There is much more meant by these two words than most think! Liberal theologians have done their best to destroy these words, while even conservative sources have not defined them completely.

8. Modern lexicons have become, in some respects, the only sources that most people can go to since they cannot read Latin or have access to the ancient lexicons. Therefore, people have no means to judge the accuracy of these lexicons and are left helpless.

9. The only way is to judge them by the ancient lexicons, the Bible, the church fathers, and others who wrote in the languages in question.

10. Modern lexicons are to be carefully judged when dealing with the fundamental doctrines of Christianity. They should not be, in these cases, the last word when dealing with these fundamental doctrines!

11. Languages have a flow to them. That flow is a means of how words should be used besides grammar and context. Also, languages have a natural rhythm and cadence, giving them a unique flow. Like a river gently meandering or a melody gracefully unfolding, languages flow effortlessly, carrying thoughts and ideas from one person to another.

The Hebrew Verbs בָּרָא and עָשָׂה

There has been much discussion about these two Hebrew verbs since much has been debated about the theories of creationism. And the things about these verbs that have been discussed are based upon the conclusions of modern lexicons, not ancient ones.

Overall, in some of the modern Hebrew lexicons, the Hebrew verb בָּרָא does not maintain its true meaning or its fullness of meaning. For example, within the AD 1800s, there began to be a rejection of the ancient view that the Hebrew verb בָּרָא in Genesis 1:1 primarily meant to create out of nothing (ex nihilo). The change of view is seen, especially in Samuel Lee's *Lexicon* done in AD 1840. He writes:

> Ex nihilo, says Castell, after the Jews and generally; but this is groundless and fanciful; and greatly is it to be regretted that any such notion was ever entertained and applied in defense of revealed religion. It is, I think, quite obvious that the Bible was never intended to teach philosophy of any sort; and hence, it supplies no explanations and offers no reason for its doctrines. It deals solely in facts or doctrines. And these it proposes as authoritative. We are nowhere told, whether matter previously existed or not, and certainly the merely supposed signification of a word must afford but little towards determining such a question and particularly when we find the usage of the Arabs taking part against us. Of late, the study of geology has again called up this question, and various have been the means had recourse to for its solution. I prefer taking the view which considers the account of the creation in Genesis, as referring to the present state of things only, leaving the question, as to any previous creation, untouched. I am then at liberty to believe, that other creations might also have existed, in many respects perhaps totally unlike this, and that these were destroyed; and hence, the strange fossil remains now found in the bowels of the earth, and as such surprising depths. If there are no human remains—and this appears to be the fact,—this might be accounted for on the supposition, that if men actually existed, they did not become subject to death, as our progenitor did; and hence, might have been translated to some happier and now glorified state, as it was the case

with Enoch and Elijah, even in this of ours. Nor is it necessary to suppose that former creation was lighted by the same sun that ours is. With them clouds of light, such as those which are now believed to cover the disk of the sun, might have enveloped the earth itself; or light might have been supplied in some other way. Nor is it necessary to suppose that, even in this our system, the disk of the sun was necessary to the purpose of affording light. If indeed light was created on the first day, and suspended somewhere in the heavens, and a rotatory motion communication to the earth, evening, and morning, would necessarily be produced, and the period of the natural day be defined. On the fourth day, when the disk of the sun was created, this light might have been located on it, as its permanent place of habitation. And, it is worth remarking that, in this case, not light, but place of light, is the term in the original. This will suffice, perhaps, to solve some of the difficulties, and to remove some of the doubts, usually felt on this question; and will, perhaps guard the philosophical reader from adopting the silly theory that בְּרָא, signifies created out of nothing; and the equally silly one, that the days of creation, as found in the early parts of Genesis, constituted periods of indefinite length, like the Yogs of the Hindoos.[28]

This same thought follows in the *New Brown, Driver, and Briggs Hebrew and English Lexicon of the Old Testament.* The Hebrew verb בְּרָא is not seen as referring to the creation of non-existing material. So the verb denotes no more creation of nothing.[29] This lexicon is based upon the *Lexicon* of William Gesenius, which was translated by Edward Robinson. In the English translation of Gesenius's *Lexicon*, there is no hint that Gesenius believed this verb meant to create out of nothing, especially in Genesis 1:1.[30] However, I have an AD 1848 edition of this lexicon written in Latin rather than English. The translator of Gesenius' *Lexicon* missed the Latin words "ex nihilo" in his translation. So Gesenius still held on to the belief that the Hebrew verb בְּרָא meant to create out of nothing.[31] In his lexicon, E.F. Leopold deletes any mention of creating out of nothing.[32] Other lexicons do the same. The last lexicon I shall bring up about this part of our discussion was done by Dr. Georg. Benedict Winer. His work, like others in the AD 1800s, weakens the Hebrew verb בָּרָא such to a state that Genesis 1:1 could mean to recreate, re-fashion, or remodel out of pre-existing material.[33] I cannot help but notice Higher Criticism here.

This Hebrew verb cannot be so misunderstood here by modern Hebrew scholars if truth is maintained. The only way that these views could work well is a dismissal or a rejection of the Hebrew verb בָּרָא and its correct meaning. However, this Hebrew verb can only mean that the absolute and original creation is before us in Genesis 1:1. It demands that God created all things and that He existed before all the things He created.

Then, we would have to look for the absolute and original creation somewhere else in Scripture. This cannot be accepted. It denies the meaning of this Hebrew verb.

The Hebrew verb בָּרָא in the piel verb pattern means cutting, hewing, forming, modeling, or remodeling. However, this verb is not found in Genesis 1:1 in the piel verb pattern but in the kal verb pattern. The kal verb pattern is employed exclusively for divine productions that are new or not previously existing in the realm of history or nature (see Exodus 34:10; Numbers 16:30.)

Indeed, it expresses before all critics the undeniable truth that its result is new, miraculous, and God-originated. It never means human production. Nor is it ever used with the accusative of matter. Its subject is always God and never man or any creature.

The point here is that this Hebrew verb means that Genesis 1:1 deals with creation out of nothing, which is called "creatio ex nihilo" in Latin.

From the early lexicons, the Hebrew scholars never saw the Hebrew verb בָּרָא as meaning anything other than creavit ex nihilo (create out of nothing) in Genesis 1:1. There cannot mean here a creation out of pre-existing material.

Robert Stephanus had a special edition of Kimchi's Lexicon done for his Edition of the Hebrew Old Testament. Instead of completely doing it in Hebrew, he had the definitions translated into Latin. Pagnius translated the work of Kimchi into Latin. In this work (AD 1548), the Hebrew verb בָּרָא in Genesis 1:1 is defined as *quae videlicet ex no esse ad esse procedit* (which is to say, proceeds from no-existence unto existence).[34]

Edmund Castell defines this verb as *creavit aliquid ex nihilo* (He created something out of nothing) in Genesis 1:1.[35]

In his Hebrew Lexicon (AD 1589), Johanne Haberman recognizes that this Hebrew verb in Genesis 1:1 means to create out of nothing.[36]

In his lexicon, Valentin Schindler likewise recognizes that this verb in Genesis 1:1 can only mean to create out of nothing.[37] The last work to be noted is the Lexicon by Johannes Buxtorf. He agrees with the rest.[38]

As seen, this Hebrew verb in question was weakened by Higher Critics for one reason or another. The most plausible reason was to explain geology.

As bad as this is, nothing compares to how the modern lexicons have treated the Hebrew verb עָשָׂה.

While modern lexicons have weakened the Hebrew verb בָּרָא, they have strengthened the Hebrew verb עָשָׂה. They make both verbs interchangeable in thought and meaning, though one is stronger than the other. So modern lexicons show that both verbs are interchangeable. Overall, both mean the same thing, and we are told there are some differences, but these differences are rare. However, through my studies, I continued to uncover the mentioning that both verbs were not interchangeable nor meant the same.

The consensus of all modern lexicons already cited follows that the Hebrew verb עָשָׂה means create in Exodus 20:11, for instance. However, that there is a difference between these Hebrew verbs is revealed in the ancient lexicons.

In no way does the Hebrew verb עָשָׂה mean to create, especially in Exodus 20:11. Not one of the ancient lexicons already cited points out that this verb means to create. For example, Robert Stephanus' Edition of Kimchi's Lexicon does not define the Hebrew verb עָשָׂה as create but at least to do, to fit, to make out of things already there, to prepare, to arrange, to assemble, or bring together.[39]

Castell, in his *Lexicon Heptaglotton* (AD 1669), defines this verb never as creavit aliquid ex nihilo (create something from nothing).[40]

In his Hebrew lexicon (AD 1589), Johanne Haberman never defines this verb by creavit. He defines it as doing, making, and perfecting. It never means creating out of nothing without pre-existing material.[41] He sees it as perfecting or completing in reference to Exodus 20:11.

In his lexicon (AD 1612), Schindler defines this Hebrew verb, especially in Exodus 20:11, as perfected or perfecting, not create. He never uses the Latin verb creavit for this word. Consequently, this Hebrew verb means to perfect when used or compared to the Hebrew verb בָּרָא. Schindler recognized that perfecting is what was meant in Exodus 20:11.[42]

All these ancient lexicons predate the invention or creation of geology. Therefore, their opinions have not been compromised by such a science. According to these ancient lexicons, the six-day period is when God perfected His creation. Exodus 20:11 pulls us back to Genesis 1:2−3. It shows us the universe (creation) when God prepared the earth for the advent of humanity or the time when God said, "Let there be light." What happened before this is not known. We only read what was about to happen to creation for the advent of humanity. There is no mention of the fall of Lucifer since that fall pre-dates Genesis 1:2−3 but does not predate Genesis 1:1.

Lucifer's fall predated the advent of man, and the time when God said, "Let there be light," was a standard view of the church fathers.[43] For instance, we should notice what Basil, the fourth century father of the church, said about Genesis 1:1−2:

Ἡ δὲ γῆ ἦν ἀόρατος καὶ ἀκατα σκεύαστος. Εἰπὼν, Ἐν ἀρχῇ ἐποίησεν ὁ Θεὸς τὸν οὐρανὸν καὶ τὴν γῆν· πολλὰ ἀπεσιώπησεν, ὕδωρ, ἀέρα, πῦρ, τὰ ἐκ τούτων ἀπογεννώμενα πάθη· ἃ πάντα μὲν ὡς συμπληρωτικὰ τοῦ κόσμου συνυπέστη τῷ παντὶ δηλονότι· παρέλιπε δὲ ἡ ἱστορία, τὸν ἡμέτερον νοῦν γυμνάζουσα πρὸς ἐντρέχειαν, ἐξ ὀλίγων ἀφορμῶν παρεχομένη ἐπιλογίζεσθαι τὰ λειπόμενα. ("The earth was invisible and chaotic." Now, by saying, "In the beginning, God created the heavens and the earth," he deliberately passed over in silence many things, including water, air, fire, and those results which were produced out of them, which all things, forming the essential parts of the world, were made altogether and within an instant as the universe. However, on the other hand, history has passed over these things in silence to train our mind with resourcefulness, giving it weak starting points so that it might consider those truthful events that were intentionally missing in our account).[44]

He concluded that the Genesis 1:1–2:24 account was incomplete, and some things that had occurred were missing.

The Hebrew noun רֵאשִׁית

In Genesis 1:1, the Hebrew noun רֵאשִׁית has been interpreted in many ways. Still, it must express the anterior to all created existence. In the ancient lexicons, this Hebrew noun is recognized to mean the beginning or origin of all things. Nothing was created before this point.

We are left completely bewildered by the silence of modern lexicons on this topic. According to their definition, this Hebrew term in Genesis 1:1 only denotes an origin or a beginning among earlier origins and beginnings. It is, at most, a beginning, but neither the original beginning nor the origin of everything that has been created. Samuel Lee believes that the Hebrew noun רֵאשִׁית can mean the beginning of time, but just not in Genesis 1:1.[45] Gesenius does define this noun in Genesis 1:1 as the beginning but goes no farther.[46] Brown, Driver, and Briggs have, "In the beginning when God created. . .", but there is no mention or statement that this was the beginning of all created things.[47]

Johanne Haberman recognizes that the Hebrew noun רֵאשִׁית refers to the absolute origin of all time and space. Therefore, nothing here means that no other creations existed before Genesis 1:1.[48]

Castell defines this same word in Genesis 1:1 as *Creatio quia eius historia ita incipit* (Creation, because its history thus so begins). He does not see anything created existing before that.[49]

Schindler defines this same word in Genesis 1:1 as *principium temporis, ordinis, numeri, et dignitatis* (The beginning of time, order, number, and dignity).[50] According to Schindler, the Hebrew noun demands a creation of order, not utter chaos. He further writes, In Primo rerum omnium creatarum exordio (In the first beginning, all things were created).[51]

The Hebrew noun רֵאשִׁית cannot be translated with its preposition, "In a former time. . ." Without the article, the noun with its preposition pulls us back to before time and space, before anything created existed.

This is very plain. Using the Greek phrase "ἐν ἀρχῇ" in Genesis 1:1 in the Greek Old Testament, the same Greek phrase "ἐν ἀρχῇ" was written by John (John 1:1). Whatever the phrase means in Genesis 1:1, it must be the same in John 1:1. And it can horribly affect how we see God the Word if we do not understand the Hebrew noun correctly. John understood that the Hebrew and Greek of Genesis 1:1 could only express before all things were created—before the creation of time and space. It is perilous to translate the Hebrew any other way.

The Hebrew noun עַלְמָה

The Hebrew noun עַלְמָה is not the problem in Isaiah 7:14 where we should read something like this, "Behold a virgin." Nor is the Vulgate or the Greek Old Testament the problem. Both translate Isaiah 7:14 as "Behold a virgin." The problem is neither Luke nor Matthew (Luke 1:27; Matthew 1:23), but the problem is the modern Hebrew lexicons. So I wonder why so many ministers deny the Virgin Birth of Christ!

Gesenius denies that this Hebrew noun can mean virgin.[52] That does not surprise me since, in his grammar, he rejects the doctrine of the Trinity.

In any digital version of *Gesenius' Lexicon* or of the N*ew Brown, Driver, and Briggs Hebrew and English Lexicon of the Old Testament*, I never run across the statement from the publisher that rejects Gesenius' view and says that Gesenius' view purposely is done to undermine the significance of virgin to this word. However, the books themselves give the publisher's warning. Many do not use the books themselves but the digital versions.

There is no question at all that the Hebrew noun עַלְמָה means virgin, especially with the article before it.

In Robert Stephanus' *Edition of Kimchi's Lexicon*, this Hebrew noun, especially with the article, is defined as *adolescetula puella, sed virgo* (adolescent girl, but a virgin).[53] Johann Habermann defines the Hebrew noun עַלְמָה in Isaiah 7:14 as *adolescentula virgo innupta quae occultata est a concubitu viri* (a young unmarried virgin who has been concealed from having sexual intercourse with a man).[54] Schinder defines this Hebrew noun as a virgin, especially in Isaiah 7:14.[55] Castell defines this same Hebrew noun, especially in Isaiah 7:14, as a virgin.[56] Finally, Johannes Buxtorf points out Genesis 24:43; Exodus 2:8; Psalm 68:25; Proverbs 30:19; Isaiah 7:14; and two other verses as places where this Hebrew noun must mean virgin.[57]

All these lexicons emphasize that by the article being before the Hebrew noun עַלְמָה, only virgin can be meant. This is a simple rule in Hebrew, which the ancient lexicons noted, but somehow most, probably not all, modern lexicons do not have. It has been known as the articular construction in Hebrew, like other languages.

Too many shipwrecked people have lost their faith because modern lexicons reject what is commonly known.

The Greek Adjective μαλακός and Greek Noun ἀρσενοκοίτης

In 1 Corinthians 6:9–12, Paul made a vice list similar to the one that he made in 1 Timothy 1:10. And as part of his vice list, he listed both the Greek adjective μαλακός and the Greek noun ἀρσενοκοίτης. Both words describe sexual deviance and Paul's condemnation of such within and outside of the lives of Christians; there is no way around that in this world of insanity. Paul set forth a general and absolute prohibition against such sexual deviance.

There has been a war over these words in the last hundred years. The words themselves mean what they say, but scholars have tried their best by their own bias to undermine the explicit meaning of these words (I have read and read almost every writing on this subject).

Primarily, for worse, I was pulled into this area of study; I never wanted to research or study sexual deviance, nor study deeply what the Bible and the ancient church said about such a topic. But too many people came to me asking questions I could not answer. For this reason, above all others, I have almost completely stopped advising people in my office since this subject is almost always discussed.

So I begin a long search, understanding marriage and understanding what sexual practices are acceptable to the Bible, the ancient church, the ancient Jews, the Hellenistic Jews, and above all, what sexual practices are acceptable unto the holiness of God. Time and time again, men and women came to me asking questions. And many read to me, "Marriage is honourable in all, and the bed undefiled: but whoremongers and adulterers God will judge" (Hebrews 13:4). Their conclusion, like others, was that if you are married, you can do what you want. But the "all" in Hebrews 13:4 there in the Greek does not include anything God has already forbidden.

Many Christians are being led astray by the question of sexuality. I remember reading an article written by two authors from a publisher. Their conclusions were not based on Greek scholarship or the views of the ancient church. What they said made me ill.

Liberal theologians and scholars state that both the Greek adjective μαλακός and the Greek noun ἀρσενοκοίτης only describe homosexuals who are slaves. In particular, the Greek adjective μαλακός is limited to those slaves who are male prostitutes. Therefore, free homosexuals, they say, are not condemned by Paul. And indeed, they say, Paul is not condemning those homosexuals who have a monogamous relationship, especially in some type of marriage.

Further, liberal theologians and scholars also interpret both words as describing only the sexual deviance known as pederasty (pedophilia) or as only having reference to those homosexuals who are male prostitutes and those homosexuals who use their services.

On the other hand, conservative theologians and scholars see homosexuals as meant, whether free or slave, whether they are in numerous relationships or one relationship, whether male prostitutes or those who use the services of male prostitutes. But that is all that they see here.

Both schemes of thought limit the overall scope of both words. They set limits within these words when there were no limits on sexual deviance, as seen by Paul.

One should notice some of the modern scholars' views and some of the reference works and how they interpreted both the Greek noun ἀρσενοκοίτης and the Greek adjective μαλακός.

As pertaining to the Greek noun ἀρσενοκοίτης, the scholar Bailey agreed that the word referred to males involved in homosexual acts but not generally to homosexuals.[58] Boswell claimed that this word only referred to male prostitutes.[59] Scroggs saw this same word as only referring to abusive pederasty.[60] He demanded that the Greek noun ἀρσενοκοίτης does not generally have reference to homosexuality, female homosexuality, or to the common understanding of the term pederasty. Martin maintained that the traditional view or how the ancients interpreted this word is false.[61] Both Scobie and Campbell argued against the restriction of the word to pederasty. They conclude that there is no evidence that the term only references pederasty. According to both, the New Testament repeats the Leviticus condemnation of all types of same-sex relationships.[62]

The Greek-English Lexicon of Liddell and Scott defines the Greek noun ἀρσενοκοίτης only by the word sodomite.[63] *The Greek-English Lexicon of the New Testament* and other Early Christian Literature defines this same word as "a male who engages in sexual activity w. a pers. of his own sex, paederast 1 Cor. 6:9. . . , of one who assumes the dominant role in same-sex activity."[64] *Thayer's Greek-English Lexicon of the New Testament* defines this same word simply as "one who lies with a male as with a female, a sodomite."[65]

The *Greek-English Lexicon of the New Testament* and other Early Christian Literature defines this Greek adjective μαλακός as "being passive in a same-sex relationship, effeminate esp. of catamites, of men and boys who are sodomized by other males in such a relationship. . ."[66] *Thayer's Greek-English Lexicon of the New Testament* defines the Greek adjective μαλακός as "a male who submits his body to unnatural lewdness, 1 Co. 6:9. . ."[67]

Lange, Schaff, Kling & Poor, in *A commentary on the Holy Scriptures*, compared both words and defined what Paul meant in 1 Corinthians 6:9 as "These express correlative ideas. The former denotes those who allowed themselves to be used as women (qui muliebria patiuntur); the latter, such as used the former in this unnatural way—a widespread vice in that period."[68]

Before entering a discussion about how the ancient lexicons dealt with both the Greek noun ἀρσενοκοίτης and the Greek adjective μαλακός, it must be remembered how Paul was writing was a commonly known technique. What is impressive is the fact that using this technique does not require using the exact words. Other words can well be used in their place. For example, Paul writes, μαλακοὶ οὔτε ἀρσενοκοῖται in 1 Corinthians 6:9 while Josephus, a Hellenistic Jew, writes, ἂν ἄρρενι τολμήσῃ πεῖραν προσφέρειν, ἂν ὑπομείνῃ παθεῖν ὁ πειρασθείς.[69] And in the work "Forms of Love" by the author Ps-Lucian, a Greek Moralist, another form of what Paul wrote is also written, συνῆλθεν δ᾽ εἰς μίαν κοίτην μία φύσις· αὐτοὺς δ᾽ ἐν ἀλλήλοις ὁρῶντες οὔθ᾽ ἃ δρῶσιν οὔθ᾽ ἃ πάσχουσιν ἡδοῦντο, κατὰ πετρῶν δέ, φασίν, ἀγόνων σπείροντες ὀλίγης ἡδονῆς ἀντικατηλλάξαντο μεγάλην ἀδοξίαν.[70] Dio Cassius, a Roman statesman and historian, followed the thinking of Paul simply by writing in one place, καὶ ἔδρασε τῷ σώματι καὶ ἔπαθε.[71]

Regardless of the words, the meaning is the same. Josephus, Ps-Lucian, and Dio Cassius used more than one adjective and noun to form this meaning. They used verbs, nouns, prepositions, and whatever they needed to create their thoughts.

In the ancient lexicons, there were several attempts to arrive at what we now understand as a Greek lexicon in all its use. Joannes Cratonus began his work on Greek lexicons in AD 1478. Therefore, Cratonus's dictionary was the first bilingual Greek-Latin lexicon to be printed, and it provided a model for future lexicons. The next step was the 75-page lexicon in the *Complutensian Polyglot* in AD 1514, which is not impressive as I have seen a digital copy of it. Andreas Cratander and Valentin Curio, in AD 1519, worked together on the first Basel Edition of the *Lexicon Graecum*. Later, Valentin Curio published his version of this work in AD 1522.

However, the most critical work on arriving at a Greek lexicon's standard and usual form was the *Commentarii linguae Graecae* by Guilielmo Budaeo (Guillaume Bude) in AD 1530. It was Bude himself who pushed us into the commencement of antiquarian lexicons. From this work, he worked on his masterpiece *Lexicon Graeco-Latinum*, which was published the same year and re-published several times. John Calvin was familiar with it. The *Lexicon Graeco-Latinum* established what a Greek lexicon should be and would be. It was Bude's lexicon that was noted by Henry Stephanus, the son of Robert

Stephanus, as the foundation of his own work done in AD 1572. Therefore, Bude's work was the foundation of all other works.

In AD 1532, the *Lexicon Graecolatinum* was published by Petrus (Pierre) Gilles, and the *Lexicon sive dictionarium Graecolatinum Dictionum, explicationum & allegationum copia uberriumum, omniaca quae alia habent, et multo plura, corrplectens* was published in the same year by Junius Hadrianus. Both works are similar to Bede's since they are based on his work.

While other works were done before AD 1572, the most outstanding work ever attempted on a grand scale was the *Thesaurus Graecae Linguae* by Henry Stephanus in AD 1572. While Bede's work must be the foundation of all works, the *Thesaurus Graecae Linguae* became the standard and received authority on Greek. And even in the twentieth century, its authority was still recognized since it had been published in a new version in AD 1831. A five-volume lexicon became a twelve-volume lexicon by AD 1831.

The first Greek Lexicon of the New Testament was Pasor's (AD 1619), known as *Lexicon Graeco-Latinum in Novum Domni Nostri Jesu Christi Testamentum*. The *Critica Sacra* by Leigh in AD 1639 was a lexicon with Latin and English definitions; the first Greek-English Lexicon of any value or worth was that of Parkhurst in AD 1769 called, *A Greek and English Lexicon to the New Testament*. All Greek-English lexicons are to be traced back, not from Liddell and Scott's *A Greek-English Lexicon*, but from Parkhurst's and Pasor's and these lexicons back to Stephanus' and Bede's lexicons.

In the ancient lexicons, there are similarities in how they define both the Greek noun ἀρσενοκοίτης and the Greek adjective μαλακός and how modern lexicons recognize them. However, each of these words, as seen by the consensus of the ancient lexicons, basically have four points that Paul is getting across to the Corinthians dealing with sexual deviance. Paul is not trying to get this across; he is doing it. Some of these lexicons have one word or a handful of words describing what is meant by these words. Yet, what is meant is clear.

These four points are missing in most, if not all, of the modern Greek lexicons. The absence of these points, in particular the third and fourth points, has brought forth much confusion about homosexuality and the acceptable sexual practices of humans. In other words, what practices are normal and what practices are unnatural and deviant. Underneath these words, there are warnings to all!

The ancient lexicons recognize that both the Greek noun ἀρσενοκοίτης and the Greek adjective μαλακός imply a mental state that is unnatural or contrary to nature. These words indicate that the persons have a mental illness at least. This point is missed by all modern lexicons that I know of. Take, for example, the Greek adjective μαλακός, Pasor saw it as describing a lustful and impure man who is sick in body and mind, whereby the things done in the body effect (affect) the mind. He writes, *Queque ponitur pro libidimuso et impuro homine, per metaph. a re corporea ad animum hominis translatum* (and also for a sexual and filthy man, by metaphor, it has been supposed to be transferred from the matter of the man's body unto the mind of a man).[72]

Also, Leigh takes 1 Corinthians 6:9 and implies that a mental sickness has been transferred into the mind so that there becomes an effeminateness of the mind.[73] Parkhurst writes in the same word, "A man who suffers himself to be abused contrary to nature, a Catamite, a Pathic; hence μαλακοὶ is by the apostle joined with ἀρσενοκοῖτα, Sodomites. These wretches [were] affected [with] the dress and behavior of women."[74]

I cannot help but be amazed at how the scholars of the AD 1600s recognized a transference of spirits, as it is called today. In both works, Pasor and Leigh saw that unnatural sexual practices by or to the body would also have terrible consequences upon the mind (and the soul). For what unnatural sexual practices are done by or to the body, those effects are transferred to the mind (and soul) also, and there becomes a change, unnatural change.

Pasor defines the Greek noun ἀρσενοκοίτης as cinaedus, but adds q*uem scriptura alibi canem vocat, per metph. a libidinosa canis natura* (whom Scripture calls elsewhere a dog by metaphor, from the sexual nature of a dog).[75]

The Lexicon Graeco-Latinum by Bude defines the Greek noun ἀρσενοκοίτης simply as one Latin word, paedico.[76] The uniqueness of this simple definition cannot be overstated; it allows the four points of the Greek noun ἀρσενοκοίτης to be emphasized. This one Latin word means that Paul is condemning anyone who commits sodomy, which will and must be defined. Petrus Giles, in his Lexicon Graecolatinum, describes the Greek noun ἀρσενοκοίτης in the same manner.[77] Junius Hadrianus defines the Greek noun ἀρσενοκοίτης as paedico and as the Latin phrase *qui masculis concumbit* (he who commits sexual intercourse with other males).[78] This translation is a simple translation. Latin means more than this, as I shall show.

Robert Constantinus' Greek lexicon, published in AD 1592, agrees with the definition of the Greek noun ἀρσενοκοίτης as defined by Junius Hadrianus.[79]

Bude defined the Greek adjective μαλακός simply as mollis. That is, someone who practices sodomy as the passive partner or in the passive role.[80] Again, the four points of this Greek adjective are emphasized. Petrus Giles, in his Lexicon Graecolatinum, defines the Greek adjective μαλακός in the same manner.[81] Junius Hadrianus agrees with both Bude and Petrus Giles.[82]

Henry Stephanus, in the "Thesaurus Graecae Linguae," defined the Greek noun ἀρσενοκοίτης as the Latin phrase *qui cum masculis concumbit vel Masculorum concubitor, ut loquutus est vetus interpr* (he who commits sexual intercourse with other males or the masculine, passive sexual partner for males, which is citing the ancient interpretation).[83]

Henry Stephanus defines the Greek adjective μαλακός as going under the name of the Greek noun κίναιδος, which is the Latin noun cinaedus.[84] Henry Stephanus understands that the Greek noun μαλακός means the same thing as the Greek noun κίναιδος or the Latin noun cinaedus. In other words, both nouns mean the same thing. Each implies the practice of sodomy, and each generally denotes the passive partner in sodomy. Still, each can well include the active, passive, or both forms of sodomy in male and female homosexuality. Further, the sexual practices of sodomy are emphasized.

The focus on the term sodomy cannot be overstated here in genuinely understanding the overall view and meaning of the Greek noun ἀρσενοκοίτης and the Greek adjective μαλακός.

The issue of sodomy, that of male homosexuality and female homosexuality, is not a political issue for our society, regardless of what politicians say. Still, it is a moral issue for our society and both ethical and theological for Christianity. Like in old times, it became a moral issue, and above all, even the Greek and Roman moralists, who were themselves still pagans, saw that paganism could not be without restraint. They saw that sodomy was part of paganism that was without restraint, like other sexual crimes were, like adultery. Even the pagans saw that unrestricted paganism was nothing but chaos.

The term sodomy has reference to unnatural and deviant sexual behavior, defined as a criminal sin against nature, which includes between men, between women, between men or women using acts of sodomy, and between men or women among or with beasts.

Sodomy is a carnal copulation by humans against nature or with a beast. It is an unnatural and lascivious act—a person who commits any unnatural and lascivious act with another person.

It includes all unnatural forms of sexual practice and behavior, including male homosexuality and female homosexuality. It expresses three main things or groups: 1. The inhabitants of Sodom; 2. Those men who practice sodomy in the form of male homosexuality; and 3. those men and women who practice sodomy in any of its forms.

The *Lexicon Novi Testament Graeci Alphabeticum*, published in AD 1700, is a mystery. On the spine, it is recorded as the *Greek Lexicon of Buxtorf*, however, it just may be the Lexicon of Joannes Dawson since there is no recorded reference of Buxtorf ever publishing a Greek lexicon. This lexicon takes the Greek noun ἀρσενοκοίτης as being defined by cinaedus.[85]

In AD 1676, Cornelius Schrevelius defined the Greek noun ἀρσενοκοίτης as being simply cinaedus.[86]

Before I conclude the preface, I would like to mention two Greek lexicons for modern Greek that sum up the four points of the Greek noun ἀρσενοκοίτης and the Greek adjective μαλακός.

First, the Dictionary of Modern Greek (Λεξικό της Νέας Ελληνικής Γλώσσας), commonly known as "the Babiniotis dictionary." This lexicon defines the Greek noun ἀρσενοκοίτης as *ἀρσενοκοτών (λόγ.) πρόσωπο που ἔχει σεξουαλικές σχέσεις με ἄντρες· ΣΥΝ κίναιδος;*

Ομοφυλόφιλος (the individual man who has sexual intercourse with men; Synonyms, active or passive homosexual; homosexual, both active and passive forms).[87] The Greek adjective μαλακός is defined by this lexicon as *Τὸ ὁποῖο ἤδη στόν Ἡροδότο δηλῶσέ τὸν ἀνηθίκο. Διεφθαρμένο ἀνθρώπο, ὅπως τὸν παθητίκο ομοφυλοφιλο 3ος αι. Π.Χ,* (which is already mentioned by Herodotus as immoral. A perverted man, as the passive homosexual, third century BC).[88]

Second, the Dictionary of Standard Modern Greek by the Institute for Modern Greek Studies of the Aristotle University of Thessaloniki defines the Greek noun ἀρσενοκοίτης as *(λόγ.) αυτός που έχει σεξουαλικές σχέσεις με άντρες· σοδομίτης. λόγ. < ελνστ. ἀρσενοκοίτης* (He who has sexual intercourse with men; sodomite).[89]

It defines the Greek adjective μαλακός as *παθητικός ομοφυλόφιλος* (passive homosexual).[90]

The ancient lexicons recognize that both the Greek noun ἀρσενοκοίτης and the Greek adjective μαλακός define four points. On the other hand, the modern lexicons omit some of these points or summarize them. The ancient lexicons describe by just a single Latin word or a phrase all four points:

1. Both words describe same-sex relationships or homosexual relationships, whether free or slave. The words argue this out absolutely. There cannot be any limit to this. There is no such thing as a monogamous relationship, especially in some types of marriage, that these words sanction.

2. The words together describe the active role or partner within the sexual practices of sodomy and the passive role or partner within the sexual practices of sodomy. Both words, standing by themselves, can mean either the active, passive, or both the active and passive roles or partners within the sexual practices of sodomy. Context is the judge here.

3. The words describe a mental sickness, at least. The ancient authorities, Hellenistic Jews, Greek moralists, Greek philosophers, and historians, the apostles, and the Greek fathers of the church recognized this. The scholars who wrote

the ancient lexicons understood this from the writings of Greek authors.

4. The words describe the sexual practices themselves, which are against nature. They have reference to unnatural and deviant sexual behavior, including at least between men and women and between men or women. They may extend to men or women with beasts.

   a. These acts were condemned by the Old Testament, the New Testament, the writings of the Greek and Latin moralists, and the Greek and Latin fathers of the church.

The words themselves, while focusing on sexual deviant behavior among men, cannot be limited to that. This fourth point includes those men who practice sodomy in the form of male homosexuality, those women who practice sodomy in the form of female homosexuality, and finally, those men and women who practice sodomy in any of its forms among themselves in a heterosexual relationship.

It is the sexual practices of sodomy, which include oral and anal copulations that Paul also condemns in 1 Corinthians 6:9–12 and 1 Timothy 1:10.

That what is described by Paul using the Greek noun ἀρσενοκοίτης and the Greek adjective μαλακός means a mental sickness, as seen by the ancients and the scholars who published the ancient lexicons can also be noted by the writing of Soranus of Ephesus as quoted by Caelius Aurelianus. Soranus was a Greek physician active in Rome during the first half of the second century. He described such behavior mentioned by these words as one who has "a wickedly narrow and utterly foul mind."[91] In his second Apology for writing to the Roman Senate, Justin Martyr also points this out in the following quote.

John Chrysostom, a Church father of the fourth and fifth centuries, recognized the sickness of the mind in such behavior.[92] He described it as "unnatural madness." He even says this about such behavior, τὸ γὰρ μεταλλάξαι, τῶν ἐχόντων ἐστίν (for the changing is demonic possession).[93] Cyprian of Carthage, (St.) Bp, AD 200–258, speaks of such behavior as the result of a mind that is not sound.[94] St. Epiphanius, in his works, makes the same case.[95]

Even pagan moralists saw such sexual behavior as a sign of mental illness. For example, Seneca the Younger mentioned that such behavior requires a sickness of the mind.[96]

Those sexual practices of sodomy, including oral and anal copulations, were prohibited and condemned by the ancient church and even ancient Greek and Latin writers can be shown by several quotes, but notice what Justin Martyr ultimately says:

Διὸς δὲ καὶ τῶν ἄλλων θεῶν μιμηταὶ γινόμενοι ἐν τῷ ἀνδροβατεῖν καὶ γυναιξὶν ἀδεῶς μίγνυσθαι, Ἐπικούρου μὲν καὶ τὰ τῶν ποιητῶν συγγράμματα ἀπολογίαν φέροντες; Ἐπειδὴ δὲ ταῦτα τὰ μαθήματα καὶ τοὺς ταῦτα πράξαντας καὶ μιμουμένους φεύγειν πείθομεν, ὡς καὶ νῦν διὰ τῶνδε τῶν λόγων ἠγωνίσμεθα, ποικίλως πολεμούμεθα· ἀλλ' οὐ φροντίζομεν, ἐπεὶ θεὸν τῶν πάντων ἐπόπτην δίκαιον οἴδαμεν. Εἴθε καὶ νῦν τις ἐν τραγικῇ φωνῇ ἀνεβόησεν ἐπὶ τι βῆμα ὑψηλὸν ἀναβάς· Αἰδέσθητε, αἰδέσθητε ἃ φανερῶς πράττετε εἰς ἀναιτίους ἀναφέροντες, καὶ τὰ προσόντα καὶ ἑαυτοῖς καὶ τοῖς ὑμετέροις θεοῖς περιβάλλοντες τούτοις· ὧν οὐδὲν οὐδ' ἐπὶ ποσὸν μετουσία ἐστί. Μετάθεσθε, σωφρονίσθητε (And also becoming the imitators of Zeus and the other gods in committing sexual intercourse with men, in the active form of male homosexuality, and in committing sexual intercourse shamelessly with women, both anal and oral sexual intercourse, really, utterly complaining, can these men bring forward in their defense about such shameful sexual practices the writings of Epicurus and the poets? Nevertheless, because we persuade men to avoid these instructions from the gods, and to avoid those men who practice and imitate them, and as now we must make every effort to persuade you through our discourse, we ourselves are attacked in various ways. But we are not concerned since we know God is a just observer of the universe. And would to God that even now someone would mount upon a lofty platform and shout with a tragic voice, 'You must immediately be ashamed; you must immediately be ashamed, attributing unto the innocent men those evil practices, which you openly commit in sexual intercourse, and putting those evil practices also, which belong to yourselves and to your gods, upon Christian men whose participation in such evil deeds is absolutely nothing, not even in any degree at all. You must immediately be converted from such evil practices; you must immediately be corrected from such evil practices and be restored unto a healthy mind').[97]

"In committing sexual intercourse shamelessly with women" comes from the Greek phrase, "καὶ γυναιξὶν ἀδεῶς μίγνυσθαι" and denotes shamelessly sexual intercourse made to be done by women for men; nothing else meant but oral and anal copulations. Further, shamelessly means unlawful, unnatural, and wholly with no grace. Justin Martyr came from paganism. He saw such acts cannot be defended morally.

In his day, Basil the Great, fourth century father of the Church, warned Christians especially about oral copulation (sexual intercourse):

Πόσα δὲ εἴδη ἄλλα τῶν ἀκαθάρτων παθῶν τὸ μὲν τῶν δαιμόνων διδασκάλιον ἐξεῦρεν, ἡ δὲ θεία Γραφὴ ἀπεσιώπησε, τὸ σεμνὸν ἑαυτῆς ταῖς τῶν αἰσχρῶν ὀνομασίαις καταρρυπαίνειν οὐχ αἱρουμένη, ἀλλὰ γενικοῖς ὀνόμασι τὰς ἀκαθαρσίας διέβαλεν; Ὡς καὶ ὁ ἀπόστολος Παῦλός φησι· "Πορνεία δὲ καὶ ἀκαθαρσία πᾶσα μηδὲ ὀνομαζέσθω ἐν ὑμῖν, καθὼς πρέπει ἁγίοις", τῷ τῆς ἀκαθαρσίας ὀνόματι τάς τε τῶν ἀρρένων ἀρρητοποιίας καὶ τὰς τῶν θηλειῶν περιλαμβάνων. Ὥστε οὐ πάντως ἡ σιωπὴ ἄδειαν φέρει τοῖς φιληδόνοις (but it is found out just how many other forms of unclean and unnatural lusts there are in the school of demons, indeed! Divine Scripture maintains its silence about them, not choosing to contaminate its dignity with the names of shameful things but bringing charges against their uncleanness in general terms! As the Apostle Paul says, "But fornication and every type of sexual shamefulness. . . . let it not be once named among you as be fitting saints" (Eph. 5:3), thus under the name of sexual shamefulness, oral copulations—oral sexual practices—of men and of women, which are unmentionable vices, are included. It follows that silence certainly does not give license to unsanctified sexual practices).[98]

Even the standard means of defining the Greek words in Latin still contain the full scope of meaning. For example, Junius Hadrianus' use of the Latin phrase *qui masculis concumbit* or Henry Stephanus' use of the Latin phrase *qui cum masculis concumbit vel Masculorum concubitor* includes all points and all sexual practices of sodomy, just by the one Latin verb concumbo. The ancient lexicons could be defined more freely in Latin than in English since there was a high level of morality, and many could not read Latin.

Sometimes, it is enough to translate such things without putting everything that the words mean. Other times, it is wise to put it all out there. For example, Paul's simple Greek phrase ἄρσενες ἐν ἄρσεσι in Romans 1:24–28, following other Greek writers, can just be translated, "men with men," or can entirely be translated so that all the things noted by this Greek phrase are present for the English reader to read.

So finally, how do we translate "μαλακοὶ οὔτε ἀρσενοκοῖται" in 1 Corinthians 6:9? And how do we translate what Josephus said, "ἂν ἄρρενι τολμήσῃ πεῖραν προσφέρειν, ἂν ὑπομείνῃ παθεῖν ὁ πειρασθείς."[99] And how do we translate the words of Ps-Lucian, a Greek Moralist, "συνῆλθεν δ᾽ εἰς μίαν κοίτην μία φύσις· αὐτοὺς δ᾽ ἐν ἀλλήλοις ὁρῶντες οὔθ᾽ ἃ δρῶσιν οὔθ᾽ ἃ πάσχουσιν ἡδοῦντο, κατὰ πετρῶν δέ, φασίν, ἀγόνων σπείροντες ὀλίγης ἡδονῆς ἀντικατηλλάξαντο μεγάλην ἀδοξίαν."[100] And how do we translate also Dio Cassius's words, "καὶ ἔδρασε τῷ σώματι καὶ ἔπαθε·?"[101]

The Greek noun ἀρσενοκοίτης and the Greek adjective μαλακός in 1 Corinthians 6:9–11 should be translated something like this, "those who are the passive partners in sexual practices of sodomy nor those who are the active partners in sexual practices of sodomy." This covers all the four points of emphasis meant by these words without adding "oral copulation" and "anal copulation." However, these sexual behavior practices are understood here and can be placed in the translations. The words of Josephus, Ps–Lucian, and Dio Cassius can follow this simple way, or we can translate a little differently and add the words oral and anal copulations in our translations if we desire since both acts are interwoven together. For example, Josephus says, "If anyone would dare have the cruelty and the nerve to attempt to have sexual intercourse with a male, being the active partner, in sexual practices of sodomy; if anyone would dare to submit himself to undergo such an experience as having been penetrated by another male, being the passive partner, in sexual practices of sodomy, that act is an outrage." This is sufficient in translation, and we need not add other words. While anal copulation is emphasized more than oral copulation here, both are understood in the words of Josephus.

Besides this, we should understand that within words or phrases like these, whether in Greek, Latin, or other languages, the ancients recognized that other unnatural sexual practices were included, which could not be done but by only artificial means. Seneca the Younger, first-century moralist, speaks of the women in his times, Libidine vero ne maribus quidem cedunt: pati natae (di illas deaeque male perdant!) adeo perversum commentae genus inpudicitiae viros ineunt (in truth, these women do not yield to men regarding excessive lust, although they had been born to be penetrated by men, being the passive partners—May the gods and goddesses extremely destroy them! So perverse is their type of invented sexual impurity; they, as active partners, even penetrate men).[102]

The words of Hebrews, "Marriage is honourable in all, and the bed undefiled: but whoremongers and adulterers God will judge" (Hebrews 13:4), do not contradict what Paul meant, nor allow what is considered sexual deviance or sexual perversion either. As said before, Hebrews 13:4 does not allow what God has already forbidden.

Conclusively, any man or woman who uses Hebrews 13:4 to give credence that all things may be done in the bedroom between husband and wife must take another look at this and the use of this verse. The all of Hebrews 13:3 is not inclusive: It does not mean all. The "all" only includes the husband and wife in marriage, no one else. Some can defile a bed within marriage. Are both marriage and the bed honorable and undefiled when a man rapes his wife? Are both marriage and the bed honorable and undefiled when perversion, pornography, sodomy, and other unnatural things are brought into the bed? God forbid! Are both marriage and the bed honorable and undefiled if a husband brings into the bedroom a prostitute? Are both the marriage and the bed honorable and undefiled if a wife brings into the bedroom her extra lover? Are the marriage and the bed honorable and undefiled if the wife or the husband brings more partners into the marriage and the bedroom? Are both the marriage and the bed honorable and undefiled if the husband believes he can have more than one wife or the wife more than one husband?

Since four groups of the demonic spirits that are destroying America work in sexual sins, I thought it would be wise to define what Paul meant in 1 Corinthians 6:9–12 here rather than in those chapters.

These pages are written to show how I struggled to ascertain just how six simple words should be defined, how the modern lexicons in these six cases did not help to explain the full scope of the phrase or failed ultimately, and how the ancient lexicons helped in understanding their meaning with the ancient writings of the Hellenistic Jews, Greek moralists, and Latin moralists, and the early church fathers.

INTRODUCTION

It has been some time since I wrote a new book. Many years ago, Charles Finney wrote about the shape of America today:

> The error that lies at the foundation of this decay of individual and public conscience originates, no doubt, in the pulpit.... Brethren, our preaching will bear its legitimate fruits. If immorality prevails in the land, the fault is ours in a great degree. If there is a decay of conscience, the pulpit is responsible for it. If the public press lacks moral discrimination, the pulpit is responsible for it. If the church is degenerate and worldly, the pulpit is responsible for it. If the world loses its interest in religion, the pulpit is responsible for it. If Satan rules in our halls of legislation, the pulpit is responsible for it. If our politics become so corrupt that the very foundations of our government are ready to fall away, the pulpit is responsible for it. Let us not ignore this fact, my dear brethren; but let us lay it to heart and be thoroughly awake to our responsibility in respect to the morals of this nation. Let the awakening begin with each one of us, especially those of us who serves as leaders in the Body and let the Jesus revolution arise in our midst until the nation is shaken with the gospel. The time has come that Christians must vote for honest men and take consistent ground in politics, or the Lord will curse them...Christians have been exceedingly guilty in this matter. But the time has come when they must act differently...Christians seem to act as if they thought God did not see what they do in politics. But I tell you He does see it, and He will bless or curse this nation according to the course they [Christians] take [in politics]. Charles Finney.[1]

We have seen America's moral decline increase exceedingly in the last months. Our moral roots are rotting.

We, as a nation, are morally in trouble. And we have forgotten God's direct involvement in our affairs. God is deeply entwined in human affairs. God will use evil and good instruments to accomplish His will. The ultimate danger is forgetting to inquire of the Lord.

Those who were born before AD 1965 are shocked, if not grieving, over the shape that America is in. America does not resemble the America that I was born in. She had the spirit of freedom and God as her foundation in past years. But no more! To me, America reminds me of the Roman Empire between AD 57 and AD 325.

America is falling continually into utter chaos; the principles that founded us are being thrown into the trash. If not careful, America will be thrown into the trash heap of history. The signs of our coming destruction are all there if we do not change. We will discuss the threats later, which will, if not stopped, cause our destruction.

The changes needed are sometimes more complex than we may think. I have prayed for certain people for years. And I have seen no change, not because of the lack of God's power, but because the people refuse to fall before the altar of God and submit to God, who will change them under His power. We must all go before the potter's wheel and submit to that working over so that we can be changed into what He wants us to be or into the very image of His son.

America today feels worse, in its fundamentals, than the one many of us remember from our youth, a society presided over by those of supposedly lesser consciousness. We perceive no greatness in our leaders and a new purposelessness in ourselves. Not long ago, America was more than the sum of its parts.

We are in a land that is not genuinely Christian but pagan. We must now remember Dorothy in the land of OZ. The land of OZ is a strange place with witches, wizards, and other strange characters. I can reasonably say, "I have a feeling we're not in Kansas

2

anymore." Numerous people in middle America are feeling this today. As a country, we sowed to the wind, and we are reaping the whirlwind. Even Kansas does not feel like Kansas anymore. It feels like we are in a different land full of wonders on the surface that will truly cause troubles and disasters.

Many Christians need a spiritual IQ examination since they believe everything is fine in Kansas when Kansas is on fire with everything that is not of God.

Most in America do not believe that there will be consequences for our actions when the Bible says that the wages of sin is death. As such, an increase in political indecency is seen, immorality has become the norm, and our children have become indoctrinated into immorality.

Because of this, immorality has become as good; morality has become seen as evil. Therefore, it is like insanity has covered the whole land! And what was up, now is down, and what was down, now is up. Our education is declining, and we are amid the dumbing down of America. Our culture has become a Satanic Cultural Revolution against God, Christ, the Holy Spirit, and the church. And we are amid a brainwashing of America against God, Christ, the Holy Spirit, and the church. There is no respect for the tradition that founded America, which is Christianity. And the founding religious beliefs of America are decaying.

Indeed, we are now more than ever replacing Christianity with ancient paganism under the disguise of the New Age. There is no such thing as a post-Christian society. There is a pre-Christian society, and that is a pagan society. Paganism has never been the answer; it has been the curse. It always brought forth judgment by God against those nations following it.

America is becoming pagan in its values, morals, and ethics. Pagan cultures have a lot of religion, but their teachings exclude the one true God. America is not post-Christian. She is becoming pre-Christian, where abortions are occurring, where murder and violence are both common, where sexuality is becoming unrestricted, and where perversion is seen as normal. Pagan cultures worship the body and sensuality. A Pagan culture sees the weaker of society as to be enslaved or to be killed. If you want a look at a post-Christian world, look at the pre-Christian world.

Lightweight Christianity has now been exposed within America; the curtain has been lifted. The lukewarmness and backsliding of the church in America has, more than anything, exposed America to the dangers of God's wrath. The true message of the cross is being bypassed if not ignored. The method and the message are changing. Where are the leaders of the church like Justin Martyr, who wrote his apologies against paganism in the second century and died for it?

I cannot help but remember Winston Churchill's words about compromising. *Each one hopes that if he feeds the crocodile enough, the crocodile will eat him last. All of them hope that the storm will pass before their turn comes to be devoured. But I fear greatly that the storm will not pass. It will rage, and it will roar ever more loudly, ever more widely.*[2]

There cannot be any more time in the churches for seeker friendliness and amusement. Our watered-down gospel has now been seen to produce evil fruit, and our attempt to become like the world has failed miserably.

If America's downfall is imminent, it is because of the church. With noted exceptions, the church in America is lukewarm, stale, depressed, and disinterested.

We are beyond the foolishness of the church and the foolishness of America. Be gone, foolishness! We are at the threshold of the most incredible time within America or the greatest calamity. We are at the threshold of the most excellent time for the church or the greatest calamity. Unquestionably, the time has come because the hour is late when we must decide. And the choice before us is plain: Jehovah or Baal, Christ or chaos, conviction or compromise, discipline or disintegration.

Christians have sought to make Jesus a mere feature, not the driving force of our lives. We have incredibly forgotten that it is all about Him or not about Him at all and are being entertained to death within the churches. We have made trivial pursuits not just a game but a lifestyle. Remaking God and the gospel into a simple means has selfish ends, which result in wealth and pleasure.

Too many Christians have made prayer a thing to do when we are in trouble or buying a lotto ticket. We have forgotten the reality of heaven and hell. We have forgotten that most who die are going to hell. We Christians fill our lives and minds with such foolishness when eternity is being carried out right before us.

The modern church in America is miles wide, but its deepness is only inches. We have made faith a contest between entrepreneurs where the winner is the one who brings in the most money. We try to convince the world that they should like us because we are like them, not because we have the answer, not because we stand for something more excellent and more splendid, and not because they are thirsty and that we have the well of living water, or because they are hungry, and we have the bread of life.

There is very little substance or no substance among the churches. I remember an elderly woman in a commercial saying, "Where is the beef?" That is a good question for the Christians in America to ask themselves. Why is evil gaining power if God is so powerful and mighty, and the church is His vessel? Yes! We are in the last days, but if we, as a church, will touch the hem of the Lord's garment, I am sure He will save our land.

The church should weep over herself and the condition of the nation. Sin and wrong have ruled the land for years. And awaiting justice sleeps. We are engaged in total war and fighting for total victory. The average church member has forgotten and forsaken the old disciplines. These disciplines must be awakened. The remedy for this sad situation will lie, I believe, in the seeking of God's will for the individual church. Our strength is limited only by our faith in asking for God's help. America's future depends upon her accepting and demonstrating God's government. If America listens to God, if America obeys God, then she can be outstanding among all nations.

Men can be in touch with God. In all situations, men can know the will of God. They can know exactly what God wants them to do and to be. God's guidance and God's power are always available.

When men seek God, they find Him and are found by Him. "According to your faith, be it unto you" (Matthew 9:29). That measure would enable us to move mountains or, if our faith is limited, cause us to stumble over molehills. So also, in the affairs of the nation. "If the Lord be God, follow him, but if Baal, then follow him" (1 Kings 18:21).

In truth, America will only change when or if the church of America changes. Today, we cannot see that the wealthiest church was the church that worshipped Christ hidden among the catacombs of Rome. Its faith was pure because it was a witness for Christ in the face of persecution and martyrdom.

William Booth, the founder of the Salvation Army, prophesied in his day that the chief danger that confronts the coming century would be a religion without the Holy Ghost, Christianity without Christ, forgiveness without repentance, salvation without regeneration, politics without God, and heaven without hell.[3]

Catherine Booth, the wife of William Booth, the more fiery preacher of the two, in her sermon *Aggressive Christianity,* shouted, "I was going to note that both texts imply opposition for, He adds, 'Lo, I am with you always, even to the end of the world.' As much as if He had said, 'You will have need of my presence. Such aggressive, determined warfare as this will raise all earth and hell against you;' and then He says to Paul, 'I will be with thee, delivering thee from the people and the Gentiles unto whom I send thee.' Why would they need this? Because the Gentiles would soon be up in arms against him, and indeed they were. Opposition! It is a bad sign for the Christianity of this day that it provokes so little opposition. If there were no other evidence of it being wrong, I should know from that. When the church and the world can jog along together comfortably, you may be sure there is something wrong. The world has not altered. Its spirit is exactly the same as it ever was, and if Christians were equally faithful and devoted to the

Lord and separated from the world, living so that their lives were a reproof to all ungodliness, the world would hate them as much as it ever did. It is the church that has altered, not the world. You say, 'we should be getting into endless turmoil. Yes ! I came not to bring peace on the earth, but a sword.' There would be uproar. Yes, and the Acts of the Apostles are full of stories of uproars. One uproar was so great that the Chief Captain had to get Paul over the shoulders of the people, lest he should have been torn in pieces. 'What a commotion!' you say. Yes; and, bless God, if we had the like now we should have thousands of sinners saved."[4]

American Christians must set the essential choices before the nation. Christians must remind the nation of the godly principles of years gone by, repentance forgotten, living for Christ forgotten, and accepting Him just because of who He is, not what we can receive from Him. A time like this demands strong minds, great hearts, true faith, and ready hands.

We need Christians with a political voice and those who proclaim God's will within and outside His church. We should encourage Christians to engage in daily repentance, expressing sorrow and regret for the nation's transgressions, direction, and state. Additionally, it extended over the church. We need those who will have the ear of America and say to her now, "How long will you halt and stand between two opinions? If the Lord be God, follow him, but if Baal be God, follow him, and go to hell!" We need those who will have the ear of America and say, "If the Lord be God, follow him, but if Baal, then follow him" (1 Kings 18:21).

Rebellion has swept over America for various years while the church was asleep.

When a nation forgets its foundation, a nation will fall. Within the writings of Zephaniah Swift, the early founders of America denounced gambling, obscenity, sodomy, other sexual sins, and men dressing like women.[5] The leaders of American cities at the time demanded that people leave their cities if they were there as a burden: if people refused to work or play a part in their local society.

Once a nation falls, it never returns to its glory and position. The only one who has returned to part of its glory and position is the nation of Israel. God's judgment comes in various types and manners, as seen in Deuteronomy 28. Deuteronomy 28 speaks of two roads for any nation. Simply, obedience leads to the road of blessing; disobedience leads to cursing. Notice the simple conditions for blessings:

1. Hearken diligently to the voice of the Lord (Deuteronomy 28:1–2,9,13,15).

2. Observe and do all His commandments (Deuteronomy 28:1,13,15).

3. Walk in His ways (Deuteronomy 28:9).

4. Do not go aside from any of the words of God, to the right or left (Deuteronomy 28:13,14).

5. Do not go after other gods to serve them (Deuteronomy 28:14).

God is seeking the prayers of the righteous. Now, the Lord will accept the prayer of repentance of a sinner. However, He has not promised sinners anything other than forgiveness if they repent (1 John 1:9).

After the revival had about died out for the time, John Wesley once prayed, *Oh Lord, send us the Old Revival, without the defects; but if this cannot be, send it with all its defects; We must have the revival.*[6]

Latimer said to Bishop Ridley as they burned on the stake for the sake of their faith, *Be of good comfort, master Ridley, and play the man. We shall this day light such a candle, by God's grace..., as I trust shall never be put out.*[7]

Yes, the truth be told, on some critical fronts, we are experiencing real opposition from the world, and some of it is vicious and angry. But we are experiencing even more opposition from spiritual sources.

Therefore, the greatest threats to America are not from outside but from within. Some of these threats include the degeneration of our Judeo-Christian moral and spiritual fiber, the disintegration of our cultural and religious institutions, and the destruction of the corner foundation of any society, the family.

In summation, the very foundations upon which America was built are currently under assault and facing significant challenges. What are the foundational pillars? They are the divine institutions— a fundamental principal God ordained for the preservation of humanity, as found in Genesis 1–11. These institutions are given to all, not just those who obey God. Any society that follows these will be maintained or preserved. They maintain a more secure society. The divine institutions are human freedom and responsibility, the family, the sanctity of life, human government, and the organization of people into a nation.

However, far greater threats are being thrown against America. These threats cannot be cured or relieved by anything human. These threats are behind all others; they are hidden amid darkness. These threats cannot be fought against by politics, medicine, fundamental secularism, communism, socialism, physical armies, or any means that human intelligence can muster. These threats are spiritual in nature and are denied by a modern man who is secure in his modernism or secularism.

America is being torn apart by something that modernism has denied and that the universities and all other higher levels of American society have tried to wash away. These threats are demonic spirits. And denying Satan does not protect you from him.

The spirits are attacking stronger than I have ever known and seen. As a result, I have seen an increase in demonic oppression, demonic possession, sickness, and disease among the people of America, and an increase in mental disease. All these things point to particular spirits that have been let loose against America. The exception today is for a Christian not to be oppressed by Satan. For those who deal with spiritual warfare, the war has intensified. Still, those Christians who fight in this spiritual war are few and greatly misunderstood, or worse, they are used, discarded, and rejected as abnormal in Christian society since they do not follow normal of Christianity. Of course, normal Christianity is abnormal. Suppose you do not feel you just fit in what is called normal Christianity. In that case, it is because you are not backslidden, and you have decided to fight against all the forces of hell for the sake of the church and your families. Such people should be honored by the church rather than thrown into the trash heap.

Many Christians want to believe that they are in a bubble of safety where they see no harm or danger. But that is an illusion. While the fight goes on, they seem safe from all danger, but the truth is that Satan has fooled them into his trap. He is awaiting the time and for the place to destroy them. If only they would fight, maybe this land and their families would be saved. If we had twenty thousand intensified warfare soldiers who would fight and not surrender, this nation and their families may be saved. But few want to step out into the battle.

Numerous years of public ministry have shown me that most Christians do not want to belong to a church that is fighting or be around a pastor who is warring against demonic oppression, demonic possession, spells, witchcraft, generational curses, and other forms of the occult. They prefer to be in a church where the illusion of safety is found, and their flesh can be entertained. This has wrought much evil and danger upon the church and America. God forbid if someone demon possessed comes into a church! What upheaval it will cause! What tithes and offerings will be lost if a demon begins to manifest within a church? And what will be lost if a godly pastor takes up the challenging prospect of confronting that demon (or demons) within the public congregation? Instead of people supporting such a difficult prospect, I have seen people run, become afraid, deny what is going on, and finally, leave the church and never come back, simply because they want a safe place where people cannot be helped in such cases. What they want is not the church! This is one of the hardest things that I deal with. Churchgoers would rather have the demon stay in a person rather than upset their view of Christianity: no harm and no use of Christianity!

Numerous churchgoers are spiritual vampires or bloodsuckers—they take and take and do not give back or help the cause of Christ. In his words, Gregory Reid sums up Christianity today best, "I wanted desperately to help hurting people. I found plenty of them. I helped a few. But then I began being hounded by living spiritual vampires (anyone who has been in ministry, especially pastors, knows what I'm talking about). They say, 'Help meeee!' and they act so pitiful and defenseless that they pull you right in, attach themselves to you, and proceed to suck every bit of spiritual life and strength they can from you, then they discard you when you fail to meet their every need and leave you, a mere hollow shell of your former self, as they move on in search of a fresh victim. They give nothing, they never grow, they just take and take and demand and whine, their problems are always emergencies, and only you can help. Well, the entire Society of Christian Bloodsuckers had found me, and within a few short years, they'd taken it all."[8]

Casting demons out made Christianity grow.

In truth, I have seen dealing with demons, in particular demonic possession, damage my public ministry. What a shame! According to Mark 6:7–13, there are only three conditions for a person to be a minister:

1.   To preach repentance.

2.   To cast out demons.

3.   To pray for the sick.

Why? Mark was writing to people who were filled with all kinds of evil and who were subject to being controlled by all sorts of evil spirits. Mark knew that the Christians had their answer for that—the authority of Christ and the power of the Holy Spirit.

Mark believed that the Gentile society needed to be aware of the unclean spirits among them and their need to be cleansed of such uncleanness and evil. Most of the Gentiles were demon possessed. Mark focuses upon the central purpose of Christ: to conquer the spirit of evil and to destroy the works of the devil, especially in the hearts and lives of men. Without this aspect of Christianity, there is no Christianity! There is no church without casting out demons.

Christians need not to be entertained in the churches. If so, they are not Christians. Churches must be places where the gospel is preached, where Christ is lifted, where we know we are depraved sinners saved by grace, and where we know that the authority of Christ and the power of the Holy Spirit are greatly needed. The shape of America rests solely upon the shape of the church. The church has allowed, without fighting, the enemy to come in like a thief in the night and take the very soul of America.

The shame is that which glitters is more important to many Christians than fighting for the soul of America and their own families.

Certainly, when America was spiritually strong and had a solid church, she could push back these spirits and restrict them or their influence within American society but not now. The weakness of the church, as the watchman on the wall, has left very little protection to defend against these spirits.

I have studied and researched much for years; I have uncovered the demonic spirits, satanic in nature, that Satan uses to destroy every nation or society that has ever existed. Every nation or society these spirits have destroyed has never been completely restored. The nation of Israel comes closest to a nation being restored completely. Every pagan nation or society had all these spirits within them. And that infection entered the nation of Israel, even in the times of Moses. Once these spirits enter a nation, it is hard to remove them but not impossible. And it is not impossible to push them back or diminish their effect upon a nation. Because of a weak church, these same spirits attacked America and almost destroyed America in the early eighteen hundreds. Chief Justice John Marshall lamented that the church was so weak it could not impact the culture. The nation's colleges, created to train preachers, had become spiritually indifferent. Mock communion services occurred. Christian students were censored. Liberal ideas triumphed. At the same time, an epidemic of drunkenness threatened the fabric of families and communities.

Further, just two types of these spirits by themselves destroyed Israel in the past. We should notice that the history of ancient Israel as laid out in the Old Testament is largely the two thousand–year struggle of the worship of the one Lord against all the various forms of pagan instinct worship that dominated the ancient Near East. Supremely, it is the story of the fight of God against Baal, the god of sacred sexuality in all perverted form, and against his sacred consort Astarte/Ashtoreth. This virgin prostitute copulates and conceives but does not give birth.

America is at war against the Baalim and their consorts, Astartes. These two groups of spirits, along with the Pythonic demons and the Kundalini demons, are the most destructive demons of all spirits.

Then, will America be returned to God, or will we continue to wander, and will our society become ever more evil by these spirits? If Christ were to tarry another several decades, the outcome could only be determined by prayer and the cries of God's saints more than anything else. A people coming back to God is critical.

Matthew gives us a picture that we should note (Matthew 24). If the problems of America cannot be solved before the coming of the Lord with His saints, Christ will solve them when He comes. The Bible also tells us He will rule all the nations (including the US) with an iron rod. Therefore, the problems with this nation (and all the nations) will be resolved. The question is how this would be resolved. Will God have to resort to judgment to beckon us to return to Him? Is there going to be another World War before He comes? Is there going to be another depression before He comes? Is there going to be another great awakening before He comes? Are there going to be one or more of these things happening before He comes?

These questions must be thought of carefully, for the soul of America hangs in the balance!

CHAPTER 1
THE SPIRIT OF LEVIATHAN

There are four theories defining what the Spirit of Leviathan is today. According to these views, the Spirit of Leviathan is a demon, a spirit of pride, or some principality. Following a thorough examination of their viewpoints, I posit a more profound implication exists. While these views have a part, they do not have the whole picture. The only means to undercover the whole picture is to go back to the fall of humanity. At that place in time, the Bible shows Satan using the serpent and tempting Eve to rebel against God.

The Fall of Man

Satan had a great victory when Adam and Eve rebelled against God. He had the souls of humans, and now he wanted their land.

God instantly moved and drove them out of the Garden, placing cherubim at the gate. "And the Lord God said, Behold, the man is become as one of us, to know good and evil: and now, lest he put forth his hand, and also take of the tree of life, and eat, and live forever: Therefore, the Lord God sent him forth from the Garden of Eden, to till the ground from whence he was taken. So he drove out the man, and he placed at the East of the Garden of Eden Cherubims, and a flaming sword which turned every way, to keep the way of the tree of life," Genesis 3:22–24.

God gave them the promise of the coming Messiah in Genesis 3:15 so that He could redeem them from their fall into sin and rescue them by the blood of Jesus. The cross would separate them from the powers of darkness and wash them clean. They would be able to return to God and to live forever. From Genesis 3, several things are learned:

1. Humanity was led into rebellion against the direct rule of God by an already existing evil and evil forces.

2. Satan outwitted and fooled the sinless but inexperienced woman of her blessings and position.

3. Adam, not fooled, willingly accepted the consequences of his rebellion against God.

4. As Adam was the head of humanity, Eve's sin would have been of no effect if he had not rebelled, and the Lord would have forgiven it.

Many Consequences Took Place; Some of Them Were:

1. The Fall defiled and contaminated the creation of God. All creation was injured by the fall of humanity (Genesis 3:17–19).

2. The cosmic rebellion has become a cosmic-earthly rebellion.

3. Humanity participates in the conflict and has become a central figure in warfare (Luke 4:4–6; John 12:31, 14:30, 16:11; Acts 26:18; Ephesians 2:1–3; Colossians 1:13).

4. Every race of humanity is affected by the Fall (Romans 5:12–15).

5. Death entered the world of Adam (Romans 5:12–15).

6. Due to the fall of humanity, all unsaved are in bondage to Satan and are open to demon possession at will (1 Corinthians 10:20–21; 2 Corinthians 4:3–4; Ephesians 2:1–3; Colossians 1:13–14, 2:8–20; 2 Thessalonians 2; Hebrews 2:14–15).

7. The unsaved are all children of Satan (Matthew 13:37–39; John 8:44; 1 John 3:3–10).

8. The unsaved are in the kingdom of Satan and the property of Satan (Matthew 12:22–29; Colossians 1:12–14).

9. The unsaved are all bound by Satan (Acts 26:18).

10. The unsaved are all blinded by Satan so that they cannot in themselves receive the gospel, except for the sake of prevenient grace working in them (2 Corinthians 4:3–4).

11. The unsaved are all under the power of Satan (1 John 5:19).

12. The unsaved are all enslaved to a world-system controlled by Satan (Ephesians 2:2; 1 John 5:19).

13. The unsaved are in the flesh (Romans 7:5), under the law (Romans 6:14, 7:6), and slaves to sin (Romans 6:6, 17–20).

14. These things indicate that humans are in a condemned state and are lost sinners under the condemnation of death, are children of the devil, and helpless in the power of the great enemy of one's soul (Romans 1–3).

The Human Condition and its Results

1. We are the property of Satan as pertaining to physical birth.

2. We were born in sin.

3. We only become the absolute property of God at the new birth.

4. Since we were the property of Satan, and Satan rules the world, bad things will happen.

5. Satan will test us.

6. Many terrible things have happened to saints, but God is there regardless.

7. Our strength is our faith, and we must understand that our ways are not God's.

8. All suffering goes back to the fall of Adam.

9. This life is a life of testing; indeed, it is a life of probation.

10. We must serve God regardless.

11. Men and women have free will.

List of Privileges That Man Lost Because of the Fall

1. The privilege to be over the power of physical death (Genesis 3:7–19; Hosea 13:14; 1 Corinthians 15:54–55; Hebrews 2:14–15).

2. The privilege to be over the power of Sheol–Hades (Psalms 16:10, 18:5, 55:15, 116:3, 139:8; Proverbs 5:5, 23:14; Revelation 1:18).

3. The privilege to be over the power of the grave (Job 5:26, 10:19, 21:32; Psalm 88:5; Revelation 1:18).

4. The privilege to have control over the soul and the spirit ultimately (Galatians 5:19–22; Ephesians 2:1–10).

5. The privilege to have eternal fellowship with God (Isaiah 59:2; Colossians 1:20).

6. The privilege to have eternal happiness (Genesis 3:16–19; Galatians 5:19–22; Ephesians 2:1–10; Colossians 1:20).

7. The privilege to have eternal salvation (Hebrews 1:14).

8. The privilege to have life in three wonderful ways: spiritual, physical, and eternal life (Isaiah 59:2; Matthew 25:46; Ephesians 2:1–10).

9. The privilege to have God's perfect image and likeness (Philippians 3:20–21).

10. The privilege to have God's perfect glory and self-respect (Romans 3:23).

11. The privilege to have God's holiness and righteousness wholly (Isaiah 64:6; Ephesians 4:22–24).

12. The privilege to have an understanding that was higher than the angels' (whether un-fallen or fallen) and demons' (Psalm 8:5; 1 Corinthians 13:12).

13. The privilege to have power independently to do good and reject evil (Genesis 6:5–7; Romans 7; Ephesians 2:10).

14. The privilege to have innocence wholly (Genesis 2:25, 3:7 3:10).

15. The privilege to eat of the tree of life (Genesis 3:1–24).

16. The privilege to have the fruits of the Spirit (Galatians 5:22–23).

17. The privilege to have an eternal home, a paradise, and a throne where to rule over all created things through the constitution and manifesto God established (Genesis 3:22–24; Psalm 8:5–6).

18. The privilege to have freedom from diseases, sicknesses, sorrows, pain, afflictions, griefs, mischief, troubles, distresses, calamities, trials, tribulations, hardships, miseries, and physical death (Genesis 3:17–19).

19. The privilege to have God's grace in its fullness and unconditionally (Genesis 3:17–19; Colossians 1:20).

20. The privilege to have fellowship with animals (Genesis 2:19, 9:2).

21. The privilege to have whatever else that God bestowed upon an un-fallen man (Colossians 1:20).

Why Do We Suffer?

1. Suffering silences Satan, as witnessed in the life of Job (Job 1:1–22, 2:1–8, 42:10–13).

2. Suffering enables one to glorify God (John 11:4–5).

3. Suffering makes one like Christ (Philippians 3:10; Hebrews 2:10, 2:18; 1 Peter 1:7, 2:21, 3:14).

4. Suffering makes one appreciative (Romans 8:28).

5. Suffering teaches one to depend upon God (Isaiah 30:15).

6. Suffering causes one to exercise great faith (Job 23:10; 1 Peter 4:12–13).

7. Suffering will cause one to be glad when Christ appears (1 Peter 1:7, 4:12–13).

8. Suffering teaches one patience (Romans 5:3–5).

9. Suffering makes one sympathetic (2 Corinthians 1:3–6).

10. Suffering makes one what he or she ought to be (Romans 8:28–29; 1 Peter 5:10).

11. Suffering keeps one humble (2 Corinthians 12:7–10).

12. Suffering persuades one to pray (Judges 16:28; Daniel 1–12).

13. Suffering in the present time will bring forth a right to reign with Christ in His kingdom and will bring forth other rewards in the afterlife (Romans 8:17–18; 2 Timothy 2:12; 1 Peter 4:12–13).

14. Suffering in the present time helps one keep from sinning (Hebrews 2:10, 11:25).

15. Suffering found in the present time is seen only as a fleeting thing when one compares it to the glory, which one will see and be revealed in him or her (Romans 8:17–18).

16. Suffering brings comfort from the touch of Christ upon one's life (2 Corinthians 1:4).

17. The more suffering one has, the more grace and comfort one has (2 Corinthians 1:5).

18. Suffering causes one not to hinder the gospel of Christ (1 Corinthians 9:12).

19. One suffers for the sake of Christ (Philippians 1:29).

20. Suffering shows that one is godly in Christ (2 Timothy 3:12).

21. It is better to suffer for good or obedience than to suffer for evil or disobedience (1 Peter 3:17).

22. One glorifies God in one's suffering (1 Peter 4:16).

23. Without suffering, one will indeed be deceived (Romans 8:28–29; Philippians 3:10; Hebrews 2:10, 18, 19; 1 Peter 1:7, 2:21, 3:14).

24. A saint triumphs in suffering (Matthew 26:6; Romans 8:35–39; 1 Corinthians 4:9; 2 Corinthians 4:8, 6:3; Philippians 1:12–30; Hebrews 11:33–40).

25. Suffering proves one is a saint and a minister of the highest God (2 Corinthians 6:4).

Why Does Satan Continue?

1. So that humanity may be tried (Job 1:11, 20–21).

2. So that the love and courage of a saint might be tried (James 1:12; 1 Peter 1:7–10, 5:8–9).

3. So that humility will be found in the saints of God (2 Corinthians 12:7).

4. So that the saints will be provided a means of conflict that they may be rewarded through overcoming (Mark 16:17–20; 1 Corinthians 4:9; 2 Corinthians 2:5–11; Revelation 2:7–28).

5. So that the character and faith of a believer will be developed and well-rounded (James 1:12; 1 Peter 1:7–13, 1 Peter 5:10; 2 Peter 1:4–9; Jude 20–24).

6. So that the very power of God will be demonstrated over the power of Satan (Mark 16:17–20; 1 Corinthians 4:9; Ephesians 2:7, 3:10).

7. So that, as an instrument of chastisement, people will repent and come to God (Job 33:14–30; 1 Corinthians 5:1–6; 2 Corinthians 2:5–11).

8. So that the very possibility of falling will be purged from the saints in the eternal future (Daniel 9:24–27; Revelation 21).

The Classic Theme of Christ's Atonement

What became known as the "classic theme" of Christ's Atonement arose from all these facts. The "classic theme" notion is as old as Genesis 3:15. Paul mentioned this theme in Colossians 2:15 and Hebrews 2:14. As shall be more discussed, the "classic theme" is best defined as "Christus Victor," which means "Christ is the Victor."

Colossians 2:15 reads, ἀπεκδυσάμενος τὰς ἀρχὰς καὶ τὰς ἐξουσίας ἐδειγμάτισεν ἐν παρρησίᾳ, θριαμβεύσας αὐτοὺς ἐν αὐτῷ (when He had stripped of arms the rulers–principalities and the authorities, He also made a spectacle of them in boldness, triumphing over them by it–by the cross).

The subject of the Greek aorist participle ἀπεκδυσάμενος (when He had stripped of arms) is not God the Father. Interpreting this aorist participle with God the Father is impossible or difficult. The participle has Christ as its subject. It is grammatical and logical to consider Christ as the subject of verses 14 and 15. Using the dative αὐτῷ in Colossians 1:16, 1:17, 2:6, 2:7, 2:9, 2:10, 2:12, and 2:13 all point to the conclusion of Christ as the subject in verses 14 and 15.

In Colossians 2:14, Lightfoot notices Christ is introduced as the new subject by the change of participles to a finite verb, the change of aorists into a perfect, and in the Greek phrase καὶ αὐτὸ ἦρκεν ἐκ τοῦ μέσου (and He took it out of the way).[1]

Further, various witnesses and scholars follow this common interpretation of Colossians 2:15. This was the common interpretation of the Greek fathers. Chrysostom, Severianus, Theodore of Mopsuestia, Theodoret, Origen, and other Greek fathers followed this interpretation. Lightfoot writes and explains Colossians 2:15 beautifully, "The meaning then will be as follows.

Christ took upon Himself our human nature with all its temptations (Heb. 4:15). The powers of evil gathered about Him. Again and again, they assailed Him, but each fresh assault ended in a now defeat. In the wilderness, He was tempted by Satan, but Satan retired for the time, baffled and defeated (Luke 4:13 ἀπέστη ἀπ᾽ αὐτοῦ ἄχρι καιροῦ). Through the voice of His chief disciple, the temptation was renewed, and He was entreated to decline His appointed sufferings and death. Satan was again driven off (Matt. 16:23 ὕπαγε ὀπίσω μου, Σατανᾶ, σκάνδαλον εἶ ἐμοῦ: comp. Matt. 8:31). Then the last hour came. This was the great crisis of all, when the power of darkness made itself felt (Luke 22:53 ἡ ἐξουσία τοῦ σκότους; see above 1:13) when the prince of the world asserted his tyranny (Joh. 12:31 ὁ ἄρχων τοῦ κόσμου). The final act in the conflict began with the agony of Gethsemane; it ended with the Cross of Calvary. The victory was complete. The enemy of man was defeated. The powers of evil, which had clung like a Nessus robe about His humanity, were torn off and cast aside for ever. And the victory of mankind is involved in the victory of Christ. In His cross we too are divested of the poisonous clinging garments of temptation and sin and death."[2] Lightfoot adds, "This interpretation is grammatical; it accords with St. Paul's teaching."[3]

Historically, when the Greek fathers wrote of Colossians 2:15, the subject was always Christ. Origen wrote, Τίς δ᾽ οὗτος, εἰ μὴ Ἰησοῦς Χριστός, οὗ "τῷ μώλωπι" "ἰάθημεν" οἱ εἰς αὐτὸν πιστεύοντες, ἀπεκδυσαμένου "τὰς" ἐν ἡμῖν "ἀρχὰς καὶ ἐξουσίας" καὶ "παρρησίᾳ" δειγματίσαντος αὐτὰς ἐν τῷ ξύλῳ (And who else is this person, except Jesus Christ, by whose stripes the ones who believe on Him are healed—acceptance as healing as part of the New Covenant as a fact, when He had stripped of arms the rulers—principalities and authorities that were over us, and He also made a spectacle of them in boldness, triumphing over them on the cross)?[4] Chrysostom, speaking about Colossians 2:15, writes, Ἀπεκδυσάμενος τὰς ἀρχὰς καὶ τὰς ἐξουσίας. Τὰς διαβολικὰς δυνάμεις λέγει· ἢ ἐπεὶ αὐτὰς ἡ ἀνθρωπίνη φύσις ἐνδέδυτο, ἢ ἐπειδὴ αὐτὰς ὥσπερ λαβὴν εἶχον, ἄνθρωπος γενόμενος ἀπεδύσατο τὴν λαβήν ('When He had stripped of arms the rulers—

principalities and the authorities.' He is speaking of diabolical powers because human nature had put on them or because they held, as it were, a grasp when He became man, He stripped from Himself that grasp).[5] Athanasius, Bishop of Alexandria, said about Christ and referring back to Colossians 2:15, Οὕτω γὰρ ὑψωθείς, τὸν μὲν ἀέρα ἐκαθάριζεν ἀπό τε τῆς διαβολικῆς καὶ πάσης τῶν δαιμόνων ἐπιβουλῆς (For, consequently, when He was lifted up, He made clean the air of the evil scheme—evil damage both of the devil and demons of all kinds).[6]

The disarming of the evil forces is complete under Christ, by Christ, and especially in the realm of the atonement. Satan and his forces have been stripped of their power to destroy the whole human race. Regardless of what men and women think and do, Satan cannot destroy the whole human race.

It is the cross which was and is the place of victory over the enemies of God. The Greek phrase ἐν αὐτῷ (by it) is tied to the Greek phrase τῷ σταυρῷ (to the cross) in Colossians 2:14. Interpreting the Greek phrase ἐν αὐτῷ (by it) as having reference to the cross makes the subject of the Greek aorist participle ἀπεκδυσάμενος (when He had stripped of arms) and the Greek aorist verb ἐδειγμάτισεν (He made a show of them) the same, which is Christ.

The sufferings of Christ upon the cross are the very manifestation of the endless suffering of God over the sins of humanity in space and time. Without the cross, this infinite suffering of God over the sins of humanity would never have truly been comprehended by men. The death of Christ is victory. It is the cross that is the sermon that is preached. It is the blood that does the preaching. Without the sufficiency of the blood, the cross is silent! Without the voice of that blood, the "Atonement of Christ" cannot be obtained. It is not the resurrection that purchases the Atonement of Christ; it is His blood!

The Greek aorist participle ἀπεκδυσάμενος (when He had stripped of arms) is found in the middle voice. Sometimes, the middle voice is used as an active voice. Still, if the middle voice is accepted, it does not limit the effect of the cross to just Christ. Instead, it is in reference to the victorious self-interest of Christ— the redemption of mankind and the taking back of what Satan gained by the fall of Adam. One theme of the Bible is "where mankind was, where mankind is, and where mankind shall be." What is meant is where man was before the fall, where man is because of the fall, and where man shall be because of the Atonement of Christ. Therefore, the middle voice, in this case, depicts an action done in the interest of the verb's subject. Accepting the middle voice, "Himself" is added to the translation. Christ, being the subject of Colossians 2:15, is also strengthened by the middle voice.

The power of the evil forces had been deprived of their armor and arms. They are helpless in front of Christ. They are not powerless before the saints but only helpless if we are in Christ and doing according to His will. The saints are not Christ; we must be careful when dealing with evil spirits, even the weak ones.

Complete victory is achieved through Christ's death, burial, resurrection, and ascension.

The saints are not reigning as kings but only as slaves (1 Corinthians 4:8). Paul wrote about the Corinthians as καὶ ὄφελόν γε ἐβασιλεύσατε (and I would to God that you did reign as kings). In Greek, this type of sentence is the indicative of an unattainable wish. The saints cannot reign as kings until the resurrection. In other words, they must go through the resurrection (First Resurrection).

The Greek phrase τὰς ἀρχὰς καὶ τὰς ἐξουσίας (the rulers— principalities and authorities) was always accepted grammatically and historically as having reference to evil forces in a general sense—all groupings and functioning are combined into two Greek words— until AD 1729 when J Peirce tried to reverse that interpretation and suggested good angels were meant.[7] Still, the more common interpretation must be retained. The Greek phrase τὰς ἀρχὰς καὶ τὰς ἐξουσίας (the rulers—principalities and authorities) are hostile potentates of evil. This view is preferable due to its simplicity, being the earliest historical view, and its agreement with the context. Therefore, it is grammatically preferable.

The Greek fathers generally took the Greek phrase τὰς ἀρχὰς καὶ τὰς ἐξουσίας (the rulers—principalities and authorities) as the object of the Greek aorist participle ἀπεκδυσάμενος (when He had stripped of arms).

The Greek phrase τὰς ἀρχὰς καὶ τὰς ἐξουσίας (the rulers—principalities and authorities) is a simpler version of the Greek in Ephesians 6:12. It covers all evil spirits, whether in heaven, in hell, or upon the earth. The Greek aorist participle ἀπεκδυσάμενος (when He had stripped of arms) has reference to conflict and conquest against hostile forces. Paul recognized Christ led a triumphal procession by the cross. When a Roman conqueror—general defeated an enemy of Rome, a triumphal procession was held in Rome; it went through the "triumphal gate" and then the streets of Rome.

There is no contradiction here between Colossians 2:15 and Ephesians 6:12. Satan and his evil spirits have been defeated as per atonement; they are still virulently active, and the saints must learn how to fight against them. The cross of Christ was and is the decisive victory over evil; the fullness of it has not been achieved but will be at the Second Coming and at the end of the Millennium when creation is restored.

Further, passages found in the New Testament about Satan and his armies and the passages of the Old Testament that speak about Satan and his armies instigating the fall of humanity and their fall all speak of one theme—Christus Victor (Genesis 1:1–2, 1:3–4:1; Isaiah 14:12–15; Ezekiel 28:11–19; Matthew 4, 16:23; John 12:31; Acts 10:38).

The earliest and most dominant position on the Atonement of Christ, though not yet genuinely formalized into a theory, was that which regarded the Atonement of Christ as a victory over sin, evil, and Satan. This is "Christus Victor." This idea is repeatedly mentioned by the apostolic fathers, the early apologists, and many Greek and Latin church leaders. Apart from incorporating this classic theme, no theory of redemption is worth anything.

Satan and all his forces have been defeated at the cross. They will be defeated at the Second Coming of Christ and wholly and finally at the Battle of Gog and Magog (John 17:4, 19:30; Colossians 1:13, 2:14–17; Ephesians 2:14–18; Hebrews 2:14; 1 John 3:8; Revelation 20:7–10, 21–22). The saints of God are seen as captives in Christ's triumphal procession of victory against the forces of evil (2 Corinthians 2:14). Paul himself sees Christ's death and the shedding of his blood as a military victory over sin, evil, and particularly Satan. This victory is now a present possession of the saints by the past act of Christ's death. It will be ultimately carried out in its fullness for the saints at the resurrection and for creation beginning at the Second Coming (Romans 8:17–39; Colossians 2:15).

The defeat of Satan and his countless forces accomplished by Christ's physical death on the cross was over man's redemption, and the ultimate result of that—to raise redeemed humanity to that place that man had before the fall. Therefore, while Satan had vanquished Adam, Christ became victorious against him. The very words of Hippolytus must echo throughout the kingdom of Satan: στεφανοῦται κατὰ διαβόλου. A translation of this in Latin and English: "Victor contra diabolum coronaris" and "He is crowned the Victor against the devil."[8] Christ fought and conquered Satan, contending not only for the very kidnapped race of humans but all creation, which was Satan's due to man's fall. In so doing, Christ bound the strong man (Matthew 12:29) and set free those his tyranny had afflicted.

All the apologists accepted the teaching of Paul concerning the fall of humanity and the entrance of sin and death into the world of Adam by Adam's transgression.

For example, to Justin Martyr, the Atonement of Christ is seen as the instrument for deliverance from the power of Satan, and principalities and powers have been overthrown and continue to be overthrown. He states that Christ utterly overthrew these principalities and powers with so much perfection that they will never be over what was done to them by Christ on the cross.

According to Justin Martyr, redemption and deliverance from all evil were and are not accomplished by anything but by the death of Christ. It was not accomplished in hell or heaven but upon the Cross of Calvary.[9] Justin Martyr said that the crucifixion was how the power of Satan was broken and how the remission of sins and redemption of death could well be procured. He saw the death of Christ as the only means to accomplish all of this.

To Justin Martyr, the total result of the death of Christ was (1) the conquest of Satan, who committed the initial sin, (2) the conquest of the fallen angels, (3) the conquest of all other evil spirits implied, (4) the conquest of death, and (5) the substitution for humanity and how those who believe in him could be purified and healed with his blood from their sins.[10]

His view of evil and the effects that Christ's Atonement (especially His death) had upon the forces of evil is remarkable. His complete insight into the effects of Christ's death upon sin, evil, and the force of evil is more advanced than those of the apostolic fathers.

Like so many in the ancient church, Justin Martyr accepted the "Christus Victor" their view on the Atonement of Christ. In its pure form, its idea traces the payment of the debt that man owed back to God Himself. Christ gains redemption for humanity upon the cross, not in hell. Neither does Christ have to be "born-again" in hell for redemption to be achieved. These modern deviations are founded not upon the classic theme of the Atonement of Christ but upon the Ransom-Theory.

This classic theme is not an invention of heathenism nor derived from Gnosticism. Heathenism and, in particular, Gnosticism were rejected by the ancient church. Also, the classic theme cannot be seen as promoting heathenistic dualism. The classic theme promotes Biblical dualism. Six points disprove that the ongoing tug-of-war between God and Satan is heathen "dualism." First, in the conflict between God and Satan, only God is eternal, while Satan is created. Second, God and Satan are personal. Third, the conflict has not been ongoing eternally, nor will this conflict last forever and ever, for it has an end (Revelation 20:7–10). Fourth, in the ongoing tug-of-war between Himself and Satan, God has already determined Himself to be the winner. Fifth, God and Satan are not equal in power. Sixth, the ongoing tug-of-war between God and Satan is allowed by God Himself, under His sovereignty and under His control, to stop at a time. The time that God has decided to end it is after the Millennium (Revelation 20:7–10).

Lastly, there should be drawn attention to the last part of Hebrews 2:14. It reads, ἵνα διὰ τοῦ θανάτου καταργήσῃ τὸν τὸ κράτος ἔχοντα τοῦ θανάτου, τοῦτ᾽ ἔστιν τὸν διάβολον (so that through death, He—Christ—could make impotent the one who had the power of death, which is the devil). This began at the cross and continues. Like before, this will be completed at the Battle of Gog and Magog after the Millennium (Revelation 20:7–10).

The aorist subjunctive καταργήσῃ opens the idea that there is not just one reason for Christ's death. Still, there are several reasons that God the Word became man and died on Calvary. And this is proven throughout the New Testament. As a consequence of Christ coming to defeat the devil and end the reign of death, the reign of sin and evil, men and women in Christ are delivered from his present tyranny since the saints are delivered and set above the kingdom of evil as God sees it and His hierarchy of things (Colossians 1:16). The men and women of Christ will be set above that in the resurrection, even above the angels. Still, right now, that does not mean that saints are not to fight against the kingdom of evil. Far from it! We must fight! The work is complete on the divine side, but on man's side, the work is progressive. Only by the Atonement of Christ can the purpose of creation be completed (Romans 5:12–21, 6:1–23, 8:2; 1 Corinthians 15:1–58; 2 Corinthians 3:6–15; Hebrews 2:14–15). Further, by the death of Christ, the claim of Satan against mankind and creation is cancelled. And to accept a considerable number of blessings from the death of Christ, the individual accepts Christ as the only means of salvation (Romans 8:18–24, 14:7–9; 1 Corinthians 6:19–20; 2 Corinthians 5:14–15; 1 Thessalonians 5:10; Hebrews 2:9–15; Revelation 21:1–22:5).

The Background of Leviathan

The word "Leviathan" appears in five places in the Bible (Job 41; 3:8; Psalm 74:14, 104:24—26; Isaiah 27:1).

The idea behind Leviathan in the Old Testament is that of cosmic warfare. Further, the Near Eastern view depicts the world as surrounded by hostile monsters. These monsters seek to destroy and devour men and women. In Canaanite imagery, Leviathan is portrayed as a twisting serpent of the sea with seven heads (Psalm 74:14).

Job saw Leviathan as a dragon or twisting serpent that periodically threatens to reverse creation (Job 3:8). The very sight of Leviathan, in Job's view, causes panic (Job 41:2—14,25). Catching, controlling, or taming Leviathan is impossible (Job 41:2—14).

Leviathan taunts the weapons of humans (Job 41:26—27). Job 41:14—30 describes Leviathan as having sharp, cruel teeth, his back filled with pointed shields, and his belly hard and horned on the sides. Job 41:18—21 states that he breathes out lightning and smoke. And lastly, he blows hot flames of fire out of his mouth.

Generally, it is held that Leviathan is hinted at in Genesis 1:2 and is seen as that which caused chaos itself.

From a Near Eastern point of view, the Leviathan is a formidable, hostile, and galactic creature. He is troublesome to control.

However, the most significant fact about Leviathan is that the Lord has succeeded in subduing him (Job 41). Only God can do what Job could never do. Only God could stand up against Leviathan and subjugate him.

Psalm 74:14 expresses the same point. The defeat of Leviathan is portrayed as a future event in Isaiah 27:1. Indeed, it is portrayed as an end-time event beginning at the Second Coming of Christ that would usher in a time of peace. The effect of this, as it concerns the problem of evil, is that we are left with a bittersweet impression that the travails of the present—indeed of all history since the present order of things—stand before rather than after the triumph of God.

It can well be seen that Leviathan is beaten and still loose. The restoration of all things lies ahead.

There is no contradiction here. A hostile force has been defeated but still opposes the Lord and threatens men and women and the earth. The Lord will continue to beat him. The supremacy of the Lord over Leviathan was always emphasized.

In Rabbinical Judaism, Leviathan is interpreted as a cosmic monster.

The biblical references to Leviathan are similar to the Canaanite Baal cycle, which comprises a confrontation between Baal and a seven-headed sea monster named Lotan.

The Christian interpretation of Leviathan is often considered to be a demon or natural monster associated with Satan or the devil and held by some to be the same monster as Rahab (Isaiah 51:9). Some hold Leviathan to be the devil himself. Some biblical scholars considered Leviathan to represent the pre-existent forces of chaos.

Several interpreters suggest the Leviathan is a symbol of mankind in opposition to God, claiming that it and the beasts mentioned in the books of Daniel and Revelation should be interpreted as metaphors.

According to St. Thomas Aquinas, Leviathan is the demon of envy and the demon who first punishes the corresponding sinners.

There are four main theories of what the Spirit of Leviathan means.

The Spirit of Leviathan: First Theory

The Spirit of Leviathan is a spirit of deception and counterfeits, which is a particular demon.

It has been described as a twisted spirit. It is coiled and ready to attack. It has been described as the spirit of the New Age, occultic views, heresies, and lies. It is a spirit behind soothsaying (Micah 5:12), astrology (Isaiah 47:13), sorcery (Revelation 9:21), enchanting (Deuteronomy 18:10), divination (Hosea 4:12), drugs (Galatians 5:20; Revelation 9:21); astral projecting, and other types of magic (Exodus 7:11, 8:7).

The Spirit of Leviathan: Second Theory

The Spirit of Leviathan is seen as a spirit of pride, trying to stop the movement of the Holy Spirit, a spirit of accusation, and a spirit of confusion. It is a group of demon spirits.

According to this view, it will tear up churches, homes, and individual lives. It will do whatever it can to destroy a house or a church: by words, by a false fire leaping out of the mouth, and by a destructive mouth. It is counterfeit smoke, worship, praise, prayer, and thanksgiving. Leviathan is buried in self.

This view sees Leviathan as pride of position, pride of power, pride of who I am, and pride of what I possess are all controlled by Leviathan. It works against the moving of the Holy Spirit and works in religion contrary to the will of God.

The Spirit of Leviathan: Third Theory

The Spirit of Leviathan is not a demon spirit but a principality. This theory sees the Spirit of Leviathan as the spirit of the Antichrist. It attacks the anointing of churches and ministries. It will attack a prophetic word. It wants to cast doubt, mistrust, and suspicion on God's Word. It intends to twist God's truth and rob us of our promise.

This spirit carries an attitude of superiority, haughtiness, boasting, and arrogance.

The Spirit of Leviathan: Biblical View

The key to understanding the Spirit of Leviathan is found in the Greek Septuagint. Every time the Hebrew noun לִוְיָתָן (Leviathan) is translated into Greek, it is translated as δράκων (dragon). Only one time should it be translated serpent.

The simple truth is that the Spirit of Leviathan is not a demon, a group of demons, satanic princes, or anything imagined by men and women. The Spirit of Leviathan is the very nature, works, and power of Satan flowing from himself to the world, throughout his kingdom, and throughout any part of God's creation that he is fighting against. The Spirit of Leviathan is simply Satan, and another name for Satan.

In Isaiah 27:1, the Greek Septuagint reads, Τῆ ἡμέρα ἐκείνη ἐπάξει ὁ θεὸς τὴν μάχαιραν τὴν ἁγίαν καὶ τὴν μεγάλην καὶ τὴν ἰσχυρὰν ἐπὶ τὸν δράκοντα ὄφιν φεύγοντα, ἐπὶ τὸν δράκοντα ὄφιν σκολιόν, ἀνελεῖ τὸν δράκοντα (In that day, the God will bring the holy and great and mighty sword upon the dragon, even the fleeing serpent, upon the dragon, the twisted serpent; He will defeat—remove the dragon). The timing is the Second Coming and the Millennium (Isaiah 2:2–4, 4:1–6). It is the removal of all evil, including Satan, from the earth and creation. All evil will be confined in the bottomless pit (Revelation 20). Therefore, the Spirit of Leviathan will be confined for a thousand years.

Revelation 12:3 reads partly, καὶ ἰδοὺ δράκων μέγας πυρρὸς ἔχων κεφαλὰς ἑπτὰ καὶ κέρατα δέκα καὶ ἐπὶ τὰς κεφαλὰς αὐτοῦ ἑπτὰ διαδήματα (Behold, a great fiery dragon, having seven heads and ten horns and seven crowns upon his heads). In the middle of the tribulation, Satan and his angels will be cast out of the heavenlies upon the earth. Revelation 12:7–8 reads, Καὶ ἐγένετο πόλεμος ἐν τῷ οὐρανῷ, ὁ Μιχαὴλ καὶ οἱ ἄγγελοι αὐτοῦ τοῦ πολεμῆσαι μετὰ τοῦ δράκοντος. καὶ ὁ δράκων ἐπολέμησεν καὶ οἱ ἄγγελοι αὐτοῦ (And there appeared a war in heaven, Michael, and his angels fighting with the dragon. And the dragon fought and his angels). This war in heaven will be the last actual struggle between Satan and God over the possession of the heavenlies where Satan reigns (Ephesians 2:2, 6:12).

In Isaiah 27:1, the sword of the Lord, written in Greek as τὴν μάχαιραν τὴν ἁγίαν καὶ τὴν μεγάλην καὶ τὴν ἰσχυρὰν, is the sword used by Christ at the Second Coming. It is the sword of vengeance and destruction. Therefore, ὁ θεὸς (the God) is a direct reference to God Incarnate, God the Word, who became man. It is Christ, both as God and as the exalted man—Second Adam who comes to battle the dragon. The Leviathan, the dragon, is a person, Satan, who has destroyed many through his works, nature, behavior, influence, and persuasion. The person of Satan is personalized in the Spirit of

Leviathan. The Spirit of Leviathan may also be known as demonically controlled behavior.

The sword used and that continues to be used is unique and particular among or including all other swords. God's sword is strong, unbreakable, mighty, invincible, and far-reaching against Leviathan–dragon, another name for Satan (Isaiah 27:1; Job 41:1, 34).

The Spirit of Leviathan has been and will be pushed back and stopped in various times, forces, and places: in the dateless past at the rebellion of Satan (Job 38:6–7; Genesis 1:1–2; Nehemiah 9:6; Ezekiel 28:15; Luke 10:18; Colossians 1:16–18), at the fall of Adam (Genesis 3:22–24), at the time of the flood (Genesis 6–8), at the time of Sodom and Gomorrah (Genesis 19:24), during the time of the Exodus and the Wilderness (Exodus 3:1–33:1; Numbers 25), during the times of the judges, during the times of the prophets, especially at the Cross of Calvary on the side of God and continuing on man's side and creation (Isaiah 53; John 17:4, 19:30; Acts 2:24–26; 2 Corinthians 4:4; Ephesians 2:1–3; Hebrews 2:14–15; 1 John 5:18; Revelation 1:18), at the Reformation, at the various Great Awakenings, at the middle of the tribulation (Revelation 12:7–8), at the Second Coming and the Battle of Armageddon (Daniel 2:35–45, 7:8–14, 20–27, 8:9–12, 23–25, 9:27, 11:36–45; Matthew 24:15–28; Revelation 6:1–18:24), in the bottomless pit for a thousand years–all evil will be confined in the bottomless pit (Revelation 20), and finally and entirely at the Battle of Gog and Magog and after that put into the Lake of Fire (Revelation 20:7–10). The Reformation and the Great Awakenings were times when the Spirit of Leviathan was weakened, stopped, and pushed back (from the AD 1500s into the AD 1900s). That is the purpose of the Great Awakening. Without these times, the Spirit of Leviathan would have destroyed everything. Each time it was stopped or held back, the stopping was complete for a time or partial.

Prayer can help weaken, stop, and push back the Spirit of Leviathan in a logical view–locally and regionally. The most excellent means of doing this by prayer is to seek God to bring forth a Great Awakening. Still, while the effects of the Spirit of Leviathan would be significantly hindered, evil spirits could work, but not as powerful as before. The greater the Spirit of Leviathan is, the greater the power and influence of demons will be. The weaker the Spirit of Leviathan is, the weaker the power and influence of demons will be. Suppose the saints can partially and locally cut off this spirit from our lives, churches, and ministries. In that case, the rest of the demonic spirits will become weaker. Significant changes can occur in our lives, churches, and ministries. If the saints can cut off this spirit, the rest will fall from their places of authority for a time.

All the biblical manners and means of fighting evil spirits can produce excellent and positive fruits against the Spirit of Leviathan. They can reduce and hold back the Spirit of Leviathan from our lives, the lives of our families, our homes, our churches, and this land. Still, the utter defeat of this most evil spirit rests out of our control. Its time of defeat—utter defeat and its complete defeat—will be manifested in the future. It is utterly removed when Lucifer is thrown into the Lake of Fire (Revelation 20:7–10).

Our warfare is limited in this world; its effects are limited. We are not kings yet. Still, Paul said beautifully in Ephesians 6:12, ὅτι οὐκ ἔστιν ἡμῖν ἡ πάλη (for our warfare is not). Our warfare is fixed; we are in a state of warfare regardless of whether we fight.

Remember that one of the most frequent and fundamental ways in which the New Testament depicts our salvation as a freeing consequence of Christ's cosmic victory over Satan is by referring to it as "redemption" (Romans 3:24, 8:23; Ephesians 1:7; Colossians 1:13–14).

In the Greek Septuagint, Psalms 74:14 and 104:26 speak of the Leviathan as a dragon. Satan is known as the dragon and serpent— the same Greek noun is used for him.

Additionally, Paul speaks of the Spirit of Leviathan in Ephesians 2:2 as κατὰ τὸν ἄρχοντα τῆς ἐξουσίας τοῦ ἀέρος, τοῦ πνεύματος τοῦ νῦν ἐνεργοῦντος ἐν τοῖς υἱοῖς τῆς ἀπειθείας (according to the ruler of the authority of the air, the spirit which now works in the sons of disobedience). It is the very spirit from which flows all evil and all evil works of Satan. It is the source of and from which all evil spirits receive organization and purpose. Those who have rebelled against God accepted this spirit and became like Satan in rebellion. It is the spirit of the world, and the flesh mentioned in 1 Corinthians 2:12 and Galatians 5.

The Spirit of Leviathan is that spirit (attitude, way of thinking, frame of mind, and way of life) of the age that is antagonistic to God. It is all habits, standards, conduct, attitude, frame of mind, and way of thinking flowing from Satan into the lives of men, influencing them to rebel and bringing forth evil upon the earth and throughout the kingdom of Satan. This spirit flowed into the angels and all other creatures that rebelled when Satan rebelled. It was this spirit that arose in Satan apart from God. It is the very likeness, reflection, and manners of Satan flowing throughout the earth and his kingdom. The same term, "god of this world," is understood to be a primary influence behind all sin (2 Corinthians 4:4).

In his Apology against the Books of Rufinus, Jerome stated Leviathan is the devil.[11] Athanasius held Leviathan as the world and the things in the world in which the saints find themselves in a war, death, and life war.[12] Gregory Nazianzen spoke of Leviathan as the devil.[13] Cyril and Ambrose both spoke of Leviathan as the devil.[14] Gregory the Great held Leviathan as the Antichrist and the devil.[15] Augustine also held that the Leviathan is the devil.[16]

Sin is a departure from God's love and grace. Satan must be seen as the originator of sin, while man succumbed to the power of sin originated by Satan. Satan was not fooled but chose to sin, while man was withdrawn from the very love and grace of God from some power outside of himself. Satan's sin was an open rebellion against God, while man was misled.

Definitions of Evil

1. It is a sinful act of breaking the covenant between God and His creatures.

2. It is a broken relationship with God, a spiritual divorce.

3. It is disordered love and grace, disordered will, a wrong relationship, nonconformity between God's will and His creatures' wills, an absence of good, a lack of something that should be there in the relationship between good things, a perversion of good, perversion of the moral order, a state of alienation to God, a discord in the universe and order of creation.

4. It is the negation or canceling out of goodness.

Evil is something much more significant, powerful, and pervasive than what transpires in our lives, in our segment of the cosmos, and through our wills. This is not to suggest that we are ourselves, not evil, for the New Testament unequivocally concludes that, apart from Christ, we are. We were, indeed, dead through our trespasses (Ephesians 2:1). We were in desperate need of a high priest to enter the sanctuary and offer up a perfect sacrifice to atone for our sins (Romans 8:34; Hebrews 7:25, 10:10; 1 John 2:2). Christ made this offering, effecting our salvation to the glory of God the Father.

In reference to Satan's fall, due to pride and ambitions to conquer God and be God, Lucifer became Satan (or the devil) and led a great rebellion against God. (See Luke 10:18; Isaiah 14:12–15). By his free act and will, Satan lost his original supremacy and dignity and turned himself into a tyrant and fiend. His great wisdom, corrupted by pride and ambitions, developed into craftiness, perversion, evilness, and wickedness. Initially, this tremendous and splendorous being was known as Lucifer. He became the great "Prince of Darkness." So evil came into being by sinless, free will beings rebelling against God. If God had not given humanity free will, nor given free will to the creatures that God tested in the dispensation of angels, then God, not Satan, would be the author of sinful evils and would be responsible for causing them. Evil is a consequence of sin, and sin comes from free will. Also, it must be seen that death is a consequence of sin. The view of the Old Testament that sin is the result of free decisions of human beings to rebel against their creator is applied to cosmic beings to explain their sinfulness (Isaiah 14:12−15; Ezekiel 28:11−17).

Characteristics of the Spirit of Leviathan

1. Pride (Ezekiel 28:17; 1 Timothy 3:6).

2. Power (Job 1:6−22, 2:1−7; Acts 10:38; Revelation 13:1−4).

3. Desires (Luke 22:31).

4. Lust (John 8:44; Ephesians 2:1−3).

5. Cunning (2 Corinthians 2:11, 11:4; Ephesians 6:11−12).

6. Wicked (John 8:44; 1 John 3:8, 5:18).

7. Malignant (1 Peter 5:8−9; 2 Corinthians 4:4).

8. Cowardly (James 4:7).

9. Tempter (Matthew 4:1−11).

10. Thief (John 10:10).

11. Slanders God (Genesis 3:1−10; Job 1:6−12, 2:1−7).

12. Presumptuous (Job 1:6−12, 2:1−7).

13. Deceitful (2 Corinthians 11:4; Revelation 12:9).

14. Fierce and cruel (Luke 8:29).

15. Aggressive (Ephesians 4:27, 6:10−18).

Its Works

1. Adultery and fornication (Matthew 15:19; Mark 7:21; John 8:3; Galatians 5:19).

2. Uncleanness (Galatians 5:19; Matthew 23:27; Romans 1:21−32, 6:19; 2 Corinthians 12:21; Ephesians 4:19, 5:3; Colossians 3:5; 1 Thessalonians 2:3, 4:7; 2 Peter 2).

3. Lasciviousness (Mark 7:22; 2 Corinthians 12:21; Galatians 5:19; 1 Peter 4:3; Jude 1:4).

4. Idolatry (1 Corinthians 10:14; Galatians 5:20).

5. Witchcraft (Galatians 5:20; Revelation 9:21, 18:23, 22:15).

6. Hatred (Luke 23:12; Romans 8:7; Galatians 5:20).

7. Variance, Emulations (John 2:17; Romans 10:2; 2 Corinthians 7:11, 9:2; Philippians 3:6; Colossians 4:13).

8. Wrath (Galatians 5:20).

9. Strife (Galatians 5:20).

10. Seditions (Romans 16:17; Galatians 5:20).

11. Heresies (Galatians 5:20–21).

12. Envyings (Galatians 5:21).

13. Murders (Matthew 15:19; 1 John 3:15).

14. Drunkenness (Galatians 5:21).

15. Revellings (Galatians 5:21; 1 Peter 4:3).

CHAPTER 2

THE PYTHONIC DEMONS

History is filled with the strangest things that anyone can well imagine. It is filled with various weird creatures—some imaginary—but many that are real. It is easily forgotten that within the same space, there are two realities: the physical world and the spiritual world (supernatural world).

As we live, walk, talk, and travel from one place to another, we will be greatly amiss to think we are alone. Every step a man and a woman make, we are apt to meet individuals exhibiting severe demonic possession. And this may not be known to us. The world is infested with evil spirits—evil entities, and it is unwise to think otherwise. Denying their existence and the existence of Satan does not save people from them.

Numerous years ago, a Christian woman wanted to see the supernatural world. She wanted to know what it contained and the workings of evil spirits. She continued to seek God. She did not know what she was asking. Still, her asking was the best thing she could have done. She should have been prepared and also sought the Lord for His protection and how to deal with them. She did not inquire.

This devout Christian woman, having placed her faith in the Lord, found her trust rewarded and was not disappointed. He sought to teach her. She failed to learn the lesson that was taught.

One day, she went to a grocery store she had gone to countless times. At that place, God turned on a light. He pulled back the curtain. And the hidden things were revealed. She could see the supernatural world. She could see all the evilness of the people that were hidden. She saw things that people had hidden—even the weapons that were hidden on their bodies while they were shopping. Above all, she saw evil entities everywhere she looked in that grocery store. Godly angels were present (at least in what she was shown). She thought she was armed and dangerous. She could reasonably deal with all the evil spirits. What she asked, God delivered. It showed that she was not reigning in the kingdom of God. This woman was ignorant of evil, the organization of the kingdom of Satan, how to fight, and when to fight. She ran out of that grocery store and never went back. Sadly, instead of pushing (or pulling) her to learn spiritual warfare, she became more ignorant of the devices of Satan and his spirits. She became more defeated.

God wanted her to understand that we were in a conflict, and she needed to learn that. He wanted her to join in the battle, but she, like so many, finally refused.

We need to know and understand the supernatural world. Too many Christians are deaf, dumb, and blind when it comes to the supernatural world, in particular, the system and groupings of evil spirits.

Background of the Defilement and Infestation

Sulpitius Severus, one of the earliest Christian Biblical Historians, wrote about the antediluvian period as follows:

> qua tempestate cum iam humanum genus abundaret, angeli, quibus caelum sedes erat, speciosarum forma uirginum capti illicitas cupiditates appetierunt: ac naturae suae originis que degeneres, relictis superioribus, quorum incolae erant, matrimoniis se mortalibus miscuerunt. hi paulatim mores noxios conserentes humanam corrupere progeniem, ex que eorum coitu Gigantes editi esse dicuntur, cum diuersae inter se naturae permixtio monstra gigneret (That at this time, when the human race became numerous, angels, whose residence was in heaven, were enslaved by the appearance of some beautiful virgins, and possessed illicit desires for them, and also departing from

40

their own nature and origin, they left behind the upper regions where they were inhabitants, and mingled themselves in mortal marriages. These angels gradually sowed deadly behaviors in order to corrupt the human race, and from their sexual intercourse with women, giants are said to have been given birth since the mixture of each other who is of a different nature would give birth to monsters).[1]

When Adam sinned, he committed high treason against God. Soon after Adam so sinned (but not right after), prevenient grace entered, with the effects already seen as taking effect in time recorded in Genesis 3:7. The time between Adam sinning and what happened in Genesis 3:7 is only seconds. So sin and death gained their dominance over the world. Still, soon afterward, prevenient grace came in, counteracting this complete dominance and spreading hope in a hopeless world. Without prevenient grace coming upon the world rapidly, sin and death would have become so ruthless and dominant that all would have been ruined.

In succession, first, man sinned; second, the power of Satan entered the world of Adam as a dominating force directed against humanity; third, spiritual death fell upon the human race; fourth (and last) prevenient grace so entered. All this took place in seconds.

In Genesis 3, it is impossible to find a place where the intellectual frame of man is seen as wholly devolved, shattered, and brought to an absolute chaos and confusion of ignorance and darkness. This is because prevenient grace entered soon after Adam sinned into the world of Adam. Prevenient grace came into the world of Adam as a force. As such, prevenient grace became a universal counterweight against sin and death (Psalm 145:9; Romans 2:4, 5:20; 2 Corinthians 9:8). According to the ancient church and their view on grace, grace had several aspects. One of those aspects was prevenient grace. It is seen in Psalm 59:10. Prevenient grace is that grace which goes before; it is that grace that imitates in God's creatures whatever good that is found therein; it is that grace which prepares the soul for the initiation of salvation, or the possibility of salvation; it is that grace which retains and preserves the free will of God's creatures, and gives them the ability to believe, whether they exercise that belief; it is that grace (which Pelagius denied), and is that grace that provides men within their depraved state an inward help, working on them, and trying to lead them to the state of conversion (or repentance).

From Genesis 1 throughout until the flood, there was continued defilement. And this defilement transgressed the boundaries of order. This is also clearly seen and assumed in Genesis 6–11. Transgressions of forbidden boundaries had taken place. The בְּנֵי הָאֱלֹהִים (sons of the gods) had contaminated almost all of humanity.

Within the antediluvian age, normalcy was abnormal. Morality became immorality; right became wrong, and good became evil. The mantras of the antediluvian people were that sexual love has no race, no labels, no gender, no limits, and lastly, no limitations to just physical creatures. It was a period of physical violence, force in opposition to the right, unrestrained lust, rapes, abortions, and universal unbelief in the messages preached by Noah and other prophets. Faith in God lost means morals lost.

The "mantra love is love" was common in this period, and there was a normalization of unnatural lusts, including pedophilia. If the "mantra love is love" is true, there would be no boundaries on who could be loved sexually. If the "mantra love is love" refers to anyone, there are no boundaries for anyone. If love is love, what stops a man from acting and claiming to be a young girl who wants to date a man? If love is love, what stops a woman from marrying a tree?

Each vice of men, women, and children achieved its most significant height and depth of activity upon the earth in this age. It was darkness combined with darkness thousands of times beyond our imagination. No vice has reached that level of activity since then.

Still, antediluvians, according to the ancient rabbis, "knew neither toil nor care. Because of their extraordinary prosperity, they grew insolent. In their arrogance, they rose against God. A single sowing bore a harvest sufficient for the needs of forty years, and using magic arts, they could compel the very sun and moon to stand ready to do their service."[2] Much good was still given to them, and the ancient rabbis described it in these verses: "Their houses are safe from fear, neither is the rod of God upon them. Their bull gendereth, and faileth not; their cow calveth, and casteth not her calf. They send forth their little ones like a flock, and their children dance. They take the timbrel and harp And rejoice at the sound of the organ," Job 21:9–12.

In the tenth generation after Adam, the depths of human evil plummeted to unparalleled levels. Moral pollution had become so pervasive that it had crossed the thresholds of divine tolerance. The corruption that had engulfed the world must be cleansed and purged.

The wickedness of mankind, which began to show up in the time of Enoch, the seventh generation from Adam, had increased monstrously in the time of Enoch's grandson Jared (Jude 14–15).

The importance of studying Genesis—especially in the first few chapters—is understanding the condition of the antediluvian age. In the antediluvian age, few saints emerged. The cost was too great; evil was too great. Persecution beyond imagination was the food of the antediluvian saints. No greater evil has ever existed on this earth since the creation of Adam and Eve. Sainthood has been, and will again be, most challenging during times of widespread wickedness, such as the antediluvian era and the tribulation to come.

If the cost for the saints were merely the sons of men and their evil doings, extraordinarily little overall was the cost. But if the cost for the saints were serving God during the appearance of the בְּנֵי־ הָאֱלֹהִים (sons of the gods) upon the earth and their offspring, the cost was the greatest yet suffered by the saints. The biblical narrative becomes a warning that the saints must endure among the evilest times and the evilest creatures.

Before the origin of evil and sin, all the wills of creatures were in conformity to God's will. This means that what God willed, wanted, and desired was the same thing that was found in all His creatures. Perfect harmony existed. However, when sin came into existence, and with that evil, the universal conformity between God's will and the wills of all His creatures was broken. Though many creatures remained obedient to God, and their wills were still in conformity to God's will, many creatures attacked and went against God's will. Due to this, their wills became in opposition to God's will. Does this mean that God must override their wills to protect and defend His holiness and to remain God, defeat evil, and not be defeated?

For God to override the will of anyone makes God a tyrant and the author of sin and evil. How does one solve this problem? For if God never overrides a person's will, would not Satan have won the rebellion against God? For Satan said, "I will" in Isaiah 14:12–14.

The defeat of Satan and his forces was in harmony with what they willingly submitted to. When these creatures rebelled against God, they willingly submitted to any or all the consequences of their actions that could fall upon them by a God of terrible judgment. And though Satan and all his forces did not, at the time of their failed rebellion, willingly desire God to defeat them, yet by their sin, they willingly submitted to all the consequences that would follow and anything that God could do to stop them. So when Satan said in Isaiah 14:12–14 "I will," he was willingly accepting the consequences of his will to try to dethrone and defeat God. Therefore, at the time of their sin, Satan and all his forces willingly submitted to the penal consequences of their sin that would come. As such, Satan and all his forces willed upon themselves all these consequences by falling and rebelling against God. Their wills determined the implications that they would face from a holy God. And no matter how much they did not consciously want these judgments, yet by their willing actions, they would suffer the consequences.

God does not have to suspend His creatures' free will nor make free will only in appearance. If God makes free will only an illusion, then God Himself is made responsible for evil, sin, and all suffering. And by God violating free will, He would become the author of evil, sin, and all suffering rather than those who rebelled against Him: the will of the past out rules the will of the present. The will of a person who violated God's will and moral law in the past overrules the will of the same person in the present who wants or does not want to suffer because of his actions. Therefore, God pays no attention to a person's will in the present, not wanting or desiring judgment to fall upon that person. But God will pay attention to that person if he repents.

Remember that God created the "tree of knowledge of good and evil" mentioned in Genesis 2:9. If evil had not existed before this time, then there would have been no reason for such a tree as this. Its very presence indicates the existence of evil before the fall of man by the fall and rebellion of Satan and his spirits.

In Genesis 6:11, the Hebrew verb שָׁחַת (corrupt) means more than generally thought of by modern theologians. Also, Genesis 6:11 speaks of the earth having been filled with violence. This was primarily due to the Nephilim, who were great warriors. The Nephilim were great in size and strength.

In the antediluvian age, moral corruption is a reversal of creation and natural law, defying nature and the limits upon which God had set the material universe and the earth. Within the Hebrew verb שָׁחַת (corrupt), the utter shamefulness of the time is seen. A fullness of depravity was seen. And a fullness of sexual perversion was practiced. The Hebrew verb שָׁחַת (corrupt) by itself points to all of this.

Moreover, the Hebrew verb שָׁחַת (corrupt) means universal corruption and the subversion of the ordered processes of law in any way imaginable. Natural law or nature itself was changed and corrupted.

In Genesis 6:11–13, the Hebrew phrase וְהִנְנִי מַשְׁחִיתָם (and look, I am going to make to be destroyed) conveys a profound message—mankind cannot undermine the moral foundation of society without putting its very civilization at risk. When corruption taints a society, it sets in motion a chain of events that ultimately leads to its own inevitable self-destruction.

In Genesis 6:12, compared to Genesis 6:5, the very DNA of creation had been corrupted. Both mankind and the animal kingdom had been corrupted.

With the invasion of the בְּנֵי־הָאֱלֹהִים (sons of the gods), we are introduced to total and absolute war against God, both fallen angels and men. Within the Flood Account, humanly wrought evil is perceived as undoing God's creativity. In other words, the flood is a cosmic catastrophe that is the undoing of creation. But God's chastisement and grace operate simultaneously, so renewal comes out of the disaster. One righteous man, Noah, his family, representative animals, and birds were to be saved to regenerate the world. No one in the line of Cain was to be saved. The action progresses in several stages:

1. Following God's detailed instructions on survival (Genesis 6:9–22), Noah meticulously carried out each and every command to ensure his safety and that of his family and animals.

2. Subsequently, the flood, with all of its intended destructive capabilities, was unleashed, as indicated by the reference (7).

3. As the narrative progresses, the flood reaches its divinely ordained conclusion, as described in verses 8:1–14.

4. In the end, the reconciliation between humanity and God is complete, bringing about a renewed and reordered world, as described in verses 8:15 through 9:17.

5. God's decision to destroy humanity, as described in the text (6:7, 1:26–27), represents His ultimate choice to undo the creative work and processes He had previously established.

6. The flood is "brought about by the release and virtual reuniting of the two halves of the primordial waters that had been separated in the beginning" (7:11, 1:1, 6–7).[3]

Even today, there is no such evil at the level that it was in the antediluvian age. The level of evil that will be present in the tribulational period will be the same as it was in the antediluvian age. Do not believe people who say that they are in the tribulation. They do not know what they are talking about. The tribulation will have the same evil as in the antediluvian age, its various forms, and its heights and depths of activity. It is hard to imagine such evil in those heights and depths.

The attempts to create a master race did not begin with Adolf Hitler. The creation of a master race occurred in the antediluvian age. Its inception is recorded in the sixth chapter of the Book of Genesis.

In the Old Testament, the New Testament, the Apocrypha, Pseudepigrapha writings, and the writings of the ancient church, archaeologists and historians almost all give the exact description of the antediluvian age. Outside sources not in the Old and New Testament will be quoted and discussed at least partly first.

The Apocrypha has a literature work entitled the "Wisdom of Solomon." The Apocrypha book was written between 100 BC and 50 BC, respectively. The writer was a Hellenistic Jew. The work gives an insight into the views and beliefs of the Hellenistic Jews at that time, especially about idolatry and the antediluvian age and after that. Only such a work as this should be used whenever it agrees with Scripture, when there is historical importance to the work, or when the writer is comparing Scripture with other works, showing the differences, and pointing out to follow Scripture rather than these works.

The work was well known by all Hellenistic Jews and even early Christians. Paul was influenced by it in his writing of the Epistles of Romans and Ephesians. Comparing the Greek text of the "Wisdom of Solomon" and the Greek text of Paul's two Epistles, there are traces of the "Wisdom of Solomon" in them.

In the Wisdom of Solomon, there is a description of the state of the antediluvian people as soon as they became ignorant of the true God. Once ignorance reigned, the people lived in continual evil warfare. In learned procedures, they knew how to murder their own children through abortion or sacrifice their children to the gods.

Learning the secret mysteries of idolatry and the occult, they celebrated and held wild ceremonial sexual orgies with various forms of unnatural practices. As sin always does, idolatry led to more and more other types of sins, especially sexual immorality, through these rituals and orgies. Simply put, idolatry, demon possession, and sexual immorality always are joined. Therefore, evil spirits, more ancient than any evil of flesh, were already present, leading humanity to the greatest depths of sins, depravities, and atrocities. Marriages were not kept pure any longer. Various forms of sexual immorality became widespread. The murder of each other was expected because of sexual immorality and betrayal.

The Wisdom of Solomon 14:22–30 reads as follows:

Εἶτ᾽ οὐκ ἤρκεσεν τὸ πλανᾶσθαι περὶ τὴν τοῦ θεοῦ γνῶσιν, ἀλλὰ καὶ μεγάλῳ ζῶντες ἀγνοίας πολέμῳ τὰ τοσαῦτα κακὰ εἰρήνην προσαγορεύουσιν. ἢ γὰρ τεκνοφόνους τελετὰς ἢ κρύφια μυστήρια ἢ ἐμμανεῖς ἐξάλλων θεσμῶν κώμους ἄγοντες, οὔτε βίους οὔτε γάμους καθαροὺς ἔτι φυλάσσουσιν, ἕτερος δ᾽ ἕτερον ἢ λοχῶν ἀναιρεῖ, ἢ νοθεύων ὀδυνᾷ. πάντα δ᾽ ἐπιμὶξ ἔχει αἷμα καὶ φόνος, κλοπὴ καὶ δόλος, φθορά, ἀπιστία, τάραχος, ἐπιορκία, θόρυβος ἀγαθῶν, χάριτος ἀμνησία, ψυχῶν μιασμός, γενέσεως ἐναλλαγή, γάμων ἀταξία, μοιχεία καὶ ἀσέλγεια. ἡ γὰρ τῶν ἀνωνύμων εἰδώλων θρησκεία παντὸς ἀρχὴ κακοῦ καὶ αἰτία καὶ πέρας ἐστίν· ἢ γὰρ εὐφραινόμενοι μεμήνασιν, ἢ προφητεύουσιν ψευδῆ, ἢ ζῶσιν ἀδίκως, ἢ ἐπιορκοῦσιν ταχέως· ἀψύχοις γὰρ πεποιθότες εἰδώλοις κακῶς ὀμόσαντες ἀδικηθῆναι οὐ προσδέχονται. ἀμφότερα δὲ αὐτοὺς μετελεύσεται τὰ δίκαια, ὅτι κακῶς ἐφρόνησαν περὶ θεοῦ προσχόντες εἰδώλοις, καὶ ἀδίκως ὤμοσαν ἐν δόλῳ καταφρονήσαντες ὁσιότητος (After that, it was not enough that they went astray from the knowledge of God, but also, as they were living in great war through ignorance of Him, they were calling such evils peace. For they were celebrating either the murdering of children in cultic rituals or in secret mysteries or raving frantic orgies of strange rituals. They were no longer guarding either their lives or the moral state of their marriages, but either one was killing another by ambushes, or one was grieving another by adultery. But everything had become a confusion: blood and murder, theft, and treachery, depravity, faithlessness, disturbance, perjury, confusion of good things, forgetfulness of gratitude, pollution of souls, interchange of sexuality, disorder in marriages, adultery, and living sexually without any moral restraint. For the religion of nameless idols is the beginning and cause and end of every kind of evil. For their worshippers either were losing their minds, or prophesying lies, or living unjustly, or hastily perjuring themselves. For they put their trust in lifeless idols. They wickedly swore by false oaths and expected not to have done anything wrong. But the righteous things shall come after both regarding these sins. Because they had thought wickedly about God after having offered unto idols. And they swore wickedly in deceit after they had already despised holiness).

The author of the Wisdom of Solomon gives us a vice list. The writer here tailored his vice list to the most prominent sins in the antediluvian age. In the writer's vice list, the absence of a sin does not give a license to commit it. Any sin not mentioned in this list is still understood as an evil practice. The sins that afflicted the antediluvian age were mentioned considerably. The sins that did not dominate that age were understood as still present but extraordinarily little problems.

The writer of the Wisdom of Solomon was a master of Greek. Many point out that a literal translation is all that is needed to understand all the nuances of Greek grammar. Not true!

The author of the Wisdom of Solomon used the α prefix and the anarthrous construction throughout his writing. Rarely did he use the article. Both constructions point out the state of evilness in the antediluvian age. The anarthrous construction points to the behavior dominating the antediluvian age. The α prefix points to the totality of wickedness without good or righteousness. Combining both the wickedness, including all its forms and atrocities, described in the times of the antediluvian age goes beyond any restraint. The wickedness was extreme, without restraint, the most significant level ever done, and the totality of ability that the forces of evil can ever achieve. It was like God did not exist. There was no human restraining force able to push back such evilness. It was a miracle that anyone could stay faithful to the Lord.

The author of the Wisdom of Solomon adds, ἦ γὰρ εὐφραινόμενοι μεμήνασιν (For their worshippers were losing their minds). Besides, the Baalim and the Astartes pre-dating the Nephilim, the appearance of the antediluvians losing their minds, in the thinking of the Hellenistic Jews, indicates that these people were turned over to reprobate minds, and that the Kundalini demons were also present. The Kundalini demons make people insane. They affect the minds either before or after God turns people into reprobates. With these three main groups of demons appearing and not being the Nephilim, other devastating demons, such as the Pythonic demons, were also advancing into the earth's realm through Adam's rebellion.

As written by the writer of the Wisdom of Solomon, insanity gripped the people of the antediluvian age. When there are no restraints on evil, insanity is one of the many fruits.

The insanity of the antediluvian people had no boundaries. Of course, they were to conclude that they were gods. Since they thought they were gods, they concluded they could change their gender and sexuality. Besides this, they were to try to change natural law and all creation. They had the power to alter profound physical realities. Besides gender transformation, they attempted to control nature and corrupt nature.

Satan is the source of heathenism and spiritism. Spiritism, which is also necromancy or the invocation of the dead, was a feature of Gnosticism that assailed the Christian Church in the apostolic era and against which Paul, by the Holy Spirit, inveighs, particularly in his Epistle to the Colossians. This practice was not a new thing. It occurred in the earliest pagan religions.

Spiritism was before the flood, and it was after the flood. With Spiritism came demonism—the worship of demons and human possession by demons. Israelites, in their practices of idolatry, like other nations, worshipped demons, sacrificed to them, and became the properties of these most evil spirits. All idolatrous worship and all practices of idolatry and the occult are inseparably connected with magic and the exercise of supernatural power. By demonic power, the human race can be held in the bondage of demonic service.

In short, heathenism is the belief in human sacrifice, death, and barbarism.

The devil increased faith in the supernatural world before and after the flood. In so doing, he was to emphasize himself, not Christ. He was to hasten the Antichrist to sit as God in the temple of God. Satan and his spirits were to become masters of signs and wonders. These signs and wonders were to become appearances of aerial forms, visions, oracles, soothsaying, necromancing, spirit-writing, voices coming from the supernatural world, magnetic healings, spirit-communications, omens, tokens, lucky and unlucky days and seasons, spells, potions, amulets, charms, fetishes, relics, images, pictures, and all the countless prescriptions of demoniacal systems. All these things were to push people away from the creator of the universe.

Evil spirits became familiar with the past, present, and future; they became masters of imitating the dead. The Pythonic demons, the Kundalini demons, the Baalim, and the Astartes are extensively used in this respect.

Invasion of the Pythonic Demons

From various sources, the defilement and infestation occurred before the flood. Disembodied evil spirits invaded the world of Adam—men and women. All these disembodied evil spirits predated the Nephilim, the product of the בְּנֵי־הָאֱלֹהִים (sons of the gods). The בְּנֵי־הָאֱלֹהִים (sons of the gods) by themselves alone contaminated almost all of humanity. But disembodied evil spirits also entered the same world.

The Pythonic demons, like that of others, were thrown upon the earth and in the lives of men and women. At the first, evil practices were introduced to men and women. And the Pythonic demons played a part in this.

Like the Baalim and the Astartes, they have at least played significant roles in Spiritism. The Pythonic demons go back to the very beginning of man's rebellion against God and our desire to learn and follow the arts of the occult. These demons were used by higher evil spirits in the arts of the occult before the flood of Noah.

Generally, the Pythonic demons possessed more people in the old dispensations than any other group of demons. They wrought destruction upon many by their mediums and seances (mediums can receive communications from another world. Their communications are from evil spirits, particularly the Pythonic demons, the Baalim, the Astartes, and the Kundalini demons).

The Pythonic demons are called three main things in the Bible: אוֹב (familiar spirit), ἐγγαστρίμυθος (a familiar spirit—a ventriloquistic spirit), and πνεῦμα πύθωνα (a Pythonic spirit) or πνεῦμα Πύθωνος (the spirit of a Python).

The Hebrew noun אוֹב (familiar spirit) follows both the common gender, the masculine gender, and the feminine gender. It is written in various ways in the Hebrew Old Testament: אֶל־הָאֹבֹת (Leviticus 19:31, 20:6; Isaiah 8:19, 19:3), אוֹב (Leviticus 20:27; Deuteronomy 18:11; 2 Kings 21:6;2 Chronicles 33:6), הָאֹבוֹת (1 Samuel 28:3), בַּעֲלַת־ אוֹב (1 Samuel 28:7), בָּאוֹב (1 Samuel 28:8; Isaiah 29:4; 1 Chronicles 10:13), and אֶת־הָאֹבוֹת (1 Samuel 28:9; 2 Kings 23:24). The Hebrew noun אוֹב (familiar spirit) in its formal and basic form expresses common gender. All genders are meant. The plural form הָאֹבוֹת of the Hebrew noun אוֹב (familiar spirit) can well be recognized as masculine or feminine. The context tells the reader what is meant.

The Hebrew noun אוֹב (familiar spirit) has several meanings: A familiar spirit, a skin-bottle (or leathern bottle), a necromancer or sorcerer who professes to call up the human dead by means of incantations to answer questions (Deuteronomy 18:11; 2 Kings 21:6), and the one who has a familiar spirit. The familiar spirit uses the victim of the possession as a bottle and a host. Familiar spirits are evil spirits impersonating dead human beings and attaching themselves to the "mediums" and those who give up their will to them (Deuteronomy 18:10–12; 1 Chronicles 10:13–14; Isaiah 8:19).

Further, the Hebrew noun אוֹב (familiar spirit) is a soothsaying demon. This term also has reference to the vessel or person in which the demon resides (Leviticus 20:27); it is a spirit who is familiar with you and those who have died; it is a spirit who is familiar with a person, a place, or a thing. It has knowledge about living persons and dead humans, and the spirit wants to pass that knowledge to those who serve him/her/it. This information follows the thinking that a familiar spirit is a demon who uses a medium as a vessel or bottle. These spirits work as spirit-guides.

These spirits are the familiars of the mediums. They reveal things about numerous dead or alive people to the mediums.

Familiar spirits work in the practice of necromancing and ventriloquism. Necromancy is the heathen, ungodly, and horrific practice of communicating with the supposed human dead to inquire into the past, present, and future. It is not the human dead, but demons like them.

It was widely practiced among all ancient peoples, particularly in Egypt, which was considered the center of all sorcery and magic after the time of the Tower of Babel. Notice all sorcery and magic can be traced back to the Tower of Babel. At one time, Babylon was the center of terrible practices before Egypt.

In the Greek Septuagint, the Hebrew noun אוֹב (familiar spirit) is translated with the Greek adjective ἐγγαστρίμυθος (ventriloquistic spirit–familiar spirit). It is written in several forms: ἐγγαστρίμυθοις (Leviticus 19:31, 20:6), ἐγγαστρίμυθος (Leviticus 20:27; Deuteronomy 18:11; I Samuel 28:7), ἐγγαστρίμυθους (1 Samuel 28:3, 28:9; 2 Chronicles 33:6, 35:19a; Isaiah 8:19, 19:3), ἐγγαστρίμυθον (1 Samuel 28:7), ἐγγαστρίμυθῳ (1 Samuel 28:8; 1 Chronicles 10:13), and ἐγγαστρίμυθων (Isaiah 44:25). The Hebrew noun אוֹב (familiar spirit) is dominantly interpreted by the scribes as one Greek adjective, but two genders: both masculine and feminine.

The development of the Greek adjective ἐγγαστρίμυθος is clearly seen throughout various sources and various ages. In the Greek Septuagint, it has a few meanings: ventriloquistic spirit—familiar spirit or Pythonic spirit, a bottle, a necromancer, or sorcerer who professes to call up the human dead by means of incantatios to answer questions (Deuteronomy 18:11; 2 Kings 21:6), one who has a ventriloquistic spirit—familiar spirit, and the ventriloquists. Ventriloquistic, Pythonic, or familiar spirit speaks from the belly. And the medium is one who prophesies through the belly.

The Greek adjective ἐγγαστρίμυθος can well be reduced to three main uses in the Greek Septuagint: demons who are called ventriloquistic, familiar, or Pythonic demons, the ability by the mediums to use ventriloquism done through Pythonic demons, and the mediums themselves who are ventriloquistic mediums, witches, or Pythonesses. Belly speaking is tied to the demons themselves. Those who do such are mediums—ventriloquistic mediums.

Notice how Clement of Alexandria used the Greek adjective ἐνγαστρίμυθος, saying, Παραπλήσιος οὖν οὗτος ἀτεχνῶς τῷ ἐγγαστριμύθῳ καλουμένῳ (This demon, therefore, is accurately similar to the one who is called the ventriloquistic demon).[4] A fragment of Philochorus of Athens, a Greek historian Atthidographer of the third century BC, has τοῦτον τὸν ἐγγαστρίμυθον νῦν τινες Πύθωνά φασι (Now, certain people say that the Python is this ventriloquistic demon).[5]

Both Hesychius of Alexandria, who lived in the fifth century AD, and Suidas, who produced one of the most comprehensive Greek lexicons in the tenth century AD, took the Greek noun πύθων and the Greek adjective ἐγγαστρίμυθος as including the idea of a ventriloquistic demon, familiar spirit, or Pythonic demon. Hesychius and Suidas define the Greek noun πύθων as Πύθων: δαιμόνιον μαντικόν (Python: a demon of divination).[6]

The ancient church fathers accepted that the Greek noun πύθων refers to the demon who speaks from the ventriloquistic medium, mediums, or Pythoness. Tertullian spoke about those spirits working in magic as scimus etiam magiae licere explorandis occultis per catabolicos et paredros et Pythonicos spiritus (we know also that magic is permitted to be explored for occultic secrets by the Catabolic, and the Paredral and the Pythonic spirits).[7] According to the interpretation of the Latin into English, the Parabolic spirits are those who throw men and women to the ground most violently; the Paredral spirits are those who haunt people or keep ever at their victims' sides; and the Pythonic spirits are those who cast their victims into trances and work in divination and ventriloquistic practices. Tertullian also said again, Et credo, quia mendacio possunt; nec enim Pythonico tunc spiritui minus licuit animam samuelis effingere post deum mortuos consulente saule. Absit alioquin, ut animam cuiuslibet sancti, nedum prophetae, a daemonio credamus extractam (And, I believe, indeed, they can lie; for this instance, it was no less than this that was permitted to the Pythonic spirit—ventriloquistic spirit than to impersonate the soul of Samuel, when Saul consulted the dead after he lost the living God. God forbid, otherwise, that we ought to think that the soul of any saint, not to speak of a prophet, can be taken out of paradise by a demon).[8] In the Recognitions of Clement, it is written, Et pythones divinare videntur et non continuo dii sunt; denique a Christianis hominibus effugantur (And the Pythones—Pythonic demons—are seen to be divine, and they are not gods; and, in summary, they are driven out of men—men and women by Christians).[9] In the Clementine Homilies, it is written, ὅτι καὶ πύθωνες μαντεύονται, ἀλλ' ὑφ' ἡμῶν ὡς δαίμονες ὁρκιζόμενοι φυγαδεύονται (For Pythones—Pythonic demon—also prophesy, yet they are overthrown—uprooted and cast out by us as demons).[10]

By the time of the first-century AD, the Greek adjective ἐγγαστρίμυθος was used in pagan and secular sources to mean ventriloquists with no supernatural or demonic power. Translating this Greek adjective simply as ventriloquists leaves no room for all that is meant by it. The Greek adjective in these sources was reduced to mere natural power and uses, nothing else. For example, by the time of Nero, the Greek adjective ἐγγαστρίμυθος began to be weakened in meaning by secular sources. In such sources, the Greek adjective ἐγγαστρίμυθος was synonymous with the Greek noun πύθων.

Erotianus Grammaticus said, ἐγγαστρίμυθοι· οὕς πύθωνάς τινες καλοῦσιν· ἔστι δὲ τῶν ἅπαξ εἰρημένων (Ventriloquists; whom certain people call the Pythones; now, it is immediately known from these words).[11] Plutarch wrote, εὔηθες γάρ ἐστι καὶ παιδικὸν κομιδῇ τὸ οἴεσθαι τὸν θεὸν αὐτὸν ὥσπερ (εἰς) τοὺς ἐγγαστριμύθους, Εὐρυκλέας πάλαι νυνὶ δὲ Πύθωνας, αγορευομένους, ἐνδυόμενον εἰς τὰ σώματα τῶν προφητῶν ὑποφθέγγεσθαι, τοῖς ἐκείνων στόμασι καὶ φωναῖς χρώμενον ὀργάνοις (For it is silly and babyish entirely to suppose that the god himself just as following in the means of ventriloquists, who were formerly called 'Eurycleis,' but now 'Pythones,' enters into the bodies of his prophets and inspires their muttering and utterances, using their mouths and voices as instruments).[12] In the Hippocratic Lexicon organized by Gallen in the second and third centuries AD, the Greek adjective ἐγγαστρίμυθος is defined as ἐγγαστρίμυθοι: οἱ κεκλεισμένου τοῦ στόματος φθεγγόμενοι, διὰ τὸ δοκεῖν ἐκ τῆς γαστρὸς φθέγγεσθαι (Ventriloquists: those who are uttering from the closed mouth, because they are believed to be speaking utterances from the belly).[13]

Outside of pagan and secular sources, the Greek adjective ἐγγαστρίμυθος (ventriloquistic spirit—familiar spirit) retains its meanings as founded by the Greek Septuagint. Like many church fathers, Clement of Alexandria held that the ventriloquists were another type of soothsayers.[14]

In the Greek New Testament, the Hebrew noun אוֹב (familiar spirit) is translated as πνεῦμα πύθωνα (Pythonic spirit) or as πνεῦμα Πύθωνος (the spirit of a Python) as recorded in Acts 16:16. The Greek noun πνεῦμα (spirit) is in the neuter gender, but the Greek noun πύθων is in the masculine gender and either the accusative case or the genitive case. The Pythonic demons are a mixture of genders.

The Pythonic demons, being unique disembodied evil spirits, were conceived by antiquity to be androgynous, hermaphroditic, or both male and female.

The Hebrew noun אוֹב (familiar spirit) in some places in the Old Testament is separately used from the Hebrew noun בְּעָלִים

(Baalim) and the Hebrew noun אֲשֵׁרוֹת (Astaroths) or the Hebrew noun עַשְׁתָּרוֹת (Astartes). Second Kings 21:1–9 and 2 Chronicles 33:1–9 separate the Baalim and Astartes from the אוֹב (familiar spirit). And these passages make the אוֹב (familiar spirit) almost exclusively the Pythonic demons. This is confirmed also by Jewish sources.[15]

When the Hebrew noun אוֹב (familiar spirit) is used separately, and there is no mention of the Baalim and Astartes, this noun moves far and wide and covers all evil spirits working in necromancy and soothsaying. Further, all evil spirits who can possess a human are meant. Pythonic demons are one of the disembodied spirits that can be used as a familiar spirit. Therefore, in the Old Testament, there is exclusiveness and inclusiveness in terms.

In the New Testament, Paul spoke of πνεῦμα πύθωνα (Pythonic spirit) or πνεῦμα Πύθωνος (the spirit of a Python) in Acts 16:16. However, Paul also spoke of Baal in Romans 11:4. And in Acts 19:34–35, both Artemis (Diana), the goddess, and Jupiter are mentioned. These are other names for the Baalim and Astartes. Therefore, there is a difference between these classes of disembodied spirits.

Further, Mark 3:11 reads, "And unclean spirits, when they saw him, fell down before him, and cried, saying, Thou art the Son of God." And Mark 6:7 reads, "And he called unto him the twelve, and began to send them forth by two and two; and gave them power over unclean spirits." The Greek phrase τὰ πνεύματα τὰ ἀκάθαρτα (the unclean spirits) mentioned by Mark and other places in the New Testament, points back to Zechariah 13:2, "And it shall come to pass in that day, saith the LORD of hosts, That I will cut off the names of the idols out of the land, and they shall no more be remembered: And also I will cause the prophets and the unclean spirit to pass out of the land." Notice the Greek phrase in the Septuagint Greek as translated from the Hebrew τὸ πνεῦμα τὸ ἀκάθαρτον (the unclean spirit). The singular is used to represent the plurality of evil spirits collectively.

Throughout the New Testament, the term unclean spirits is mentioned over twenty times (Matthew 10:1, 12:43–45; Mark 1:26–27, 3:11, 5:1–13, Luke 4:36, 6:18, 11:26; Acts 5:16, 8:7). The bottom-line is that the Greek phrase τὰ πνεύματα τὰ ἀκάθαρτα (the unclean spirits) with the definite articles is a Jewish formulation. Primarily, with the article before each adjective and noun, there cannot be any interpretation other than a particular type of demon, the vilest and the most unclean, the Baalim. It was these spirits that infested the Jewish people. With these spirits, other demons are included. The Astartes, the Pythonic, and the Kundalini demons were considered unclean spirits but less recognized than the Baalim. The best way to describe the Baalim is a cesspool.

The Greek phrase τὰ πνεύματα τὰ ἀκάθαρτα (the unclean spirits) has a meaning that many do not notice. According to this Greek phrase, these spirits can appear in various forms besides the forms of humans and the human dead. They can take upon the forms of unclean animals: the swine, owl, bat, raven, weasel, mouse, lizard, snail, hawk, kite, jackal, vulture, goat, frog, and others (Leviticus 11; Isaiah 13:21; Revelation 16:13, 18:2).

In the Gospel of Mark, Mark was writing to a people filled with all kinds of evil who were subject to being controlled by all sorts of evil spirits. The Gentile society needed to be aware of the unclean spirits among them and their need to be cleansed of such uncleanness and evil.

All the Gentiles, except those who accepted Judaism and hence became proselytes, were at least daemonically influenced, but most, if not all, were demon possessed. It is impossible to be connected to idolatry, and especially that of the cult of the Baalim and the cult of Astartes, without being demon possessed. The Greeks and the Romans had exorcists to deal with their gods, but the exorcists did not have the power to drive them out of the persons. They tried various ways to limit the damage to the persons that the demons possessed. In truth, the Greeks and Romans did not want their gods out of the persons but just wanted to keep them under somewhat control so that the victims of possession would not die.

Further, the Pythonic demons, the Baalim, the Astartes, and the Kundalini demons are involved in pagan prophecies, prophesying in frenzies, communication with the supposed dead, or necromancy. Overall, the Pythonic demons almost exclusively worked in necromancy, as recorded in the Old and New Testaments. Other demons can work in the same occultic practices. Sometimes, it can reasonably be hard to identify which evil spirit is working at a time.

The ancient church saw the Pythonic demons as a group of demons, the most powerful and the most dangerous. They saw them as familiar spirits that could represent the souls of the dead through their power. They can also possess people by their divination and ventriloquistic arts. They are driven out of the bodies of the victims. They give words and words of prophecy. They bless those who serve them with blessings in various ways, including financial. They attack those that they do not control. They are cast out and put to flight. They are said to work in cures or healings. They have remedies for sickness and disease. There are not one but many.

Delphic Oracles and the Pythonic Demons

The Delphic oracles, occurring back in history before 600 BC, are examples of the infestations of the Pythonic demons among the pagans. At least five hundred examples of the prophecies given at Delphi by the Greek female mediums through these Pythonic demons have survived. The oracles—prophecies—were commonly done in poetic forms.

The term "oracles" was both the verbal responses of a god—Pythonic demon, and the place where they were consulted.

Cicero once said, Numquam illud oraculum Delphis tam celebre et tam clarum fuisset neque tantis donis refertum omnium populorum atque regum, nisi omnis aetas oraculorum illorum veritatem esset experta. idem iam diu non facit (That oracle at Delphi would never have been so celebrated and so well known, nor it would have been so filled up with so many offerings from all the peoples and the kings unless every age had experienced the truth of those prophecies. For a long time now, that has not been the same case in point).[16]

According to myth, Python was a soothsaying serpent of Delphi that dwelled in the caves of Mount Parnassus and was slain by the Greek god Apollo, who then founded the sacred oracle at Delphi or took it over from Python's guardianship. Apollo slew this serpent and was called Pythius, becoming celebrated as the foreteller of events. It was believed that all who predicted future events through occultic powers were influenced, controlled, or possessed by the spirit of Apollo Pythius.

The term Python, used as a reference to a serpent, was transferred to soothsaying demons, which gave the response in the name of Apollo (Satan).

The Pagan Oracle of Delphi was located about 75 miles NW of Athens on the Corinthian Sea, 5 miles inland, and 10 miles south of Mount Parnassos' (Parnassus) summit. Here, the Pagan Temple of Apollo was located.

Tradition has it that Delphi was found by Coretas, a shepherd boy, who discovered that his sheep and goats acted strangely when they approached the area. He soon began uttering prophetic statements, which came true. However, the priestesses of Daphoene gave an oracle at Delphi during Cretan times, which were at least 200 years and possibly 400 years before Apollo. The shepherd, Coretas, obviously did not discover the sight.

The people believed that the god Apollo spoke through the Pythoness as his vessel. He used her vocal cords to express his wishes and advice. Divination was founded on Python worship. This snake was worshipped for thousands of years before Apollo established his famous oracle and temple, and it was the very symbol of this region.

Centuries before Christ's birth, devout pilgrims made the arduous journey to Delphi to ask for advice from the famous oracle. They sought answers for planting crops, preparing for war, or resolving a moral dilemma. The city-states made generous contributions, some even establishing treasuries on the site. For over six centuries, until the Christian emperor Arcadius destroyed the shrine in AD 398, Delphi truly shaped the history of the world.

At Delphi, multitudes of well-bed beggars were present, seeking the favors of Apollo and the food upon the altar. The god Apollo demanded the first fruits of all things. Slaves were also present at Delphi, where they served their new masters.[17] Many wives were present to confide their family sorrows. Embassies from every city with offerings were present.[18]

Some females from their childhood were put into Apollo's service here. Others were forsaken by their mothers and fathers and left at the temple and the service of Apollo at Delphi. Illegitimate children were commonly found. Many of the most beautiful male and female youths had been sent as gifts to the Apollo.

Before messengers could enter the temple and speak to the god Apollo through the Pythoness and the Pythonic demons, they were to wait and prepare themselves. "Then, binding round their brows the mystic branch of bay, they rose, and in silence entered upon holy ground. . . . Fronting them rose the high altar, crowned, like the rest, with laurel, on which all must lay tribute who would inquire aught of Phoebus. Here the priests took of their offering and burned it upon the slab. If the day were one of consultation, lots then were drawn for precedence, and he whom fortune favoured moved on, past the Omphalos, where Apollo had reposed in early days, past the tomb of Neoptolemus, past the image of Pallas, to the steps of the shrine itself. At the foot he left his train of servants, and mounted all alone, wondering at the marvels round, the open colonnades, the wondrous sculptures filling the pediments of the noble tympana, each commemorating the life and labours of a god. . . . And now the jubilant trumpets of the priests pealed out, with notes that rang round the valley, and up among the windings of the Hyampeian cliff. Awed into silence by the sound, he crossed the garlanded threshold: he sprinkled on his head the holy water from the fonts of gold and entered the outer court. New statues, fresh fonts, craters, and goblets, the gift of many an Eastern king, met his eye: walls emblazoned with dark sayings rose about him as he crossed towards the inner adytum. Then the music grew more loud: the interest deepened: his heart beat faster. With a sound as of many thunders, that penetrated to the crowd without, the subterranean door rolled back: the earth trembled: the laurels nodded: smoke and vapour broke commingled forth: and, railed below within a hollow of the rock, perchance he caught one glimpse of the marble effigies of Zeus and the dread sisters, one gleam of sacred arms; for one moment saw a steaming chasm, a shaking tripod, above all, a Figure with fever on her cheek and foam upon her lips, who, fixing a wild eye upon space, tossed her arms aloft in the agony of her soul, and, with a shriek that never left his ear for days, chanted high and quick the dark utterances of the will of Heaven."[19]

The people beheld statues, heard pagan hymns, and tragedies won their tears. The sentiments of a lifetime came crowding upon them. They could feel all that Greek poets and others wrote.

Delphi, overloaded with gifts, had to have storage facilities for treasures. It displayed masterpieces. Delphi became a museum. Sacrifices became more and more lavish. The priests became part of the upper-class politicians and intellectuals.

A Pythoness (priestess) is any woman supposed to be possessed of the spirit of prophecy. Pythonism is divination, diving, augury, soothsaying, fortune-telling, crystal gazing, astrology, or sorcery.

For a long time, the Pythoness, also called Pythia, was a young virgin who continued in that state for the rest of her life. This was important since her virginity was greatly emphasized for her union with the god Apollo—the Pythonic demon or demons that would possess her. However, a law was later decreed that the Pythoness at Delphi was to be an elderly woman of fifty. The law was decreed because Echecrates the Thessalian defiled the Pythoness, who was a virgin.[20]

Both young and aged Pythonesses (female mediums) were present at Delphi. However, one, and no more than up to three at a time, could be the official Pythoness and become the voice of Apollo through the Pythonic demons. The officiating Pythoness— the head and high Pythoness—was chosen at the death of her predecessor from among a company of temple priestesses. These women were all natives of Delphi and were required to have had a sober life and be of good character.

While it was expected to have one practicing Pythoness at a time, there was a time when three practicing Pythonesses were employed. By the end of the first-century AD, this was no longer needed.

It was rare, but some Pythonesses were married, at which time they ceased all family responsibilities, marital relations, and individual identity. Each may have been a woman chosen from an influential family, well-educated in geography, politics, history, philosophy, and the arts. However, uneducated peasant women were chosen for the role in later periods.

From their beginning at Delphi, the women, regardless of age, were introduced into the atmosphere of the Pythonic demons and taught how to enter their presence and become possessed.

The Pythonesses were possessed much like mediums today. Questions were given to the Pythoness, and they were written on slips. She spoke back gibberish, which had to be interpreted by the priest.

The Pythoness was opened to the spiritual world and demonic possession by inhaling the vapors. The inhaling of these vapors began the process of demonic possession. Even drugs today are used as a means to open a person up to demonic possession.

Archaeologists have identified the vapors as coming from hydrocarbon gases. Three types of gas—ethane, methane, and ethylene—have been in spring water located near the oracle. Ethylene is known to produce euphoric effects like those described by Plutarch. These gases leaked from cracks in the floor of the fissure, which allowed the Pythoness to be pushed into a state where she could become possessed. These gases changed her state of mind, left her vulnerable to evil spirits, and shortened her life. The gases alone did not cause the trance of the Pythoness. Plutarch and others spoke of the vapors coming from the earth.[21]

Under the influence of the vapors and under the influence and control of the Pythonic demons, the Pythoness, who was inside a cave, was sitting on a three-legged stool over a cleft in the earth from which the oracle was supposed to proceed. Through her possession, the Pythoness became a ventriloquist and belly speaker. She could change and throw her voice so much so that people present thought that the voice came from a nearby image of Apollo.

The Greek god Apollo was a demon that expressed itself as many other strongholds in ancient mythology and was also known as the god of healing diseases. Apollo was considered the Destroyer and the Conqueror, and he is recognized as another name for Satan and the coming Antichrist.

The Pythonic demons have led many to their destruction. For example, Croesus, the King of Lydia, based his whole life and fate upon the Delphic oracles and the Pythonesses.[22] To Croesus, after testing all the prophetic centers of the ancient societies, the Delphic oracles and the Pythonesses at Delphi were more remarkable than all other places. He explored strategies for evaluating the extent of Persian influence. The Pythonic demons gave him the wrong advice, which led to his utter destruction.

In Greece, all people held the infallibility of Delphic oracles.

Background to Samuel and Saul

In 1 Samuel 9:15–17, the revelation was introduced, which Samuel received the day before the arrival of Saul. Samuel based this revelation upon his prayerful hopefulness on how God would establish the monarchy, which was promised to the Israelites regretfully. The phrase "in his ear a day" in 1 Samuel 9:15 means that God breathed His divine thoughts to the human spirit of Samuel, which became words.

The words "I will send to thee a man" set forth the Divine Providence that directs the ways of a man so to the point that he must come to Samuel, the head of Israel and mediator between God and His people. Both Hebrew and Greek do not have the article before man. Samuel is not told just whom the man was to be but simply said that a man was to be sent from the Tribe of Benjamin. The general or conditional element of this prophecy is seen here from the start. The two conditions were a man and coming from the Tribe of Benjamin. The man who finally came from the Tribe of Benjamin was the one who submitted to the Divine Providence of God. Not all the details were given to Samuel.

The man, the chosen king, who became Saul, had to come to a prophet rather than a prophet had to go to him. Men and women must seek out the men of God usually unless God demands that the prophets go to them to give them a word. The words from God meant to history that Saul's mission was a warlike mission, a deliverance of Israel from the dominance of the Philistines.

The words "that he may save my people out of the hand of the Philistines" indicate the main reason for anointing Saul as the leader and king over Israel (1 Samuel 9:16). How the words are translated from the Hebrew is unfortunate. There is no idea of plausibility (possibility) here. The Hebrew text reads, וְהוֹשִׁיעַ אֶת־עַמִּי מִיַּד פְּלִשְׁתִּים (and he will deliver my people from the hand of the Philistines). The Greek Septuagint reads, καὶ σώσει τὸν λαόν μου ἐκ χειρὸς ἀλλοφύλων (and he will deliver my people from the hand of the Philistines). The idea is that he must deliver the people of God. That is his mandate. Further, his mandate is for him to be the king and continue to be king. He must fulfill that.

Further, there is no contradiction here when comparing this to 1 Samuel 7:13, since the Philistines had been subdued but recovered enough in strength to recover their lost dominion.

The looking of God upon His people and their circumstance (suffering) is more than just a causative look (1 Samuel 9:16); it is a look, complete and absolute, with much energy attached as understood from the Hebrew and Greek. A long look is inferred, now complete. Until the completion of this look, God did not move for His people. And the look of the Lord was not due to Him hearing the prayers of His people.

It was only when Samuel saw what Saul did that he knew the man from the Tribe of Benjamin was Saul. For God told him that

Saul was the man whom He had chosen (1 Samuel 9:17). From that point, Samuel greeted Saul, talked with him, ate with him, and told him that he was called by God to be the king over Israel (1 Samuel 9:17–21). Saul was greatly surprised that he was the focus of all Israel's hopes. At that time, Saul was very humble and could be used as a vessel of God's glory.

Then, Samuel privately anointed Saul to be the king of Israel, which was a truthful confirmation of what Samuel had already said. While Samuel anointed Saul with the holy oil and holy practice of anointing a high priest, it was not that act that made Saul the king of Israel. God anointed Saul to be king of Israel by His favor, grace, power, Divine Providence, and divine power. The anointing of Saul with the holy oil was the only means that a person could be physically consecrated to become a theocratic king.

After that, three signs were given to show that what Samuel had foretold came from the Lord (1 Samuel 10:2–6):

1. Saul would meet two men of his native place. They would inform him that his donkeys were found and that his father was fearful about him.

2. Saul would meet three men on the way to the holy place at Bethel. There, the men were to sacrifice. One man would have three kids, another three loaves of bread, and the other a bottle of wine. The three men would salute Saul and bestow on him two loaves of bread.

3. Saul would meet a company of prophets with musical instruments, and they would be prophesying; then, the Spirit of God would fall upon Saul, and he would prophesy with the prophets and become a new man.

The company of prophets was a society of prophets, an organized company of prophets under the guidance and direction of Samuel. They belonged to the schools of the prophets, which better would be named prophetic unions, or an assembly of prophets. These prophetic unions were first founded by Samuel and, under his direction, he presided over them (1 Samuel 10:8, 19:19–20). Later, there were prophetic unions in different places, especially at Bethel and Gilgal (2 Kings 2:3, 4:38). The origin of these schools of the prophets, which the Greek Septuagint also calls τὴν ἐκκλησίαν τῶν προφητῶν (the assembly of the prophets), came from what Samuel awoke among the Israelites in his times. These schools leaned heavily into a relationship with the movements, actions, practices, and atmosphere of the Holy Spirit. The schools were to teach the prophets to cherish and develop prophetic inspiration and spiritual life by exercising their faith through prayers, entering the presence of the Holy Spirit, studying the written law, music, and sacrifices, and practicing the gift of prophecy. Either all the time or from time to time, the prophetic gift came upon the prophets continually.

The words "and they were prophesying" in 1 Samuel 10:5 should be understood as the focal point. The prophets were amid giving words of prophecies under the influence and power of the Holy Spirit, with no need for Samuel to stand in and help them to determine that it was the Spirit of the Lord who influenced them rather than another spirit. They had already learned to distinguish between the Spirit of God and contrary spirits.

Their state was a constant state of inspiration and divine thoughts coming from the Lord and becoming words that were spoken in the honor of the Lord God. The prophetic gift had now been expanded and fell upon more persons than just one person at a time.

"The Spirit of the Lord" not only had fallen upon the prophets, but now the Spirit fell upon Saul in their midst. The Spirit of the Lord followed the company of prophets wherever they went, and as they were walking and met Saul, the Spirit fell upon Saul (1 Samuel 10:6). Then, the term "Spirit of the Lord" excludes every earthly type of inspiration and every form of occultism.

The importance of the Holy Spirit falling upon Saul was that by this act, he became part of the divine inspiration and prophetic words of the prophets. The holy fire of the divine inspiration and providence that rested upon the company of the prophets now jumped upon Saul. The holy fire immediately fell upon Saul coming from the prophets, and it caused him to be another man, a new man changed internally. The Spirit of the Lord wreaked this internal change upon the heart of Saul with sanctification and the subordination of his will to the Lord's will and law.

As seen, the Spirit of the Lord during this time fell upon the persons rather than communed with them or dwelt with them continually. It was rare for the Spirit to dwell continually upon or in a person's life.

The significance of the occurrence of these signs was to show that God was with Saul. It is incorrect to read 1 Samuel 10:7 as giving Saul permission to do whatever he liked, but what seemed most proper or what agreed with the will of God. The restriction is found in the subjunctive mood being used and the text of the conditional statement used, אֲשֶׁר תִּמְצָא יָדֶךָ or ἐὰν εὕρῃ ἡ χείρ σου (whatever your hand may find). The subjunctive mood is clearly stated in the Greek Septuagint and understood in the Hebrew text.

The prophetic gifts, ministry, and office of the prophets were not by birth, and so bodily paternity meant nothing. They came from the Lord. And this is true even today.

In the next part of this selection, Samuel was represented as having summoned all the tribes of Israel upon Mizeph, where he cast lots until the lot fell upon Saul. This was a firm proof that providence was upon Saul and his calling (1 Samuel 10:17–27). Out of this passage, the words of prophecy from Samuel coming from the Lord are these, "I brought up Israel out of Egypt, and delivered you out of the hand of the Egyptians, and out of the hand of all kingdoms, and of them that oppressed you: And ye have this day rejected your God, who himself saved you out of all your adversities and your tribulations; and ye have said unto him, Nay, but set a king over us. Now therefore present yourselves before the LORD by your tribes, and by your thousands," 1 Samuel 10:18–19. The change of pronouns, from the first person to the second person in verses 18 and 19, gives the whole problem of the Israelites wanting and having a king over them. The change is from the powerful assistance of the Lord to the sinful practice and conduct of the Israelites asking for a king. It is a change from depending upon the assistance of the Lord and His provision to depending upon your own independence from the Lord. The Israelites were proclaiming that they could take care of themselves when the opposite for hundreds of years had been the truth. It was as if they were putting a finger in the eye of God and saying something like, "We can make it without You." The emphatic pronouns, it should be known, are used in the texts, and they doubly indicate the abhorrence of the Lord God over this and the sinful conduct of the Israelites. Out of all the sins that the Israelites could commit, this was one of the gravest ones since they refused to depend upon God completely. In truth, it was the worst.

The next part of the election of Saul as king came forth as having Saul seen as a bold patriot who rose to the occasion when a call came from the men of Jabesh Gilead for help against the Ammonites, who were about to devastate their city. Saul sent out a ringing challenge to the surrounding country that met with a hearty response, organized the volunteers into three divisions, fell suddenly upon the Ammonites from three directions, and utterly routed them. In due reason, the Israelites hailed Saul as king and proceeded to Gilgal, where they made him king before the Lord and rejoiced greatly (1 Samuel 11:1–11, 15).

From 1 Samuel 12:6–25, several things took place:

1. The Israelites had not learned from their lessons of history.

2. Samuel gave them a brief historical review.

3. Their disobedience always brought catastrophe upon them.

4. Their repentance had always brought forth nothing but restoration and prosperity.

5. God was their true King.

6. Yet, the history of Israel did not have to be repeated if they would listen to Samuel.

7. If the Israelites and their new king would obey and follow the Lord, they would be blessed.

8. If not, then nothing but catastrophe would follow them.

9. Samuel sought to call upon the Lord to send a rainstorm to prove these words.

10. The Lord agreed and sent a storm, which wrought fear in the hearts of the Israelites.

11. The Israelites became fearful of the Lord and Samuel.

12. One more time, Samuel warned the Israelites that their prosperity would depend upon their obedience to their only true King.

13. In times of disobedience, God would still be merciful to the Israelites, and Samuel would continue to pray for them as long as he lived.

Two things worth noting from this passage are more than just a summary. First, Samuel reminded the Israelites of his innocence, faithfulness, and blamelessness before the Lord God and all of them during his life (1 Samuel 12:1−4). Next, the Israelites added unto all their sins against the Lord God, the sin of asking for a king (1 Samuel 12:18−19). According to the grammar of 1 Samuel 12:18−19, the Israelites accepted both another sin among their sins and the additional consequences of those sins. They wanted a king more than wanting God to cover over their sins and wanting God to remove the coming consequences of having evil men rule them.

On the next occasion, Samuel and Saul were seen together in the Lord God rejecting Saul as king. The rejection of Saul occurred in several acts (1 Samuel 13:1−28:10):

1. Saul offered a sacrifice without being a priest (1 Samuel 13:9).

2. He made an excuse for breaking the commandment of God (1 Samuel 13:8−10).

3. He ordered the death of his own son, though the Israelites did not carry it out (1 Samuel 13:9—14:45).

4. He opposed the commandment of God, which demanded the destruction of Agag and his city (1 Samuel 15:2—12). This cost Saul his crown.

5. He lied to Samuel about obeying God and what God wanted done with the Amalekites (1 Samuel 15:13—20).

6. He sought to blame his own people for his failure (1 Samuel 15:10—21).

7. He became exalted in pride (1 Samuel 15:17).

8. He denied and rejected the Word of God (1 Samuel 15:23—26).

9. While still blaming the Israelites, his own people, he somewhat repented of his actions (1 Samuel 15:24—35).

10. Because of his actions, the Holy Spirit was lifted from him, and he became demon possessed (1 Samuel 16:14—18:12).

11. He became envious of what David did by the Lord God and made many attempts, twenty-one attempts, on his life (1 Samuel 18:6—26:25).

12. He became very bitter toward his own son because of David (1 Samuel 20:30—34).

13. He drove David away from his presence, home, and inheritance (1 Samuel 21:1—30:31).

14. He sought spiritual help from the witch of Endor, who was possessed by a Pythonic demon (1 Samuel 28:7—25).

15. He swore to the witch of Endor that he would protect her from death, contrary to the Lord God (1 Samuel 28:10).

The words of Samuel to Saul are utterly remarkable and prove that the words of the Lord to Saul through Samuel were conditional words, though no condition was noticed, "Hath the Lord as great delight in burnt offerings and sacrifices, as in obeying the voice of the Lord? Behold, to obey is better than sacrifice, and to hearken than the fat of rams. For rebellion is the sin of witchcraft, and stubbornness is iniquity and idolatry. Because thou hast rejected the word of the Lord, he hath also rejected thee from being king," 1 Samuel 15:22–23. The words of Samuel are simply that it is better to obey the words of the Lord, being in a state of obedience, than to sacrifice for sins committed, being in a state of sins.

Saul could have well refused to accept the calling and election of king. For the blessings given to Saul became his own downfall and curses because of his disobedience. It was his choice, accept the blessings but be obedient, accept the blessings but become disobedient, or reject being king and the blessings that follow.

The repentance of God and Samuel's reaction to God's repentance were very important to the lives of Samuel and of Saul and allow us to see deep into the interworking of the Lord's nature. In 1 Samuel 15:11, the words of the Lord were, נִחַ֫מְתִּי כִּי־הִמְלַ֫כְתִּי אֶת־ שָׁאוּל֙ לְמֶ֫לֶךְ כִּי־שָׁב֙ מֵאַחֲרַ֔י וְאֶת־דְּבָרַ֖י לֹ֥א הֵקִֽים (I have repented My own self that I made Saul to be king, for he has turned away from following Me and he did not make himself to keep My commandments) or παρακέκλημαι ὅτι ἐβασίλευσα τὸν Σαουλ εἰς βασιλέα ὅτι ἀπέστρεψεν ἀπὸ ὄπισθέν μου καὶ τοὺς λόγους μου οὐκ ἐτήρησεν (I have repented My own self with much regret because I have crowned Saul to be king, since he has turned away from following Me and he has not kept My commandments).

The repentance of God means that God changed His will and mind about Saul. The change of the divine will and mind was determined by the change in the conduct of a man, Saul. God, being a holy God, could not stand by and allow someone whom He had chosen to become evil and keep him as the chosen king of Israel. It became the purpose of God to remove Saul from being the king of Israel. Indeed, the conduct of a man cancelled or suspended the prophetic words of the Lord, and that conduct made the words of non-effect. The fault was the evil conduct of Saul.

The change within the will and mind of God was not a change of nature but was a change wrought upon by an outside source, the conduct of a man, which was contrary to the state of a holy God. The conduct of a man changed first and became the opposite of what God was and always is. As seen here, the condition of a man or woman can change the will and mind of God about a circumstance.

In addition, repentance of God is a change within the administration and direction of God. And the repentance of God always supposes an evil change within man or some other creature. So the evil conduct of a man can change that administration and direction and make the words of God be canceled, suspended, and given to another. This change is always sorrowful for the Lord.

The grounds (reasons) for God's repentance were that Saul turned away from following the Lord and that he had not kept His commandments. Both clauses express the total apostasy from the Lord, including internal and external. And God's repentance caused a judicial decision against the evil conduct of Saul. This made Saul become an illegitimate king over Israel and become an apostate and not part of Israel.

The reaction of Samuel to the words of the Lord about Saul is more than distress. Here, there appeared a word that fell to the ground and had to be picked up and given to another. The words "it grieved Samuel; and he cried unto the LORD all night" in 1 Samuel 15:11 indicate a twofold reaction that came upon Samuel because of the revelation of the Lord coming upon him. Both the Hebrew and the Greek do not express grief, instead, both express the reaction of anger, red-hot anger. It was the holy anger of God since Samuel did pray while angry. He was furious about Saul's apostasy and disobedience.

Further, he was angry about the intentional attempt of Saul to violate and thwart the purposes of the Lord in his life and in the national life of the Israelites. The object of Samuel's crying was not only the apostasy and disobedience of Saul, but that God would not exempt Saul from his sinful actions—Saul sowed something that could not be unsowed. God refused to hear the prayers of His priest and prophet. Since there was no repentance in Saul, Samuel became an avenging prophet against him rather than remaining a mediator as a priest, seeking God's mercy for Saul.

In simple terms, both 1 Samuel 13 and 1 Samuel 15 state that Saul was rejected as king firstly because he had not carried out faithfully the command of the Lord to exterminate the Amalekites. Secondly, he offered up the sacrifices necessary before launching a battle against the Philistines without waiting any longer for Samuel.

Because of these two reasons and other ones, Samuel himself in the office of a prophet removed Saul out of the kingship. In a summary, the reason given is that Saul has "not kept the commandment of the Lord God" 1 Samuel 13:13. Why? The rejection according to chapter 15 is to the effect that Samuel communicated to Saul the order of the Lord God that he should destroy the Amalekites, leaving neither human being nor animal alive, but devoting the whole people and all that they possessed as an offering (reward) unto the Lord. However, Saul brought back some of the livestock as spoil and led the captive King Agag in triumph back to Gilgal. Samuel met Saul on the way and rebuked him for this disobedience (1 Samuel 15:22−23).

After that, Samuel himself "hewed Agag in pieces before the Lord in Gilgal" (1 Samuel 15:33). The point of view and spirit of this are simple enough to point out the horrible thing done by Saul in the eyes of the Lord. From this point, the prophecies, promises, and blessings were going to be suspended and then transferred from Saul to another, even David (1 Samuel 16:1−13). Samuel must appoint him since he had anointed Saul. The only other contact of Samuel with David is relayed in 1 Samuel 19:18−24.

The great virtue of Samuel was that he saw the need of his times, found the man capable of meeting that need, and inspired in him the courage and faith necessary for the successful accomplishment of his task. The importance of Samuel is seen in the fact that so much is written under his name.

The rejection of Saul as king and his process of backsliding ended and consummated with Saul seeking a medium—one who was trafficked with familiar spirits (Pythonic demons). The Witch of Endor was one of the greatest mediums mentioned in Scripture. She had escaped the sword of Saul. And now Saul resorted to her instead of the Lord God. She belonged to Satan. She was highly possessed; she was accustomed to doing her work with occultic powers. She, like the mediums at Delphi, was a Pythoness. When she had a customer, she willingly handed herself over to the Pythonic demon, who lived in her, to talk for the supposed dead, or she could do it herself in a way to deceive.

Saul was a backslidden king. He had called upon God for information but refused to hear him. He was determined to discover what he wanted to know, so he called on the devil. This was the last step in his backslidden state. He had become a reprobate.

Many oracles existed in Canaan. This is evident from the number Saul himself is said to have suppressed. Such a one, with its Pythoness, was this at Endor. It was a city in the Tribe of Manasseh.

According to I Samuel 28:3–25 and 1 Chronicles 10:13–14, Saul sought after a medium who was possessed of a Pythonic demon. He did not ask the Lord but wanted to ask from the evil spirits that the woman had. Why? God did not answer Saul by any means. Therefore, if God refused to answer Saul by these means, it is firmly stated that God did not answer him in a way that the Scriptures forbid. And God did not allow Samuel to communicate through a witch (Leviticus 19:3–11, 20:6; Deuteronomy 18:11; 2 Kings 21:6, 23:24; 2 Chronicles 33:6; Isaiah 8:19, 19:3, 29:4).

1 Samuel 28:7 indicates that Saul sought occultic information from evil spirits. In 1 Samuel 28:13, the woman seeing gods ascending out of the earth tells the answer here. These gods are none other than demons.

It is also understood here that the old man who came out of the earth is also a demon. And it is understood from the demon, whom the woman was possessed with, that he left her, went down into the earth, and then rose up from the earth. Then, he appeared as Samuel. After that, he returned to her and began to speak through her in the voice of Samuel. The reason this occurs is because the vision was not for Saul but for a woman. Therefore, how could Saul, who did not see this imitation by the demon, speak to this demon and get answers he could understand unless the demon was going into the woman and was speaking through her, for spoken words were clearly used?

That God had become Saul's enemy confirms this. Therefore, if Samuel helped him, he would also become God's enemy. God had stopped dealing with him (1 Samuel 28:6,16). How could a woman filled with a demon have power over a saint who is in the hand of God to make him come up from the underworld (John 10:28)? Second Samuel 12:23 and Job 10:21 reveal that the dead cannot come back in soulish forms to appear to humans on earth. However, these verses do not show that a person cannot return to be resurrected in mortality, as shown in the Scriptures.

Saul and the Witch of Endor

The section about the Witch of Endor in 1 Samuel 28 begins with a clear statement about the present state of Samuel in verse 3, וּשְׁמוּאֵל מֵת or Καὶ Σαμουὴλ ἀπέθανεν (and Samuel died). What is meant by 1 Samuel 28:3–25 is intended to reference a time after Samuel's death.

As from the death of Samuel, it is said that Saul הֵסִיר הָאֹבוֹת וְאֶת־הַיִּדְּעֹנִים מֵהָאָרֶץ׃ (made the mediums and the soothsayers both who had in them Pythonic demons to be removed by death from the land) or περιεῖλεν τοὺς ἐγγαστρίμυθους καὶ τοὺς γνώστας ἀπὸ τῆς γῆς (removed by death the mediums, also known as ventriloquists, and others who had occultic knowledge—both possessed with Pythonic demons). The mediums and soothsayers both were possessed of evil spirits—Pythonic demons; the mediums also were ventriloquists. Therefore, ventriloquists are the same as mediums. First Samuel 28:3 covers all types of occultists who had been attempted to be killed by the efforts and orders of Saul. Therefore, many, not all, were removed by death from among the land.

After the death of Samuel, the Philistines saw weakness in the land of Israel. There appeared to be a great opportunity to attack the Israelites. The enemies always attack when there are signs of weakness. So the Philistines threatened war in the Jezreel Valley.

Saul became afraid of the army of the Philistines and all that was meant if Israel lost the war. His life, for example, would be forfeit (1 Samuel 28:4–5). His fear and bewilderment were beyond measure. Both were exceeding. The last part of 1 Samuel 28:5 reads, וַיִּרָא וַיֶּחֱרַד לִבּוֹ מְאֹד (he was afraid and his heart—mind was exceedingly disturbed) or ἐφοβήθη καὶ ἐξέστη ἡ καρδία αὐτοῦ σφόδρα (he was afraid, and his heart—mind was exceedingly bewildered). Besides the coming appearance of the Pythonic demon that Saul was to experience, the disturbance of his mind points to the appearance of more types of evil spirits, the Kundalini demons, and even more, as well as his awful state of reprobation. His awful state was exceeding. He was abandoned by evil, and evil consumed him simultaneously.

Still, Saul inquired of the Lord. The inquiring was not once but a continual state that was past. None done by him did any good. The Lord—the Covenant-God—rejected him because of his sins and evil. Saul had broken the covenant with the Lord. The Lord had not broken the covenant with him.

For reprobates, even just for common backsliders, the words of 1 Samuel 28:7 must be a warning, וְלֹא עָנָהוּ יְהוָה or οὐκ ἀπεκρίθη αὐτῷ Κύριος (the Lord did not respond to him). The Lord had permanently rejected any communication between Himself and the living Saul. No form of divine communication was permitted to Saul: dreams, Urim and Thummim—divine lots, and prophets (1 Samuel 22:5–23, 23:6, 9, 30:7). Saul saw that the Philistine army was numerous. Since the Lord did not answer him, he wanted to learn the fate of himself and his army.

After seeking assistance from the Lord and communication between the Lord and himself and finding no answer, Saul immediately sought occultic knowledge and information. This is the expected behavior, conduct, disposition, and attitude of someone who tries the Lord, finds no help, and turns to the devil and his evil spirits.

In 1 Samuel 28:6, the repetition of the Hebrew adverb גַּם (neither) or the Greek conjunction καὶ (or) points out the three lines of inquiry of the Lord from Saul: dreams, Urim and Thummim and the prophets. The dreams were not to come upon Saul but those the Lord blessed with these supernatural abilities. These persons could hold the office of a prophet or work in the prophetic without holding the office (Numbers 12:6 with Jeremiah 23:25–32, and Deuteronomy 13:2). And other persons without being actual prophets could well receive dreams from the Lord (Joel 3:1).

In 1 Samuel 28:6, the persons who had revelations in dreams were distinguished from the prophets. The passage gives an order of divine revelation. There was a progression from less to greater.

The term Urim here in this passage is the abbreviation of Urim and Thummim (Exodus 28:30; Numbers 27:21). The Ephod with the Urim and Thummim were in David's camp since the murder of the priests in Nob (1 Samuel 22:18, 23:6, 30:7). However, Saul made a new Ephod with the breastplate and the Urim and Thummim. It is also possible that a copy of the Ephod with the Urim and Thummim had been left behind when Abiathar fled (1 Samuel 14:37, 23:9–12; 2 Samuel 8:17, 15:24, 29, 35; 1 Chronicles 15:11; 18:16).

The relationship between Saul and the prophets had been broken because of his persecution against David and because of his constant rebellion and sins.

Knowing that he had ordered the deaths of all mediums in the kingdom of Israel, Saul still sought from his servants to see if any remained alive. Speaking to his servants, Saul said, בַּקְשׁוּ־לִי אֵשֶׁת בַּעֲלַת־אוֹב וְאֵלְכָה אֵלֶיהָ וְאֶדְרְשָׁה־בָּהּ (You must immediately and extremely seek for me a female medium who is possessed with a Pythonic demon so that I may go to her and may seek of her) or Ζητήσατέ μοι γυναῖκα ἐγγαστρίμυθον, καὶ πορεύσομαι πρὸς αὐτὴν καὶ ζητήσω ἐν αὐτῇ (You must immediately seek for me a female medium who is possessed with the Pythonic demon, so that I may go to her and seek in her) in 1 Samuel 28:7. The imperative mood with the piel verb pattern used in the Hebrew point out the awful state of Saul. He sought an immediate and robust response. He wanted his servants to go immediately and seek every place possible to find any medium that had not been killed. These words include desperation, impatience, hopelessness, force, and command. The Greek Septuagint also has the imperative, and the rest is implied. The imperative shows his mental, spiritual, and emotional state.

Grammatically, 1 Samuel 28:7 is formed by two cohortatives: וְאֵלְכָה (so that I may go) and וְאֶדְרְשָׁה־בָּהּ (may seek of her). These cohortatives indicate Saul's intention, but his intention did not have to be fulfilled. The imperative and the waw + cohortative all point to a potential, contingent, or conditional element to this passage. The piel verb pattern stresses the greatest of his desire to locate a medium that had a Pythonic demon. Still, according to the cohortatives, he could refuse to go any farther than what he had so far done.

In the Greek Septuagint, the simple future is used to express the cohortatives.

The Hebrew phrase אֵשֶׁת בַּעֲלַת־אוֹב (a female medium who is possessed with a Pythonic demon) includes seven main ideas: a woman, a female medium, a female owner or possessor of, a mistress of a Pythonic demon, demonic possession, a Pythonic demon—familiar spirit, or ventriloquistic spirit, and the practice of ventriloquism through the demon. This Hebrew phrase considerably indicates a satanic covenant between the medium and the Pythonic demon that she was using for her benefit and the benefits of Satan's kingdom. The Witch of Endor whispered, peeped, or chirped like a chicken coming out of its shell.

The Hebrew noun בַּעֲלָה has various shapes of meaning here. Basically, it means a medium who possesses a Pythonic demon; a woman who consults the supposed dead but a Pythonic demon. Therefore, she is also a necromancer. Still, the woman has a relationship with the Pythonic demon. At least, in some respects, she has control over the demon coming and going. She owned and had mastery over this demon to do her bidding. She had authority over the magic arts and evil spirits. And she consulted with evil spirits.

All these things point to a satanic contract or covenant between herself and the kingdom of evil and a partnership between herself and evil spirits, especially the one mentioned in 1 Samuel 28:7.

The uniqueness of her relationship with this Pythonic demon must be carefully studied here. According to the Hebrew noun בַּעֲלָה, the Witch of Endor was the owner, possessor, and mistress of that Pythonic demon. It is translated better as "the mistress of the Pythonic demon." There is represented here a relationship that cannot rule out some type of sexual connotation, even an illicit sexual relationship, and the witch prostituting herself unto this demon.

At least, the Hebrew noun בַּעֲלָה promotes the idea of spiritual fornication (whoredom). This was what the witch was practicing. In Nahum 3:4, the Hebrew noun בַּעֲלָה is associated with כְּשָׁפִים (witchcraft) and בִּזְנוּנֶיהָ (harlotries). So both words are tied to spiritual fornication, and with that comes always sexual fornication. Simply, idolatry, demon possession, and sexual sin are all tied together.

A type of marriage between a demon and a medium is not unheard of in the stories of philosophers, historians, theologians, and even occultists. In occultic circles, it is known that spirits have appeared to women and claimed to be their husbands for eternity. For example, a demon appeared to a woman and claimed to be a man who previously died. The spirit sought to marry her, even in this life.[23] Pember mentioned a work of a medium done in the AD 1800s, in which the medium experienced many evil things.[24]

The servants of Saul knew about a medium who lived in Endor. They should have turned her in so that she could have been executed for practicing the black arts, including necromancing. His servants not turning her in was itself an abomination and a sin (Leviticus 19:31). Both Saul and his servants hardened their hearts and went after the abominations of the Gentiles and those things that the law of God had forbidden (Leviticus 19:31). And this did not make them humble themselves before God.

To seek the Witch of Endor out, Saul disguised himself and wore clothes other than his royal clothes. At night, he was to go to the Witch of Endor in order to disguise himself from his own people and the posts of the Philistine army. He was accompanied by two men who assisted him in finding the witch and protecting him (1 Samuel 28:6−8). This journey was terrible; the night was also awful. Step-by-step and moment by moment, Saul was moving away from what he had been. There more and more a change from what he had been to what he was on this journey. Self-darkening and inner self-hardening were both present.

Saul appeared before the witch in disguise. 1 Samuel 28:8 begins with the Hebrew phrase וַיִּתְחַפֵּשׂ (he completely disguised himself). The idea of the hithpael verb pattern is that Saul disguised himself, no other. But the hithpael verb pattern also stresses the completeness of his masquerade for a time.

In the appearance before the witch, Saul asked, קָסוֹמִי־נָא לִי בָּאוֹב וְהַעֲלִי לִי אֵת אֲשֶׁר־אֹמַר אֵלָיִךְ: (I pray you−please−you must immediately consult for me by the Pythoness demon, and you must immediately cause to be brought up for me whoever I may say unto you) or Μάντευσαι δή μοι ἐν τῷ ἐγγαστριμύθῳ καὶ ἀνάγαγέ μοι ὃν ἐὰν εἴπω σο (Surely, you must immediately perform divinations for me by the Pythonic demon and you must immediately raise up for me whoever I may say to you) in 1 Samuel 28:8. The Hebrew phrase קָסוֹמִי־נָא (I pray you−please−you must immediately consult) and the Greek phrase Μάντευσαι δή (Surely, you must immediately perform divinations) both occur here in a bad sense of the predictions of false prophets (Deuteronomy 18:10−14; 1 Samuel 6:2). Also, necromancy is meant here and is practiced. Necromancy is forbidden on pain of death (Exodus 22:18; Leviticus 19:31, 20:27; Deuteronomy 18:10, 11). Therefore, the Witch of Endor was a necromancer.

This Pythoness, medium, claimed through the practices of divination to be able to raise the dead. Saul sought to have her bring up whoever he wanted to be raised. As a medium, she spoke through a mysterious tone of voice, like the voice of the departed dead from the depth of the earth, the voice of another or her own voice (Leviticus 19:31, 20:6, 27; 1 Samuel 28:3–8; 2 Kings 23:24; Isaiah 29:9).

Saul knew what the Witch of Endor was. He knew what information he was seeking. He was seeking information from a Pythonic demon working through this medium. First, 1 Samuel 28:8 shows that Saul did not have complete confidence in her. The extent of her powers and occult abilities remained unknown to him, as did the Pythonic demon's capacity to mimic the deceased through its vessel. Saul harbored skepticism regarding the far-fetched possibilities presented by this woman and her methods. He hoped that she could apparently attempt to call up a departed spirit from Sheol. Saul sought to hear Samuel's voice through the Pythonic demon and ventriloquistic acts. He sought that the woman would give prophecy by the Pythonic demon in the voice of Samuel. This demon had ventriloquistic arts.

In 1 Samuel 28:8, the Hebrew phrase אֲשֶׁר־אֹמַר אֵלֶיךָ: or the Greek phrase ὃν ἐὰν εἴπω σο (whoever I may say to you) stresses the limitations of the medium's abilities in the mind of Saul. He understood the Pythoness's occultic abilities were limited. While real occultists have supernatural powers, these powers are limited. Even the backslidden Saul understood this.

At first, the Pythoness, the Witch of Endor, refused to do as Saul wanted. She thought that this was a trap to kill her (1 Samuel 28:9). Saul had made a law and a command that all mediums and other occultists were to be sought out and exterminated. This Pythoness had escaped death so far. In his earliest period of rulership, Saul sought to purify divine worship from all idolatry.

The Hebrew phrase הָאִשָּׁה and the Greek phrase ἡ γυνὴ (the woman) in 1 Samuel 28:9 point out that the Witch of Endor was speaking. It was not any other witch, nor was it the Pythonic demon indwelling her. In her speech to Saul, she repeated what was also mentioned in 1 Samuel 28:3.

Saul swore by the Lord to her that no harm or her death would come to her (1 Samuel 28:10). The oath showed just how far gone Saul was. Also, it showed just how hardened Saul's heart was. It should be noticed the Covenant-God statement, בַּיהוָה (by the Lord) and חַי־יְהֹוָה or Ζῇ Κύριος (As the Lord eternally lives). The Greek Septuagint could well have ἐν Κυρίῳ (by the Lord) like the Hebrew text. Origen in his recension adds this. The scribes simply saw "by the Lord" as unnecessary in Greek.

It is one thing to make an oath by God, but to make an oath by the Covenant-God sealed Saul to his fate. It was the last assault against God, the previous disrespect, contempt, and blasphemous thing done by Saul, at least in this context. And he made this oath to one of the most heinous creatures—Pythoness. Saul was bringing the Witch of Endor into a covenant with God. Impossible! But what Saul was trying to do was beyond blasphemy.

In 1 Samuel 28:11, once Saul gave the Pythoness the oath, she asked the question, אֶת־מִי אַעֲלֶה־לָּךְ (Whom should I make to be brought up for you) or Τίνα ἀναγάγω σοι (Whom should I bring up for you)? Even in these words, there is some doubt that she can bring up anything (1 Samuel 28:10). Overall, she believed that she had some sovereignty over the realm of the dead in Sheol. She saw her mediumship as a business in soothsaying and conjuration. Her occultic practice was not free. She demanded payment.

In the Hebrew question אֶת־מִי אַעֲלֶה־לָּךְ (Whom should I make to be brought up for you), the hiphil verb pattern, is used with the imperfect form. In her words, she would participate in this event as understood by the hiphil verb pattern. In the mind of the Witch of Endor, the departed spirit, summoned up by soothsaying, was to be progressively brought up, foot by foot.

The Pythoness believed that she could call up a departed spirit from the realm of the dead. She thought that the departed dead appeared. She did conjuring, and she was to be aided by her Pythonic demon. She claimed power and authority, which no human and evil spirit have. If anything could be done, it would be done through her Pythonic demon, and this spirit disguised himself as a departed person, male or female.

The use of the Witch of Endor by Saul to try to contact the spirit of Samuel affirms that necromancy can bring contact with spiritual beings (1 Samuel 28:7–19).

The rituals of conjuring up the supposed dead followed the same procedures throughout various forms of paganism. In Homer's *Odyssey*, Mesopotamian, and Hittite literature, the details are provided: 1) Necromancing was generally done at night, 2) a ritual pit was dug with a special tool, 3) either food or the blood of a sacrificial animal was placed in the pit so that the spirits would be enticed into the pit, 4) an invocation ritual, 5) the name of the spirit summoned for was chanted, 6) giving a water sacrifice was part, 7) after that, the pit was covered in order to make sure that the spirits do not escape after the rituals were concluded, and 8) a skull was used and questions were asked and the spirit gave answers. Both the Pythoness and the client had roles to play in these procedures. The spirits who came up were in human form; they could communicate with the client or with the ventriloquistic medium. And sometimes, the ventriloquistic medium could see the spirit conjured up in the vision state.[25]

In Homer's *Odyssey*, the rites of a necromancer must be performed around a pit with fire at night, and various sacrifices must be offered.[26]

Saul demanded that the Witch of Endor אֶת־שְׁמוּאֵל הַעֲלִי־לִי (You must immediately cause to be brought up Samuel) or Τὸν Σαμουὴλ ἀνάγαγέ μοι (You must immediately bring up Samuel), not from the grave but in Sheol. At this time, both godly and ungodly were in this place. Sheol is beneath the earth. The dead were supposed to rise from Sheol to the earth's surface and answer the Pythoness (Exodus 22:18; Leviticus 20:27). Saul was precise about what he wanted. He wanted to see the departed spirit of Samuel (1 Samuel 28:11). Samuel had died and was buried (1 Samuel 25:1, 28:3). The burial site was a grave owned by Samuel near Ramah, in the territory of Benjamin.

At the end of the conjuring—bringing up a spirit—verse 12 says, אֲשֶׁר־אֹמַר־ אֵלֶיךָ: or καὶ εἶδεν ἡ γυνὴ τὸν Σαμουήλ (and the woman saw Samuel). A principle of Scripture is to interpret one part of Scripture by another part. This is especially true if many Scriptures point out something and another part of Scripture seems to say the reverse. Various Scriptures indicate that necromancing is forbidden.

Before verse 12, the Pythoness was using her conjuring arts. A form appeared to the woman. Saul did not see it. This apparition was not anticipated. She was in a vision state and a state of clairvoyance. In this state of clairvoyance, she recognized people who, like Saul, were in his disguise.

According to the Pythoness, who was possessed and a reprobate, she saw Samuel. Easily, the Pythonic demons deceive and make themselves appear in various forms, especially the forms of the dead and the forms of the righteous dead. The magical and black arts of the Pythoness could not at her will make a righteous man leave Paradise and appear before her. She did not see Samuel. She saw the Pythonic demon who imitated him. In all respects, the Pythonic demon represented Samuel.

When she saw the apparition, she cried in a loud voice. Therefore, the cause of her reaction was what she saw. Her response indicated that she rarely had a vision state and seldom saw anything (1 Samuel 28:12–13).

In this state, the Pythonic demon possessed or entered her, and she said to Saul, לָמָּה רִמִּיתָנִי וְאַתָּה שָׁאוּל or τί παρελογίσω με; καὶ σὺ εἶ Σαούλ (Why have you deceived me? Now you are Saul). The emphatic pronoun stresses that she was in shock, desperation, and utterly bewildered. By the Pythonic demon, she could know just who this man was. Before the entrance of the Pythonic demon, she was unaware of who the man was. The knowledge came from the evil spirit.

At this time, she knew just who the man was, and she was reminded of her danger of violating the prohibition of the king. She thought she was deceived, tricked, and given over to death. The appearance of the form and the sudden perception of her danger caused great terror for her.

In 1 Samuel 28:12, the question was to be answered positively. It was a question of fact rather than a probable question of fact. Within a few seconds, the knowledge of just who was before her was revealed to her.

A Pythonic demon cannot, by an urge, whether himself or through a ventriloquistic medium, demand the soul of a righteous man or woman come from Paradise, which was part of the netherworld. Nor can an evil spirit demand that the spirit of a righteous man or woman come from heaven.

When the Pythonic demon revealed to her the person before her, Saul calmed her fear about her life. She was fearful that she was going to be killed.

The question מֶה רָאִית or τίνα ἑόρακας (What person have you seen?) in 1 Samuel 28:13 means that Saul did not see what she saw. Further, the Pythoness and Saul were in the room but somewhat distant from each other. Saul knew that she had seen someone. That was taken for fact.

The Pythoness saw in the vision state and in a state of clairvoyance spirits ascending, אֱלֹהִים רָאִיתִי עֹלִים מִן־הָאָרֶץ or Θεοὺς ἑόρακα ἀναβαίνοντας ἐκ τῆς γῆς (I saw the gods coming up from the ground). The spirits of the dead to be conjured up in necromancy are אֱלֹהִים (gods), which are the same as demons. In the Hebrew text, the Hebrew noun אֱלֹהִים is accompanied with the plural participle עֹלִים (ascending). This indicates that more than one spirit was ascending. Grammatically, this view is very sound. Historically, it is sound as well. Only one spirit is described in what follows by the notice of the Hebrew phrase מַה־תָּאֳרוֹ (What is his appearance). The Greek Septuagint has both the plural Θεοὺς and the plural participle ἀναβαίνοντας. Both indicate more than one spirit was ascending.

The Pythoness first saw the form of Samuel before her, and now she saw various gods coming up from the earth (1 Samuel

28:13). The gods were not the souls of the wicked nor the souls of the righteous. What is represented here is the progressive and ongoing appearance of various demons coming from the bottomless pit, one of whom was the one who appeared in the form of Samuel. The form of Samuel, whom the witch saw, was the first demon to arise from the netherworld: the bottomless pit. He was first among the rest of the group coming from the earth.

She described the spirit as an old man, appearing upright and wrapped in a cloak like the one Samuel wore in his lifetime. Saul prostrated himself in reverence before that spirit, which was unseen by him (I Samuel 28:14). Such experiences and communication with spirits were forbidden and most evil.

Among many, Saul and the spirit summoned communicated with each other through the Pythoness. The spirit spoke through the woman where she was standing. First Samuel 28:15–20 proves that the Chronicler supposed the magical practices were used and that the spirit's presence excluded God's miraculous power. The apparition did not ascend before her employment of witchcraft but due to it. The use of witchcraft occurred especially between verses 11 and 12. The words of the apparition confirm this. The spirit was disturbed by the conjurations of the Pythoness (1 Samuel 28:13–14). When an occultist uses incantations, the spirits will always be troubled.

Saul gave three reasons for disturbing the apparition: 1) I am very anguished because the Philistines war against me; 2) God has left me and does not give an answer to me anymore; and 3) I have called you so that you may tell me what to do (1 Samuel 28:15).

Saul mentioned the Lord did not give him revelation through any prophet (1 Samuel 28:15). In Saul's mind, the apparition was not a prophet. However, the spirit looked like Samuel, spoke like Samuel through the Pythoness, and had supernatural powers that Saul recognized. If this person were Samuel, there would have been a contradiction here. Saul could use no prophet, none. The word of Saul crosses out the person before him as a godly prophet, whether living or dead.

Clearly, Saul said in 1 Samuel 28:15, וֵאלֹהִים סָר מֵעָלַי וְלֹא־עָנָנִי עוֹד גַּם בְּיַד־הַנְּבִיאִם גַּם־בַּחֲלֹמוֹת וָאֶקְרָאֶה לְךָ לְהוֹדִיעֵנִי מָה אֶעֱשֶׂה (God has turned aside from me and has not given me an answer, neither anymore by the hand of the prophets nor by the dreams; and therefore, I have summoned you to make known to me what things I must do) or καὶ ὁ θεὸς ἀφέστηκεν ἀπ᾽ ἐμοῦ καὶ οὐκ ἐπακήκοέν μοι ἔτι καὶ ἐν χειρὶ τῶν προφητῶν καὶ ἐν τοῖς ἐνυπνίοις· καὶ νῦν κέκληκά σε γνωρίσαι μοι τί ποιήσω (and God has gone from me and has not given to me an answer, still both by the hand of the prophets and by the dreams; and now I have called you to make known to me what things I must do). In Greek, the words of Saul especially stress the departure of the real and absolute God of the universe. Also, God the Word in his pre-incarnate state had disappeared. All things of the Abrahamic Covenant were cut off from Saul, including the Shekinah glory. All that could commune with Saul now was the false and pagan gods and all their practices and rituals. Through incantations of witchcraft, Saul summoned a spirit by his Pythoness. Nothing here represented came from God.

Through practices of abominations, Saul only had somewhat of a hope that he could well receive answers from the spirit, especially summoned, לְהוֹדִיעֵנִי מָה אֶעֱשֶׂה or τί ποιήσω (what things I must do).

Recorded in Isaiah 8:19, God spoke of the abomination of necromancy in a question as בְּעַד הַחַיִּים אֶל־הַמֵּתִים: (Must they seek after the dead for the living) or τί ἐκζητοῦσιν περὶ τῶν ζώντων τοὺς νεκρούς (Why do they summon the dead about the living)?

The definite articles used with the Hebrew phrase בְּיַד־הַנְּבִיאִם גַּם בַּחֲלֹמוֹת or the Greek phrase ἐν χειρὶ τῶν προφητῶν καὶ ἐν τοῖς ἐνυπνίοις emphasize that all forms of divine revelation had been taken from Saul. Both parts of the Hebrew and Greek phrases cover all forms of divine revelation. Therefore, he understood that the answers he sought were not to come from the revelation of God (1 Samuel 28:13–20). Since God did not answer Saul by any means, the communication of the spirit cannot be of God. The spirit, like all evil spirits, knew some of the future. The communication of this spirit did not help Saul at all. This is true for all such communication. The end will always be like this.

The real God, the Lord, had departed from Saul and became his enemy (1 Samuel 28:13–15). The Lord had departed from Saul several times. This proves that this is possible with anyone who goes into sin and disobedience. Not only did the Lord depart from Saul and take the Holy Spirit from him (1 Samuel 16:13–14), but He became an enemy of Saul and cut him off in his sins (1 Samuel 28:16; 1 Chronicles 10:13–14). Both these facts were stated several times by inspiration and also spoken by a demon. Evil spirits and wicked men can tell the truth about some things. The lies must be rejected and not the truth.

The apparition spoke truth with lies. He knew the kingdom had been rent out of Saul's hand and been given it to David. God determined this several years before when Saul rejected Him (1 Samuel 28:16–18, 15:26–28, 16:1–13).

First Samuel 28:17 explains and confirms the words of 1 Samuel 28:16.

In 1 Samuel 28:18, the apparition told Saul that he did not listen to בְּקוֹל יְהוָה or φωνῆς Κυρίου (the voice of the Lord). Whatever voice Saul was listening to now, it did not come from the Lord. Therefore, the apparition was not a saint or a prophet but an evil spirit.

The fate of Saul had been settled due to his disobedience (1 Samuel 28:18). Notice the words, עַל־כֵּן הַדָּבָר הַזֶּה עָשָׂה־לְךָ יְהוָה הַיּוֹם הַזֶּה: or διὰ τοῦτο τὸ ῥῆμα ἐποίησεν Κύριός σοι τῇ ἡμέρᾳ ταύτῃ (therefore, the Lord has done this thing to you this day). The Hebrew verb עָשָׂה in the perfect form or the Greek verb ἐποίησεν in the aorist tense all point to that which is already settled. The results were immediate, which were complete fulfillment of the judgment against Saul.

First Samuel 28:19 is a prophecy, but the prophecy is unique. It is like the oracles given at Delphi. The source of the prophecy came from the Pythonic demon. Even an evil spirit knows much about the supernatural world, which men and women cannot find out until later, except through revelation. The Pythonic demon knew about the defeat of Israel before it happened. The defeat of Israel was accomplished by evil spirits in the heavenlies (Daniel 10:13). Deuteronomy 13:1–3 teaches that demons and false prophets can predict some true things well. Two predictions by this demon:

1. The Lord will deliver Israel with you into the hands of the Philistines.

2. Tomorrow, you and your sons will die.

The soul of the real Samuel was not in the place Saul went to at death. He was in the righteous compartment, whereas Saul went to the wicked compartment; the two places had a great gulf.

The tragedy affected not only Saul but also the whole Israelite community. The Hebrew phrase וְיִתֵּן יְהוָה גַּם אֶת־יִשְׂרָאֵל עִמְּךָ (And the Lord will give also Israel with you) or the Greek phrase καὶ παραδώσει Κύριος τὸν Ἰσραὴλ μετὰ σοῦ (And the Lord will hand over Israel with you). By one man, all Israel was going to suffer and enter the judgment of God. The act of God was done according to His holy will. The judgment was going to fall upon Saul and Israel. As the king, so did the people. If the king was holy, God saw the people as holy. If the king was disobedient and evil, God saw the people as disobedient and evil. Therefore, there was ethical and theocratical unity between the king and the people.

The message was tragic enough. Saul was overcome and fell at full length upon the earth. Part of this reaction was due to physical exhaustion. Again, the words of Samuel were the words of the Pythonic demon impersonating Samuel. This information came to Saul through the Pythoness; he did not see or hear anything himself. He merely took her word for what she saw and heard.

In 1 Chronicles 10:13–14, the same information is given that 1 Samuel 28 has, but in an abrupt manner. The Greek Septuagint does have this, καὶ ἀπεκρίνατο αὐτῷ Σαμουὴλ ὁ προφήτης (and Samuel the prophet gave an answer to him). The Hebrew text does not have this. This is more an interpretation than a literal interpretation and translation of the Hebrew. Then, this is a redundant addition.

The Pythoness came to the prostrate Saul and understood his mental disturbance. She offered him a morsel of meat (1 Samuel 28:21–22). He first refused, but his servants and the woman urged him on to eat. He rose up from the ground and sat on the couch—one of the four articles of furniture in her house. She had a fatted calf in the house and baked unleavened cakes for the entertainment of her guests. The description here is like the description of Abraham's hospitality.

Historically, various fathers, reformers, and earlier Christian theologians denied that an evil spirit brought up Samuel himself. This was the traditional view. Origen wrote, giving a reply of defender of traditional view, Καὶ μὴν γοῦν ἴσμεν τινὰς τῶν ἡμετέρων ἀδελφῶν ἀντιβλέψαντας τῇ Γραφῇ, καὶ λέγοντας, Οὐ πιστεύω τῇ ἐγγαστριμύθῳ. Λέγει ἡ ἐγγαστρίμυθος ἑορταμέναι (5) τὸν Σαμουὴλ, ψεύδεται· Σαμουὴλ οὐκ ἀνήχθη· Σαμουὴλ οὐ λαλεῖ. Ἀλλ᾽ ὥσπερ εἰσί τινες ψευδοπροφῆται λέγοντες· «Τάδε λέγει Κύριος,» καί· «Κύριος οὐκ ἐλάλησεν (6)·» οὕτω καὶ τὸ δαιμόνιον τοῦτο ψεύδεται, ἐπαγγελλόμενον ἀνάγειν τὸν ὑπὸ τοῦ Σαοὺλ προτασσόμενον (And indeed, we well know that certain ones of our brothers look skeptically at the Scripture and say, I do not believe in the ventriloquistic medium. The ventriloquistic medium says that she saw Samuel. She tells lies! Samuel was not raised up. Nor did Samuel speak. Just as there are certain false prophets who say, "Thus says the Lord," and "The Lord did not speak," So too does this demon lie when it announces that it is bringing up the one pointed out by Saul).[27] Generally, the Greek fathers follow this interpretation. For example, Gregory of Nyssa interpreted this as πρὸς τὸν Σαοὺλ τὰς ἐπιζητουμένας ψυχάς, θεοὺς ἑωρακέναι φησίν (for Saul the spirits which he inquired about, saying that "she saw gods").[28]

Martin Luther once said as follows:

> Dr. Luther was asked whether the Samuel who appeared to king Saul, upon the invocation of the Pythoness, as is related in the first Book of Kings, was really the prophet Samuel. The doctor answered: " No, 'twas a spectre, an evil spirit, assuming his form. What proves this is, that

God, by the laws of Moses, had forbidden man to question the dead; consequently, it must have been a demon which presented itself under the form of the man of God. In like manner, an abbot of Spanheim, a sorcerer, exhibited to the emperor Maximilian all the emperors, his predecessors, and all the most celebrated heroes of past times who defiled before him, each in the costume of his time. Among them were Alexander the Great and Julius Caesar. There was also the emperor's betrothed, whom Charles of France stole from him. But these apparitions were all the work of the demon").[29]

There are various examples of the practice of necromancy given throughout history. In the AD 1600s, several examples were mentioned in the work by Joseph Glanvil.[30] He was a Chaplain to the king. A spirit, claiming to be a murdered woman, appeared to James Graham.[31] In the section on the "Collection of Relations," there was a demon mentioned that appeared as the father-in-law of a man and said, "I am Edward Avon, your father-in-law, come near to me. I will do you no harm."[32] In the late AD 1800s, an explosion of necromancy occurred in England, America, and other countries, where numerous people sought to communicate with their departed loved ones. A private letter was given to a Christian writer, where the author of the letter said, "My wife saw her boy in his spiritual body permitted to come once to comfort."[33]

Paul Confronted by a Pythonic Demon

Paul was now on new ground—Greece. He was in a Greek city, a Roman colony. A new scene now opens before him, a new era in the history of the church. He has not only gone to war with Jewish prejudice. Now, he must encounter Satan in other forms. He now must confront him with the idolatries and superstitions of the West. There was a new spiritual territory with all its pitfalls and struggles on this new ground.

When Paul preached in Ephesus, he had to deal with unknown gods and the goddess Artemis, who was supposed to be the sister to Apollo (Acts 19:34–41). Of course, different names are given, but the same gods—Baalim and Astartes are meant. At Ephesus, a riot broke out against Paul since he rejected worshipping all pagan gods.

What happened in the city of Philippi with the possessed slave girl was a natural picture and manifestation of the ruling spirits in the region that went back thousands of years (Acts 16:13–18). One of the most significant difficulties that the gospel had to contend with arose from the power exercised over the Greek and Roman minds through oracles, enchantments, divination, soothsaying, and sorcery. The Pythonic demons revealed that power. Paul met this power face-to-face in the streets of Philippi.

The Pythonic demons were ministers of the old serpent (2 Corinthians 11:3; Revelation 12:9). They were and are agents of Satan.

In many respects, the Pythonic demons were the ones who worked chiefly as familiar spirits in the Old Testament. These demons continue to do so in modern times.

Remarkably, this last-named passage contains a prophecy concerning the victory to be achieved against the Great Serpent at the Second Coming and finally at the Battle of Gog and Magog.

At Philippi, a young slave girl, a Pythoness (priestess and prophetess) of Apollo, met Paul. This young damsel, possessed by the Pythonic demon, continued to harass Paul as he went on his way, proclaiming the gospel of Jesus Christ. The Pythonic demon spoke through the young damsel these words, "These men are the servants of the most high God, which shew unto us the way of salvation" (Acts 16:17). There was an evil spirit of deception within her. Note four things:

1. The testimony of the evil spirit was a true testimony. Paul and the others were "the servants of the highest God."

2. The testimony of the evil spirit was also a false testimony. This is seen in the Greek, which reads, "a way of salvation," not "the way." The word "the" (the definite article) is not in the Greek.

93

3. The evil spirit proclaimed that Paul preaches only one of the numerous ways to reach God.

4. The testimony, although partly true, is unacceptable.

The casting out of the Pythonic demon by Paul may be seen as a visible manifestation of Christ's authority bruising the head of Satan. Every time this occurs, we see Satan fall again from heaven.

This one Pythonic demon sought after Paul at the time of prayer and as they were going to the place of prayer. Paul and his companions did not seek after the Pythonic demon. This shows that it will try to undermine, destroy, control, stop, or hinder your prayer life. It was during this time that the conflict occurred.

The text does not mean that the young woman would meet with Paul and his companions. Still, the young woman was seeking them out to fight against them, to oppose, and engage them in spiritual warfare.

These Pythonic demons, like many others, will seek a fight. They will use false prophecy against true prophecy, counterfeits against the genuine, the counterfeit presence of God against the authentic presence of God, and counterfeit glory against the authentic glory. These Pythonic demons often initiate warfare. They are more active than passive and seek to keep the saints on the defensive.

The Pythonic demons seek someone to serve. They will bless their master with blessings of various kinds and try to destroy the blessings of those they are attacking. The blessings include gain, profit, and business.

The Pythonic demons will make sure that their masters (or those that they serve) are blessed financially and blessed in their endeavors, especially when their masters are false prophets, antichrists, or false teachers.

Scripture says that the young slave girl was possessed by an evil spirit, which gave her the power of fortune-telling (Acts 16:18). As a result, people went to her in the hope of that:

1. Their desires would be fulfilled.

2. Their futures would be good.

3. Their confidence would be restored.

4. Their fortunes would be at hand.

5. Their lost items would be found.

6. Their past would be unraveled.

7. Evil spirits cause people to trust such things instead of God.

8. Evil spirits keep people away from the Word of God and the faithful promises of God.

9. Evil spirits blind people to the reality of prayer.

10. Evil spirits keep people away from the grace of God, the grace of the only living and true God, the Sovereign Majesty of the universe, the only Sovereign Spirit who can truly save them.

The point to see is the power of sin to enslave and bind a person in the dark world of divination, fortune-telling, witchcraft, black magic, sorcery, and astrology. All false approaches to the truth are similar.

The spirit of greed and materialism possessed the men. The young girl was a slave exploited by men to make money. They used her fortune-telling ability to play upon the needs of people for hope and confidence, self-esteem, and direction.

The Pythonic demon worked through the young woman by giving her false prophecies.

The Pythonic demons will speak the truth to bring forth confusion. They sought to talk about bringing forth about confusion and deception. Every word of this is true, but the purpose of Satan in it was to discredit the message of the apostles by making the people think they were in league with demons who were making this announcement through a demon possessed medium. The people would conclude that they were doing miracles by the devil and so discount the gospel. When the demon was cast out in the name of Jesus, it proved that they were of God and not of demons (Acts 16:18).

The Pythonic demons will not give up. They are determined and persistent.

Paul had to put a stop to the Pythonic demon. The saint, many times, must retreat from these Pythonic demons until the Holy Spirit moves them. Then the saint must turn back to confront those Pythonic demons. The Pythonic demons are too strong to fight on their own terms.

Paul became furious and annoyed before he turned to face this demon spirit. The Pythonic demon was cast out almost immediately and quickly and did not take days or hours.

Acts 16:16–19 in the Light of Greek Grammar

The slave damsel, a Pythoness, was possessed by a Pythonic demon. She met Paul and his companions as they were going to the place of prayer, which they went to regularly.

The Pythonic demon, through the slave girl, also known as a young damsel, was trying to hinder their prayer life so much that this Python demon sought after them at the time of their prayer and as they were going to their place of prayer.

The Greek noun προσευχή (place of prayer) used in the article indicates a particular place of prayer and a specific time of prayer. Paul and his companions were that precise in their prayer life. They chose a place and a time and continued to keep it.

The young slave girl had a part in her possession. According to the text, she was possessed by the Pythonic demon. Translating the Greek as "a certain damsel possessed with a spirit of Python" is incorrect. Acts 16:16 reads, Ἐγένετο δὲ πορευομένων ἡμῶν εἰς τὴν προσευχὴν παιδίσκην τινὰ ἔχουσαν πνεῦμα πύθωνα ὑπαντῆσαι ἡμῖν, ἥτις ἐργασίαν πολλὴν παρεῖχεν τοῖς κυρίοις αὐτῆς μαντευομένη (Now it came to pass as we were going to the place of prayer, a certain female slave having a Pythonic spirit—a ventriloquistic spirit—did meet us, who brought a great profit unto her masters by her occultic prophesying). Her will is seen to be a part of this. She is actively choosing to allow this Pythonic demon to demonize her, to possess her, to enter her body, to take control of her mind and thoughts for a time, and to take over as it sees fit.

Origen described how the Pythonesses—priestesses and prophetesses of Apollo became possessed. Origen wrote. Ἱστόρηται τοίνυν περὶ τῆς Πυθίας, ὅπερ δοκεῖ τῶν ἄλλων μαντείων λαμπρότερον τυγχάνειν, ὅτι περικαθεζομένη τὸ τῆς Κασταλίας στόμιον ἡ τοῦ Ἀπόλλωνος προφῆτις δέχεται πνεῦμα διὰ τῶν γυναικείων κόλπων· οὗ πληρωθεῖσα ἀποφθέγγεται τὰ νομιζόμενα εἶναι σεμνὰ καὶ θεῖα μαντεύματα (So it is recorded about the Pythian priestess, whose prophecies—oracles supposed to have been the greater wonderful than others, that as she was sitting down at the mouth of the Castalian cave, the prophetess of Apollo received the spirit through her female genitalia—vagina).[34]This is the case for all female mediums.

Virgil also gave a description of the Pythonic demon entering a Pythoness—female medium and how she reacted to that, cui talia fanti ante fores subito non voltus, non-color unus, non comptae mansere comae, sed pectus anhelum, et rabie fera corda tument, maiorque videri nec mortale sonans (As such, she spoke before the doors suddenly, no face nor color was the same nor her hair remained braided, but her chest was gasping hard for air. And her heart swelled with wild frenzy like one who has rabies—madness, and her appearance seemed to be greater in stature, and her voice did not sound like a mortal).[35] The Pythoness became mad and took upon herself the appearance of someone with rabies.

The "having" comes from the Greek verb ἔχω, which is an active participle. The Pythoness had an active part in this demonization of herself. She was submitted willingly to this possession, holding on to the Pythonic demon, keeping the Pythonic demon, and cooperating with it. It is like she was treating this demon as a pet.

This is a clear example of a medium in cooperation with her demon spirit. The relationship here is not passive on either side but active. The damsel and the Pythonic demon are active and working together to continue this bond. She had not totally lost her mind or will, as in some cases of demon possession. She had some control.

It is incorrect to say that the female slave met Paul and his companions. The very Greek infinitive ὑπαντῆσαι translated "did meet us," cannot mean a friendly meeting, an accidental meeting, or a meeting by chance. The meeting was more than a meeting. According to this Greek infinitive, the Pythonic demon and its vessel or host sought after Paul and his companions for warfare or battle. The Pythonic demon and the female slave were both active in this, the young slave wanting to confront them, especially the Pythonic demon wishing to engage them.

The Pythonic demons seek confrontation more than any other demon does. And as said before, they will bless their mediums. The imperative of command is used. That indicates this fact very well.

The phrase "who declare to us the way of salvation" must be carefully examined. In Acts 16:17, the Greek text has ὁδὸν σωτηρίας (a way of salvation). The Pythonic demon believed and pushed that Paul and his companions only promoted one way of many ways to salvation. And that was not true. The way the Pythonic demon spoke was one of many. The salvation spoken of was not from God but from what the pagans understood. The Pythonic demon spoke the truth in the first part. In the last part, the demon lied, but in a subtle manner. So the Pythonic demon, talking through the young damsel, lied and said that Jesus Christ is only a way of salvation rather than the way of salvation. The difference between heaven and hell can be the presence or absence of the definite article "the."

The female slave continued to follow Paul and his companions for several days. Paul and his companions had been retreating from confronting the Pythonic demon. They would not confront that demon on its own terms but were waiting on God the Holy Spirit to tell them when to confront that demon. Sometimes, it is wise to retreat from confronting evil. This is so true if the Holy Spirit has not told you to. There is a time and a place to confront evil.

Paul was following the strategy of warfare. The plan was a tactical retreat. The forces of evil must have been laughing at Paul and his companions. They would not fight or give any opportunity for warfare.

Notice the Greek text in verse 18. Two things are contrasted. The young girl was following; at the end of those days, Paul turned around. The retreat was over; the Holy Spirit had given Paul the commission and the right to act now. The very Greek participle διαπονηθείς (became greatly annoyed) shows this to be true. Paul was grieved and annoyed, but much more is understood. Notice the Greek phrase ἐπιστρέψας τῷ πνεύματι (having turned around to the spirit). Paul had prepared himself to confront the spirit. It was not just any spirit, but the spirit following him in that young girl. Paul was filled with a Holy Spirit indignation, wrath, and anger against the Pythonic demon. It was not Paul fighting against that demon, but the authority of Christ and the power of the Holy Spirit through Paul that were fighting against the Pythonic demon.

Paul was not fighting alone. Paul was not fighting on the terms of the Pythonic demon but on the terms of Christ and the Holy Spirit. Paul did not speak to the slave girl but directly to the Pythonic demon.

Functions/Works/Forms of the Pythonic Demons

1. The Pythonic demons, whose primary forms are pythons, are ones of the spirits that can be used as familiar spirits.

2. They can appear in any form or any form of a human.

3. Their primary purpose is that of witchcraft, necromancy, and divination.

4. They are soothsaying demons that can possess mediums.

5. They are the most dangerous demons of all the others.

6. They can work as familiar spirits in divination, necromancy, and false or counterfeit religions.

7. They are multi-faceted, smothering and crushing their victims in many ways and manners.

8. They are very subtle and sneaky.

9. A necromancer generally works with these spirits when they are used as familiar spirits.

10. They are spirits of witchcraft and divination that are sent as a fiery dart to destroy, oppress, and attack the saints of God.

11. They are those spirits that work to squeeze the life out of what God is doing, just like the serpent squeezed the life out of what God said in the Garden of Eden.

12. They are religious spirits, backwardness, monitoring spirits from hell, divination and un-seriousness.

13. They make people forget revelations and dreams coming from the Lord in order to expose the enemy.

14. They can imitate the dead.

15. They can possess their victims.

16. They can oppress their victims.

17. They work in divination, necromancy, and in false or counterfeit religions.

18. They try to deceive us when studying the Word of God.

19. They operate through our thoughts or try to control our thoughts.

20. They give thoughts to men.

21. They are the source of witchcraft and divination.

22. They were the leading occultic spirits in the West for a time. Still, there is a great mixture of the Pythonic spirits and the Kundalini demons. This mixture has been ongoing for some time.

23. They work with shamans.

24. They play on the will of the flesh and the ignorance of men, leading people away from the plan of God.

25. They plant a seed in our hearts, hoping that it will grow.

26. They attack the plan of God in our lives.

27. They are used to keep us out of the position God intended for us.

28. They openly come against what God is revealing to His church.

29. They work in deception.

30. They manifest themselves in possession.

31. They have a few manifestations in common with the Kundalini demons, but the Kundalini demons have much more.

32. They crush the life out of any Christian.

33. They are haughty.

34. They are one of the strong men.

35. They possess victims, but they do not have the same victims as the Kundalini demons.

36. They sneakily condemn Christians.

37. They bless those who serve them in multiple ways.

38. They attack those whom they do not control.

39. They are conquered through the name of Jesus and His blood.

40. They work by drugs and cause their victims to be bound to them.

41. They seek to kill their victims gradually.

42. They want to kill their victims themselves.

43. They work to plague people with a lifetime of infirmity or frequent bizarre and freak accidents, near drowning, traumatic situations, and choking manifestations.

44. They work in counterfeit gifts, including tongues, prophecy, and healing.

45. They reside in the belly and use a victim as a vessel.

46. They can destroy everything in a person's life with no need for any other spirit.

47. They are sexual spirits; they have sex with those whom they possess, whether by consent or by force.

48. They are behind European and African philosophy, religion, meditation, etc.

49. Total deliverance is possible from them.

50. They do very little damage to the mind.

51. They play on the will of the flesh and the ignorance of men, leading people away from the plan of God.

52. They work in our lives daily.

53. They affect everyone and are manifested in and through people.

54. They can preach things contrary to the Word.

55. They can deny the existence of other spirits.

56. They can operate through our thoughts.

57. They work in the secular world.

58. They work against our spirit.

59. They like a spiritual atmosphere since they function best there.

60. They can serve people.

61. They crush the life out of any Christian who falls into its trap.

62. They belittle and hate Jesus, the work of the cross, the blood, the word, and all the saints.

63. They whisper in our ears.

64. They are used in inflicting pain, sickness, and disease.

Pythonic Demons, Ventriloquism, and Puppets

Ventriloquism is equal to necromancy; puppetry involves familiar spirits. Both are evil, as seen in the Old and New Testaments and from the writings and thoughts of the ancient church. The ancient church condemned the use of puppets. The use of puppets by pagans to cause their supposed gods to speak through was common, the puppets of Pan, for example. The panes were also used as playthings for children.

Habakkuk 2:18–20 reads:

> What profiteth the graven image that the maker thereof hath graven it; the molten image, and a teacher of lies, that the maker of his work trusteth therein, to make dumb idols. Woe unto him that saith to the wood, Awake; to the dumb stone, Arise, it shall teach! Behold, it is laid over with gold and silver, and there is no breath at all in the midst of it. But the Lord is in his holy temple: let all the earth keep silence before him.

Psalm 135: 15–18 says:

> They have mouths, but they speak not; eyes have they, but they see not; They have ears, but they hear not; neither is there any breath in their mouths. They that make them are like unto them: so is every one that trusteth in them.

The art of ventriloquism has been around for thousands of years, but it has not always enjoyed the respect it has today. History discloses that ventriloquists were stoned as witches and sorcerers, and they were burned at the stake. Some people even say that the very first user of this art was Satan himself when he spoke to Eve through the serpent. The users of the art of ventriloquism were outcasts from God; ventriloquists were feared and hated by pagan socialites. Many people who saw their act or knew that they were ventriloquists ran away, fearing that evil itself had come to their place or habitation.

Ventriloquism is found in Egyptian and Hebrew archaeology and the later writings of the Greeks and the Romans. Confucius knew about it. However, it was not used just for entertainment in those ancient cultures. Priests of numerous religions would seemingly project their voices into a rock, statue, or tree. Then, they would "talk" through these inanimate objects and claim they had performed miracles! They use this "voice throwing" to make people believe their god or gods were alive and powerful. Priests were the only ones permitted to use ventriloquism. If others attempted to put it into practice, they were accused of being witches and were burned at the stake.

Some still use ventriloquism in the same manner as the ancients. They are part-civilized Zulus and Maoris in the Pacific Islands and —startling as it seems—the gentle Eskimos.

Historically, there are contrasting views about who first used ventriloquism to entertain people. Some say it was Louis Brebant in the household of King Francis I of France in the AD 1500s. And others claim it was a Viennese named Baron Merger who lived around the year AD 1770. Others believe Le Sieur Thiement, who entertained Napoleon and Josephine, was the first ventriloquist in the entertainment field.

Some businesspeople credit Frenchman Nicholas Marie Alexandre for first attracting public attention using this medium. Contrary to most ventriloquists today, though, neither Alexandre nor his peers used dummies in their acts. Each used the ventriloquial voice. Alexandre's acts, for instance, were a one-man show. By changing costumes and voices, he could play several characters on stage. By "throwing his voice," he created the illusion of other characters offstage. Thus, he could present a whole family of characters with just his one voice. One might wonder if ventriloquists and impressionists have the same roots. At any rate, there is some similarity.

It is not known precisely when the first dummy was made to incorporate with the art of ventriloquism. However, one of the earliest known records states that in the AD 1700s, a Spanish court, who knew the art quite well, had a doll made with a moving mouth so that he could entertain his friends at court. In those days, the doll was known as an "automata" rather than a dummy.

Long before the Spanish entertained with the automata, Italians tinkered with puppets and marionettes and created the "Punch and Judy" show. An Englishman named Arthur Prince made ventriloquism a big-time act in show business at the turn of the last century. Arthur toured Europe and the United States with his dummy Sailor Jim and made much money from his weekly shows. Yet Arthur Prince knew of the gruesome history of his medium because he said that years earlier, ventriloquism was used in connection with religious ceremonies instead of state entertainment. He knew ancient pagan priests had also profited from the power they gained through ventriloquism.[36] He was aware of the evil beginnings but preferred the fame and profit he gained from the arts.

Harry "the Great" Lester followed Arthur Prince, who appeared on the stages of our leading Vaudeville theatres.[37]

After Harry Lester retired, talking movies rendered ventriloquism almost extinct until Edgar Bergen revived the art with Charlie McCarthy and Mortimer Surd in the AD 1930s. After his death in recent years, other artists have cunningly entertained and educated the world through ventriloquism, dummies, and puppets.

Ventriloquism means "belly speaking" and has its birthplace in Latin. Ventriloquist is derived from two Latin words: "venter" meaning "belly" and "loqutus" meaning "to speak." The Romans linked the two words together to make the word "ventriloquus." Later, in English, it became ventriloquist.

As said before, in such cases as here, ventriloquists were also recognized as mediums (Leviticus 19:31;1 Samuel 28:9; 2 Chronicles 33:6; Isaiah 8:19, 19:3).

Within the Greek Septuagint, these passages have the Greek adjective ἐγγαστρίμυθος, and it means ventriloquists—ventriloquistic mediums who are possessed of Pythonic demons. There are numerous examples illustrating the diverse perspectives of ancient church fathers regarding ventriloquism and its potential connection to demonic forces, specifically those described as Pythonic. The words of Clement of Alexandria have previously been cited in this discussion.[38] And Tertullian has already been mentioned in two passages.[39]

Origen wrote, Εἴπερ οὖν τῶν ἐθνῶν χρωμένων μαντείαισ εἴτε διὰ "κληδόνων" εἴτε δι᾽ οἰωνῶν εἴτε δι᾽ ὀρνίθων εἴτε δι᾽ ἐγγαστριμύθων εἴτε καὶ διὰ τῶν τὴν θυτικὴν ἐπαγγελλομένων εἴτε καὶ διὰ Χαλδαίων γενεθλιαλογούντων (If after all, therefore, the pagans make use of various types of divination either by oracles or by omens, or by birds, or by ventriloquists—ventriloquistic mediums, or also by those who proclaimed the practice of the diviner, or by Chaldean genealogists).[40] Gregory Nazianzen wrote, ἐγγαστρίμυθοί τινες ὄντες καὶ κενολόγοι, τὰς ἑαυτῶν ἡδονὰς θεραπεύοντες λόγοις ἐκ γῆς φωνουμένοις καὶ δυομένοις εἰς γῆν (certain people became ventriloquists—ventriloquistic mediums, and chatterers—empty talkers, who do service to their own unrestrained pleasures by words speaking out from the earth, and sinking into the earth).[41]

CHAPTER 3

THE KUNDALINI DEMONS

Ecclesiastes 10:8, "He that diggeth a pit shall fall into it; and whoso breaketh an hedge, a serpent shall bite him."

The serpentine power comes from the Spirit of Leviathan, the Pythonic, and the Kundalini demons (Genesis 3; Isaiah 27:1; Acts 16; Revelation 12). In occultic literature, the Kundalini demons are considered to be equal to and the same as the Holy Spirit in the Bible. These demons work to imitate or impersonate the Holy Spirit and His workings.

In AD 1934, an Indian Christian named Jeevartnam held several meetings in Poona City, India. In these meetings, various signs and wonders occurred. Besides godly manifestations, demonic manifestations also appeared. In one manifestation, a demon-like cobra manifested, and it is written as follows:

> Another woman under possession stood swaying and hissing exactly like a cobra snake-the demons stated they were seven and gave each name and the name of the woman herself-all were names of Hindu goddesses-they said they had killed two of her children. (You know how babies are killed in various ways, in India, surely at the prompting of the devil). After prayer, and repeating after us "Victory through Jesus' blood," the demons came out, contorting the poor body of the woman, as in the Bible. But her face changed; peace came, she smiled; she was delivered! Case after case like this, until we stood around moved to tears and the power of God filling us mightily-Yes, Jesus is over all the power of the enemy, and we have seen and know it. In every case, the victims had no

knowledge of what had happened from the time they went under the power of the devils until they were delivered-they denied having spoken or screamed or answered any questions-but they knew they were free![1]

Jerome reports in his biography of St. Paula about the demon possessions that she saw.

amque cernebat daemones uariis rugire cruciatibus et ante sepulchra sanctorum ululare homines luporum uocibus, latrare canum, fremere leonum, sibilare serpentum, mugire taurorum, alios rotare caput et post tergum terram uertice tangere suspensis que pede feminis uestes non defluere in faciem (for she saw demons roaring under various tortures and before the tombs of the saints, men were howling like the voices of wolves, barking like dogs, roaring like lions, hissing like serpents and making loud deep noises like bulls. Still, others distorted their heads, and they touched the ground with the top of their heads behind their backs—bending themselves backwards; and women were suspended by their feet first—from the feet to the head—and their clothes did not fall on their faces).[2]

The Kundalini demons have two primary forms: the cobra and the black snake. The Sacred Cobra is well-known to every Hindu student. Actual worship is paid to the serpents throughout India and many other parts of the world. The Indian people have festivals every year when they worship the cobra snake. Even the physical cobras have become enemies unto preachers, revivalists, and missionaries. There have been reports that men preaching Christ have been bitten, and some have died by the cobras.

In India, snakes, especially the cobras, are encouraged to dwell in order to ensure the family's freedom from many types of evils and misfortunes. Milk, eggs, and boiled rice are commonly offered to the snakes—shrines in the form of a hooded cobra rudely carved out of granite.

Historically and archaeologically, pharaohs wore crowns decorated with the Uraeus snake, black-necked cobra, protecting from the front.[3] It was supposed to drive away demonic forces.

Moses, as a youth, saw the Uraeus snake for what it represented: Satan.

Also, the staff was a sign of authority, while the serpent represented emblematically divinely protected sovereignty. The staff having become a serpent meant that the power of the Cobra-Kundalini demons was no match for the power behind Moses. The fear of Moses seeing his rod turn into a serpent set the stage for his act of faith by taking the serpent by the tail (Exodus 4:3–4). This sign was to convince Israel that Moses's message came from God (Exodus 4:5).

The Hebrew phrase וַיְהִי לְנָחָשׁ and the Greek phrase καὶ ἐγένετο ὄφις (and it became a serpent) point out that the staff became, in all means, a real serpent—a living serpent. Both the Hebrew and the Greek stress the staff was just that—a staff. Then, it changed from that to a serpent within seconds. And then it changed back. This was due to the power of God. The anarthrous construction within Hebrew and Greek stresses that the character of the staff had changed to that of a living serpent completely. The staff was transformed into a cobra and then back into a staff.[4] Josephus writes, τὴν κεφαλὴν ἐπανέτεινεν (erected—held up its head).

The Hebrew noun תַּנִּין (serpent) has reference to a general term for serpents or snake-like animals. The creature mentioned by this Hebrew noun is generally monstrous in size (Genesis 1:21) and the creature is used parallel to "cobra" in two places (Deuteronomy 32:33; Psalm 91:13). The Hebrew noun תַּנִּין (serpent) is tied directly together with the "cobra" by means of archaeological findings. In archaeological sites, clay cobra figurines, known by this Hebrew noun as well, were discovered. The cobra figurines were breasted. The Egyptians believed that there were cobras known as the "breasted cobras." The cobra figurines had "tiny, button-like nodules on the torso." This had been interpreted as breasts. Such figurines were used in spells.[5] The serpents transformed from the staffs were all poisonous.

Psalm 91:13 reads, "Thou shalt tread upon the lion and adder: The young lion and the dragon shalt thou trample under feet." Luke

10:19 reads, "Behold, I give unto you power to tread on serpents and scorpions, and over all the power of the enemy; and nothing shall by any means hurt you." Colossians 2:15 reads, "And having spoiled principalities and powers, He made a show of them openly, triumphing over them in it."

These days, having no power to meet the assaults of Satan will cause our defeat. Suppose we do not know how to take victory over Satan, who is so powerful and crafty and cunning in his movements. In that case, we shall be stranded spiritually and physically. Who stands behind the darkness that surrounds us when we attempt to pray? Satan. Who stands back on the bondage of Spirit upon many of God's children? Satan. Shall we then throw our hands in despair and say we cannot avoid some things, and that defeat is sure on all things? No! We have a Victor, and His name is Jesus Christ.

Psalm 91:13 describes our enemies clearly. God has given us the power to tread over all the forces of the devil. The Hebrew text reads, עַל־שַׁחַל וָפֶתֶן תִּדְרֹךְ תִּרְמֹס כְּפִיר וְתַנִּין: (You will tread on the lion, which is in its prime, and the horned viper—cobra; you will trample with your own feet the young lion and the serpent—dragon). Behind this thinking is spiritual warfare and the darkness of evil that covers our lives and our duties to fight against them. In this listing, the Hebrew פֶּתֶן in Psalm 91:13 represents the Cobra (Cobra Naja Haje).

Psalm 91:13 is tied together directly with the demons who appear as the black snakes or the cobras. And those are the Kundalini demons. Other names, such as the black snake demons, the cobra demons, or the cobra-Kundalini demons, may be given. The Lord has given us the power to tread upon all these spiritual, slimy, and poisonous snakes.

There are other passages where the cobra is mentioned in Scripture or at least has reference to it (Deuteronomy 32:33; Job 20:14–16; Psalm 58:3–5; Isaiah 11:2–8). James refers to the tongue of the cobra when he says, "But the tongue can no man tame; it is an unruly evil, full of deadly poison," (James 3:8).

In the culture of Egypt, there was the cult of the cobra. This cult occurred in the earliest times. The amulet of the cobra was used as a personal or house-protecting amulet throughout the history of Egypt. The image of the cobra was placed on the Egyptian kings' foreheads or crowns. Priests and priestesses of Ra carried its representative. The cobra symbolized the power of life and death. And it became identified as the eye of the god Ra. The spirits formed as cobras were used to guard the groves and gates of Amenti and the pylons of the heaven of Osiris.

Almost every Egyptian house was filled with images of the cobras, and this was also true for various other types of structures. The image of the cobras was commonly found on the doorposts of the Egyptians.[6] The reared cobra was found on the headdresses of various gods and pharaohs. The image was an amulet for protection.[7] The cobra Uraeus was a symbol of the pharaoh, which appeared on some crowns and in various works of art. The image of the cobra on the crown of the pharaoh was supposed to overthrow the enemies of Egypt.[8]

Further, in the wilderness, the golden calves were not representations of the Lord God—Jehovah, but they represented the Apis—another one of the Baalim, like or the same as Baal-Peor in practices. Therefore, the golden calves (bulls) were the worship of the bulls among the Baalism. Golden calf (bull) worship was prominent in the times of the Old Testament (1 Kings 12:28; 2 Kings 10:29; 2 Chronicles 11:15, 13:8). The calf (bull) symbolized power, lordship, strength, fertility, and the like. As one of the Baalim, Apis was frequently represented by a solar disc and sometimes by a rearing cobra between its horns. Therefore, the Baalim and the cobras were linked but not in the same groupings of evil spirits in history.

In early Jewish texts from the Bible, the cobra and other types of serpents are seen in a negative light. In the document (work) known as the "Thanksgiving Hymns," the cobras denoted the poison that the men of Belial threw out.[9] And in that document is a notice of "spirits of the viper (cobra)."

Also, Kundalini worship and demons are seen to have appeared against the ancient church. There were Naasenians, a serpent-worshipping Gnostic sect, and the Ophites. The Ophites saw the Serpent as the Great Mother, goddess, or wisdom (Sophia)— a group of Gnostics in the second century.

One of the most significant signs that someone is under the influence or possession of the Kundalini demons is due to the loss of the mind, confusion of the mind, or at least the deception of the mind (Leviticus 18:23, 20:12; Ezra 9:7; 1 Samuel 20:30; Psalms 31:12, 44:15, 71:1; Isaiah 24:10, 41:29, 45:16; Jeremiah 7:19; Daniel 9:7–8; Luke 8:35, 12:29; Acts 19:29, 32; Romans 1:28; 1 Corinthians 14:33; Ephesians 4:17; 2 Thessalonians 2:3; Titus 1:15). Experiencing these demons gives pain, makes depression, and produces madness. Even the gurus have been negatively affected by Yoga, Hindu Meditation, and the Kundalini Awakening. Origen wrote about the spirit of madness upon those who submit to these evil spirits, aliquotiens eos, quos vates appellant, subito insaniae cuiusdam spiritu esse subpletos (several times, those whom they call oracles/soothsayers were unexpectedly filled with a certain spirit of insanity/madness).[10]

In people submitting to Yoga, Hindu mediation, the Kundalini Awakening, and other pagan techniques and methods, there has been an overwhelming category of separate negative experiences. And these are in the sense of evil.[11] Therefore, those who follow the paths of the occult, sooner or later, are affected negatively by spiritual experiences and evil entities. In addition, the devotees, even the godmen and godwomen, the gurus, have horrible experiences of evil by following the paths of the occult.

Describing his own experiences, Gura Muktananda said as follows:

> Soon after sitting for mediation, I started feeling restless and uneasy. Within moments strange things were happening to me. I could not understand it. I was perturbed mentally and emotionally. My mind seemed deluded. By the time evening came this delusion became

worse. Generally, I am a man of great courage but that day I was overcome by fear...I felt I would soon become insane. My mind was terribly agitated.[12]

Again, he wrote about another experience of the Kundalini as follows:

As I sat again for mediation, I felt there was great commotion around. My entire body started aching and automatically assumed padmasana, the lotus-posture. The tongue began to move down the throat and all attempts to pull it out failed as I could not insert my fingers into the mouth. My fear grew; I tried to get up, but I could not, as my legs were tightly locked in padmasana. I felt severe pain in the knot (manipur chakra) below the navel. I tried to shout but could not even articulate. It seemed as if something was stuck in my throat. Next, I saw ugly and dreadful demon-like figures. I thought them to be evil spirits. Strangely, I was fully aware all this time of what was happening to me. I was consciously witnessing everything.

I then saw blazes of fire on all sides and felt that I too was burning. After a while I felt a little better. Suddenly I saw a large ball of light approaching me from the front; as it approached, its light grew brighter and, brighter. It then entered unobstructed through the closed doors of my kutir and merged into my head. My eyes were forcibly closed, and I felt a fainting sensation. I was terrified by the powerfully dazzling light, and it put me out of gear.[13]

This Kundalini Awakening and yogic experience should be a warning to anyone. A great Siddha, named Harigiri Baba, defined Yoga to Gura Muktananda as "Good times have come for you not bad. You are going to be better-off soon. You will attain the Godhead." This is the purpose of Yoga—to try to obtain the Godhead.[14] In his yogic experiences, Gura Muktananda saw "various types of temples, gods and goddesses."[15]

The Kundalini Awakening has been defined in the work of Gura Muktananda as "This spiritual awakening of the latent divine power in an aspirant is also known as the awakening of Kundalini."[16]

The Kundalini Awakening was also called "diabolical mysticism" by William James.[17] He writes as follows:

> So much for religious mysticism proper. But more remains to be told, for religious mysticism is only one half of mysticism. The other half has no accumulated traditions except those which the textbooks on insanity supply. Open any one of these, and you will find abundant cases in which "mystical ideas" are cited as characteristic symptoms of enfeebled or deluded states of mind. In delusional insanity, paranoia, as they sometimes call it, we may have a diabolical mysticism, a sort of religious mysticism turned upside down. The same sense of ineffable importance in the smallest events, the same texts and words coming with new meanings, the same voices and visions and leadings and missions, the same controlling by extraneous powers; only this time the emotion is pessimistic: instead of consolations we have desolations; the meanings are dreadful; and the powers are enemies to life. It is evident that from the point of view of their psychological mechanism, the classic mysticism, and these lower mysticisms spring from the same mental level, from that great subliminal or trans-marginal region of which science is beginning to admit the existence, but of which so little is really known. That region contains every kind of matter: "seraph and snake" abide there side by side. To come from thence is no infallible credential. What comes must be sifted and tested and run the gauntlet of confrontation with the total context of experience, just like what comes from the outer world of sense. Its value must be ascertained by empirical methods, so long as we are not mystics ourselves.[18]

Guru Ramakrishna, who worked as a priest in the temple of Kali, went insane. Ramakrishna wrote as follows:

Kali was waiting for him. Hardly had he crossed the threshold than divine delirium in its most violent form was rekindled... The legion of Gods swooped upon him like a whirlwind. He was torn in pieces...His madness returned tenfold. He saw demonic creatures emerging from him— Horror paralyzed his limbs... Two years went by in this orgy of mental intoxication and despair.[19]

Others also have spoken about their negative experiences with the Kundalini. There are many Kundalini casualties. Once invoked, there can be no way to reverse the expansive consciousness of the Kundalini except by and through the authority of Christ, the power of the Holy Spirit, the power of the word, the power of the blood, and the power of the cross.

The Kundalini demons transcend Hinduism, but Hinduism, more than any other vehicle, has been used to spread their influence and the demons themselves throughout the world in the last two hundred years, respectively.

Since the Kundalini is not impersonal nor a group of techniques but a group of evil spirits, they, like the other evil spirits, can work well in various systems of religion.

Because too many Christian scholars, theologians, apologists, and occult experts focused on the Kundalini demons working in the system of Hinduism, it does suggest these demons cannot work out of Hinduism or use any other techniques.

The term Kundalini Awakening, used in Hinduism and borrowed and used by Christian authors, describes what people are experiencing under another Jesus, another spirit, and another anointing. The Kundalini Awakening is another term for demonic oppression and demonic possession. It opens a person up to evil spirits.

Yoga is one means that the Kundalini demons can enter a person for possession. The seven Chakras (seven wheels along the spine—seven energy centers), associated with Yoga, the Shakti (Universal Life Force), and the Shaktipat (Divine Touch) are terms of Hinduism. Shaktipat has been defined as "a subtle spiritual process by which the Guru transmits his divine power into the aspirant."[20] The Kundalini demons can work through these techniques, but they can work through other methods.

The Kundalini Awakening in Hinduism occurs through yogic postures, hand positions, and breath-control exercises. It is not a force that is awakened. Demons do not wake up but come into the person's life through these techniques. These demons, however, are not limited to these techniques. They have various ways to enter a person's life. According to Hinduism, the mind must be emptied of its contents for this awakening. The victims of the Kundalini demons must empty their minds, and finally, their minds will be useless and void.

The most effective method to awaken the Kundalini is a combination of meditation and yogic postures. Certain drug experiences, near-death experiences, and certain ritualized sexual practices—Tantric sex—intensive chanting and dancing can be used to become possessed by these spirits. Sexual activity or enjoyment is possible in the process of the arousal of the Kundalini.

The gurus also lay hands upon their devotees to receive spiritual enlightenment so that they can well become gods. Of course, they are becoming possessed by these evil spirits. Not every instance of laying on hands is biblical. There is such a thing as transference of spirits, and Christians must be careful in allowing anyone to lay hands on them (Leviticus 16:21–22; Numbers 27:12–21; Deuteronomy 34:9; 1 Timothy 5:22).

If Hinduism had not gained a firm foothold and acceptance in the United States, the invasion of the Kundalini demons would have been less. The acceptance of the gurus in the 1960s made a blending of the smoke. Yoga, meditation, and other Hindu techniques have entered the churches and the United States. Yoga, which is used by the Kundalini demons to possess people, is used for physical exercise. But that is not its purpose. Its purpose is to open a person for demonic possession. It is the uniting of humans with strange and evil entities.

Even before the AD 1960s, Hinduism appeared in the West in the eighteenth century. Hinduism heavily influences the New Age movement.

In AD 1989, Walter Martin wrote as follows:

> The great English apologist and writer C. S. Lewis saw the battle lines clearly drawn. He noted that in the final conflict between religions, Hinduism and Christianity would offer the only viable options because Hinduism absorbs all religious systems, and Christianity excludes all others, maintaining the supremacy of the claims of Jesus Christ![21]

Therefore, Hinduism is a fluid religion. It is a perfect example of the religious system known as the Great Whore of Babylon. Still, the Great Whore of Babylon will be a more complete restoration of goddess worship. Salvation in Hinduism is the supposed realization that individuals can become gods or are gods. And it is believed that Christ became God, not that He was and is always God. The old lie is present in Hinduism.

Hinduism, with its 330 million gods, has no official founder, no creedal statements of faith, and no universal agreement among Hindus.[22] John Ankerberg and John Weldon wrote, "In its most simple definition, Hinduism may be defined as the religious beliefs and practices common to India. Defining Hinduism in a more precise manner is difficult because of the wide number of practices and teachings it offers."[23] Hundreds of sects founded by individual teachers have sprung up, flourished for a time, split, fused, fallen into decay, and died out. Hinduism is an adjustable phenomenon.

Idolatry is traced back to the Tower of Babel. Hinduism is traced back to the Egyptian religion and the religion of Canaan, which then goes back to the Tower of Babel. The techniques invoking the Kundalini demons are more than just found in Hinduism. The names may change, but the methods are the same.

The Arrival of the Kundalini Demons

One wall that Satan must tear down so that the Antichrist and his religion can come forth is around the supernatural. He is doing it with Christian Yoga, breathing prayers, Hindu-like breath praying exercises, imagining, vision casting, visualizing, etc.

The term "Experiencing God" is often used to imply a person's pursuit of God-consciousness, with the underlying belief that they can attain godhood. Empirical evidence is supplanting divine authority. The act of experiencing has taken precedence over Jesus.

Scripture has said and commanded us to test the spirits. We must test every experience. Without exception, the most potent New Age teachers, voodooists, or other types of occultists have experience. Their experiences is commonly accompanied by a vision, dream, or a voice to be God, Jesus, Ascended Masters, or angels. Their experience overrides common sense, reason, and objective truth.

For decades, unchecked, untested, and unscrutinized phenomena have led to a breach in the church's only genuinely untouched area: the supernatural.

God desires individuals, unknown and without personal ambitions, driven solely by His purpose. As they preach about the King and His Kingdom, and pursue Him supernaturally, signs and wonders follow. The issue is that a lot of people look for a sign; they may get the chills and frills but leave with nothing more than goosebumps and little spiritual change, if any. The pursuit of God's kingdom and righteousness initiates a transformation of the heart. This is God's way and always has been.

In the 1980s, the occult experts warned that the Christian faith was being attacked from within. Christianity is being remade right before our eyes. Many modern theologians, clergy, and seminaries are remaking the Christian faith into the very form of New Age pantheism, Gnosticism, scientific reductionism, ancient superstition, and sexual license.

Today, the level of deception is so extreme and even beyond the discernment in the church that survival is scary. Men and women who have been "rocks" of spiritual courage are being deceived.

Many are wondering if the church can survive. Our enemies are declaring the end of Biblical Christianity. The very foundations of Christianity, in particular that of the New Testament and the Old Testament, have tried to become perverted.

Few are entirely set free; few are without a curse, a spell, or demonic oppression. The completely free are the exception rather than the rule today.

Now, it is like the whole world is off in some confused state. There are multitudes of excuses or arguments against the holy living. Seeing souls weeping at the altar of repentance becoming a new person has become rare. There are too many people who confess (profess) Christ but do not possess Him. Families that were once bound together in faithfulness to share their burdens are being torn apart. The world is full of self.

Therefore, these days, compromise is full in the air. We are being pushed very hard to compromise the very basics of Christianity. We are being forced to accept every wind of doctrine and every bizarre manifestation that can be seen or felt. The church must come back to her sanity. In particular, the Pentecostals and Charismatics must again face the very fact that little discernment is found within their circles. We must seek God for a renewal of discernment. In many respects, we have no discernment. We have become so gullible that no one can discern what is of God and what is not.

The mind snatchers—that is, the Kundalini demons—have now already arrived. People are losing their minds, becoming irrational and lifeless in their faces because of accepting the spirits of the ancient world. These evil spirits are taking over the minds and even bodies of human beings. The people being taken over by these spirits are seen to maintain the Christian labels, words, and appearances, but what is inside has been replaced with something alien, strange, and loony. People have been so contaminated with these spirits that they cannot even think. The minds have been snatched. Their rational behavior has been jeopardized. No spirit can be of God that keeps you from praying and reading the Word of God.

These evil spirits are working behind a false anointing. The Apostle John spoke of the spirit of the Antichrist. This term deals with the power to produce the personal Antichrist in the last days. Still, this very term also means that there is a counterfeit anointing out there being controlled and released by evil spirits working behind the scenes to deceive and destroy the people of God in the churches.

The anointing transferred in many circles today is not that of the Holy Spirit. Still, it is the transference of the Kundalini demons. They cause Christians to be transformed into silly Christians who no longer possess God's power to convert people to the real Jesus. Instead, they are being conquered by alien spirits. When Jesus and His blood sacrifice are no longer at the center of one's message, it no longer is the Christian gospel.

The Kundalini demons were and are one of the most contagious spirits. They mimic the Holy Spirit very closely; it is hard to determine which is of God and which is not. Then, there are Astral-projection, Death Magic, Soul Force, and other such techniques in the occult that supposed Christians are teaching today. Finally, when you deal with these demon spirits, another evil spirit becomes even more dangerous. That spirit is called the "Oni."

Misinformation and ignorance have led many to surrender themselves to evil spirits unwittingly. The Kundalini demons feel great when they enter a person. They want to hypnotize people to order to bypass their will! They do not want the people to resist their control to possess them. God never commands blind faith from His followers. We gladly accept Him and His Word. We are not empowered by God to battle Him for spiritual control (Matthew 11:28–30).

A born-again Christian must make it a habit "to give no place to the devil" (Ephesians 4:27).

The Kundalini demons and other spirits have sought to enter many revivals. In some cases, the discernment of the leaders saved them. The church in America is being overwhelmed by these spirits.

The Apostle Paul told us in 1 Corinthians 1:23 to seek God, "We preach Christ crucified, unto the Jews a stumbling block and unto the Greeks foolishness; but unto them which are called, but Jews and Greeks, Christ the power of God and the wisdom of God."

Jesus came down to earth and lived among men. Jesus also suffered, was crucified, and He died on the cross for us. You can find Him when you seek Him with all your heart.

Many no longer preach about the cross of Jesus or the importance of His sacrifice. Jesus said, "If I be lifted up, I will draw all men unto me" (John 12:32). The problem we face today is millions have been drawn away to receive another spirit other than the Spirit they had previously received (2 Corinthians 11:4).

Paul reproved these Corinthian Christians for receiving another spirit. The Christians at Corinth were looking for a "new move" or a God to do something new. They no longer had their faces toward Christ and focused on Him. Every time we get our eyes off Christ, we are bound to fall, be deceived, be broken, and be destroyed. While God will do a new thing and has done it repeatedly, under the banner of the Bible and in its boundaries, many have thrown away the Bible, looking for manifestations and crying out words that have an occultic sound to them.

In the occultic literature of Hinduism, it is known that the gurus constantly cry out "fire, fire, and fire" to invoke and awaken the Kundalini demons. They can take your mind away. They can put you in an altered state of consciousness, like a trance. The experience of coming from Kundalini demons is one of the strangest phenomena.

God gave men and women the promise of the coming Messiah in Genesis 3:15 so that He could redeem them from their fall into sin and rescue them by the blood of Jesus. The cross would separate them from the powers of darkness and wash them clean. They would be able to return to God and live forever.

The Kundalini demons have been able to capture many upon many through false manifestations. Still, these evil spirits, like others, have been defeated at the cross and will be defeated at the Second Coming of Christ and finally at the Battle of Gog and Magog (Revelation 20:8). We must now choose the Spirit of the Living God, not false spirits.

Many Christians are insensible to spiritual things and are lukewarm in their love for the Lord and His kingdom's work. They are usually led to follow another Jesus and another gospel led by another spirit. These false spirits supernaturally imitate the Holy Spirit. They give spiritual gifts, such as dreams, visions, and deviating prophecies. The powers of darkness bind millions of Christians. Few Christians realize that for thousands of years, gurus have operated with gifts of healing, miracles, knowledge, and intense displays of spiritual consciousness as they stretch out and connect with a cosmic power that, though demonic in origin, is very real.

When the Kundalini demons leave a person, that person experiences immediate relief from the commanding bondage over their lives. Only Jesus can set the captives free.

Functions/Works/Forms of the Kundalini Demons

1. Kundalini demons, whose primary forms are cobras and black snakes, are ones of the spirits that can be used as familiar spirits.

2. Their primary purpose is to imitate the Holy Spirit and His moving (manifestations). The occultists speak of these spirits as the Holy Spirit of the Bible.

3. They can appear in any form or any form of a human.

4. A necromancer works with these spirits when they are used as familiar spirits.

5. They are religious spirits, backwardness, monitoring spirits from hell, divination, and un-seriousness.

6. They make people forget revelations and dreams coming from the Lord in order to expose the enemy.

7. They can imitate the dead.

8. They can possess their victims.

9. They can oppress their victims.

10. They work in divination, necromancy, and in false or counterfeit religions.

11. They try to deceive us when studying the Word of God.

12. They operate through our thoughts or try to control our thoughts.

13. They give thoughts to men.

14. They affect everyone and are manifested in and through people.

15. They can preach things contrary to the Word.

16. They can deny the existence of other spirits.

17. They can operate through our thoughts.

18. They work in the secular world.

19. They work against our spirit.

20. They like a spiritual atmosphere since they function best there.

21. They can serve people.

22. They belittle and hate Jesus, the work of the cross, the blood, the word, and all the saints.

23. They whisper in our ears.

24. They try to stop people from studying and reading the Word of God. They also try to stop the prayer life of the people.

25. They try to destroy the minds of their victims instead of just sending thoughts of their own.

26. They give thoughts to men to destroy our minds.

27. They are the leading occultic spirits in the East, but as Eastern philosophy has spread, so has their dominion.

28. They are under the spirits of Python.

29. They work with shamans, witches, and other occultists.

30. They attack the plan of God in our lives.

31. They are used to keep us out of the position God intended for us.

32. They secretly come against what God is revealing to His church.

33. They work in deception.

34. They manifest themselves in possession.

35. They have various manifestations associated with them: physical, mental, emotional, and spiritual.

36. They are one of the strong men.

37. They condemn Christians by having them accept the false manifestations as coming from the Holy Spirit.

38. They bless those who serve them with blessings in various ways.

39. They attack those whom they do not control.

40. They can inflict pain, sickness, and disease.

41. They are conquerable through the name of Jesus and His blood.

42. They work by drugs and cause their victims to be bound to them.

43. They work to plague people with mental, emotional, physical, and spiritual disorders.

44. They open people to destruction and death by other spirits, including the Oni and the Pythonic demons.

45. They set up the person before these other demons as a helpless victim.

46. They work in counterfeit gifts, including tongues, prophecy, and healing.

47. They reside on their victims' spines.

48. They work to destroy all things in a person's life. Other spirits will come in and finish the job when this is accomplished.

49. They are sexual spirits. They promote sexual immorality.

50. They commonly cause people to lose their minds, so much so that many are sent to mental hospitals.

51. They are behind all forms of Eastern philosophy, religion, meditation, Yoga, and Martial Arts. When a person does Martial Arts, there is great potential for opening himself up to the Kundalini demons.

52. Total deliverance is possible from them.

53. Kundalini demons do much damage to the mind.

54. Only by deliverance can this be reversed. It is possible that a person can wait too long for a total reversal of the demonic consequences.

Symptoms Coming from the Kundalini Demons

1. Dramatic increase in premature deaths, cancers, marriage break-ups, sickness, and disease.

2. Non-lucid mind; cloudiness; irrational behavior; confusion of the mind.

3. Unable to pray, read the Word of God, and focus.

4. Expulsion of evil spirits coming from people.

5. Strong anger and intense hatred, not believing that this is of the devil or wrong.

6. Many have spoken of a hissing sound that follows them.

7. Demon possession.

8. If you accept it, you will be blessed for a season and destroyed. If you reject it, you will be attacked. If you have true anointing, you will be saved and protected.

9. Churches will be destroyed if they follow it; if a church does not, it will lose some members.

10. People have a kind of childlike drunken stupor that does not go away.

11. Descriptions of being washed back and forth like the waves in the ocean.

12. Young men are whistling repeatedly, holding their heads, and claiming they "feel the Holy Spirit about to split them in two."

13. People with their eyes rolled in the back of their heads, weaving around like they're lost.

14. Women are just gyrating and pulsating like they're being ravaged from behind by some unseen force.

15. Hearing voices in the head telling people to drown themselves.

16. Animal noises. People sound and act like animals.

17. People act like they are urinating within a church or building.

Manifestations from These Demons

1. Energy rushes, or immense electricity circulates the body.

2. Itching, vibrating, prickling, tingling, stinging, or crawling sensations.

3. Intense heat or cold.

4. Strange activity and blissful sensations in the head, particularly in the crown area.

5. Vibrating, tingling sensations.

6. Uncontrollable laughing.

7. Spontaneous vocalization of animal sounds.

8. Jerking, tremors, shaking.

9. Postures or moving one's body in unusual ways.

10. Muscle twitches, cramps, or spasms.

11. Mental confusion, difficulty concentrating.

12. Altered states of consciousness: heightened awareness, spontaneous trance states, mystical experiences.

13. Psychic experiences: extrasensory perception, out-of-body experiences, past life memories, astral travel, contact with spirit-guides through inner voices.

14. Spontaneous trance states.

Other List of Manifestations from These Demons

1. Feeling an inner force pushing one into postures or moving one's body in unusual ways.

2. Alterations in eating and sleeping patterns.

3. Episodes of extreme hyperactivity.

4. Conversely or overwhelming fatigue.

5. Intensified or diminished sexual desires.

6. Headaches, pressures within the skull.

7. Racing heartbeat, pains in the chest.

8. Digestive system problems.

9. Numbness or pain in the limbs (particularly the left foot and leg).

10. Pains and blockages anywhere, often in the back and neck.

11. Emotional outbursts, rapid mood shifts, seemingly unprovoked or excessive episodes of grief, fear, rage, and depression.

12. Spontaneous vocalizations (including laughing and weeping) – are as unintentional and uncontrollable as hiccups.

13. Hearing an inner sound or sounds is classically described as a flute, drum, waterfall, birds singing, or bees buzzing. Still, it may also sound like roaring, whooshing, booming noises, or ringing in the ears.

14. Heat, strange activity, and blissful sensations in the head, particularly in the crown area.

15. Visions, dreams, and trances not coming from God.

Other Problems with the Kundalini Demons

1. Death.

2. Pseudo death.

3. Psychosis.

4. Pseudo psychosis.

5. Confusion.

6. Anxiety.

7. Panic attacks.

8. Depression.

9. Sadness.

10. Suicidal thoughts.

11. Urges to self-mutilate.

12. Homicidal urges.

13. Irregular heartbeat.

14. Insomnia.

15. Inability to hold a job.

16. Inability to talk.

17. Inability to drive.

18. Sexual pains.

19. Temporary blindness.

20. Headaches.

21. Disability injury.

22. Job loss.

23. Personality changes.

24. Loss of healing.

25. Multiple doctor visits.

26. Divorce.

27. Serious health issues.

28. New illness.

29. Visitations of evil spirits for months.

30. Inability to eat.

31. Going to a mental institution.

32. Mental breakdowns.

33. Impaired vision.

34. Migraines.

35. Loss of property.

36. Becoming completely destitute.

CHAPTER 4

THE BAALIM AND ASTARTES

The Baalim and the Astartes should be a central part of this work. After all, most of the infestation in any society rests upon these two groups. Besides these two groups, the Pythonic demons and Kundalini demons are generally associated with them.

This chapter covers all that the Baalim and the Astartes control and are in charge of in a variety of ways. This chapter covers a number of subtopics because they fall under the topics of the Baalim and the Astartes. It is necessary to talk about almost every aspect of Israel's history that the Baalim and the Astartes have impacted. There will be some duplication in this chapter. For instance, as prostitution has been discussed throughout Israel's and the pagans' history, it will be brought up multiple times. It's critical to recognize these spirits' infestation at different times and understand their actions throughout that time.

Both the Spirit of Jezebel and the Spirit of Religion are under the subjects of Baalim and the Astartes. The spirits of fornication are under the subjects of the Baalim and the Astartes.

Comparing how the Greek Septuagint translated the Hebrew noun בְּעָלִים (Baalim) and the Hebrew noun אֲשֵׁרוֹת (Astaroths) or the Hebrew noun עַשְׁתָּרוֹת (Astartes) must be clearly noticed. Both names Astaroths and Astartes refer to the same group of evil spirits. These spirits can also be called Ashtoreths and Asherahs.

The Baalim and the Astartes

Comparing how the Greek Septuagint translated the Hebrew noun בְּעָלִים (Baalim) and the Hebrew noun אֲשֵׁרוֹת (Astaroths) or the Hebrew noun עַשְׁתָּרוֹת (Astartes) must be clearly noticed. Both names Astaroths and Astartes refer to the same group of evil spirits. These spirits can also be called Ashtoreths and Asherahs.

The Greek noun Βααλιμ (Baalim) is found with the masculine article: τοῖς Βααλίμ (Judges 2:11, 3:7, 10:6; 1 Samuel 12:10; 1 Kings 22:54; Hosea 11:2); τῶν Βααλείμ (Judges 8:33; 1 Kings 18:18; 2 Chronicles 34:4; Hosea 2:13, 2:17); τῷ Βααλίμ (Judges 10:10). The Greek noun Βααλιμ (Baalim) has the feminine article before it as well: τὰς Βααλείμ (1 Samuel 7:4); ταῖς Βααλίμ (Judges 10:6; Judges 10:10; 2 Chronicles 24:7; 2 Chronicles 33:3). The Codex Alexanderius in some cases has the feminine article rather than the masculine. For example, Judges 10:6 in the Codex Alexanderius, the feminine gender is found. The Greek noun Βααλιμ (Baalim) is found with the masculine article or in the feminine article in the singular form: ὁ Βάαλ (Judges 6:32; 2 Kings 18:26); τῷ Βάαλ (Judges 2:13, 8:33, 1 Kings 16:31–32, 19:18, 2 Kings 1:2, 1:3, 10:18, 10:19–20, 17:16, 23:4–5); τὸν Βάαλ (2 Kings 10:28); τοῦ Βάαλ (Numbers 22:41; Judges 6:25, 6:28, 6:30, 6:31, 2 Kings 18:22, 18:26, 18:40; 2 Kings 1:18, 3:2, 10:19, 10:21, 10:22–23, 10:25, 10:26, 10:27); τῆς Βάαλ (2 Kings 21:3; 2 Chronicles 23:17; Zephaniah 1:4; Jeremiah 2:23, 23:13); τῇ Βάαλ (2 Kings 1:6, 1:16, 21:3; Hosea 2:8, 13:1; Jeremiah 2:8, 2:28, 7:9, 11:13, 11:17, 12:16, 19:5, 23:27, 39:29, 39:35).

The Greek noun Ασταρωθ (Astaroths) is only with the feminine article: ταῖς Ασταρωθ (Judges 10:6). The Greek noun Ασταρτη (Astarte) is written with the feminine article: ταῖς Ἀστάρταις (Judges 2:13; 10:6); τῇ Ἀστάρτῃ (1 Kings 11:6, 11:33; 2 Kings 23:13; 2 Chronicles 15:16). In several cases, however, these names are not used in the Greek Septuagint. Instead, the Greek noun ἄλσος (grove) is used as a substitute for the names given for these spirits (1 Samuel 7:3). It is used with the neuter article in two verses: τοῖς ἄλσεσιν (Judges 3:7; 1 Samuel 12:10).

Both the Baalim and the Astartes, being unique disembodied evil spirits, were conceived by antiquity to be androgynous, hermaphroditic, or both male and female. Fallen angels are not both male and female but wholly masculine. And neither were the Nephilim of old hermaphroditic. Whatever the Baalim and the Astartes are, they are not angels.

Both the Baalim and the Astartes seek to confuse gender and make one gender act and conduct itself as two genders, especially in sexual sin. This confusion is more profound with the Baalim. Astartes generally are female but using the neuter article in Judges 3:7 and 1 Samuel 12:10, they have been recognized also as androgynous. The Baalim, like many of the chief deities of the pagans, were understood to be each male and female.

Whenever a society has confusion over gender, it is due to these spirits alone. And it is these spirits that push all forms of perversion more than any other.

The deities under the names Venus, Astaroths, Astartes, Ashtoreths, Asherahs, and other ones were all understood to be hermaphrodites, having both male and female genitalia. It was these spirits whom the apostate Israelites worshipped on the Mount of Olives and practiced vile orgies there (1 Kings 14:23–24, 15:12–13, 22:46; 2 Kings 23:4–14).

The priests of the Baalim and the Astartes, also known as prophets, served these demons and ultimately sought to mimic them in their hermaphroditic character. They sought to represent in their persons the character and practices of these deities so much that they mutilated themselves and confounded the sexes. They imitated the dress and manners of women. Thus, priests of these evil spirits wore dresses and took upon the character of women in every manner sexually.

In other words, it was common for the priests and priestesses of the Baalim and the Astartes to personate these deities, whom they worshipped and served. They took upon themselves their titles and imitated their character. Then, the priests, taking upon the hermaphroditic nature, wore the dress and copied the manners of women; they stopped being men, tried to take upon themselves both sexes, and failed to partake of either sex. In addition, the priestesses of the Baalim and the Astartes assumed the dress and manners of males and, at the same time, tried to maintain their effeminacy while appearing as men. The institution of prostitution, whether male prostitution or female prostitution, was for the uniting of this hermaphroditic nature, bringing together the hermaphroditic demons and the phallic processions that followed.[1]

In so doing, the father and mother principles were united, generating even worse forms of iniquity. The father and mother principles were generally represented under the sun and moon. Many times, the father principle was expressed under the phallus (penis). And the mother principle was expressed under the symbol of the female genitalia—vagina. To the pagans, pillars, altars, high places, groves, mountains, heathen temples, pyramids, and other monumental statutes were symbols of the phallus, representing the father principle. The moon, the earth, and the Ark of Noah represented the mother principle. Above all, the phallus was worshipped as the giver of life when united with hermaphroditic nature. In truth, the pagans saw one hermaphroditic deity when both principles were united. They sought repeatedly to unite both sexes together through sex (sex magic) or by means of them being possessed apart from sexual relationships with other humans.

All who practice male homosexuality, lesbianism (female homosexuality), and other forms of sexual perversions are attempts to unite the hermaphroditic nature by being possessed of these demons, whether male to male, female to female, male or female to the beast, or even male to female. In such cases, where heterosexual sex is accomplished outside of God's institution, order, and limitations for such a practice, it is an attempt to unite the hermaphroditic nature since the Baalim and the Astartes are united to or involved in heterosexual sexual sin like almost all other sexual sins. This is so clear from Numbers 25 and 1 Corinthians 6:9–15. All these evils are attempts of the Baalim and the Astartes to unite that hermaphroditic nature with others of their own kind.

Since the Baalim and Astartes can change their genders instantaneously and according to their wills, the uniting of these demons with humans always stresses the hermaphroditic nature. If they possess males, these demons become females so that the female gender can be obtained through the males. If they possess females, they become males again so that the male gender can be obtained. This phenomenon is recognized by how the males change into the manners of the opposite gender and how the females change into the manners of the opposite gender. So, the blurring of the two genders occurs. The original gender of a human takes upon itself another gender by demonic possession, which becomes dominant. The genders of demons become united with the biological genders of humans.

Scripture gives several allusions to these practices. This was at the heart of the evil by prohibiting men from dressing as women or women to dressing as men (Deuteronomy 22:5).[2] The dressing of men as women or women as men, men wanting to take upon the habits of women or women taking upon the habits of men, or the utter confusion of persons in understanding their gender (sex) is the infestation of these Baalim and the Astartes in a society. Those who follow suit end up becoming the modern priests and priestesses of these demonic spirits—something that neither God nor God's nature ever intended.

The worship of the Baalim and the Astartes, with its emphasis on hermaphroditic practices and sexual perversions, is an apparent distortion of God's design for human sexuality. It is a form of idolatry that seeks to unite male and female energies in a way that goes against the natural order established by God. This kind of worship ultimately leads to confusion and perversion in society, as individuals are led astray from God's intended purpose for their gender and sexuality.

As believers, we must be vigilant in guarding against the influence of these demonic forces that seek to distort and pervert God's design for gender and sexuality. We must stand firm in the truth of God's Word and reject any teachings or practices that go against His divine order. By staying faithful to God's design for gender and sexuality, we can resist the temptations of the Baalim and the Astartes and remain steadfast in our commitment to living holy and righteous lives before the Lord.

The prophets of Baalim, numbering four hundred and fifty, and the prophets of the Astartes, numbering four hundred, were all also priests of these deities (demons). These men ate at the table of Jezebel dressed as women and faced Elijah and the God of Elijah on Mount Carmel dressed as women (1 Kings 18:18—46). Nothing eviler could have been done but to meet the prophet Elijah in such clothes and mimic the habits of women!

It is utterly false that Adam was originally a hermaphrodite—a being who has both sexes. Genesis 1 deals with the creation of Adam (man). Man was originally only a male (Genesis 1:26—27). Genesis 2 deals with the formation of the feminine gender by taking from man a part and making a female from that while Adam still retained his masculinity. The female to be human had to have been formed from man. In Christian circles, the Gnostics proposed the doctrine that Adam originally was a hermaphrodite, and the ancient church denounced such as utter heresy.

The strict and stern view on sexual sin in the Old Testament and the New Testament, and the ancient church, for example, was solely based upon the fact that such sins are tied to these evil spirits. If not checked, these evil spirits, especially the Baalim and the Astartes, would bring pestilence upon whole societies and cause all these sins to be a contagion. There was and is no better remedy for such a pestilence than fire, and God rained down fire upon Sodom and Gomorrah because of such evil sins.

The Groupings of the Occultists

In Deuteronomy 18:10—11, there is a list of occultic groups within the pagan world. The list is fuller and was designed to be almost exhaustive. There are nine forms of occultism mentioned here and their practitioners under each term. There is a mingling of practices among these groups. Some practices were used by more than one group. Both males and females were involved in the occultic practices meant here, and that is true before that time and afterward. The godly prophets were in opposition to these occultic groups. The first group was known as מַעֲבִיר בְּנוֹ־וּבִתּוֹ בָּאֵשׁ (a practitioner who made his son or daughter be thrown into the fire as a human sacrifice). The causative verb pattern points out that a practitioner, a parent, or another, was the one who toss the children into fire—human sacrifice. The Moloch practice is here stressed. Both Moloch and Baalim are one and the same group of evil spirits (Leviticus 18:21, 20:2). Under the practice of human sacrifice, especially the murdering of children, there is the darkest arts, and it is filled with the demon possessed. These practices were especially done for fertility and purification, as seen by the interpretation of the Hebrew in the Greek Septuagint περικαθαίρων τὸν υἱὸν αὐτοῦ καὶ τὴν θυγατέρα αὐτοῦ ἐν πυρί (a person who purifies his son and daughter by the fire). The worship of Moloch (Baalim) was the worst kind of idolatry, except the worship of the Astartes. The second group was known as קֹסֵם קְסָמִים or μαντευόμενος μαντείαν (a practitioner who gives pagan divinations/oracles). It means a group that practices witchcraft by natural knowledge or human prudence or sagacity. Divination is forbidden, abominable, and execrable. Such a practice was real, not fake. Evil spirits accompanied the practice. The divinations were occultic and demonic controlled prophetic utterances. It was the pagan oracles. This group of occultists had many senses: geomancy, necromancy, oneiromancy, gastromancy, lithomancy, catoptromancy, and others. It may be seen as a general phrase that introduces the rest of the occultic groups that follow. But overall, it is used to denote false prophets and their false utterances (Micah 3:3, 3:6−11). The third group was known as מְעוֹנֵן or κληδονιζόμενος (a practitioner who observes the times and omens). Under the Hebrew poel participle, this occultist was declarer of signs, seasons, omens, and times. He observed natural signs, and he could foretell the future or other things by the behavior of birds (ornithomancy). He could divine by watching clouds, thunders, and lightnings. He was an imposter. This terminology permits the manipulation of visual perception by both sexes, potentially resulting in the belief of attainable self-transformation. The occultist was able to convincingly portray himself in a multitude of guises and forms. This group also included the stargazers (astronomers). The use of the Greek participle κληδονιζομενος indicates that this pagan practitioner possessed a strange voice in which he worked this practice. The fourth group was known as נָחַשׁ (an enchanter). In the Greek Septuagint, this fourth group is defined as οἰωνιζόμενος (a person who enchants). This type of occultist told the future by the drinking cup, radiation from the water, from gems and from crystal divining-globes. As time went on, it was to include other methods of witchcraft, like Ouija boards. A person under this occultic group was able to control and entice other people by their whispering and hissing. And a practitioner was able to kill serpents by their whispering, and he was able to foretell by serpents. Under this term, there was included "serpent-charming" (ophiomancy). This type of practitioner had an occultic voice. The fifth group was known as כָּשַׁף (a witch). In the Greek Septuagint, this group is known as φαρμακοῖς (sorcerer/magician). In Exodus 7:11, the female version is used. This group is a general name for the occultists. Under this term also, the occultists work their miracles by mechanical or chemical (drugs) means, by mere handiness, or by demonic assistance. The practitioner worked also in supposed healing. This name covers another property of the occultists. It does cover the purpose of finding water by divining rods. And there is meant here the foretelling of the rise and setting of the sun, moon, and stars, and the prediction of eclipses. The sixth group was named חֹבֵר חָבֶר or ἐπαείδων ἐπαοιδήν (a practitioner who casts magical spells). Besides other types of occultic practices, it deals with a type of occultic practice where the practitioner weaves spells, uses spellbinders by tying magic knots, foretells by rings, and uses love spells and other spells, especially for violence or harm. And under this group also, there was a charming of serpents as seen in Psalm 58(57):5(6). There is a sexual component here where the women were known to blow on knots as a form of loving making spells.

137

The seventh group was named שֹׁאֵל אוֹב (a practitioner who consults with a familiar spirit—a demon either acting like the dead or other familiar). The Greek Septuagint has ἐγγαστρίμυθος (ventriloquist who consults with a familiar spirit). Both the Hebrew and Greek point to the evil spirit (familiar spirit) using the belly and using the victim as a bottle. A peculiar sound came from the person possessed that represented the voice of the dead. This group included a ventriloquist who pretended to have communication with the invisible world. A practitioner mentioned here and throughout these groups is one who is possessed by an evil spirit. The practitioner can tell hidden things or things to come to pass. The demon generally can be the Pythonic demons, the Baalim, or the Astartes. An old expression describes the occultists and their association with evil spirits as "Nothing can come out of the sack that was not in the sack." The evil spirits are in the human victim and work through that victim. All people possessed with evil spirits are their victims. The eighth group was known as יִדְּעֹנִי (wizard/medium)—someone who was wise in the occultic practices and in association with evil spirits. Such term is highly tied to evil spirits and can be translated as "a practitioner who has a familiar spirit." There is a blending of the practitioner and the evil spirits using him or her. Speaking of one and both are meant. This group is always ranked with those who deal with the familiar spirits as the dead. The ninth group was known as דֹּרֵשׁ אֶל־הַמֵּתִים (a necromancer or a practitioner who inquires to the dead). The demon manifests in the form of the dead. This association with evil spirits is limited to the demons appearing in the forms of the dead.

The groupings of the occultists here represented are all-inclusive and cover all forms of the occult and all groups of the occultists mentioned and not mentioned. All forms, potential operations, and other manifestations are within these groupings, whether said or not. Every actual and imaginable action and practice of the occult is here represented.

Some manifestations, powers, operations, and practices of the occultists in the Middle Ages, the times of the Reformation, and modern age are hinted at in some of the Hebrew words mentioned in Deuteronomy 18 and other places.

In the sixteen hundreds, from ancient Hebrew scholars, the Hebrew noun כָּשַׁף (a witch), the Hebrew participle מְעוֹנֵן (a practitioner who observes the times and omens) in Deuteronomy 18:10–11, and the Hebrew participle מְכַשֵּׁפָה (a witch) in Exodus 22:18 express manifestations, actions, operations, and practices, which are hinted about and can be done by the occultists. For example, physical transformations from one place to another place is under these words. Raping and molesting men and women sexually are understood by these words. And demons having sexual relationship with humans is understood as well. All that Satan and his evil spirits can do in an occultic manner are understood. God is not surprised by what any of them can do. He alone can restrict their power and manifestations.

The idea that occultists were then and now united in a covenant with their evil spirits was commonly held by the reformers and the church fathers. To prove his point, Walter Raleigh quoted Sixtus Senensis (AD 1520–1569), a Jew who converted to Roman Catholicism and became a Roman Catholic Theologian. Sixtus believed that an occultist was united in covenants with demons. Therefore, witches, sorcerers and others were in a covenant relationship with demons.

> That the testimonies of Theophilus and Polychronius (saith he) may not move any man, it is to be understood that Magick is of two sorts, the one everywhere condemned by Origen, which worketh (whether truly or seemingly) by covenants made with Devils: the other commended by Origen which appertained to the practice part of natural Philosophy, teaching to work admirable things by the mutual application of natural virtues, agent and suffering reciprocally![3]

Augustine writes, et pacta quaedam significationum cum daemonibus placita atque foederata, qualia sunt molimina magicarum artium (and certain pacts agreed upon in the proper manner and ratified with demons, such are the endeavors of magical arts).[4] Thomas Aquinas writes about how real satanic miracles come about, magi per privatos contractus cum daemonibus (Magicians by private contract with demons).[5] Those who make a pact with the devil and evil spirits are well demon possessed.[6]

The act of demonic sex is often linked to covenants or pacts that individuals make with the devil. The act is ritualistic in nature, suggesting a deeply ingrained practice. Although the devil is sometimes implicated, demonic activity is a more frequent and commonly accepted explanation for such occurrences. Therefore, the covenant that occultists make with evil spirits fundamentally and obligatorily includes sexual intercourse as its essential and defining element. Engaging in sexual intercourse with an evil spirit is considered a powerful and significant action that is believed to solidify and seal the satanic covenant and ensure its continuation. Such a state with evil spirits is liken to a form of marriage.

Various other phenomena can be recognized among these same groups from the Hebrew words: crystal gazing, reading in magic mirrors, slate-writing, planchette, the quasi-scientific study of apparitions, table turnings, rappings by unseen dowers, telepathy, subliminal self, hypnotism, trance mediums, speakers on theosophy, palmistry, fortune tellers, and clairvoyants.

Prevalence of Demonism and Demon Possession

From the very moment that Adam's fall from grace occurred within the Garden of Eden, humanity irrevocably entered a state of subjugation under the merciless dominion of malevolent entities, resulting in the loss of its purity and making it vulnerable to the pervasive and extensive effects of evil. Without divine intervention, humanity would have been completely subjugated by evil entities, losing all power and becoming entirely at their mercy, subject to their unpredictable whims and tyrannical rule.

The Old Testament paints a haunting picture of the ancient world, a landscape persistently scarred by the ongoing, dramatic conflict between divinely established order and the encroaching, chaotic forces of darkness. Against this historical backdrop, the ancient saints found themselves engaged in a very real and tangible spiritual war, one where demonism was not an abstract philosophical concept but a powerfully present and actively malevolent force.

The historical works of the ancient peoples were brimming with accounts of demon possession and malevolent spirits emphasized a world where the unseen realm exerted considerable power over human existence. The belief in and widespread experience of demonism and demonic possession were characteristic features of the era. Because their idolatry was both widely known and easily understood, they were rarely discussed. In both Antediluvian and Diluvian societies, demonism and demon possession were so pervasive and commonplace that no explicit mention or explanation was necessary. Everyone alive during those tumultuous periods was acutely aware of the unfolding events.

The background of the Old Testament and New Testament describes evil on the rampage; demons were almost everywhere; the sorceries and other forms of the occultism made most men and women weak spiritually, mentally, and sexually. As a ragdoll, the demons entered men and women and children, controlling every aspect of them.

Through a thorough and detailed study of both the Old and New Testaments, combined with extensive scholarly research into the religious practices, including the various cults, idolatries, and pagan rituals of the ancient world, a significant and persuasive collection of evidence emerges, strongly suggesting the pervasiveness of demon possession in the periods before the birth of Christ. The arrival of demonic possession brought with it the cruel weight of demonic oppression, a dark and inescapable burden. Amidst the turbulent and chaotic spiritual landscape, it appeared as though succumbing to demonic possession had become the prevalent and accepted standard. As a direct consequence of this event, most of humankind tragically fell victim to possession, resulting in widespread moral corruption and depravity that affected nearly everyone.

During those wicked times, an environment ripe for demonic possession was fostered, making it frighteningly easy for nearly anyone to succumb to such malevolent forces. Without God's special grace and divine protection, the world's population—men, women, and children—would be utterly defenseless against evil spirits, left vulnerable and exposed to their malevolent schemes and whims, becoming easy prey for their wicked designs.

One cannot reasonably study the ancient cults, the diverse manifestations of occultism, and the religious customs of ancient paganism—especially when considering the depiction of paganism within the Old Testament—without arriving at the undeniable conclusion that demon possession was a pervasive phenomenon among pagans before the arrival of Christ, and before the flood as well. Because paganism is inherently associated with the risk of demonic possession, pursuing this path presents an insurmountable challenge for those who seek to remain free from the corrupting influence of evil spirits.

Moreover, the groupings of occultists and the practices of the occultists retain precise phrases or words that indicate mass amounts of demon possessions in the Old Testament times (Deuteronomy 18:10–11). These have already been defined.

The Hebrew verb גָּעַר, meaning "to rebuke," reveals a fascinating historical intertwining of language and spirituality, as its usage is strongly associated with ancient exorcism practices and the cultural belief in demonic possession. The Hebrew verb גָּעַר, used during the practice of exorcism, conveys a meaning that extends beyond the mere control and subjugation of malevolent spirits; it also emphasizes that such subjugation is absolutely necessary for the complete and unwavering establishment of God's ultimate reign and authority over all things. In technical usage, the term signifies the authoritative word, uttered by God or a divine agent, which subjugates malevolent powers, thereby establishing God's just and righteous rule over all creation. This verb aptly captures the powerful act of overcoming obstacles that stand in the way of God's plan's successful completion.

In Zechariah 3:2, the use of the Hebrew verb גָּעַר within the Old Testament passage establishes clear examples of both exorcism and demonic possession, providing illustrations of each phenomenon. The Old Testament frequently depicts God as the primary agent of exorcism, suggesting that such acts were considered divinely ordained and only undertaken when absolutely necessary. It was extremely rare in the Old Testament for individuals to receive freedom through divine intervention from God. It was the general consensus that only a miraculous intervention, a divine act from God Himself, possessed the power to resolve the situation without requiring the services of a human exorcist. This event, acting as a premonition and symbolic representation, foreshadowed the future actions and ministry of Jesus Christ, who, in His incarnation, embodied deity in human form.

The Hebrew verb גָּעַר reveals that, before the arrival of Jesus, the prevalence of demon possession in society was so widespread that it led to the creation of specific terminology and the establishment of a formal exorcism process to deal with it. Had there been just a few accounts of demon possessions in the Old Testament era, there would have been no need for such terminology. The Hebrew verb גָּעַר suggests that rebuking was not merely an act of reprimand but an assertion of power in the face of perceived demonic influence and possession. The frequent appearance of this term can indeed indicate a societal familiarity with demon possession and the need for a structured response to it, particularly in the prophetic and healing narratives. Moreover, the absence of extensive formalized processes for dealing with spiritual disturbances in earlier texts may hint at varying degrees of prevalence and public acknowledgment of such phenomena. By the time of the Second Temple period and into the New Testament, one can observe a more organized approach to exorcism, suggesting an escalation in both reported cases and societal engagement with the concept of demonic possession. The emergence of specialized terminology and rituals would imply that these issues were not merely fringe experiences but were woven into the fabric of the community's lived reality.

The New Testament exhibits numerous accounts of Jesus performing exorcisms, further indicating that addressing demon possession had become a significant aspect of religious practice. This continuity from the Old Testament to the New Testament highlights a transformation in the understanding and treatment of demonic forces, reflecting broader societal beliefs and fears. The increasing emphasis on exorcism as a formal and recognized process signals that the issue was widespread and required communal and spiritual intervention, as societal perceptions of the supernatural evolved over time.

Consequently, the pagan practices of idolatry resulted in the prevalence of demonization in the period before the arrival of Christ and His teachings. This statement remains true and accurate as of today's date. Through the practices of pagan idolatry, coupled with other sinful practices such as sexual immorality, men, women, and children became vulnerable to demonic possession, leaving them susceptible to demonic influence and control at the whim of malevolent entities. Before Christ, and particularly within the state of reprobation, demon possession was understood to be one of the most significant and prevalent consequences of this spiritual condition. Most individuals living before the Great Flood were not only morally corrupt but also possessed by malevolent spirits, a situation that characterized the Antediluvian era.

Hermaphroditic Nature of Demonic Possession

Within this phenomenon of demonic possession by the Baalim and the Astartes, there appears what has been known as "gender fluidity" in a limited state.

The Baalim and Astartes possess the extraordinary ability to switch genders effortlessly. They have the amazing ability to change their gender with ease. They become feminine when they live in male bodies, which allows the female gender to express itself through the male host. On the other hand, they assume a male gender when they inhabit female bodies, which allows them to acquire a male gender.

So when they inhabit male bodies, they transform into females, granting the potential for the female gender to manifest through the male host. Conversely, when they occupy female bodies, they revert to a male gender, enabling the male gender to be acquired.

The demons subvert social conventions and induce a hermaphrodite state in those under their control by taking on the opposite genders. A deep merging of the genders of demons and humans is made possible by this transcendence of conventional gender boundaries.

Moreover, feminine gender adoption occurs when Baalim or Astartes entities take possession of males, enabling the male host to experience femininity. On the other hand, these demons take on a male gender when they inhabit females, giving the host the opportunity to experiment with masculinity. The boundary between conventionally linked gender attributes is further blurred by this entire shift in mannerisms and behaviors, which is part of this gender metamorphosis rather than just cosmetic changes.

As the original gender of a human takes on another gender through demonic possession, the dominant gender becomes one that is determined by the demon. This fluidity results in the blurring of gender boundaries and the creation of a hermaphroditic nature within the possessed individual. For instance, a male possessed by a female demon would now be perceived as and behave predominantly as a female. This dominance of the possessed gender highlights the transformative power and influence of the demons in shaping the individual's gender identity.

As the demons possess individuals of the opposite gender, profound behavioral changes can be observed in the possessed hosts. Males inhabited by female demons adopt feminine mannerisms, speech patterns, and even physical attributes. Similarly, females inhabited by male demons exhibit masculine traits, vocal inflections, and physical characteristics. This transformative process not only manifests in external appearance but also influences internal psychological states, prompting a shift in the individual's perception of their own gender identity. Through this intricate interplay of possession and behavior, the boundaries between male and female become blurred, further reinforcing the unified nature of the demonic and human genders.

Demons, Humans, Sexuality, and the Occult

While these things have and will be discussed in one form or another, they must at least here be defined.

Sex magic—phallic ritual—is the combination of magic, the occult, and the sexual act. In such a practice, the orgasm and sexual energy are used to cast spells to produce any number of desired outcomes. Sex done in rituals increased the power of the rituals, spells, and incantations. For example, sex magic was used in the Egyptian occultism and the Babylonian occultism. The cults of the Baalim and the Astartes incorporated it into their rituals. Sorcery, spells, incantations, sacrifices (especially human sacrifices), and sexual orgies were all present. Combining sexual orgies with the occult is sex magic. Since sex is done, nudity is part of sex magic.

Sex magic may be called "ritual sex." It symbolizes the regeneration of the universe. This ritual brings with it demon possession. Therefore, sex magic was and is the sexual orgies that accompanied the fertility and other rites of the pagans. The orgies of Adonis or Baal-Peor and of Astartes were completely established in Palestine prior to the time of the Exodus.

Demonic sexual assault is when demons—disembodied spirits— use their powers and force to attack a woman or a man and go through every sensation of the sexual act upon that person. The sensation is like a real act of sex without any seed or other fluids being brought forth. These evil spirits, since they are disembodied spirits, cannot, through this union, produce children; the union is spiritual with physical effects like force, being slipped, hit, beaten, and bloodied. Demonic sexual assault or rape is going through the activities of sex without there being a physical partner. Historically, there have been various cases when an unseen evil force, having no physical genitalia, attacks men and women and a physical sexual rape is sensed and experienced. Augustine wrote, et quoniam creberrima fama est multi que se expertos uel ab eis, qui experti essent, de quorum fide dubitandum non esset, audisse confirmant, siluanos et panes, quos uulgo incubos uocant, inprobos saepe extitisse mulieribus et earum appetisse ac peregisse concubitum; et quosdam daemones, quos dusios galli nuncupant, adsidue hanc inmunditiam et temptare et efficere, plures tales que adseuerant, ut hoc negare inpudentiae uideatur (And since it is a very frequent report, which many persons have confirmed that they have also experienced it themselves, or have heard from such as has experienced it, whose trustfulness is without doubt, that sylvans and fauns, who are generally named "incubi," had frequently done evil assaults upon women, and they have satisfied and also performed sexual intercourse with them; and there are certain demons, named Duses by the Gauls, who are constantly trying and completing this sexual dirtiness—foulness, so many amount of people acknowledge it that to deny this must be considered to be shameless).[7]

Demonic sexual submission is when people submit to the lusts of evil spirits. They allow them to have the similarity of sexual intercourse with them. Occultists submit to this. This becomes part of the occultic lifestyle.

Sexual sin is an act of idolatry; it is accompanied by demon possession. The union of two humans in such sinful acts unites them with their evil spirits; therefore, the evil spirits participate in the acts of sexual sin as well; the humans are having a sexual relationship with each other, and the demons are satisfying their lust in these activities. Such demonic activities here are not demonic rapes. The human partners have given their bodies over to evil spirits; the evil spirits are using their bodies to satisfy their lusts. The demons work in corporation with their human vessels. Logically, historically, and grammatically, as seen in various works, both in the Bible and outside of the Bible, a human in such a state is having physical sex with his human partner but also having sex with evil spirits, whether the manifestation is only spiritual, physical, or both.

In such cases, as demons interfering into sexual intercourse between men and women, their purposes are not mild nor good. The demons have their vessels, hosts, or victims at their mercy. With their sovereign will, they conquer every bit and every part of humanity; nothing is left. They control the mind, soul, spirit, and especially the bodies. The bodies of men and women become playthings unto the demons. The bodies of men and women, even children, have no power to do anything in this state. It is the demons themselves that operate, influence, and make all gestures and movements through the bodies of their victims. The victims are like marionettes, their lives controlled by unseen forces and manipulated with callous disregard. Every aspect of these sexually explicit acts is meticulously planned by demons, who seek to fulfill their depraved lust through the suffering and violation of their victims. Every joy or sexual pleasure caused by the men and women having sexual intercourse is kidnapped and taken away by the demons. The sexual pleasure is not gained by the men and women, but the demons are the ones enjoying; they are working in and operating every part of this incident to gain sexual pleasure from their victims.

So, the act of sexual intercourse, often seen as an intimate exchange of energy and trust between partners, becomes tainted by the presence of evil spirits. This can lead to a perversion of relationships, breeding distrust, guilt, and further immoral behavior. As these demons partake in sexual sin, they simultaneously spread their malevolent influence on others, amplifying the consequences of such acts.

The idea that evil spirits could experience sexual communion alongside their human hosts introduces a chilling perspective on the nature of sin. Such unions are not merely isolated incidents of immorality; they symbolize a broader cascade of corruption that has the potential to infect both the individual and the collective community. Sexual pleasure is one of fundamental aspects of human sexuality; through the relationships of demon spirits through this practice, sexual pleasure is not only corrupted but annihilated altogether. When demons obliterate all avenues for sexual fulfillment, they leave behind only an echo of what once was—a haunting reminder that in this realm, pleasure is piped through violence and violation.

Further, the involvement of demons in sexual activity with men, women, and children was and is attempts to destroy the moral concept of sex. This is true especially with demons seeking after women for their sexual enjoyment. It is attempts to destroy the place of the women among the human race and among the establishment of marriage. And it is often linked to the promiscuity of women.

There are many different stories from the medieval period about Christian women who were involved with demons but who still considered themselves devout Christians. In the minds of these women, the events were not evidence of demonic possession, nor were they considered sinful in any way, shape, or form. Despite everything, however, they remained victims of demonic possession. They did not believe, nor did they feel, that this action constituted a renunciation of their faith. They took shelter within the hallowed halls of the churches, remaining hidden until a divine intervention, a smoking out by God himself, revealed their true identities.

It was not necessary for demons to manifest themselves in a human form. They have the ability to transform into a range of animal forms to engage in sexual activities with individuals of all ages and genders.

Tertullian, as previously translated in reference to the daughters of Moab, and Hosea in Hosea 4:12–17 and in the Greek Septuagint also Hosea 2:5, 7 (9), 10 (12), 2:12 and 2:15, just to name these two sources, all see the union of those who practice sexual sin also being united with evil spirits at the same time. So as Tertullian pointed out when sexual immorality is committed, there is both a unifying of the persons who commit these sins together as one person, and there is a unifying of those spirits who work in these practices. Therefore, people who commit such sins are united with demons, and, besides, having sexual intercourse with their companions, they are also having sex with the spirits themselves.

In the Old Testament, beside mentioning the workings of the Baalim and the Astartes in its method of possession and torment, another entity, is mentioned. In Isaiah 34:14, the Hebrew noun לִילִית (Lilith) is used; it demotes a demon seeking after humans to have sexual intercourse. This spirit, which takes upon the form of a woman and seen as one of the Astartes can well be seen as a man or a woman. It can well be used as an incubus-succubus.

Furthermore, in Hosea 4:17, the Hebrew noun עָצָב (idol) and the Greek noun εἴδωλον (idol) have more meanings that can well be arrived just by a translation. These nouns include the idols themselves, the cults of the idols, the demonic powers behind the idols, the gross immoralities practiced by those devotees to the idols, idolatry, sex magic, and demon possession of those devotees to the idols. In the minds of the Jews and the ancient church, idols meant more than what modern people think.

In Hosea 4:18, the fornication here is both spiritual and corporal (sexual) without ceasing from the time of Jeroboam. The Israelites in the kingdom of Israel were involved in the sacrilege and unbridled insanity of the Canaanites. They added promiscuity to promiscuity beyond the bounds of restraint and modesty. They added practices of insanity to their list of vices. Sex magic is included. Therefore, the allowance of demons using the bodies of those whom they possessed for sexual means is included. There can never be any person practicing idolatry without being demon possessed and without sex magic. Demon possession, sexual sin, and idolatry always go together.

In Hosea 4:12–17, the Hebrew phrase רוּחַ זְנוּנִים (spirit of fornications) denotes that both this sexual intoxication and addiction are means whereby the demons unite with their human vessels. The union of the demons and their human vessels, besides spiritual, are physical by possession and sexual by that same possession. The possession opens a means by which evil spirits become partakers of sexual sin along with their human vessels and spread their evil to others. They experienced sexual intercourse with both their partner and their human vessel simultaneously.

It should be heavily noticed, in particular, a part of the Latin text of Tertullian. ut et spiritu fnicarentur (so that they also committed sexual fornication with the spirit).[8] In the ancient church's view, the depth of the occult practices, the clear involvement of evil spirits, the presence of demonic sexual acts within those practices, and the disturbing participation of humans in such acts were all indisputable.

In the writings of Eusebius, the ancient Christian women especially and the Christian fathers held that sexual sins brought one under the slavery of demons. They held that such evil sexual practices brought forth demon possession. They were to become the temples of the vilest.[9]

In Judges 8:27, the Hebrew verb זָנָה and the Greek verb ἐκπορνεύω (commit fornication) include spiritual fornication—the worshipping of the idol, sexual fornication, the committing of sexual sins between Israelites and at the same time the Israelites having sex with those demons possessing their partners—sex magic. So these verbs interpret sexual sin, idolatry, and demon possession occurring at the same time. A person commits sexual sin with one partner (at least); both have committed idolatry; both are demon possessed; both are instruments where demons can experience and satisfy their sexual lusts; both can be possessed with male or female evil spirits. So the spirits gratify their lust through the human instruments and each human instrument is experiencing a sexual relationship with another human and evil spirit, which possesses another human. Further, these verbs include the prostitution of both sexes and finally, the mutilation of males to become the worshippers and the initiates to the Baalim and the Astartes. The mutilation of the male Israelites meant that all their masculinity was cut off, including penises and testicles, and their transformation into women for their gods and goddesses was accomplished along with dressing the part of women.

In the Testament of Solomon 2:3 (first-century AD), it is told that the demon Ornias appears as a man to have sexual intercourse with young boys: μὲν ὡς ἄνθρωπος ἔχων ἐπιθυμίαν εἴδους παιδίων θηλυκῶν ἀνήβων (At times, I am a man who excessively craves the body (form) of young effeminate boys). In the Testament of Solomon 14:4, it is recorded that a demon was having sexual intercourse with women through their buttocks: συγγινόμενον διὰ γλουτῶν (having sexual intercourse with them through their buttocks). This is anal copulation. And the other demon craving the body or form of young boys means that he sought after to have sexual relations with boys in the forms of oral and anal copulations. Moreover, the Testament of Solomon 14:4 describes demonic rape: καὶ ἡ μὲν βαστάζει ἢ ἐφώρμησα (and one woman I raped was bearing a child). The Testament of Solomon is a work done by Hellenistic Jews and Christians. It reveals their thinking about this topic.

Justin Martyr, Origen of Alexandria, Tertullian, Augustine of Hippo and others held that demons were lustful and lascivious beings.

St. Jerome mentions what happened to St. Hilary several times. Succubi appeared to him in his sleep. In one particular time, Jerome wrote, multae sunt temptationes eius et die noctu que uariae daemonum insidiae; quas si omnes narrare uelim, modum excedam uoluminis. quoties illi nudae mulieres cubanti, quoties esurienti largissimae apparuere dapes (Many were his temptations, and various kinds were the traps of demons, day and night, that if I wished to tell them all, I would far exceed the limit of a volume. How often when he went to sleep did naked women appear to him, how often lavish feasts appeared to him when he was hungry).[10] Such temptations were common to occur to the ancient saints.

In AD 1608, Francesco Maria Guazo wrote, Solent Malefici, & Lamiae cum Daemonibus, illi quidem succubis, hae vero incubis actum venereum exercere, comunis est haec sentenia partum Theologorum, & Philosophorum doctiorum, & omnium fere faeculorum, atque nationum experiential comprebata (Almost all the Theologians and learned Philosophers are agreed, and it has been the experience of all times and all nations that sorcerers and witches copulate—practice committing sexual intercourse—with demons, those men with succubi and those women with the incubi).[11] The author of this work adds that Plato, Philo, Josephus, the old synagogue, Cyprian, Justin Martyr, Clement of Alexanderia, Tertullian, and others held the same view. The author lastly adds, quod voluerunt Daemones posse cum mulieribus rem habere (that demons are able willingly to commit sexual intercourse with women). Such demons are called the familiars of the sorcerers and witches. Historically, nuns were also the victims of such evil.

The denial of cooperation or copulation between demons and witches necessitates the acceptance of a degree of unreality for demons themselves, which includes the possibility of their complete nonexistence since their reality is demonstrated through their interactions.

Lastly a modern writer, named Edward F. Murphy, once wrote about this phenomenon, "Demons which specialize in having sex with human beings, both male and female, are very common. They have been known and written about for centuries. They are called incubi and succubai. The former take on the male sexual role and the latter the female. While incubi and succubai spirits do engage in full sexual relationships with humans, they do not produce sperm, and are thus incapable of procreating children and producing a race of beings half demon and half human."[12]

The Golden Calves and Sexual Orgies

Moses had great reverence for God. He also had tender care of his people in the pains taken to impress on them the sanctity of the Mount while God's presence was upon it. There repeatedly was the understanding that there was the danger of approaching too near it while there was attaching to them any sort of defilement (Exodus 19:14—25). Moses taught and showed that there must be the absence of all jealousy or self-seeking in his readiness to share the honor of approaching near to God (Exodus 24:9—13).

The experiences of Moses on the top of the mountain, mentioned in Exodus 25 throughout to 31, were not known by the Israelites at the bottom of the mountain. The experiences of the Israelites are mentioned in Exodus 24:1—11 moving toward Exodus

32:1. They had confidence and commitment unto God with Moses. However, with the absence of Moses, the Israelites turned away from the Lord God (Exodus 24:18). They saw an opportunity to rebel, commit apostasy, practice idolatry, and make molten gods that they were going to worship. They sought another leader, which temporarily was to be Aaron. With the absence of Moses, the protecting and helping presence of God had vanished. The Israelites were determined to have gods made for them and return to Egypt (Exodus 32:1–22; Acts 7:39–40). Therefore, they became vulnerable, unstable, annoyed, impatient, rebellious, and stiff necked. Evil used this time to make the Israelites long to return back to the practices of the Egyptians. They were not as sold-out unto the Lord as Moses was.

Aaron had no backbone when Moses was not present. He went along with their plan to return to Egypt (Exodus 32:1–6). Therefore, the Israelites sought Aaron to fashion their gods that they were going to worship (Exodus 32:1–5). After making their gods, Aaron constructed an altar right before the large (national) golden calf and proclaimed that there was going to be a festival unto the Lord tomorrow (Exodus 32:5–6). The next morning, the people rose early, set up whole burnt offerings and other sacrifices; they ate, drank, danced, and indulged themselves in pagan carousing (Exodus 32:6).

In Exodus 32:6a, the Greek Septuagint uses singular verbs rather than plural, as in the Hebrew text. Some point out that Aaron, rather than the Hebrews, was the one who offered up whole burnt sacrifices. Then, the scribes who translated the Hebrew text into Greek may have interpreted Exodus 32:6 this way to make sure that the appropriate cultic practice is written.[13] However, the rest of the Greek translations use the plural forms of the verbs, which refers to the Israelites themselves. The singular Greek verb does not have to refer to Aaron alone; it can reasonably refer to ὁ λαὸς (the people), which is singular. Therefore, a plural number of Israelites were involved in making and offering up the whole burnt sacrifice.[14] Common cultic practice, or what may be known as the common religious and pagan practice, was thrown out the door. Both Aaron and the Hebrews made and offered up whole sacrifices. Aaron, as priest, generally was the one who made and offered up sacrifices, but in this climate, general is key; both Aaron and other people could and did offer up whole burnt sacrifices.

This occurred on the thirty-eighth or thirty-ninth of the forty days that Moses spent on the mount (Exodus 32:5). In Exodus 32:5, it is stated that tomorrow was going to be the feast. The molding of the golden calves was done in one day. The day of the feast was the day Moses came down (Exodus 32:5–28).

After seeing the continued delay of Moses, the Israelites spoke to Aaron, עֲשֵׂה־לָנוּ אֱלֹהִים or ποίησον ἡμῖν θεοὺς (You must immediately make for us gods) in Exodus 32:1–5. Next, notice the wordings of verse 4, וַיַּעֲשֵׂהוּ עֵגֶל מַסֵּכָה וַיֹּאמְרוּ אֵלֶּה אֱלֹהֶיךָ (he made it—gold into a cast image of a young bull-calf, and he said, these are your gods) or καὶ ἐποίησεν αὐτὰ μόσχον χωνευτὸν καὶ εἶπεν Οὗτοι οἱ θεοί σου (and he made them—golden rings into a molten young bull-calf, and said, these are your gods). The golden idol, which here stood for the whole nation of Israel, was the same as the chief Egyptian god, a young bull called Apis, which was worshipped at Memphis near the land of Goshen. Israel did worship idols in Egypt (Joshua 24:14; Ezekiel 20:8, 23:3–8).[15]

The plurality of calves is also seen in Exodus 32:31 in the phrase "made them gods of gold," not god.

By blasphemous words, Aaron credited the miracles and the deliverance of the Israelites from Egypt to the golden calves, in particular to the national golden calf (Exodus 32:5). Therefore, Aaron and the apostates called the golden calf Jehovah (Exodus 32:1–6). So to them, Jehovah and Apis were one and the same. Aaron said before the national golden calf about a feast, לַיהוָה מָחָר or τοῦ κυρίου αὔριον (unto the Lord tomorrow). The golden calves were not representations of the Lord God—Jehovah, but they represented the Apis—another one of the Baalim, like or the same as Baal-Peor in practices. Therefore, the golden calves (bulls) were the worship of the bulls among the Baalism. Golden calf (bull) worship was prominent in the times of the Old Testament (1 Kings 12:28; 2 Kings 10:29; 2 Chronicles 11:15, 13:8; Hosea 3:1–2). The calf (bull) symbolized power, lordship, strength, fertility, and the like.

The plurality of calves—one national and twelve tribal—are violations of idolatry rather than the violations of polytheism. The duplication of the golden idol is not various gods—thirteen different gods, but only one demon-god represented by thirteen golden idols. Comparing Exodus 20:4–5 with the phrase "who brought you out of Egypt" in Exodus 32:7, idolatry rather than polytheism is stressed heavily. All the idols were in the shape of a calf (bull) as seen in Exodus 32:4–8.

The golden calves were made from the golden earrings, which were in the ears of wives and daughters (Exodus 32:2–3). The wives and daughters took them from their ears, and all gave them to Aaron.

Aaron's golden calves were modeled after Apis, an Egyptian bull god. Apis related to another Egyptian god, Osiris. All holiness was pulled away, and the Israelites became nude, offering up burnt offerings, peace offerings, and finally, according to the Hebrew and Greek Septuagint texts, went full into heathen worship.

The golden idol—golden young bull, the one represented for the whole nation of Israel, like those made for each tribe of Israel, was believed by the Israelites to have been the gods which brought them out of Egypt. The golden calves did not represent the Lord God, but the Israelites replaced the true God with these false gods. Simply, the Israelites had forgotten their God and replaced Him (Psalm 106:16–20).

The idea that there was one golden calf idol is true, as it pertains to the people of Israel. However, Jewish sources, like the term "gods" in Exodus 32, state while one golden calf stood for the whole of Israel, there were twelve other golden calves, one for each tribe of Israel. Ginzberg writes:

> But the people worshipped not only the golden calf, they
> made thirteen such idols, one each for the twelve tribes,

156

and one for all Israel. More than this, they employed manna, which God in His kindness did not deny them even on this day, as an offering to their idols. The devotion of Israel to this worship of the bull is in part explained by the circumstance that while passing through the Red Sea, they beheld the Celestial Throne, and most distinctly of the four creatures about the Throne, they saw the ox. It was for this reason that they hit upon the notion that the ox had helped God in the exodus from Egypt, and for this reason did they wish to worship the ox beside God.[16]

Further, according to the Jerusalem Talmud, R. Simon B. Yohai taught this, and said, "Thirteen golden calves did the Israelites make, and there was one which was common property for all of them. What is the Scriptural basis for this statement? [And he received the gold at their hand, and fashioned it with a graving tool, and made a molten calf; and they said,] 'These are your gods, O Israel, [who brought you up out of the land of Egypt]' (Ex. 32:4). Lo, they were for the twelve tribes. [Even when they had made for themselves a molten calf and said,] 'This is your God [who brought you up out of Egypt,' and had committed great blasphemies]" (Neh. 9:18). [The reference to "this is your god"] indicates the one which was common property for all."[17]

Why was the golden calf so accepted as the God that brought Israel out of Egypt? That question was a wonder. Just why? According to Jewish sources, several key events occurred while Moses ascended to the Mount and stayed there. First, at noon on the fortieth day of Moses staying on the mount, Satan came and gave a vision to the people that Moses was dead. Second, the multitude that fled Israel was not only Jews but also a mixture of people who fled with the Jews for one reason or another. Therefore, there were pagans among the Israelites.

Moreover, some of these pagans were magicians. Two magicians demanded that Aaron made them these idols, and both magicians along with others killed Hur. Third, soon after the making of the golden calf—the one that was made for the whole camp of Israelites—both magicians made the golden calf move about like it was alive.

157

This was no trick, while the magicians did not give life to the golden calf, they did cause it to move. And that was enough for the mixed multitude to cry out, "This is thy God, O Israel."[18]

The Israelites were not that holy in Egypt. They accepted and played the fool before the pagan gods and practiced the abominations of the Egyptians. Indeed, following the practices of the pagan gods will always make us fools since they were beaten by the true God, and the true God hates those practices. Further, it is impossible for the Israelites to have played the fool before the pagan gods without becoming demon possessed, and it was impossible for them to commit sexual sin without them being demon possessed. The Israelites, then, would have to have been delivered from the power of evil, including demon possession before the beginning of their exodus from Egypt.

Heathen worship included all acts of licentiousness. The Israelites had become like mad dogs.

Clement of Alexandria speaks of those heretics who follow the Canaanite Rites:

> γὰρ τρισάθλιοι τὴν [τε] σαρκικὴν καὶ [τὴν] συνου σιαστικὴν κοινωνίαν ἱεροφαντοῦσι καὶ ταύτην οἴονται εἰς τὴν βασιλείαν αὐτοὺς ἀνάγειν τοῦ θεοῦ. εἰς τὰ χαμαιτυπεῖα μὲν οὖν ἡ τοιάδε εἰσάγει κοινωνία καὶ δὴ συμμέτοχοι εἶεν αὐτοῖς οἱ σύες καὶ οἱ τράγοι, εἶεν δ᾽ ἂν ἐν ταῖς μείζοσι παρ᾽ αὐτοῖς ἐλπίσιν αἱ προεστῶσαι τοῦ τέγους πόρναι ἀνέδην εἰσδεχόμεναι τοὺς βουλομένους ἅπαντας (For the three times more perverted make the rites of a religion both out of physical union and sexual intercourse and think that this practice will bring them up into the kingdom of God. Therefore, it is such as this Communion that leads unto the brothels. Indeed, both herded swine and he-goats should be their partners. But it is the prostitutes who are presiding over the brothel and freely receive all willing customers who should be in greater hopes from them).[19]

The best definition and explanation of the most evilness of idolatry comes from Tertullian:

Principale crimen generis humani, summus saeculi reatus, tota causa iudicii idololatria (The chief crime of the human race, the highest guilt of the world, the whole procuring reason of judgment, is idolatry).[20]

The best description of paganism and idolatry and its effects upon Roman culture comes from John Chrysostom:

Τότε ἦν θρῆνος, τότε πανταχοῦ βωμοὶ, πανταχοῦ καπνὸς, πανταχοῦ κνῖσαι, πανταχοῦ πορνεῖαι, πανταχοῦ τελεταὶ, πανταχοῦ θυσίαι, πανταχοῦ δαίμονες βακχεύοντες, πανταχοῦ ἀκρόπολις τοῦ διαβόλου, πανταχοῦ πορνεία στεφανουμένη· καὶ εἷς ἦν ὁ Παῦλος. (Then there was lamentation, then there were altars everywhere, everywhere smoke, everywhere smells of burnt sacrifice, everywhere fornications, everywhere unclean rites, and mysteries, everywhere sacrifices, everywhere demons holding their sexual rites of Bacchus, everywhere a citadel of the devil, everywhere fornication which was decorated with garlands of honor; and Paul was alone).[21]

George Stanley Faber said about paganism:

In the corrupt theology of paganism, prostitution was not accidental, but systematic. It flowed naturally from the doctrines and formed a constituent part of the ritual. The violation of female chastity was not the mere result of unrestrained licentiousness but was esteemed the surest mode of propitiating the two great principles of generation, from whose mysterious union was produced the world and all that it contains.[22]

In Exodus 32:6, the Hebrew phrase לְצַחֵק and the Greek infinitive παίζειν both depict sexual immorality here, sexual magic, and the most gross forms of idolatries. Sexual orgies were occurring. Further, cultic prostitution is here seen; female prostitution is understood. Female virgins offered themselves unto these gods and men, like the daughters of Moab so did.

159

Further, male prostitutes must be included and especially male virgins giving themselves over to men as cultic prostitutes. Men to men, women to women, and men to women were giving themselves to each other. Once each gave up their virginity, they continued in these sexual immoralities, deed by deed. Like Baal-Peor, Apis incorporated into its practices the worship of the phallus.

All pagan idol gods had consecrated women devoted to immoral practices (Exodus 34:13; Deuteronomy 7:5, 12:3, 16:21; Judges 3:7, 6:25–30; 1 Kings 14:15, 23, 15:13, 16:33, 18:19; 2 Kings 13:6, 17:10, 16; 2 Chronicles 17:6, 19:3, 24:18, 31:1, 33:3, 19, 34:3–7; Isaiah 17:8, 27:9; Jeremiah 17:2). The Lord accused the Israelites of corrupting themselves by sexual sins. Various commandments did the Israelites break here (Exodus 20:1–7, 12, 14, 16, 17).

Both depictions have reference to the veneration of the idols by various ill behaviors, especially sexual sin. Dances, games, eating, and drinking were part of these pagan venerations. Dancing around the altar of Baal is mentioned in 1 Kings 18:26. First Corinthians 10:7 quoting Exodus 32:6 stands under the whole weight of the repudiation of all pagan cultic forms by Judaism. The Hebrew phrase לְצַחֵק has reference to cultic dances, has an erotic sense, has cultic licentiousness (sexual immorality), and cultic prostitution.

Irenaeus wrote, Sedit populus comedere et bibere et surrexerunt ludere. Neque fornicentur, sicut quidam ex illis fornicati sunt (The people sat down so that they could eat and drink and they rose up to practice pagan carousing–orgies. Neither let us commit fornication, as some of them also committed fornication).[23] Tertullian connected this incident to that of Numbers 25; he also connected it with the same offenses done by the daughters of Moab, selling themselves in prostitution for their god. He connects sexual whoredom with the evil spirits.[24] Also, Tertullian describes the playing (pagan carousing) as lusum nisi impudicum (game unless it was a shameless one).[25]

Moreover, in Exodus 32:25, the Hebrew passive participle פָרֻעַ and the Greek perfect verb διεσκέδασται portray the Hebrews as a people without any moral restraint, out of control morally, like the

Egyptians, the Canaanites, and their other enemies. Nakedness, drunkenness, partying, violence, rape, and all forms of sexual orgies present themselves here. Historically, this has been the interpretation of the Hebrew and Greek.[26] To the shame of Aaron, he permitted these types of behaviors. Moses must stop the orgies—the filthy, sexual, perverted practices—at any cost.

Simply put, Moses knew nothing would cause the wrath of God to arouse more than filthy, sexual, and perverted practices combined with idolatry. Even these sexual practices by themselves were enough, far enough. However, such sexual practices regardless are tied to idolatry, whether those who practice such know it. It is impossible to separate such practices from idolatry. Even adultery and fornication among different sexes are tied to idolatry. Such practices that are contrary to nature or those that are according to nature done outside of a holy marriage are tied to idolatry. It is impossible to commit a sexual sin without it being tied to idolatry, and it is also impossible to commit a sexual sin, whether unlawful or unnatural, without it being tied to the Pythonic demons, the Kundalini demons, the Baalim and the Astartes. A sexual sin is tied directed to the cults of the sun and the moon and phallic worship. Phallic worship and the cults of the sun and moon are associated with a sexual sin.

According to the Targums, Aaron helped the Israelites in their sins of idolatry because the Israelites had killed Hur, who had been left in charge of the Israelites while Moses was away before the Lord. And Aaron was so afraid that they would kill him.

The Canaanites Preoccupied the Land

The work which Moses was not allowed to accomplish Joshua had now to undertake and carry to completion. This task was a difficult one, but not impossible through Divine Providence and help.

Joshua did not have to conquer, possess, and colonize an uninhabited country, nor did he have to drive out or subdue simple barbarians of an inferior race and culture. On the contrary, the people already preoccupying the country of Canaan, in many respects, were far advanced and more civilized than the Israelites, and were extremely their superior in using arms and in all matters pertaining to military experience. The struggle against the preoccupied Promised Land was not going to be easy now.

Too many look upon the ancient civilizations as barbarians, ignorant and highly uncivilized. Many civilizations were far more advanced than we give them credit. Archaeologists have uncovered these facts. Pagans the Canaanites were, but not stupid—without intelligence.

The country of Canaan, which Joshua was expected to conquer, was already and had long been inhabited by Phoenicians—Canaanites. Their nation was the most significant commercial nation of antiquity. The letters of Europe trace themselves back to the Phoenicians. They also entered beyond the bounds of the Mediterranean Sea in boats and carried off stores of minerals from the shores of Britain.

When the Israelites were residing in Egypt, the Promised Land became more and more under the control of pagan nations. A substantial struggle was required for the Israelites to acquire the land as their rightful inheritance. *Like almost always, Satan sends his forces and people to preoccupy what God has given to others.*

At the time of Joshua, at least the Promised Land was under the occupation of seven powerful and pagan nations. They were the following, as numbered by Joshua to his assembled army: the Canaanites, or Lowlanders who dwelt on the seacoast and the Jordan valley; the Hivites, a peaceful tribe who inhabited Shechem and its vicinity; the Perizzites, agriculturists dwelling in the unwalled villages of Central and Southern Palestine; the Girgashites, who are supposed to have taken their name from Gergesa or Gerasa on Lake Gennesareth; the Amorites, or mountaineers, the most powerful of the Canaanite peoples, who in close connection with the Hittites, had established themselves both east and west of the Jordan in various localities; the Jebusites, who held the central highlands around their impregnable capital, Jerusalem, and were of the Hittite or Amorite race (Genesis 10:1−19, 15; Numbers 13:26−33; Deuteronomy 1:28, 9:1−2; Joshua 3:10).

These Canaanite nations were completely depraved in terms of morality and religion. The state of opulence−luxury and commercial prosperity resulted in an extreme moral depravity that demanded punishment and oppression by the Lord God. His holiness demanded it. Even nature itself demanded it.

Depravity itself causes creation to cry out for punishment and oppression (Romans 8:22).

In the Scriptures and other historical resources, the overall essence of pagan religion is stamped and defined by cruelty, bloodlust, lustfulness, perversion, and an explicit disregard for the laws of nature. In Canaan, the worship of multiple gods, such as the Baalim and the Astartes, was prevalent, with the use of the plural form in Scripture emphasizing their plurality.

These deities were associated with practices of sexual perversion, including homosexuality, bestiality, and various forms of intercourse. Followers of the Baalim and the Astartes were encouraged to engage in prostitution, homosexuality, and lesbianism, leading to temptation and moral transgressions among the Israelites (Judges 2:11, 3:7, 10:6). The cults of the Baalim and the Astartes promoted male and female prostitution, as well as same-sex relationships, which some Israelites found themselves unable to resist, falling into these sinful practices.

The biblical writers and authors rejected the homosexual cult prostitutes, and by doing this, they were rejecting four significant things: the worship of all goddesses, the worship of any pagan god, the whole phenomenon of homosexual practice, and all other unlawful or unnatural forms of sexual immorality. The source of sexual sin, regardless of its type, is traced back to the Pythonic demons, the Kundalini demons, the Baalim, and the Astartes. Once a nation has been taken over by the Baalim and the Astartes in particular, it is almost impossible to rid the nation of them.

Israel was progressively and steadily established in the country of Canaan. The Scriptures portray the Israelites as receiving a long-awaited inheritance and carrying out divine retribution upon a multitude of sinners deemed unworthy of life. The transgressions of the Canaanites rendered almost all unsuitable for existence. Those who engaged in such behavior have been labeled as reprobates because of the consequences.

Several centuries in the past, the land of Canaan was pledged to Abraham and his descendants. This hope had been consistently presented to the patriarchs. It was this ambition that prompted Jacob, who was near death, to request his sons to entomb his remains in the cave of Machpelah—the moment had arrived for the Israelites to assume their inheritance and establish themselves in the place where God's Providence was guiding them.

Many have often questioned the morality of this dispossession and wholesale destruction of the Canaanites. The abhorrent evil that the Canaanites practiced was so vile that the salvation of the world necessitated their destruction!

In order to make room for Israel, nations which had long inhabited Palestine were exterminated. This ruthless slaughter was attributed to the express command of God: "But of the cities of these people, which the LORD thy God doth give thee for an inheritance, thou shalt save alive nothing that breatheth: But thou shalt utterly destroy them" (Deuteronomy 20:16–17).

The blessings bestowed upon Abraham hold the secret and the key to unlocking this difficulty. He was told that since the transgression of the Amorites had not reached its peak, he and his descendants could not immediately take ownership of the country of Canaan. Initially, the territorial demarcation was perceived and handled as a legal transaction. God has reserved for Himself the authority that all sovereigns are required to reserve, namely the authority to expunge criminals from the earth and seize their belongings (Genesis 15; Joshua 24:15).

The Amorites were the most powerful of the Canaanite nations. The sin of the Amorites was to reach its full measure.

The claim of the Canaanites to the land, based on their long possession, was nullified because of their wickedness. As a result, the responsibility of safeguarding it was bestowed upon the Israelites, considering it as the central aspect of genuine faith and the tangible representation of God's dominion on earth. This cause applies to any race that God displaces.

In addition, the four hundred years of delay that His own people endured highlight the severe and silent process of God's justice. The Lord God knew the Canaanites would not make any progress. Their wrongdoing had reached a level that even the neighboring heathens voiced their grievances about them. Their reputation also extended to the most detestable forms of idolatry and the most crude and brutal behaviors. He knew that from the time of Abraham, their fate was sealed.

And by judging the moral state of the Canaanites on the implications made in Leviticus, there is no other action than what God demanded and what the Israelites were ordered to do. Under such circumstances, it must be acknowledged that the land was forced to "spue out" the abhorrent and unclean people.

This was a judicial punishment, and clearly a fair one. The realization of Israel that they were the executors of a terrible punishment decreed by God upon the Canaanites served as a safeguard against any potential dehumanizing impact that the invasion could have had on them.

God has made it abundantly clear through the destruction of the Canaanites that it is better to wipe out the wicked several times over rather than entice the innocent to associate with them.

In truth, the preservation of Israel depended on the destruction of the Canaanite idols, all their idolatry, and all their sexual practices. The world would have faced destruction if they had been saved. Despite their small number, the remaining remnants of those individual Canaanites caused Israel to apostatize, and repeatedly, the fate of the entire world relied on a few devout families who maintained their understanding of the only true God.

The depraved rituals and practices of the Canaanites permeated the polluted atmosphere. Foul smells permeated the land: the smells of decaying corpses, the smells of sacrificing various sacrifices, and the foul smells of sex in different forms. The entire land smelled like a brothel.

Also, the taint of idolatry seemed to infect the very air of the defiled land; contamination breathed from the trees of the groves, which were still stained with the blood of human sacrifices, and about which still hung the odor of their intoxicating incense.

If God's goal was to keep all of humanity in sin and disobedience, if He wanted to disprove all His promises and laws, and if He wanted to cut off His creation from Himself permanently, then sparing the Canaanites was the most effective strategy to accomplish these goals.

The extermination campaign of Joshua may be seen as sacred considering the enemies he faced—their morally depraved state, their allegiance to demonic forces like Satan, the Baalim, and the Astartes, who sided with the Canaanites and the giants, both human and supernatural.

As for the population of Canaan, as we have seen previously, the great majority were considered reprobates—the vilest creatures who have existed since the time of the flood until that point. Nothing spiritually positive can be said about them.

The entirety of their civilization, regardless of its level of advancement, was inherently evil. Through Joshua's leadership in exterminating and the complete destruction of Sodom and Gomorrah during Abraham's time, God bestowed upon us a blessing. In addition, archaeologists have documented the moral degradation of the Canaanites residing in Sodom and Gomorrah, expressing their appreciation to God for the complete annihilation of these cities and their inhabitants. In one case, archaeologists investigating the ruins of the Canaanites uncovered the remains of tens of thousands of newborn children that had been offered up to the Baalim and the Astartes. In a separate instance, archaeologists hastily exited the caves they were exploring because of the discovery of explicit depictions on the walls, particularly those involving bestiality. These fully grown men hastily vacated the premises, experiencing episodes of vomiting.

Whether the intended eradication of the Canaanites was brought about by warfare, famine, pestilence, or earthquakes, it is believed that it was orchestrated by God as an instrument and guided by His providence.

The Israelites were explicitly chosen and saw themselves as instruments in carrying out the Lord's mission of retribution against deliberate sinners. Their sense of morality was clearly apparent in the situation.

During a period where human life held little value, the extermination of a population did not provoke disgust or was seen as a terrible or monstrous act. There was no tactful mercy that stopped the application of the death penalty. This devastation, whether human-caused or not, is both relentless and irrational.

Many causes of death, such as illness, accidents, and old age, claim the lives of men, women, and children. These events are commonly perceived to be normal, and we hardly ever voice our displeasure over their unfairness. If the Canaanites had been gradually eliminated by famine or pestilence, the divine plan would not have faced criticism, even though their suffering and distress would have been intensified. However, if they were to be executed, the use of a sword as the method of execution was not only the quickest but also the most humane.

In those times, it was customary to execute the entire population of a captured town or region. The Assyrian monuments consistently document the widespread massacre that accompanied the conquest of a city. The concept of showing mercy towards an opposing enemy was unfamiliar to those engaged in combat during that era.

The destruction of the Canaanites was not complete, as the terms used seem to imply. For various reasons, such as lack of interest, or cowardice, or disobedience, the Israelites failed to obey God completely. They left large districts unconquered or lived on peaceful terms with the original inhabitants. And many of these later avoided extermination by fleeing from the country, or into parts yet unconquered, or took refuge in cities on the seaboard.

Indeed, the lack of total submission to the will of God and His plan by the Israelites in the destruction of the Canaanites continued to produce evil consequences that plagued the Israelites for centuries. And their non-compliance to the unconditional will and plan of God concerning the Canaanites had dire consequences for all mankind.

It is a matter of daily experience that innocent people should be involved in destroying the guilty. Because of the vilest crimes of the Canaanites, almost everyone should and must perish. If not, their vileness would be transferred from one nation to another nation. Here is the transference of spirits. Rather than letting the leg damage the entire body, it was preferable to amputate the whole leg and preserve life. From a divine standpoint, all Canaanites were culpable, regardless of age.

In the sight of God, though, the Canaanites, regardless of age, were not innocent. Most of the Canaanites were accursed, or they were utterly accursed, of God at birth. In other words, they were born reprobates, like many of the antediluvian people. Wickedness can well reach such a height that God will cause ones to be reprobates at birth.

For example, everything in Jericho was cursed, excluding Rahab and her household and those things that could be placed in the treasury of the Lord. And they destroyed all that was in the city, both man and woman, young and old, and ox, and sheep, and ass, with the edge of the sword (Joshua 6:21). And they burned the city with fire, and all that was therein (Joshua 6:24).

Remember that the crimes against nature, the horrible cruelty, and the demeaning idolatry all screamed out for divine retribution. The grace and mercy of God had waited long for the repentance of these nations. However, there no hope of the Canaanites improving. Their right to the land of Canaan, whatever it was, was originally the gift of God. Now that right was revoked. God, who had given, now reclaimed the gifts and put them into the hands of the Israelites by the execution of His fiat word. It only took His word to change ownership of the land.

The Israelites, demanded by God to put to death the whole inhabitants of city after city, could not but see that these victims were abominable in the sight of God, and that wickedness such as theirs was certain to meet with severest punishment.

Practically, the Israelites were taught various things by having to deal with the Canaanites. They were taught the danger of evil communication, there cannot be any truce between them and the paganistic nations, and isolation was their duty and safety. Even the partial accomplishment of the divine sentence against the Canaanites had an enduring and widely extended effect but was not complete. For a time, the pagans did not grow up intermingled with the people of God; the spark of true religion was not smothered by the overpowering blight of paganism, and the knowledge of God and His pure worship was retained and kept forward the era of full salvation. To the Israelites alone was confided the pure idea of God; the pagans had taken the idea and corrupted it.

Jewish authorities have consistently referenced Deuteronomy 10:14 as evidence of Joshua's attempts to negotiate with the inhabitants before invading the land. However, our history does not record any such negotiations.

Joshua understood very well the difficulties that accompanied the great responsibility he inherited when Moses died. In a period of thirty days following the death of Moses, Joshua was divinely instructed to begin the task ahead, either through direct revelation or through the high priest as an intermediary. He was told to commence his labors by leading the host across the river Jordan; the boundaries of the future kingdom were pointed out, from the desert of Arabia to the mountain of Lebanon which they could discern in the far north, from the Mediterranean Sea to the River Euphrates in the distant east; all should be theirs (Joshua 1:5–7).

Joshua dedicated the remaining years of his life to fulfilling the plan of God and showing his claim to be the worthy successor of Moses, the servant of the Lord God.

The Israelites were themselves deeply impressed with this view of the matter about the Canaanites, as shown by the remarkable passage in the following apocryphal book:

Καὶ γὰρ τοὺς παλαιοὺς οἰκήτορας τῆς ἁγίας σου γῆς μισήσας ἐπὶ τῷ ἔχθιστα πράσσειν ἔργα φαρμακειῶν καὶ τελετὰς ἀνοσίους, τέκνων τε φονέας ἀνελεήμονας, καὶ σπλαγχνοφάγων ἀνθρωπίνων σαρκῶν θοῖναν καὶ αἵματος, ἐκ μέσου μύστας θιάσου, καὶ αὐθέντας γονεῖς ψυχῶν ἀβοηθήτων, ἐβουλήθης ἀπολέσαι διὰ χειρῶν πατέρων ἡμῶν, ἵνα ἀξίαν ἀποικίαν δέξηται θεοῦ παίδων ἡ παρὰ σοὶ πασῶν τιμιωτάτη γῆ (Also, for the old inhabitants of Your Holy Land, whom You have hated as a result of their most detested practices of evilness, the works of sorceries, and the ungodly rites of the mysteries, and the merciless murderers of children, and a feast of eating the internal organs of sacrificial human flesh and blood, with these mystics—priests—from the midst of their idolatrous orgy, and those parents who are the murderers of the helpless lives of their own babies, You willed that they would be destroyed by the hands of our fathers in order that before You the most valued land above all lands might receive a praiseworthy colony of God's servants).[27]

The most effective approach to convey this information to contemporary individuals is by depicting the population of Canaan prior to and during the conquest as an epidemic, highly infectious, that very few, if any, could endure. The sole solution to halt the highly contagious pestilence was to eliminate it entirely.

There is no detailed account of the chaotic wars that followed the great battle of Merom, nor do we know precisely how long they lasted. The conquest of the Promised Land took approximately seven years.

The results, which are enumerated in Joshua 12, were achieved after long-continued efforts encompassing expeditions, battles, and sieges, yet unfortunately, no detailed account of these events has been preserved.

Many times, territory once conquered was reoccupied by the original inhabitants on the withdrawal of the victorious Israelites and had to be removed by further contests. This was the case with Hebron and the towns in its vicinity, with Debir and Anab.

The Anakim had seized these places—the giants of demonic origin—who had to be dispossessed before the families to whom they were allotted could colonize them. The Anakim were a race of colossal stature, either aboriginals or very early immigrants from the region of Babylon, who had settled at first on the eastern side of Jordan, in the territories afterward known as Edom and Moab, and subsequently had occupied the hill country of Judaea, and taken refuge in the cities of the Philistines.

If we lose sight of the demonic origin of the Anakim, for example, and the state of reprobation that almost all Canaanites were under, we lose sight of just how Canaan was and just how difficult the conquering of Canaan was, and what a task God has set before Joshua and the Israelites to accomplish.

The normal and the mundane were not part of what Joshua was running after to have in his life and the lives of the Israelites. There was no settling for halves, nor what every other person had from God. He was after the extreme; the very conquests without God were to be impossible. Great was the difficulty, but greater were the blessings that were to be gained for Joshua if he hung on.

When the spies entered the Valley of Hebron on an investigative mission, the sight of these Anakim terrified them. It made them flinch from a victory that required a struggle with such dreadful and demonic enemies. The more significant part of these people was exterminated at this time, both for the benefit of the Israelites themselves and the rest of mankind. A minority of the Anakim was combined with the Philistines of Gaza, Gath, and Ashdod. A family of them existed in the time of Saul when the shepherd led with his sling and stones to overcome the blustering champion Goliath, and even later when David's chosen warriors encountered and slew the brethren of the giant. Their size and strength decreased as they adapted their free mountain air and habits to the atmosphere and depleted the life of lowland cities. They gradually died out and are never mentioned in subsequent histories (Number 13:31−33).

A broad assessment of the scope of the conquests may now be conducted. The subjugation of all the districts named was not complete at this time, nor were the former inhabitants annihilated. This is demonstrated by the Anakim. Under Joshua's leadership, at least for a moment, all opposition was effectively subdued, and armed resistance was at an end. The group of nations that once inspired fear was now non-existent. The possession of the land was a gradual process, but one that might now advance unchecked and with certainty.

Because of the triumphs achieved by the Israelites, the remaining Canaanites were willing to live at peace in the territories that were left to them, and they demonstrated compliance through reluctant submission. Simultaneously, the invaders distributed out the land. Except for the Gibeonites, no one attempted to conquer the conquerors (Joshua 11:20).

The process of hardening is a consequence of sin. There was no interference with free will, since almost all the Canaanites had become reprobates because of their evilness; they had chosen their path and consequences.

Men initially harden their own hearts before God hardens them. And when He does this, He acts in a manner consistent with justice, penalizing transgressors according to their sin.

The Canaanites who had persisted in their idolatry and degrading vice, like all forms of unlawful and unnatural sexuality, were blinded to their own interest and recklessly hurried to their own destruction. Therefore, they failed to recognize the clear signs of God's intervention on behalf of the Israelites.

The nations of the Canaanites on the east of Jordan had been conquered toward the close of the life of Moses, as we should remember. As already said, some portions were left unsubdued. The Ammonites, in the center of the country, with their formidable capital city, Rabbah, were not troubled at this time, nor were the Moabites, south of the Arnon and the Dead Sea, disinherited. And even someone from the Midianite settlements was allowed to stand.

Joshua 12 provides a comprehensive list of the kings who were vanquished in wars.

The content of Joshua's statement in Joshua 11:23 requires modification through a comparison with the listing provided in Joshua 13:1–6. In such instances, certain districts remained unconquered and resistant.

Joshua successfully had marched from one end of the country to the other and, for a time, prevented all resistance. However, there was still territory to be seized. The complete transference of possession was now rendered possible; it only remained for Israel to follow up the advantage gained, and all should be theirs. But there was much to be done. In the first place, the powerful association of the Philistines, in the southwest region, encompassing the Shephelah and the maritime plain, with their five cities, Ekron, Gaza, Ashdod, Ascalon, and Gath, remained unsubdued. The Geshurites were left unaffected. And other little kingdoms and their cities were left unconquered.

A significant portion of Western Palestine remained unconquered. No offensive had been launched. However, the path was cleared for full occupation, and circumstances were bound to provide opportunities for the expansion of the dominion of the Israelites. There was a prohibition given against the Canaanites about attacking the Israelites. Also, in these conquests, idolatry must be put down at any cost; no treaty or covenant or intermarriage was to be made with the Canaanites.

The clashes and wars arising from the adherence to such strict and offensive laws would force vigorous measures, which ultimately resulted in the gradual subjugation of the entire land. From this point on, the work of the combined forces of all Israel was over; it remained for each tribe to make a firm foothold in the territory that had been assigned to them. Even when Saul and David united the tribes, there was still division, and each tribe was on its own in some respect.

Daughters of Moab, Baal-Peor and Sexual Orgies

The daughters of Moab are a clear example of women being physically pure but spiritually unclean and demon possessed. These women were priestesses of Baal-Peor (Numbers 25). To be priestesses meant they were demon possessed, wore clothes like men in some instances, and were, for a time, virgins. Later, they simply became female prostitutes for Baal-Peor. The Baal, who was worshipped at Peor, was a Moabitish Priapus, whose temple was situated on Mount Peor. The phallic ritual was carried out to the most extreme. The worship of the penis was its focus. Both virgins and women prostituted themselves unto this god, but at least in the times of Hosea, the phallic rituals included male prostitutes. Baal-Peor is written in Hebrew as בַּעַל פְּעוֹר and Greek as Βεελφεγώρ. The very term, being a combination of Baal and the mountain Peor, especially in Greek means the "Lord of the Penis." Baal-Peor was worshipped in the image of the penis. The Greek form of Baal-Peor, Βεελφεγώρ, is derived partly, the last part, from the old Greek noun πέος (penis) and other old forms πέορ, and ποῖρ standing for παῖς in the Laconian dialect.

Philo spoke about this incident of the daughters of Moab as follows:

§ 295 φέρε δ' οὖν καὶ τὰς καλὰς αὐτοῦ παραινέσεις ἐξετάσωμεν, ὡς τετεχνιτευμέναι πρὸς ὁμολογουμένην ἧτταν τῶν ἀεὶ νικᾶν δυναμένων εἰδὼς γὰρ Ἑβραίοις μίαν ὁδὸν ἁλώσεως παρανομίαν, διὰ λαγνείας καὶ ἀκολασίας, μεγάλου κακοῦ, πρὸς μεῖζον κακόν, ἀσέβειαν, ἄγειν αὐτοὺς ἐσπούδασεν ἡδονὴν δέλεαρ προθείς § 296 "εἰσὶ" γὰρ εἶπεν "αἱ ἐγχώριοι γυναῖκες, ὦ βασιλεῦ, διαφέρουσαι τὴν ὄψιν ἑτέρων· ἀνὴρ δ' οὐδενὶ μᾶλλον εὐάλωτος ἢ γυναικὸς εὐμορφίᾳ ταῖς οὖν περικαλλεστάταις ἐὰν ἐπιτρέψῃς μισθαρνεῖν καὶ δημοσιεύειν, ἀγκιστρεύσονται τὴν νεότητα τῶν ἀντιπάλων § 297 ὑφηγητέον δὲ αὐταῖς, μὴ εὐθὺς ἐμπαρέχεσθαι τοῖς ἐθέλουσι τὴν ὥραν· ὁ γὰρ ἀκκισμὸς ὑποκνίζων τὰς ὁρμὰς ἐπεγείρει μᾶλλον καὶ τοὺς ἔρωτας ἀναφλέγει· τραχηλιζόμενοι δὲ ταῖς ἐπιθυμίαις πάνθ' ὑπομενοῦσι δρᾶν τε καὶ πάσχειν. § 298 πρὸς δὲ τὸν οὕτω

174

διακείμενον ἐραστὴν λεγέτω φρυαττομένη τις τῶν ἐπὶ τὴν θήραν ἀλειφομένων· "οὐ" θέμις ὁμιλίας σοι τῆς ἐμῆς ἀπολαῦσαι, πρὶν ἂν ἐκδιαιτηθῇς μὲν τὰ πάτρια, μεταβαλὼν δὲ τιμήσῃς ἅπερ ἐγώ. πίστις δέ μοι τῆς βεβαίου μεταβολῆς γένοιτ᾽ ἂν ἀρίδηλος, ἢν ἐθελήσῃς μετασχεῖν τῶν αὐτῶν σπονδῶν τε καὶ θυσιῶν, ἃς ἀγάλμασι καὶ ξοάνοις καὶ τοῖς λοιποῖς ἀφιδρύμασιν "ἐπιτελοῦμεν" § 299 ὁ δ᾽ ἅτε σαγηνευθεὶς πάγαις πολυειδέσι, κάλλει καὶ στωμυλίας χειραγωγίαις, οὐδὲν ἀντειπών, ἐξηγκωνισμένος τὸν λογισμόν, ἄθλιος ὑπηρετήσει τοῖς προσταττομένοι ἀναγραφεὶς τοῦ πάθους δοῦλος." § 300 ὁ μὲν δὴ τοιαῦτα συνεβούλευεν ὁ δ᾽ οὐκ ἀπὸ σκοποῦ νομίσας εἶναι τὰ λεχθέντα, τὸν κατὰ μοιχῶν νόμον παρακαλυψάμενος καὶ τοὺς ἐπὶ φθορᾷ καὶ πορνείᾳ κειμένους ἀνελών, ὡς εἰ μηδὲ τὴν ἀρχὴν ἐγράφησαν, ἀνέδην ἐπιτρέπει ταῖς γυναιξὶ τὰς ὁμιλίας πρὸς οὓς ἂν ἐθέλωσι ποιεῖσθαι. § 301 δοθείσης δὲ ἀδείας, τὴν πληθὺν τῶν μειρακίων ἐπήγοντο πολὺ πρότερον τὴν διάνοιαν αὐτῶν ἀπατῶσαι καὶ τρέπουσαι ταῖς γοητείαις πρὸς ἀσέβειαν, ἕως υἱὸς τοῦ ἀρχιερέως Φινεὲς ἐπὶ τοῖς γινομένοις σφόδρα χαλεπήνας δεινότατον γὰρ αὐτῷ κατεφαίνετο, εἰ ὑφ᾽ ἕνα καιρὸν ἄμφω τά τε σώματα καὶ τὰς ψυχὰς ἐπιδεδώκασι, τὰ μὲν ἡδοναῖς, τὰς δὲ τῷ παρανομεῖν καὶ ἀνοσιουργεῖν ἐνεανιεύσατο νεανίαν ἀνδρὶ καλῷ καὶ ἀγαθῷ προσήκουσαν § 302 ἰδὼν γάρ τινα τῶν ἀπὸ τοῦ γένους θύοντα καὶ εἰσιόντα πρὸς πόρνην, μήτε κεκυφότα εἰς τοὔδαφος μήτε λανθάνειν τοὺς πολλοὺς πειρώμενον μήθ᾽ οἷα φιλεῖ κλέπτοντα τὴν εἴσοδον, ἀλλὰ μετ᾽ ἀναισχύντου θράσους τὴν ἀκοσμίαν ἐπιδεικνύμενον καὶ φρυαττόμενον ὡς ἐπὶ σεμνῷ πράγματι τῷ καταγελάστῳ, πάνυ πικρανθεὶς καὶ πληρωθεὶς ὀργῆς δικαίας ἐπεισδραμὼν ἔτι κατ᾽ εὐνὴν κειμένους ἀμφοτέρους τόν τ᾽ ἐραστὴν καὶ τὴν ἑταίραν ἀναιρεῖ προσανατεμὼν καὶ τὰ γεννητικά, διότι σποραῖς ὑπηρέτησαν ἐκθέσμοις § 303 τοῦτο θεασάμενοί τινες τὸ παράδειγμα τῶν τὴν ἐγκράτειαν καὶ θεοσέβειαν ἐζηλωκότων προστάξαντος Μωυσέως ἐμιμήσαντο καὶ πάντας τοὺς τελεσθέντας τοῖς χειροποιήτοις συγγενεῖς καὶ φίλους ἡβηδὸν ἀνελόντες τὸ μὲν μίασμα τοῦ ἔθνους ἐκκαθαίρουσι διὰ τῆς τῶν προηδικηκότων ἀπαραιτήτου τιμωρίας, τοὺς δ᾽ ἄλλους παρασχόντας ἀπολογίαν ἐναργεστάτην ὑπὲρ τῆς αὐτῶν εὐσεβείας περιεποιήσαντο μηδένα τῶν ἀφ᾽ αἵματος κατακρίτων οἰκτισάμενοι μηδ᾽ ἐλέῳ τἀδικήματα αὐτῶν παρελθόντες, ἀλλὰ καθαροὺς νομίσαντες τοὺς αὐτόχειρας· ὅθεν οὐδενὶ παρεχώρησαν τὴν ἐπέξοδον φέρουσαν τοῖς δρῶσιν ἀψευδέστατον ἔπαινον § 304 τετρακισχιλίους δέ φασι πρὸς τοῖς δισμυρίοις ἀναιρεθῆναι μιᾷ ἡμέρᾳ, συναναιρεθέντος εὐθὺς τοῦ κοινοῦ μιάσματος, ὃ πᾶσαν τὴν στρατιὰν ἐκηλίδου τῶν δὲ καθαρσίων ἐπιτελεσθέντων ὡς ἀριστεῖ γέρας ἐπάξιον τῷ υἱῷ τοῦ ἀρχιερέως, ὃς πρῶτος ἐπὶ τὴν ἄμυναν ὥρμησεν, ἐζήτει παρασχεῖν Μωυσῆς· φθάνει δὲ χρησμοῖς δωρησάμενος ὁ θεὸς Φινεεῖ τὸ μέγιστον ἀγαθόν, εἰρήνην, ὃ μηδεὶς ἱκανὸς ἀνθρώπων παρασχεῖν, πρὸς δὲ τῇ εἰρήνῃ καὶ παγκρατησίαν ἱερωσύνης, αὐτῷ καὶ γένει κλῆρον ἀναφαίρετον § 305 ἐπεὶ δὲ τῶν ἐμφυλίων οὐδὲν ἔτ' ἦν ὑπόλοιπον κακῶν, ἀλλὰ καὶ ὅσοι πρὸς αὐτομολίαν ἢ προδοσίαν ὑπωπτεύοντο πάντες ἀπωλώλεσαν, ἔδοξεν εἶναι καιρὸς ἐπιτηδειότατος τῆς ἐπὶ τὸν Βαλάκην στρατείας, ἄνδρα μυρία καὶ βεβουλευμένον ἐργάσασθαι κακὰ καὶ δεδρακότα, βεβουλευμένον μὲν διὰ τοῦ μάντεως, ὃν ἤλπισεν ἀραῖς τισι δυνήσεσθαι καθελεῖν τὴν δύναμιν τῶν Ἑβραίων, δεδρακότα δὲ διὰ τῆς τῶν γυναικῶν ἀσελγείας καὶ ἀκολασίας, αἳ τὰ μὲν σώματα λαγνείαις τὰς δὲ ψυχὰς ἀσεβείᾳ τῶν χρωμένων διέφθειραν (Anyway, come, therefore, let us also examine strictly into his excellent suggestions, as they use cunning ways for the most sure and certain defeat of our always triumphant enemies. For knowing that the only way of conquest against the Hebrews was lawlessness, Balaam purposed in his mind and hastened using sexual pleasure as a bait—means of enticement—to lead them on by means of fornication—unrestrained lust—and intemperance, that great evil in themselves, to the still greater crime of ungodliness. § For he said, "O king, the women among the inhabitants surpass the beauty of all others, both men and women, and there is no other thing by which a man is more easily subdued than by the beauty of a woman; therefore, if you permit the very beautiful women to serve and be public prostitutes for a price unto men, they will ensnare and overcome on their hooks as fishes the youth of your enemies." § But you must give guidance unto them not to surrender their beauty immediately unto those men who lust after them; for prudishness tickles a little and excites the passions more active and arouses more sexual practices of love; and so, when they are wholly overpowered by their unrestrained sexual lusts, they will submit to do and to experience anything. § Now, let any unrestrained woman say unto any affected sexual lover among other Hebrew men stimulated in such a manner for the snare, "It is not lawful for you to enjoy the benefits of sexual intercourse with me unless you can change your traditional observances—ancestral habits, and change your heart, and hold in honor the observances of the same practices which indeed I do. And the proof of a change which is real would be manifested to me, only if you could desire lustfully to participate with me in both the same liberations and sacrifices which we do at the idols and statues, and other erections—temples—in honor of our gods." § And just as the sexual lover was taken into the dragnet of her manifold and multiform snares, he could not resist the pressure of her beauty and small seductive conversion, being bound and wholly subdued in his sound judgment, and being a miserable man, he will serve the commands which she laid upon him and be registered as the slave of passion. § Now indeed, were such suggestions which Balaam gave unto Balak. And the king considered that what things were spoken to him were not unreasonable, repealed the law against adulterers, and took away all penalties which have been established against seduction and fornication and as if they had never been written at the beginning, permitted without any restraint women to have sexual intercourse with any men whom they would please. § Consequently, when liberty was given, the women brought forward a multitude of young Hebrew men—long beforehand the women deceived—and by trickeries and allurements, under the power of witchcraft, they perverted them toward impiety; until Phinehas, the son of the chief priest, being above measure embittered at such deeds which were taking place (for it seemed unto him that both their bodies and souls were willingly being surrendered unto the most disgraceful things—on the one hand, by sexual and unrestrained lusts, and on the other hand, by transgressing the law and committing works of wickedness), undertook with youthful boldness, such an action that was befitting unto a good and moral man. § For when he saw a particular man of his race participating in sacrificing—belonging to the priestly order—and afterward entering unto the tent of a prostitute, not hanging his head downward unto the ground in shame, nor attempting to hide these practices from the notice of the multitude, nor concealing in secrecy the way entering into such practices that he longed to do, but instead showing his disorderly behavior (wrought by idolatry and sexual sin) with shameless impudence and making himself proud as if he were participating in a respectable feat, which only deserves laughter and ridicule—Phinehas, I say, altogether was embittered and was filled with righteous anger, rushed and busted into the tent, and as both the sexual lover and the prostitute were still lying on the bed, he slaughtered them, cut them into two pieces and additionally cut off his sexual organs, since they satisfied his unlawful lusts—the unlawful sowings of his seeds. § When some persons among the Hebrew men who strove after the self-control—the inner power to control their desires and cravings, especially sexual—and the godliness—both internal and outward morality, saw this example, by the command of Moses, they imitated it, and slaughtered from the youth upward all their own family relatives and friends who performed sacrifices unto idols that were made with hands, and they cleaned off the stain which was the defilement of the nation by this unmerciful punishment against wrongdoers. And they spared the rest who gave a clear defense of themselves and preserved their own piety. They showed pity on none of the others from their blood who were condemned unto death, nor condoned their crimes in pity, but held that their slayers were free from any guilt. Consequently, they did not allow for anyone to escape the punishment whosoever who sinned in this way, which type of thinking is the most truthful praise. § And they say that twenty-four thousand men were slaughtered in one day, the common pollution that was destroyed altogether with them at the same moment, which defiled

178

the whole army. But when the purification was accomplished, Moses sought that he would offer an honor deserving to the son of the chief priest in excellence who was first that rushed to pay vengeance against the wrongdoers. But God preceded him, having given unto Phinehas, by His oracles, the greatest good, specifically peace, which no suitable one among men can well give; and, in addition unto this peace, he gave unto him the perpetual possession of the priesthood, and an inheritance unto his family, which could not be taken away. § 305 Since now, when none of the public evils was remaining any longer, but also as many of the men who were suspected either by desertion of the faith or by treachery had perished, it seemed to be a most advantageous time for an expedition against Balak—a man who deliberated to do, and also implemented innumerable evil deeds, since he had planned them through the agency of the prophet, who expected to be able, by means of curses, to pull down by force the power of the Hebrews, and who accomplished his purpose by means of the unrestrained lust and self-gratification of the women, who destroyed the bodies of those men who made use of them for sexual intercourse, and their souls for impiety).[28]

The Pseudo-Targum Jonathan reads Numbers 25:1 as וִיתֵיב יִשְׂרָאֵל בְּאַתְרָא דַהֲוָה מִתְקְרֵי שִׁיטִין עַל שְׁטוּתָא וְקִלְקוּלָא דַהֲוָה בְּהוֹן וּשְׁרִיאוּ עַמָּא לְאוֹפָסָא קְדוּשַׁתְהוֹן וּלְמִפְעַר נַרְמֵיהוֹן לְטוֹפְסָא דִפְעוֹר וּלְמַטְעִית בָּתַר בְּנָת מוֹאֲבָאֵי דְמַפְּקָן יַת טוֹפְסֵיהּ דִפְעוֹר מִתּוֹתֵי פְּסִקְנֵיהוֹן (And Israel settled in the land, which is itself called Shittim, in consequence of the stupidity and reprobate state which were among them. And the people extremely began to defile their holiness, and to uncover their bodies to the form of Peor, and to seduce themselves after the daughters of the Moabites, who brought out the form of Peor from under their girdles). The "form of Peor" was that of the Penis.

Tertullian wrote about this incident, In Arithmis cum diuertisset Israel apud Sethim, abeunt libidinatum ad filias Moab, inuitantur ad idola, ut et spiritu fornicarentur, edunt denique de pollutis eorum, dehinc et adorant deos gentis et Beelphegor initiantur (In Numbers,

179

when Israel would have turned aside at Sethim, the Israelites went unto the daughters of Moab to indulge in their own lusts; they were enticed unto the idols, so that they also committed sexual fornication with the spirit; lastly, they ate of their polluted sacrifices—dead bodies, then they both venerated the gods of the nation and were initiated into the rites of Baal-Peor).[29]

In reference to the attendants of Baal-Peor, Hosea speaks of female prostitutes—the priestesses of Baal-Peor—and male prostitutes who were the initiates of the Baal-Peor (Hosea 4:12–14), especially how the Hellenistic Jews interpreted it. Cyril of Alexandria in his commentaries on Hosea and following the Greek Septuagint version of Hosea, writes, Πόρνας δέ φησιν ἰδικῶς τὰς τοῦ Βεελφεγὼρ ἱερείας. Βεελφεγὼρ δέ ἐστιν, ὁ καλούμενος Πρίαπος. αἱ δὲ τὸ οὕτως αἰσχρὸν τιμῶσαι βδέλυγμα, πόρναι λοιπὸν ὁμολογουμένως. τετελεσμένους δὲ ὀνομάζει πάλιν τοὺς ἱερομύστας τοῦ Βεελφεγὼρ, ἄνδρες δὲ ἦσαν εἶναι μὲν οὐκ ἀνεχόμενοι τοῦθ’ ὅπερ εἰσὶ, μεταφοιτῶντες δὲ μᾶλλον εἰς φρόνημα τὸ θηλυπρεπὲς, λόγοις τε καὶ τρόποις ἀνοσίως μαλακιζόμενοι. θηλυδρίας δὲ καὶ μαλθάκωνας τοὺς τοιούτους ἀποκαλοῦσί τινες, οἳ γυναικείαις ὀλολυγαῖς καὶ κυμβάλοις χρώμενοι, περιθέοντες τε τινὰς δαδίσιν ὁμοῦ, μυσταγωγεῖν ὑπεκρίνοντο, τῆς τοῦ Βεελφεγὼρ αἰσχύνης πληροῦντες τὰ παίγνια. ἔθυον τοίνυν φησὶ μετὰ τῶν τετελεσμένων, τουτέστι, μεμύηνται τὰ ἐκείνων, καὶ ὁμοῦ τοῖς οὕτω κατεφθαρμένοις προσῆγον θυσίας τῷ Βεελφεγὼρ (Now, in reference to prostitutes, He speaks explicitly about the priestesses of Baal-Peor, and Baal-Peor also being named Priapos. But after another manner, the remaining of the women who honored such a horrible abomination were undeniably only prostitutes. By Initiates, who are male prostitutes, he terms again those who are initiated into the religious mysteries and rites of Baal-Peor; though males, they were unable to accept what they were, but instead passed from males unto womanly thinking, and became effeminate, like women, both with unholy words and behaviors. Consequently, some people also call such ones both men-women and soft; these men-women make use of the loud crying and cymbals of women, run around with some feast-torches together and pretend to guide others into the religious mysteries, performing in purpose the playthings of shamefulness for Baal-Peor. Then, He says, *They were sacrificing with Initiates, which are male prostitutes*, that is, they were initiated into their religious mysteries and rites, and so together with those corrupted men-women, they were offering sacrifices unto Baal-Peor).[30]

The true intention of the Baalim, as witnessed by the term Baal-Peor, is the exaltation of the penis and the exaltation of all forms of sexual sin, especially that of heterosexual and homosexual sin. The focus is more on heterosexual sin. However, under the worship of Baal-Peor, male prostitutes were included.

Phallic worship was a common feature in paganism. The worship of Baal-Peor is but one example, and such worship was accompanied by sexual excesses and perversions, during which the wearing of attire belonging to the opposite sex was sometimes part of the ritual. The Israelites were warned against phallic worship and forbidden to make "a graven image, the similitude of any figure, the likeness of male or female" or to "rear up a standing image" or to go a whoring after the gods of others, and the donning of clothes of the opposite sex was clearly forbidden (Exodus 34:15; Leviticus 26:1–5; Deuteronomy 4:16, 22:5; Judges 2:17).

At an annual festival in honor of Baal-Peor, young women gave up their virginity to the first comer. At this festival, the Midianites invited the Hebrew men. There was more than one Hebrew man and one Midianitish woman involved. But Numbers 25 gives one case of it and what happened. It is said that a Midianitish woman committed fornication with a Hebrew. She did that to honor Baal-Peor, and she was a virgin. In the view of the Mosaic Law, fornication was an act of idolatry, a private transgression of the law of chastity, and an act contrary to the fundamental law of the Hebrew state. Such an act by a Midianitish woman was the sacrifice of her virginity for the sake of Baal-Peor. She was demon possessed and a reprobate despite virginity. She was a priestess of Baal-Peor. Her acts of sexual immorality were tied directly to that god.

The spirits of lust and licentiousness seized, oppressed, and even possessed almost the entire group of Hebrew men. These spirits were so destructive that the ancestral institutions were in danger of being abandoned altogether. The Hebrew men were led astray by the daughters of the Moabites, and both practiced fornication with them and made sacrifice in their temples to the god of the country, whose priestesses, as Balaam declared, were noticeable above other women for their beauty. God's judgment was immediate and twenty-four thousand were killed (Numbers 25:5). In 1 Corinthians 10:8, Paul gives the number that fell as twenty-three thousand. One thousand of the chief men of Israel were included in the twenty-four thousand count of Numbers 25:9 and excluded from the twenty-three thousand mentioned in 1 Corinthians 10:8. Twenty-three thousand fell in one day; twenty-four thousand were slain altogether. Only twenty-three thousand perished from pestilence. Moses includes in his record those who were executed by the judges.

The plague of Numbers 25 was a judgment of God upon the young Hebrew men who took part in the worship of Baal-Peor (Joshua 22:17; Psalm 106:28–30; Hosea 9:10). It was a venereal disease wrought by their sexual intercourse with the Moabitish women. The disease affected the genital organs, and the ulceration of the genitals during this time caused many fatalities. It was an acute form of the most terrible disease known to medical science– Syphilis. The command of Moses to slay the "worshippers" was not merely a sad and terrible necessity; it was a mercy to the victims.

This acute form of Syphilis was widely propagated by the Moabitish women. It was very infectious, and death could occur fast, especially among men. While it was transmitted from sexual contact, it was also transmitted from women to their children. Children being affected by this type of Syphilis could well die before birth, at the point of birth, die soon after birth, or simply suffer various health issues from this disease. Therefore, despite their virginity and lack of sexual intercourse prior to corrupting the young Hebrew men, the Moabite daughters, infected with syphilis by their mothers, passed it on to the young Hebrew men.

Miscarriages, stillbirth, prematurity, enlarged liver and spleen, deformed bones, anemia, low birth weight, and death immediately after birth are some consequences of the children who were infected with Syphilis through their mothers.

Idolatrous worship was commonly accompanied by sexual immorality, especially that of unlawful and unnatural sexual practices. In such cases, both men and women sunk to the level of beasts and still worse, even below that. The penalty of sin is sin itself, with all its unavoidable consequences. Few truly want to suffer the consequences. Or they want to practice sin, hopefully without suffering the dire consequences of this practice. Still, the consequences do come as sure as the rain comes.

The women who corrupted the young Hebrew men were executed later, along with Moabite men (Numbers 31:15–18). The Jews had slain many thousands of Moabite men in their previous wars.

The Moabitish women were not as old as many think. Commonly, women who offered up their virginity unto the gods or the goddesses by giving themselves up to sexual intercourse with men and by becoming prostitutes were so young that they had not had their first menstruation. For example, Strabo also wrote, δὲ Διὶ ὃν μάλιστα τιμῶσιν, εὐειδεστάτη καὶ γένους λαμπροτάτου παρθένος ἱερᾶται, ἃς καλοῦσιν οἱ Ἕλληνες παλλάδας· αὕτη δὲ καὶ παλλακεύει καὶ σύνεστιν οἷς βούλεται μέχρι ἂν ἡ φυσικὴ γένηται κάθαρσις τοῦ σώματος· μετὰ δὲ τὴν κάθαρσιν δίδοται πρὸς ἄνδρα (And unto Zeus, whom they honor above all, a virgin, most beautiful and of highest ancestry, is a venerated as a priestess, and these priestesses the Greeks call Pallades. And she also acts as a concubine and has sexual intercourse with whom she wills until the natural purification—menstruation—of the body can begin first time. And after the natural purification had begun, she is given in marriage to a man).[31]

It was known that among some Asiatic nations, every woman before her marriage was required to uncover herself in the temple of a certain deity, and even publicly. Later, she was forced to give up her virginity to the first person who asked her to have sexual intercourse for the benefit of the temple. The Phoenicians also made a gift of the prostitution of their daughters before they married them to a husband. And the Babylonians had a custom where women prostituted themselves at the Temple of Venus.

Functions/Works/Forms of the Baalim

1. The Baalim are spirits that can be used as familiar spirits.

2. They work in sexuality and are demons of sexuality, especially heterosexuality and sometimes homosexuality.

3. As already said, they are both sexes. They can appear as men and women or as male and female.

4. They blend the genders of men and women less than the Astartes.

5. They are cesspools.

6. They work in fertility, especially in the rites and rituals of fertility.

7. They are gods of rain and water and storms.

8. They bless in prosperity.

9. They bless in health.

10. They war against righteousness, the saints, and above all God.

11. They make a nation forget God.

12. They try to banish God in society.

13. They seek after the children to destroy them.

14. They promote child sacrifice.

15. They promote abortions.

16. They can cause schizophrenia.

17. They cause apostasy.

18. They try to deify the objects of a culture.

19. They work to try to change perception.

20. They work to overturn the truth.

21. They try to make the truth a lie and the lie to be the truth.

22. They try to merge both man and animal as one being.

23. They try to change humans' genetic code.

24. They try to make a culture increasingly driven, restless, conflicted, obsessed, and addicted.

25. They push God away more so that they can be more consequential.

26. They blur reality.

27. They blur the line between man and machine.

28. They can appear in any form or any form of a human.

29. A necromancer works with these spirits when they are used as familiar spirits.

30. They are religious spirits, backwardness, monitoring spirits from hell, divination and un-seriousness.

31. They work to make people forget revelations and dreams given by the Lord in order to expose the enemy.

32. They can imitate the dead.

33. They can possess their victims.

34. They can oppress their victims.

35. They work in divination, necromancy, and false or counterfeit religions.

36. They try to deceive us when studying the Word of God.

37. They operate through our thoughts or try to control our thoughts.

38. They affect everyone and are manifested in and through people.

39. They can preach things contrary to the Word.

40. They can deny the existence of other spirits.

41. They can operate through our thoughts.

42. They work in the secular world.

43. They work against our spirit.

44. They like a spiritual atmosphere since they function best there.

45. They can serve people.

46. They belittle and hate Jesus, the work of the cross, the blood, and the word, besides all the saints.

47. They whisper in our ears.

48. They try to stop people from studying and reading the Word of God. They also try to stop the prayer life of the people.

49. They give thoughts to men and women.

50. They work with shamans.

51. They attack the plan of God in our lives.

52. They are used to keep us out of the position God intended for us.

53. They secretly come against what God is revealing to His church.

54. They work in deception.

55. They have numerous manifestations associated with them: physical, mental, emotional, and spiritual.

56. They are one of the strong men.

57. They condemn Christians by having them accept the false manifestations as coming from the Holy Spirit.

58. They bless those who serve them with blessings in various ways.

59. They attack those whom they do not control.

60. They can inflict pain, sickness, and disease.

61. They are conquerable through the name of Jesus and His blood.

62. They work by drugs and cause their victims to be bound to them.

63. They work to plague people with mental, emotional, physical, and spiritual disorders.

64. They work in counterfeit gifts, including tongues, prophecy, and healing.

65. They work to destroy all things in a person's life.

66. They are sexual spirits; they have sex with those whom they possess, whether by consent or by force.

67. They promote sexual immorality.

The Cult of the Astartes (Diana or Venus)

In the cult of the goddess, whatever the names given, morality is threatened more than in the cult of the Baalim. All morality is destroyed, and the idea of moral restraint is stopped. The blending of the genders is incredibly stressed; changing men into women is essential. The reversal of creation itself is attempted.

The cult of the goddess introduced men to a more significant form of femininity; the females they had in their arms could not equal or even bypass the image of the goddess. Therefore, this cult pushed men to an image of a female that cannot be had. The perfection of the goddess is an illusion that men have swallowed for years. That perfection has destroyed numerous men, cultures, and nations. Behind the use and creation of pornography is this cult and the various goddesses. Men run after the image of the goddess that can never be obtained by marrying or running after women. The cult promotes a perversion of creation and the relationship between men and women.

The Astartes predate the Nephilim that lived during the Canaan invasion by the Hebrews. They even predated Nephilim before the flood.

An ancient Greek poem reads, Οὐρανίη, πολύυμνε, φιλομμειδὴς Ἀφροδίτη, ποντογενής, γενέτειρα θεά, φιλοπάννυχε, σεμνή, νυκτερία ζεύκτειρα, δολοπλόκε μῆτερ Ἀνάγκης· πάντα γὰρ ἐκ σέθεν ἐστίν, ὑπεζεύξω δέ <τε> κόσμον καὶ κρατέεις τρισσῶν μοιρῶν, γεννᾶις δὲ τὰ πάντα, ὅσσα τ' ἐν οὐρανῶι ἐστι καὶ ἐν γαίηι πολυκάρπωι ἐν πόντου τε βυθῶι {τε}, σεμνὴ Βάκχοιο πάρεδρε, τερπομένη θαλίαισι, γαμοστόλε μῆτερ Ἐρώτων (Heavenly, abounding in many songs, smiling Aphrodite, sea-born, revered Mother Goddess of generation—parent of all—, a friend of the night long festivals. You couple lovers at night, O Cunning Mother of Necessity; for all things come from you, you have subjugated (yoked) the world. And you rule over all three realms; you give birth to all things in heaven, the fruitful earth, and the depth of the ocean. You are enthroned with Bacchus in great respect. You delight in festivities, O Harbinger of marriage, Mother of the Erotes—sexual lovers).[32] Homer wrote also about Aphrodite, κυπρογενῆ Κυθέρειαν ἀείσομαι, ἥτε βροτοῖσι μείλιχα δῶρα δίδωσιν, ἐφ' ἱμερτῷ δὲ προσώπῳ αἰεὶ μειδιάει καὶ ἐφ' ἱμερτὸν θέει ἄνθος (Cyprus-born Cytherea, I will sing a song forever. She gives sweet gifts unto mortals and there is always a smile on her lovely form, and she is looked upon as a lovely blossom of love).[33] The Trojan women used to go to the river Scamander, bathe in it, and then forsake their virginity for the sake of the goddess, which represented the river Scamander to men.

Further, there was a lustful worship of Venus among the Babylonians. Babylonians had a religion that was divorced from morals and had free love and marriage.

Various classes of prostitutes lived within the temple precincts, plied their trade there, and amassed, some of them, great fortunes. Such temple prostitutes were common in Western Asia; we find them in Israel, Phrygia, Phoenicia, Syria, and other places; in Lidia and Cyprus, the girls earned their marriage dowries in this way.

Cultic prostitution continued in Babylonia until it was abolished by Constantine (AD 325).

Making men become like women for sexual purposes could well be tolerated by the pagan societies, and pagans concluded that the changing from men to men-women was the doing of their goddess.

It was known that among some Asiatic nations, every woman was required to uncover herself in the temple of a specific deity and even publicly before her marriage. Later, she was forced to give up her virginity to the first person who asked her to have sexual intercourse for the benefit of the temple. The Phoenicians also made a gift of the prostitution of their daughters before they married them to a husband. And the Babylonians had a custom where women prostituted themselves at the Temple of Venus.

In Babylon, the cult of Venus originated as Mylitta worship, spread over the inland parts to Mesopotamia as the Sabaean religion, and was passed on by the Phoenicians to the seaboard peoples as Astarte worship.

So the woman was to offer herself as a gift at the holy place so that Aphrodite would be glorified in her and participate in the highest happiness of a woman, the joys of motherhood. The woman entered the temple and followed the priest to her lover's arms. In the temple, her lover drew his darling to the sacred couch bedecked with fragrant blossoms, and she was deflowered. And the defloration was unto the goddess.

There were the female Hieroduli who, as prostitutes of Aphrodite, resided in the vicinity of her temple and performed the necessary rituals in her honor. At Corinth, there were more than a thousand female Hieroduli who were presented as slaves and prostitutes to the temple. A significant number of strangers went to the temple. And the prostitutes were used in trying to seduce all the visitors of Corinth, especially all those who were sea-faring visitors.

Strabo wrote, τό τε τῆς Ἀφροδίτης ἱερὸν οὕτω πλούσιον ὑπῆρξεν ὥστε πλείους ἢ χιλίας ἱεροδούλους ἐκέκτητο ἑταίρας, ἃς ἀνετίθεσαν τῇ θεῷ καὶ ἄνδρες καὶ γυναῖκες. καὶ διὰ ταύτας οὖν πολυωχλεῖτο ἡ πόλις καὶ ἐπλουτίζετο (And the temple of Aphrodite was so wealthy that it possessed more than a thousand Hetaerae, prostitutes–temple servants, committed to its service as Hieroduli, whom both men and women were dedicated to the goddess. And so consequently, the city was visited by multitudes and grew wealthy).[34] The term Hieroduli represents the prostitutes of the temple; the Hetaerae were Lady-Companions and were handmaids of Aphrodite. The Hetaerae were for the goddess. The Hieroduli were for the men.

Herodotus wrote, Καὶ τὸ μὴ μίσγεσθαι γυναιξὶ ἐν ἱροῖσι μηδὲ ἀλούτους ἀπὸ γυναικῶν ἐς ἱρὰ ἐσιέναι οὗτοι εἰσὶ οἱ πρῶτοι θρησκεύσαντες. οἱ μὲν γὰρ ἄλλοι σχεδὸν πάντες ἄνθρωποι, πλὴν Αἰγυπτίων καὶ Ἑλλήνων, μίσγονται ἐν ἱροῖσι (And the practice of not having sexual intercourse with women in temples, and not entering into holy places unwashed after having sexual intercourse with women, these practices were the first to be observed religiously; for almost all other men, except Egyptians and Greeks, have sexual intercourse in the temples).[35] Clement of Alexandria wrote, Αἰγύπτιοι γοῦν πρῶτοι ἀστρολογίαν εἰς ἀνθρώπους ἐξήνεγκαν, ὁμοίως δὲ καὶ Χαλδαῖοι. Αἰγύπτιοι λύχνους τε αὖ καίειν πρῶτοι κατέδειξαν καὶ τὸν ἐνιαυτὸν εἰς δώδεκα μῆνας διεῖλον καὶ ἐν ἱεροῖς μίσγεσθαι γυναιξὶν ἐκώλυσαν μηδ᾽ εἰς ἱερὰ εἰσιέναι ἀπὸ γυναικὸς ἀλούτους (Hence, the Egyptians together with the Chaldeans were the first to produce astrology for humankind. The Egyptians were also the first to discover how to light lamps, divide up the year into twelve months, prohibit sexual intercourse with women in holy places, and not allow entry into temples unwashed after having sexual intercourse with a woman).[36] Quintus Curtius Rufus wrote about the city of Babylon, Nihil urbis eius corruptius moribus, nihil ad inritandas inliciendasque inmodicas cupiditates instructius. Liberos coniugesque cum hospitibus stupro coire, modo pretium flagitii detur, parentes maritique patiuntur (Nothing can well be more corrupt than the customs of this city, nothing more cleverly modified to excite the lustful desires and give enticement to voluptuous excesses. Parents and husbands suffer for their children and their wives to have sexual intercourse with strangers, provided the price of shame is forthcoming).[37] Strabo wrote, ἀλλὰ καὶ θυγατέρας οἱ ἐπιφανέστατοι τοῦ ἔθνους ἀνιεροῦσι παρθένους, αἷς νόμος ἐστὶ καταπορνευθείσαις πολὺν χρόνον παρὰ τῇ θεῷ μετὰ ταῦτα δίδοσθαι πρὸς γάμον (Moreover, the highest men of the nation consecrate their virgin daughters as sacrifices, and it is the law for these women, after committing these practices of prostitution for a longtime to the goddess, to be given in marriage).[38] Athenagoras also wrote, Γυναῖκες γοῦν ἐν εἰδωλείοις τῆς Φοινίκιας πάλαι προκαθέζοντο ἀπαρχομεναι τοῖς ἐκεῖ θεοῖς ἑαυτῶν τὴν τοῦ σώματος αὐτῶν μισθαρνίαν, νομίζουσαι τῇ πορνεια τὴν θεὸν ἑαυτῶν ἱλάσκεσθαι (Consequently, women used of old to sit as prostitutes in the idolatrous temples of the Phoenicians, offering from there as first fruits to the gods the leasing of the prostitution of their own bodies, thinking that by fornication their own goddess was to be appeased).[39] Marcus Junianus Justinus Frontinus wrote, Mos erat Cypriis virgines ante nuptias statutis diebus dotalem pecuniam quaesituras in quaestum ad litus maris mittere, pro reliqua pudicitia libamenta Veneri soluturas (It was a custom among the Cyprians to send their virgins before their marriage on established days to the shore of the sea, there to sit for leasing themselves as prostitutes and so earn money for their dowry; for the rest of their purity—what remained of their purity— was going to be rendered as sacrifices to the goddess Venus).[40]

Also, Herodotus said as follows:

199. Ὁ δὲ δὴ αἴσχιστος τῶν νόμων ἐστὶ τοῖσι Βαβυλωνίοισι ὅδε· δεῖ πᾶσαν ηυναῖκα ἐπιχωρίην ἱζομένην ἐς ἱρὸν Ἀφροδίτης ἅπαξ ἐν τῇ ζόῃ μιχθῆναι ἀνδρὶ ξείνῳ. πολλαὶ δὲ καὶ οὐκ ἀξιεύμεναι ἀναμίσγεσθαι τῇσι ἄλλῃσι, οἷα πλούτῳ ὑπερφρονέουσαι, ἐπὶ ζευγέων ἐν καμάρῃσι ἐλάσασαι πρὸς τὸ ἱρὸν ἑστᾶσι· θεραπηίη δέ σφι ὄπισθε ἕπεται πολλή. αἱ δὲ πλεῦνες ποιεῦσι ὧδε· ἐν τεμένεϊ Ἀφροδίτης κατέαται στέφανον περὶ τῇσι κεφαλῇσι ἔχουσαι θώμιγγος πολλαὶ γυναῖκες· αἱ μὲν γὰρ προσέρχονται, αἱ δὲ ἀπέρχονται. σχοινοτενέες δὲ διέξοδοι πάντα τρόπον ὁδῶν ἔχουσι διὰ τῶν γυναικῶν, δι᾽ ὧν οἱ ξεῖνοι διεξιόντες ἐκλέγονται· ἔνθα ἐπεὰν ἵζηται γυνή, οὐ πρότερον ἀπαλλάσσεται ἐς τὰ οἰκία ἤ τίς οἱ ξείνων ἀργύριον ἐμβαλὼν ἐς τὰ γούνατα μιχθῇ ἔξω τοῦ ἱροῦ· ἐμβαλόντα δὲ δεῖ εἰπεῖν τοσόνδε· "Ἐπικαλέω τοι τὴν θεὸν Μύλιττα." Μύλιττα δὲ

καλέουσι τὴν Ἀφροδίτην Ἀσσύριοι. τὸ δὲ ἀργύριον μέγαθος ἐστὶ ὅσου ὦν· οὐ γὰρ μὴ ἀπώσηται· οὐ γάρ οἱ ἐστί. γίνεται γὰρ ἱρὸν τοῦτο τὸ ἀργύριον. τῷ δὲ πρώτῳ ἐμβαλόντι ἕπεται οὐδὲ ἀποδοκιμᾷ οὐδένα. ἐπεὰν δὲ μιχθῇ ἀποσιωσαμένη τῇ θεῷ ἀπαλλάσσεται ἐς τὰ οἰκία, καὶ τὠπὸ τούτου οὐκ οὕτω μέγα τί οἱ δώσεις ὥς μιν λάμψεαι. ὅσαι νυν εἴδεός τε ἐπαμμέναι εἰσὶ καὶ μεγάθεος, ταχὺ ἀπαλλάσσονται, ὅσαι δὲ ἄμορφοι αὐτέων εἰσί, χρόνον πολλὸν προσμένουσι οὐ δυνάμεναι τὸν νόμον ἐκπλῆσαι· καὶ γὰρ τριέτεα καὶ τετραέτεα μετεξέτεραι χρόνον μένουσι. ἐνιαχῇ δὲ καὶ τῆς Κύπρου ἐστὶ παραπλήσιος τούτῳ νόμος (Now, indeed, the obscenest of customs by the Babylonians is this: every woman of the country must once in her life be made to sit down in the temple of Aphrodite and have sexual intercourse with some foreign—strange man. Also, many women such being wealthy, proudful, and still not condescending to associate with the rest—other women, drive to the temple in enclosed carriages drawn by teams of animals—horses, and they stood there a great number of servants following them. But the greater number of women were made here to sit down in the shrine of Aphrodite, with crowns of a cord on their heads; for there is a great number of women that were coming and going away. The routes were kept by a straight line running every way and in every manner through the women, by which the foreign—strange men pass and chose. When a woman has formerly been made to sit down in her place, she does not escape (go back) to her house before some strange men have thrown down money into her lap and had sexual intercourse with her outside the temple; but when they have thrown down the money, they must say, "I call upon you in the name of the goddess Mylitta" (that is the Assyrians call Aphrodite by Mylitta). The amount of money does not matter whatever; the woman will never refuse, for that was to be seen as a sin; for the money became by this act holy. Therefore, she follows the first man who throws it down and rejects none. After she had sexual intercourse, she became purified in the sight of the goddess and departed to her home. And from this, there are no gifts however great that will acquire her. So then the women of fair and tall form are quickly to depart, but the unsuitable ones of them have a long time to wait because they are unable to fulfill the law; and for some of them stay there for three or four years. There is a custom coming near to this in some areas belonging to Cyprus).[41]

Prior to this statement of history, Herodotus wrote about what happened to the Babylonian women after the Persians captured Babylon, ἐπείτε γὰρ ἁλόντες ἐκακώθησαν καὶ οἰκοφθορήθησαν, πᾶς τις τοῦ δήμου βίου σπανίζων καταπορνεύει τὰ θήλεα τέκνα (for since they were conquered, they were afflicted and poverty-stricken, every single one of the people that wanted a livelihood prostitutes his female children).[42] The poorer classes, dreading the forcible abduction of their daughters for the sake of Aphrodite, turned their female children into harbor prostitutes. Those types of prostitutes were some of the poorest and lowest types of prostitutes.

Herodotus' use of Greek is noteworthy here. The last Greek phrase καταπορνεύει τὰ θήλεα τέκνα should be interpreted and defined as "prostitute down their female children." The idea is for the female children to become prostitutes and sit down at a house of ill-fame, brothel. The brothels and the prostitutes generally lay near the harbor.

The sum of money offered to the women became bribes and indulgences for sexuality. The brides and indulgences became fornication fees, and the temples became brothels. Besides the regular brothels, women were also kept at taverns.

For instance, the priestesses of Astartes stood calling all strangers to come and enjoy the prostitution. And all strangers and visitors were required to pay fees. It was almost impossible to be in a pagan city where these prostitutes of the goddess were and not see them. They made a point to be seen. For example, prostitutes lived in brothels and taverns. They stood at the doors with no clothes on, in almost transparent dresses or fine-woven robes, which were practically transparent robes, very tight. Still, other prostitutes did their prostitution at the marketplace of the harbor or in that neighborhood. For the sake of the goddess, many surrendered themselves wherever they were and did not go to any type of house or brothel.

Further, the women of Byblus were bound in honor of Venus for one whole day so that they would abandon their bodies to strangers. This was also true among the Carthaginians.[43]

As seen, prostitution, brothels, and pedophilia with various types of perversions are tied to the Astartes and the ancient cult of the goddess. Besides this, the first fruits of everything were to be offered up and consecrated to the gods and the goddesses. The virginity of the young girls was offered up to the goddesses. Bluntly, the virgin gave up her virginity to the goddess, sometimes unto a god, not to the stranger. He was just a means to fulfill it. In some customs, the stranger did not choose the woman. It was the woman who chose her stranger.[44]

The virgin followed a ceremony and an act of self-surrender. One was for religion, but the other was the sexual act itself that was deflowered here. Both the hymen and the blood of a virgin were offered to the goddess. The defloration of a woman was given to the goddess.

In such pagan customs, the defloration of a virgin was not the proper function of the bridegroom. It was given to a stranger as a gift to the goddess. And so, in some cultures, brides offered their virginity to the wedding guests.[45] These pagan cultures held that the defloration of the virgin could well harm the bridegroom. Of course, this was not permitted by the Jews and the Christians.

Pederastia (pedophilia) and homosexuality, regardless of form, appeared in history directly connected to the cult of the goddess. The natural ways of sexual intercourse became insufficient for the masses of men and women. And then, unnatural love, contrary to nature, was manifested in the world under the control of evil spirits.

Both natural sexual intercourse and unnatural sexual intercourse became part of the practices of the goddess. Castration became a part of the practices of the goddess. Its purpose was and is to try to destroy the image of masculinity.

In another way of saying this, natural sexual intercourse formed a part of the temple service of the goddess. Over time, pederastia, the corruption, and defilement of young boys became part of the service of the goddess. Therefore, the defilement of young boys was carried out in honor of Aphrodite in her temples.

Athanasius said well, Γυναῖκες γοῦν ἐν εἰδώλοις τῆς Φοινίκης πάλαι προεκαθέζοντο, ἀπαρχόμεναι τοῖς ἐκεῖ θεοῖς ἑαυτῶν τὴν τοῦ σώματος ἑαυτῶν μισθαρνίαν, νομίζουσαι τῇ πορνείᾳ τὴν θεὸν ἑαυτῶν ἱλάσκεσθαι, καὶ εἰς εὐμένειαν ἄγειν αὐτὴν διὰ τούτων. ἄνδρες δέ, τὴν φύσιν ἀρνούμενοι καὶ μηκέτι εἶναι θέλοντες ἄρρενες, τὴν γυναικῶν πλάττονται φύσιν, ὡς ἐκ τούτων καταθύμια καὶ τιμὴν τῇ μητρὶ τῶν παρ᾽ αὐτοῖς λεγομένων θεῶν ποιοῦντες. πάντες δὲ ὁμοῦ τοῖς αἰσχίστοις βιοῦσι, καὶ τοῖς χείροσιν ἑαυτοῖς ἁμιλλῶνται (Consequently, women long time ago set before the idols of Phoenicia, there offering the price of their own bodies unto the gods, thinking that they have made propitiation unto their goddess by sexual immorality and that they would hold onto her favor by these sexual practices. And males, rejecting their own nature and no longer desiring to be males, fashion themselves into the nature of women, with the result that they are doing their desires and honoring the mother of their gods. But all lived together with the most disgraceful and competed with the worst among them).[46] Eusebius wrote in his Life of Constantine about a temple standing on the peak of Mount Lebanon and what went on in it, σχολή τις ἦν αὕτη κακοεργίας πᾶσιν ἀκολάστοις πολλῇ τε ῥαστώνῃ διεφθορόσι τὰ σώματα. γύννιδες γοῦν τινες ἄνδρες οὐκ ἄνδρες τὸ σεμνὸν τῆς φύσεως ἀπαρνησάμενοι θηλείᾳ νόσῳ τὴν δαίμονα ἱλεοῦντο, γυναικῶν τ᾽ αὖ παράνομοι ὁμιλίαι κλεψίγαμοί τε φθοραί, ἄρρητοί τε καὶ ἐπίρρητοι πράξεις ὡς ἐν ἀνόμῳ καὶ ἀπροστάτῃ χώρῳ κατὰ τόνδε τὸν νεὼν ἐπεχειροῦντο. φώρ τ᾽ οὐδεὶς ἦν τῶν πραττομένων τῷ μηδένα σεμνῶν ἀνδρῶν αὐτόθι τολμᾶν παριέναι (There was a certain school of wickedness for the shameless persons of every description; for all such persons ruined their bodies with great indulgence—easy and lust; then certain womanish men, who were no men at all, annulled their respect of nature and appeased the goddess—demon by the disease of effeminate behavior; and again the unlawful sexual

195

relationships among women—women to women, those who are seeking after illicit sexual love—adulteries, and rapes, and both unspeakable and infamous practices were all pampered in this temple, as in a place without law and without restraint. And no one could overlook their practices, for no honorable man among men dared to go near that place).[47] Eusebius' Greek words "γυναικῶν τ' αὖ παράνομοι ὁμιλίαι κλεψίγαμοί τε φθοραί, ἄρρητοί τε καὶ ἐπίρρητοι πράξεις" stress heavily the evil character and behavior to the extreme that were found in the temple of Aphrodite. The translation is given, "and again the unlawful sexual relationships among women—women to women, those who are seeking after illicit sexual love—adulteries, and rapes, and both unspeakable and infamous practices were all pampered in this temple" helps point this out. The Greek noun φθοραί describes the raping of virgins. This was and is a common occurrence in the cult of the goddess.

Such evil came from the place that Emperor Constantine abolished it.

Eusebius, like Paul, knew the anarthrous construction in Greek well. In 2 Timothy 3:2–6, Paul is stressing the behaviors, the demonically controlled behaviors that will dominate the last days. These same behaviors dominated the ancient world, especially the Baalim and Astartes cults. Above both cults, the most extreme and far-reaching to destroy men and women, all cultures, nations, and civilizations, was and is the cult of the goddess (Astartes). Paul describes satanic strongholds that were, are, and will be in the last days of a spiritual nature, physical nature, emotional nature, mental nature, generational nature, and behavioral nature.

In 2 Timothy 3:2–6, according to Greek grammar, all the behaviors mentioned are satanic in origin, controlled by the devil, and are not of God. The idea of the Greek is the totality of strength within these strongholds, complete in themselves. And Eusebius followed suit in his description of the men and women who visited the temple of Aphrodite. The behaviors mentioned by Paul ultimately enslave the wicked or the unsaved and work to enslave the saved. They corrupt, pollute, and work in men and women, in the world, and under the power or influence of evil spirits to destroy, kill, and steal. The idea here of Paul is not someone, even a Christian, who bothered with, opposed with, or even attacked with these strongholds of behavior, but someone who has fallen into their power completely. That would imply someone who is not saved. The behaviors noted here by Paul are the very opposite of the behavior or character of genuine Christians.

Before the statute of the goddess, like that of Venus or Aphrodite in Cyprus, offerings were given by men dressed as women and women dressed as men. The eunuch priests of Cybele were also dressed as women to lead the worshippers to the evilest rites.

To the ancient writers, a woman having effeminate behavior was no disease, but it was proper for her. But for a man to have an effeminate behavior was itself seen as a disease.

Most pagan authorities suggest that pederastia is less the activity of the goddess and more the acts of divine wrath by her, so it is tied directly to the vengeance of the goddess. Regardless, pederastia is tied directly to the cult of the goddess. Therefore, it is tied to the Astartes. In rare cases, the Baalim are associated with prostitution, pederastia, and homosexuality. Still, the Astartes are overwhelmingly associated with all these things. Pederastia was considered a form of insanity, like other forms of perversions. The deterioration of the body follows the deterioration of both the mind and the character of the people. This was understood by Paul, Hellenistic Jews, and others. Various writers made mention of this insanity.[48]

The main focus of the Baalim was the nature of masculinity, its phallus, and heterosexuality. Rarely did the Baalim and their cult step out of this boundary. The main focus of the Astartes was the nature of the feminine, homosexuality, the perversion and the disfiguring of the image of the masculine, and the attempt to reverse creation itself.

Baalim dogmatically focus on the phallus (penis) of the men, while the Astartes dogmatically focus on the vagina of women. In a nutshell, that is the difference.

Baal and Astarte formed a couple. In every societal manifestation, they presented a unified force of malevolent intent, a pairing of male and female. This process is replicated on a substantial scale. Contemporary and ancient societies alike grapple with a significant shared predicament. Each analysis focused singularly on one facet of the malevolent entities' contamination, neglecting their dual nature, encompassing both Baalim and Astartes.

Functions/Works/forms of the Astartes (Venus)

1. The Astartes are one of the spirits that can be used as familiar spirits.

2. They work in sexuality and are demons of sexuality, especially in all forms of sexual perversions.

3. As already said, they are both sexes. They can appear as men and women or as male and female.

4. They blend the genders.

5. They are seducers and temptresses and are the deities over alcohol and sexuality with intoxication.

6. They work in magic and sorcery.

7. Their cults reflected their nature.

8. Their worship is saturated with sensuality, sexuality, and open sexuality.

9. They promote brothels.

10. They are the authors of brothels, cult prostitution, temple sex, and sex magic.

11. They are the deities of prostitution.

12. They have created a pornification of the American Culture.

13. They are the Porn Goddesses.

14. They are behind sex, drugs, and rock and roll.

15. They are the ones leading the invasion of occultism into America.

16. They promote the idea that a man can be both a man and a woman.

17. They change or turn a man into a woman.

18. They promote the masculinization of women.

19. They promote the feminization of men.

20. They promote the reprogramming of boys and girls.

21. They are androgynous.

22. They promote the deconstruction of sex and the destruction of women.

23. They are tied to the Sexual Revolution of the 1960s in America.

24. They seek to destroy morality.

25. They promote the deification of sex.

26. They promote the destruction of marriage and the family.

27. They are the deities of Hollywood.

28. They have sexualized the American Culture.

29. They are the goddesses of sexuality, war, and destruction.

30. They promote unrestrained sexuality and unbridled passion and lust.

31. They wreak havoc and destruction of nations and cultures.

32. They break all rules and trespass all boundaries.

33. They can appear in any form or any form of a human.

34. A necromancer works with these spirits when they are used as familiar spirits.

35. They are religious spirits, backwardness, monitoring spirits from hell, divination and un-seriousness.

36. They make people forget revelations and dreams coming from the Lord in order to expose the enemy.

37. They can imitate the dead.

38. They can possess their victims.

39. They can oppress their victims.

40. They work in divination, necromancy, and false or counterfeit religions.

41. They try to deceive us when studying the Word of God.

42. They operate through our thoughts or try to control our thoughts.

43. They give thoughts to men.

44. They affect everyone and are manifested in and through people.

45. They can preach things contrary to the Word.

46. They can deny the existence of other spirits.

47. They can operate through our thoughts.

48. They work in the secular world.

49. They work against our spirit.

50. They like a spiritual atmosphere since they function best there.

51. They can serve people.

52. They belittle and hate Jesus, the work of the cross, the blood, the word, and all the saints.

53. They whisper in our ears.

54. They try to stop people from studying and reading the Word of God. They also try to stop the prayer life of the people.

55. They try to destroy the minds of their victims instead of just sending thoughts of their own.

56. They work with shamans.

57. They attack the plan of God in our lives.

58. They are used to keep us out of the position God intended for us.

59. They secretly come against what God is revealing to His church.

60. They work in deception.

61. They manifest themselves in possession.

62. They have many manifestations associated with them: physical, mental, emotional, and spiritual.

63. They are one of the strong men.

64. They condemn Christians by having them accept the false manifestations as coming from the Holy Spirit.

65. They bless those who serve them with blessings in various ways.

66. They attack those whom they do not control.

67. They can inflict pain, sickness, and disease.

68. They are conquerable through the name of Jesus and His blood.

69. They work by drugs and cause their victims to be bound to them.

70. They work to plague people with mental, emotional, physical, and spiritual disorders.

71. They work in counterfeit gifts, including tongues, prophecy, and healing.

72. They work to destroy all things in a person's life.

73. They are sexual spirits; they have sex with those whom they possess, whether by consent or by force.

74. They promote sexual immorality.

75. They work to reverse creation.

The Oppression by the Ammonites

The next part of the period of the judges begins in a terrible light as witnessed in Judges 10:6. The Hebrew text reads, וַיֹּסִפוּ בְּנֵי יִשְׂרָאֵל לַעֲשׂוֹת הָרַע בְּעֵינֵי יְהוָה וַיַּעַבְדוּ אֶת־הַבְּעָלִים וְאֶת־הָעַשְׁתָּרוֹת וְאֶת־אֱלֹהֵי אֲרָם וְאֶת־אֱלֹהֵי צִידוֹן וְאֵת אֱלֹהֵי מוֹאָב וְאֵת אֱלֹהֵי בְנֵי־עַמּוֹן וְאֵת אֱלֹהֵי פְלִשְׁתִּים וַיַּעַזְבוּ אֶת־יְהוָה וְלֹא עֲבָדוּהוּ׃ (And the children of Israel caused—made—themselves to repeat in doing the evil in the eyes of the Lord and they gave service unto the Baalim and the Astartes and the gods of Aram and the gods of Sidon and the gods of Moab and the gods of the children of Ammon and the gods of Philistines, so they abandoned—separated themselves—from the Lord and did not give service to Him) or Καὶ προσέθεντο οἱ υἱοὶ Ἰσραὴλ ποιῆσαι τὸ πονηρὸν ἐνώπιον Κυρίου, καὶ ἐδούλευσαν τοῖς Βααλεὶμ καὶ ταῖς Ἀσταρὼθ καὶ τοῖς θεοῖς Ἀρὰδ καὶ τοῖς θεοῖς Σιδῶνος καὶ τοῖς θεοῖς Μωὰβ καὶ τοῖς θεοῖς υἱῶν Ἀμμὼν καὶ τοῖς θεοῖς Φυλιστιείμ· καὶ ἐνκατέλιπον τὸν κύριον καὶ οὐκ ἐδούλευσαν αὐτῷ (And the children of Israel repeated to do the evil before the Lord and they gave service—became the slaves of—unto the Baalim and the Astartes the gods of Arad and the gods of Sidon and the gods of Moab and the gods of the children of Ammon and the gods of the Philistines, and they abandoned—separated themselves—from the Lord and did not give service unto Him).

In the Hebrew text, the hiphil verb pattern is used to describe the repetition of apostasy and idolatry; Israelites caused themselves to repeat these behaviors of apostasy, sin, evil, and idolatry. They surrendered themselves to these evil practices and to the evil demon-gods before all these practices.

Apostasy was very gross and aggravated. The Israelites became almost universal idolaters, adopting the gods of the surrounding nations, and scarcely acknowledging the Lord at all as one of the gods they worshipped (Judges 10:6). In other words, the Israelites served all gods, except the true God. They ran after everything, every superstition, every delusion, every sexual practice, and every self-deception, but they forgot the truth of God. In addition, they continually sought after false friends rather than keeping the only true friend.

The grouping of various gods with the Baalim and the Astartes as the first in the list sets the other gods simply as different names for the Baalim and the Astartes or as sub-groups among the Baalim and Astartes. For example, Solomon went after the goddess of the Sidonians (1 Kings 11:5), and this goddess was one of the Astartes. The Moabites served Chemosh, another Baal (Numbers 21:29; 1 Kings 11:33); Molech, which is found in the singular and plural in the Greek Septuagint, is another name for the Baalim (Leviticus 18:21, 20:5). Here, the focus is that the Baalim and the Astartes of one nation were not enough for the Israelites; they wanted to worship the Baalim and the Astartes of seven nations (Judges 10:11–12).

The Periods of the Kings and the Prophets

The period of the kings and the prophets was a condition, at least like the period of the judges. More probable though, the condition was, indeed, worse than that time of the judges. The kings were very little help for the complete deliverance of Israel from their enemies, their idolatry, and the rites of the Canaanites. and from the judgments of God. Out of the kings of the northern kingdom (kingdom of Israel), all were inferior and wicked. Not even one of the nineteen kings was righteous; all did evil before the Lord. In fact, only three kings were righteous and all from the southern kingdom: David, Hezekiah, and Josiah. The Apocrypha Book Sirach 49:1 reads, παρὲξ Δαυεὶδ καὶ Ἐζεκίου καὶ Ἰωσείου πάντες πλημμελίαν ἐπλημμέλησαν· κατέλιπον γὰρ τὸν νόμον τοῦ ὑψίστου, οἱ βασιλεῖς Ἰούδα ἐξέλιπον (Except for David and Hezekiah and Josiah, all committed sin exceedingly; for they abandoned the law of the Most High. The kings of Judah failed).

The Bible speaks of nine kings that which did not become evil in the sight of the Lord God: David (1 Kings 11:4,33), Asa (1 Kings

15:11), Jehoshaphat (1 Kings 22:43), Jehoash (2 Kings 12:2), Amaziah (2 Kings 14:3), Uzziah (2 Kings 15:3), Jotham (2 Kings 15:34), Hezekiah (2 Kings 18:3), and Josiah (2 Kings 22:2). However, only three followed the law of God completely. For the six did not remove the high places (1 Kings 15:11–14, 22:41–43; 2 Kings 12:2–3, 14:1–4; 2 Chronicles 24:27; 2 Kings 15:1–5, 32–35; 2 Chronicles 27:2).

Several epistles are spurious in the Epistles of Ignatius or those referred to as belonging to Ignatius. One of these is the epistle known as "The Epistle of Maria the Proselyte to Ignatius." Neither Ignatius nor Maria wrote this epistle. It was written later. Still, the epistle signifies the view about the period of the kings and prophets, quite well, held by the ancient church.

Ἰωσίας δὲ ὁ θεοφιλής, ἄναρθρα σχεδὸν ἔτι φθεγγόμενος, ἐλέγχει τοὺς τῷ πονηρῷ πνεύματι κατόχους, ὡς ψευδολόγοι καὶ λαοπλάνοι τυγχάνουσιν· δαιμόνων τε ἐκκαλύπτει τὴν ἀπάτην, καὶ τοὺς οὐκ ὄντας θεοὺς παραδειγματίζει· καὶ τοὺς ἱερωμένους αὐτοῖς, νήπιος ὤν, κατασφάζει, βωμούς τε αὐτῶν ἀνατρέπει, καὶ θυσιαστήρια νεκροῖς λειψάνοις μιαίνει, τεμένη τε καθαιρεῖ, καὶ τὰ ἄλση ἐκκόπτει, καὶ τὰς στήλας συντρίβει, καὶ τοὺς τῶν ἀσεβῶν τάφους ἀνορύττει, ἵνα μηδὲ σημεῖον ἔτι τῶν πονηρῶν ὑπάρχῃ· οὕτω τις ζηλωτὴς ἦν τῆς εὐσεβείας, καὶ τῶν ἀσεβῶν τιμωρός, ἔτι ψελλίζων τῇ γλώττῃ. Δαβὶδ δέ, ὁ προφήτης ὁμοῦ καὶ βασιλεύς, ἡ τοῦ σωτηρίου κατὰ σάρκα ρίζα, μειράκιον χρίεται ὑπὸ Σαμουὴλ εἰς βασιλέα· φησὶν γάρ που αὐτός, Ὅτι μικρὸς ἤμην ἐν τοῖς ἀδελφοῖς μου, καὶ νεώτερος ἐν τῷ οἴκῳ τοῦ πατρός μου (Josiah also, Beloved of God, when he could barely speak articulately, convicts those persons who were possessed by an evil spirit as speaking falsely in their speech and falling in with the corrupters of the people. He too discloses the deception of the demons and publicly shames those persons who are not gods. And yet while being a little child, he slaughters their priests and ruins their altars and defiles the altars where sacrifices were offered with dead bodies, and throws down the temples, and cuts down the sacred groves of the Astartes, and breaks into pieces the pillars, and digs up the tombs of the ungodly, in order that no artifact of the wicked might any more exist. Indeed, he was to a great extent zealous in the purpose of godliness and a punisher of the ungodly, while he still spoke awkwardly in speech as a little child).[49]

Overall, the period of the judges was based upon the transgressions of the Israelites, the repentance of the Israelites, the rising up of a judge who became the deliverer for the Israelites, the death of the judge, and the re-occurrence of apostasy and committing evil against the Lord God.

The reformations during the times of kings and prophets were not complete in their intentions or in their consequences. Despite many people turning to God, the rapid return to more profound immorality during this period demonstrates the widespread wickedness of the time (Amos 5: 16, 7:17, 8:6; Isaiah 1:23, 10:1; Hosea 9:15). At best, the reformations localized the effects of idolatry and paganism while undermining and weakening the influence of the Baalim and the Astartes.

The reformations during the times of kings and prophets were not complete in their intentions or consequences. Many people did no doubt turn in truth to God. Still, the rapidity with which each effort was followed by a return to deeper depths of immorality gives evidence of the abounding wickedness of the period (Amos 5:16, 7:17, 8:6; Isaiah 1:23, 10:1; Hosea 9:15). At best, the reformations localized the effects of idolatry and paganism while undermining and weakening the influence of the Baalim and the Astartes.

Rise of the Prophets

The rise of the prophets made a period of growth for the prophetic ministry and office beyond any parallel time that had occurred before in the history of Israel. Within this period, the prophetic ministry and office were allowed to become a permanent establishment of Israel. Before this time, both Moses and Joshua were prophets of God, stood alone as the representatives of the living God, and spoke for God alone unto the Israelites. From Joshua to Samuel, no prophet was individually named. Undeniably, the prophetic ministry and office had been put in the background of the Israelites' lives; both the prophetic ministry and office had been diminished and almost forgotten in their importance. Further, both the prophetic ministry and office had become obscure, inactive, dimmed, ignored, and diminished in the minds and lives of the Israelites. As a result, the Israelites had become insensitive to the movement of the Holy Spirit.

Therefore, the age of the prophets began with Samuel and the establishment of the monarchy and continued to almost the very end of the Old Testament times. Beginning with Samuel, the Scriptures give a list of the prophets respectively:

1. Samuel (1 Samuel 3:20)

2. Schools of prophets under Samuel (1 Samuel 10:10–12, 19:20–24)

3. Gad (1 Samuel 22:5; 2 Samuel 24:11–19; 1 Chronicles 29:29; 2 Chronicles 29:25)

4. Nathan (2 Samuel 7, 12; 2 Chronicles 9:29, 29:25)

5. David (2 Samuel 16:1; 1 Kings 2:11; Hebrews 11:32)

6. Solomon (2 Samuel 12:24; 1 Kings 1:10–11:43)

7. Ahijah (1 Kings 11:26–40, 14:1–18)

8. The man of God from Judah (1 Kings 13)

9. Shemaiah (1 Kings 12:21–24; 2 Chronicles 11:2–4, 12:1–8)

10. Iddo (2 Chronicles 12:15, 13:22)

11. Azariah (2 Chronicles 15)

12. Hanani (2 Chronicles 16:7–10)

13. Jehu, son of Hanani (1 Kings 16:7; 2 Chronicles 19:1–3)

14. Elijah (1 Kings 17–2 Kings 2)

15. Micaiah (1 Kings 22:8–28; 2 Chronicles 18:7–27)

16. Obadiah (1 Kings 18; Obadiah 1:1)

17. Ahijah the Shilonite (1 Kings 11:29−30, 12:15, 14:2−18, 15:29)

18. Unknown prophet encouraged Ahab (1 Kings 20:13−15)

19. Unknown prophet rebuked Ahab (1 Kings 20:35−43)

20. Jahaziel (2 Chronicles 20:14−17)

21. Eliezer (2 Chronicles 20:37)

22. Asaph (2 Chronicles 20:14)

23. Hosea (Hosea 1:1)

24. Amos (Amos 7:14−15)

25. Micah (Micah 1:1)

26. Amoz (the father of Isaiah)

27. Elisha (2 Kings 2:8)

28. Prophetic School of Elisha (2 Kings 9:1−13)

29. Jonah (2 Kings 14:25; Jonah 1:1)

30. Isaiah (2 Kings 19:2; Isaiah)

31. Joel (Acts 2:16; Joel 1:1)

32. Nahum (Nahum 1:1)

33. Habakkuk (Habakkuk 1:1)

34. Zephaniah (Zephaniah)

35. Zechariah, son of Jehoiada (2 Chronicles 24:20−22)

36. The man of God forbade Amaziah's league with Israel (2 Chronicles 25:7−10)

37. Unknown prophet rebuked Amaziah (2 Chronicles 25:15)

38. Zechariah (2 Chronicles 26:5)

39. Oded (2 Chronicles 28:9)

40. Huldah, the prophetess (2 Kings 22:12–20)

41. Urijah (Jeremiah 26:20–23)

42. Jeremiah (Jeremiah 20:2)

43. Baruch (Jeremiah 32, 36, 43 and 45)

44. Neriah (father of Baruch)

45. Daniel (Daniel; Matthew 24:15)

46. Ezekiel (Ezekiel)

47. Seraiah (Jeremiah 51:61–64)

48. Mehseiah (father of Neriah)

49. Haggai (Haggai 1:1)

50. Agur (Proverbs 30:1)

51. Zechariah (Zechariah 1:1)

52. Malachi (Malachi 1:1)

53. Esther (Esther 1:1)

The importance of Samuel and his place within Israel was recognized by various means. For example, Samuel, as a prophet, was more important to Israel than Saul. Also, Samuel was more important and far-reaching in godly influence on Israel than what David would become. Samuel did not receive the counsel, direction, advice, warning, and the rebuke of other prophets, but David was frequently advised, counseled, directed, warned, and rebuked by the prophets. While the prophets played an important part in the life of David, the importance of the prophets was diminished in the life of Solomon. However, one Ahijah of Shiloh appeared in the latter part of his career and affected the life of Solomon.

Within this period, the prophets were Samuel, Gad (1 Samuel 22:5; 2 Samuel 24:11), Nathan (2 Samuel 7:2–17, 12:1–12; 1 Kings

1:8–24), Iddo (2 Chronicles 9:29, 12:15, 13:22) and Ahijah (1 Kings 11:29–39). No written teachings of these prophets survived, except the story of Nathan and a few fragments. Nevertheless, much about their lives is given.

Beyond any other man, Samuel was the man of the hour in one of the evilest periods of Israel's history. From the era of Moses and Joshua to the times of Samuel, there was undeniably no greater man than Samuel. Unquestionably, everything about his life indicated that he was the man of God for that desperate hour. The supernatural means of his conception and birth, his explicitly consecrated life for the sake of the Lord God, his specific training in the affairs of God, and the specific time of his life all pointed to the fact that a new development within the history of the Israelites had begun, and a new highly significant spiritual effort was about to begin in Israel. During the time that Samuel was born, it was an age consisting of heavy immorality, lax morals, fundamental secularism, moral rationalism, selfishness, and very weak government. It was a generation morally sick and unwilling to be disciplined by God's law. For a deliverer to help such a generation as this, he must have the authority and power of God; he must be a man who knew his position and state with God. And he must be a man who was utterly fearless when dealing with God and with men.

Further, the leader would have to be disciplined, sensitive to the voice of God, living in a state of unconditional obedience to God, and have that state of unconditional obedience become his main purpose and rule of life. There was none who could fit all these requirements, except Samuel. Samuel alone was that leader. It is very unlikely that a person could be found like Samuel.

As such, Samuel became a leader that stood in the same category and style as Moses and Joshua. Samuel was immovable from God and from the law of God. Instead of allowing the Israelites to move him, he worked on moving the Israelites away from sins and idolatry to the Lord God. The age of Samuel was a countless immoral struggle and drag upon the common people; the age pulled them down and moved many toward sin, rebellion, and apostasy. Even Samuel's sons were not like their father. They fell into sin, rebellion, and apostasy.

Generally, the Jewish writers saw a difference between Moses and other prophets coming after him. For example, Maimonides held that there were four differences between Moses and the other prophets. First, God spoke to other prophets by a mediator, like an angel. But God spoke to Moses himself without a mediator or any other intervention. Second, the other prophets never prophesied but their senses were all joined to visions or dreams. However, Moses was perfectly awake and conscious as one speaking to another. Third, when the dream or vision was over, the other prophets were often left weak and feeble, so much so that they could hardly stand upon their feet (Daniel 8:18). But Moses spoke with divine dignity without any alteration of his person. And fourth, no other prophet could know the mind of God whenever he wanted to, because God communicated to him only whenever it was proper. However, Moses was able to communicate with God and receive an answer at any time.[50]

With Samuel, the prophetic ministry and office became distinct parts of the national life of Israel. Two reasons for this occurrence are obvious. In the first place, the whole priesthood had become too formal, with no spirit or life, and vile in corruption. The priesthood had become untrustworthy as a means of communicating the will of God unto Israel. In the second place, the institution of the prophetic ministry and office became a safeguard for the kingly office of the monarchy, since most kings and princes were not men of God. Accordingly, God continued to communicate truth and righteousness unto Israel through the prophetic ministry and office.

The chief glory of Samuel is a prophetical dispensation, which is traced back to him. While Samuel was not the earliest prophet regarded by future generations, he was one of the most prophetic figures in the history of the Jews. However, the great development of the prophetic ministry and office in Israel, troubled with such earth-shattering consequences, was owed to his initiative, dedication, consecration, simplicity, purity, faith, and unconditional obedience.

While God may call and elect anyone to the prophetic ministry and office, Samuel recognized that those who could withstand the burden of such a ministry were those who prepared for it. The preparation for the calling and election is through deep communion with God, which includes dedication, consecration, simplicity, purity, faith, and unconditional obedience. For this sake, men were united together in the schools of the prophets. These schools gave a constant supply of prophets for Israel; these individuals were taught the ways of the Lord God and sought to receive the Holy Spirit. In so doing, Samuel sought to make a complete national apostasy from the Lord God impossible. Furthermore, they learned how to enter the atmosphere of the Holy Spirit, commune with Him, submit unto the Holy Spirit, become a vessel of passive receptibility for the Holy Spirit, and become the very mouthpiece of God.

In addition, Samuel continued to give place for the offering up of sacrifices as part of the religious life of the Israelites. If not for Samuel, the offering up of sacrifices may have been suspended for a time. Samuel sought to encourage and permit sacrifices unto the Lord God. And he was present customarily when the people sacrificed on a hilltop and in or near a city. Samuel was present generally when sacrifices occurred at Gilgal, at Bethlehem and at Ramah, the home of Samuel.

The Prophetic Ministry and Office

From the days of Elijah and Elisha to the Babylonian captivity, there were many prophets. The prophets were leaders of Israel during the most horrible times of Israel. Much was required from the prophets, especially unconditional obedience and a destitute lifestyle. Exclusively from the beginning of the Jewish monarchy to centuries after its collapse, the preaching of the prophets became a significant event for the future of all humanity. Throughout these many centuries, the words of the prophets proclaimed by the prophets have stood as encouragements for all of humanity, shining lights toward the Cross of Calvary and the truth of God. Between the prophets and the best pagan philosophers and other truth-seekers, there stands a significant difference, even a great impenetrable abyss, which is unable to be affected or spoiled by sinful humanity. The teachings of the prophets were not the result of human knowledge or wisdom; their teachings came from the knowledge of God and their fellowship with the living God. Their words were filled with an authority and a power that are far off to the words and thoughts of sinful humanity.

Consequently, prophets "were men of a good education and moderation but void of all deceit and dissimulation. They exposed themselves to infinite hazards and difficulties carrying out their holy office. They taught doctrines impressed upon them by the Highest Lord and made discoveries that go beyond men's comprehension. They foretold events, which none but God could know. They performed works, which none but God could do. They gave all imaginable evidence of the truth of their commission and sealed it very often with the testimony of their own blood. It will truly follow then that they were messengers sent from God, to supply the intermediate space between Moses and Christ; consequently, that the revelation of God's will in the Old Testament that they presented is indubitably true."[51]

The prophets, coming after the period of the patriarchs, "preserved the purest tradition of the true religion; their employment was meditating upon the law of God, praying to him often day and night, both for themselves and others; and inuring themselves to the practice of every virtue. They instructed their disciples, explained to them the spirit and meaning of the law, and opened to them the sublime mysteries relating to the state of the church, either upon the earth, or in heaven, after the Messiah should come, that were hidden under allegories of things sensible and seemingly mean. They instructed the people too who came to hear them upon Sabbath and other feast days. They reproved them for their vices, and exhorted them to repent, often foretelling, from God, what was to happen to them (1 Kings 21:20). This liberty which they took of speaking the most disagreeable truths even to kings, caused them to be hated, and cost many of them their lives."[52]

Origen, denouncing Celsus, an ancient critic of Christianity and the Holy Scriptures, writes about the prophets:

> Τῶν δ᾽ ἐν Ἰουδαίοις προφητῶν οἱ μὲν πρὸ τῆς προφητείας καὶ τῆς θείας κατακωχῆς ἦσαν σοφοί, οἱ δ᾽ ἀπ᾽ αὐτῆς τῆς προφητείας φωτισθέντες τὸν νοῦν τοιοῦτοι γεγόνασιν, αἱρεθέντες ὑπὸ τῆς προνοίας εἰς τὸ πιστευθῆναι τὸ θεῖον πνεῦμα καὶ τοὺς ἀπὸ τούτου λόγους διὰ τὸ τοῦ βίου δυσμίμητον καὶ σφόδρα εὔτονον καὶ ἐλευθέρριον καὶ πάντῃ πρὸς θάνατον καὶ κινδύνους ἀκατάπληκτον. Τοιούτους γὰρ καὶ ὁ λόγος αἱρεῖ δεῖν εἶναι τοὺς τοῦ ἐπὶ πᾶσι θεοῦ προφήτας, οἵτινες παίγνιον ἀπέφηναν τὴν Ἀντισθένους καὶ Κράτητος καὶ Διογένους εὐτονίαν. Δι᾽ ἀλήθειαν γοῦν καὶ τὸ ἐλευθερίως ἐλέγχειν τοὺς ἁμαρτάνοντας (But in regard to the prophets, among the Jews, some of them were wise men before prophesying — exercising the prophetic office and receiving that of divine inspiration, while other such persons as these prophets became wise by the illumination through revelation that their minds received from prophesying itself. They were chosen by Divine Providence to have been entrusted with the Divine Spirit and the depositors of His Holy Words on account of them living a life, which can scarcely be reproduced, and which was very much vigorous and upright and unyielding altogether in death and in dangers. For even reason proves that such ought to be the moral conduct of the prophets of God, as much as the determination of Antisthenes, Crates, and Diogenes has proven to be child's play compared unto the prophets. Therefore, it was for truth and their uprightness in rebuking the wicked).[53]

Origen accepted as a fact that the prophets were people of the highest moral conduct, their life "can scarcely be reproduced" by others, and their life was "much vigorous and upright and unyielding altogether in death and in dangers." And the determination of the pagan moralists, philosophers, and historians is child's play compared to the ancient prophets.

Without the presence of the prophets, there would be a great abyss in the very national life of the Israelites. Their lives would have become greatly diminished and a shadow of God's promise and life for the Israelites. Consequently, the period of the prophets made the prophets be one of the highest glories of Israel; apart from this period, the prophets would be ignored in history. These prophets began their life among the mists of the sea-level; they ended it upon the tops of the mountains. The unique marks of Israel's spiritual life—their religious faith and religious character originated at least in part by the prophetic ministry and office of the prophets. In fact, the prophets lifted the lives of the Israelites to a higher level. They gave an imperishable distinction and value to the record of the Hebrew life.

The prophets of God, though prosperous with the things of God and the movement of the Holy Spirit, were destitute in life, since they lived in poverty and want; still, they did not hunger after worldly wealth and riches (1 Kings 14:3; 2 Kings 4:1, 38, 42, 6:5; Hebrews 11:37). Their appearance and dress were that of poor men (1 Kings 21:27; 2 Kings 1:8). Their dress commonly was "sackcloth or haircloth, that is, mourning, to show they were always in affliction for the sins of the people. Thus, to describe Elijah, they said, 'he was a man clothed in a hairy garment and girt with a girdle of leather about his loins' (2 Kings 1:8). Thus, when God bids Isaiah undress himself, he orders him to lose his sackcloth from off his loins'" (Isaiah 20:2).[54]

Prestigious, impressive, and admired are words that the wicked and most people in Israel could not see belonging to the prophets. The prophets were not prestigious or sophisticated at all for the Israelites. Nor were they the epitome of what people thought was hip, stylish, sophisticated, fashionable, or current. The prophets were out of the norm, as seen by the wicked and the other people in the commonwealth of Israel.

A life of humility and humiliation was theirs. Such conditions were represented in the lives of Samuel, Elijah, Elisha, and Jeremiah. Such difficulties were upon the life of Jeremiah that he cursed the day that he was born and cursed his mother for having him, "Cursed be the day wherein I was born: let not the day wherein my mother bare me be blessed. Cursed be the man who brought tidings to my father, saying, A man child is born unto thee; making him very glad. And let that man be as the cities which the LORD overthrew and repented not: and let him hear the cry in the morning, and the shouting at noontide; because he slew me not from the womb; or that my mother might have been my grave, and her womb to be always great with me. Wherefore came I forth out of the womb to see labour and sorrow, that my days should be consumed with shame?" (Jeremiah 20:14—18).

Comparing the lives of the prophets to the greatest of sinners, the lives of the prophets were humiliated lives; their lives were lives of burden. They carried the burden of the world upon their shoulders. More correctly, they carried the burden of the Israelites upon their shoulders. Most miserable were their lives, living in a world filled with great sinners and reprobates. In many respects, the pagans saw the lives of the prophets as cursed rather than blessed. Their rewards for godly lives in this world were insult, persecution, imprisonment, death, and countless other evils.

Paul in Hebrews 11:36—38 writes, ἕτεροι δὲ ἐμπαιγμῶν καὶ μαστίγων πεῖραν ἔλαβον, ἔτι δὲ δεσμῶν καὶ φυλακῆς .ἐλιθάσθησαν ἐπρίσθησαν ἐπειράσθησαν, ἐν φόνῳ μαχαίρας ἀπέθανον περιῆλθον ἐν μηλωταῖς ἐν αἰγείοις δέρμασιν ὑστερούμενοι θλιβόμενοι κακουχούμενοι ὧν οὐκ ἦν ἄξιος ὁ κόσμος - ἐν ἐρημίαις πλανώμενοι καὶ ὄρεσιν καὶ σπηλαίοις καὶ ταῖς ὀπαῖς τῆς γῆς (But others had received a trial of mockings and scourgings, and even that of bonds and imprisonments. They were stoned to death; they were cut asunder; they were tempted by their enemies through their tortures; they were killed by being murdered with the sword; they went about wandering in sheep-skins and goat-skins, being destitute, being afflicted, and being evil-treated with torments of whom the world was unworthy; they went about wandering, like lost sheep, aimlessly over deserts, and mountains, and in caves, and in the clefts of the earth).

Paul had many in mind but here are some examples. Zechariah, son of Jehoiada, was stoned (2 Chronicles 24:20–22) and Jeremiah was stoned as understood by tradition;[55] Isaiah was cut asunder as understood by tradition; Urijah and other prophets were slain with the sword (1 Kings 19:10; Jeremiah 26:23; 2 Maccabees 7:4); many prophets were hidden out (1 Kings 18:4,13, 19:9,13; 1 Maccabees 2:28; 2 Maccabees 5:27); Elisha, Jeremiah, Micah, and others experienced the mockings (Jeremiah 20:2, 37:15), and mockings and scourgings also have reference to the times of the Maccabees (2 Maccabees 7:1, 7:7, and 7:10).

In essence, the genuine prophets became outcasts of Israel. They were banished from Israel and were rejected to have fellowship with that society. Treated by other men as animals, the prophets wandered throughout the wilderness, straying aimlessly over deserts, over mountains, in caves and in clefts. The condition of the prophets was destitute, afflicted, evil-treated, subjected to all dangers and evils, and death itself. Some faced death, while others faced persecution without death.

The ὁ κόσμος (the world) does not concern itself with the evil world system, but ὁ κόσμος (the world) mentioned by Paul in Hebrews 11:38 means the whole society of humanity, humanity as a world as witnessed by Hebrews 11:7.

The three Greek present tense participles ὑστερούμενοι θλιβόμενοι κακουχούμενοι (being destitute, being afflicted, and being evil-treated with torments) can be understood to be adverbial or adjectival. As adverbial participles, all three underline the circumstances of the prophets and the continual existence of these circumstances; this is the best interpretation. As adjectival participles, they simply give a description of their lives. The participles as adverbial participles may be translated like this, to emphasis the circumstances and the continual existence of these circumstances in the lives of the prophets, "while they were destitute, afflicted, and evil-treated with torments." The prophets did all their work and spoke all their messages, while being simultaneously destitute, afflicted, and evil-treated with torments.

Sometimes having a little is far more important that having the whole world, "A little that a righteous man hath is better than the riches of many wicked" (Psalm 37:16), "Better is little with the fear of the LORD than great treasure and trouble therewith" (Proverbs 15:16), "Better is a little with righteousness than great revenues without right" (Proverbs 16:8), and "God is far from the ungodly; but he hearkens to the prayers of the righteous. Better are small receipts with righteousness, than abundant fruits with unrighteousness. Let the heart of a man think justly, that his steps may be rightly ordered of God" (Proverbs 15:29, from the Greek Septuagint).

The difficulties facing the prophets were commonly categorized as coming from: (1) those who were part of the anti-prophetic party, which opposed the prophets; (2) the objection of the prophets to idolatry; (3) the political objection to prophets; (4) the objection of the prophets unto the immoral state of the commonwealth of Israel; (5) the war of the prophets against the Baalim and the Astartes; (6) the Baalim and the Astartes waging a war against them.

The anti-prophetic party sought to persecute any prophet who did not follow the royal line or the views of the court. The anti-prophetic party was headed by the king, and not only set aside the prophet, but persecuted him. The fact that the true prophets objected to idolatry made the prophets fight against heathenism and those evil spirits backing it, especially the Baalim and the Astartes. They believed that all these things would ruin the nation.

Generally, the prophets were married (1 Kings 19:6; 2 Kings 4:10, 4:38; Matthew 3:4). The widow, whose oil Elisha multiplied, was the widow of a prophet (2 Kings 4:1).[56] Nevertheless, the lives of the prophets were stern and harsh; if the prophets had children, that was no guarantee they were to become prophets, since the prophetic ministry, gifts, and office cannot be inherited. They submitted to these difficulties, for they knew the cost of receiving the prophetic ministry, office, and anointing upon their lives. They generally possessed homes of their own, but the homes were just something to cover and protect them from the harsh weather and from the harshness of nature itself. It was meek, small, and often, a cave or a den in the mountains. Indeed, they "lived separate lives from the world, distinguished by their habit and manner of life; they dwelt upon mountains, as Elijah and Elisha did upon Carmel and Gilgal. The rich woman, who lodged Elisha when he went to Shumen, had a chamber, as I said, built and furnished for him; where he lived so retired that he did not speak so much as to the person who entertained him, but made his servant Gehazi speak to her for him; and when she came to intreat him to raise her son to life again, Gehazi would not let her touch the prophet's feet. When Naaman, general of the Syrian armies, came to him to be cured of his leprosy, he sent him word what to do, without being seen by him."[57] Two other miracles of Elisha "shew that his disciples lived in societies; that of the herb-pottage which he made wholesome, and that of the barley bread which he multiplied; which shews also the plainness of their food. There were a hundred prophets that lived together in this society, and they wrought with their hands; for, finding their lodgings too strait, they went themselves to cut down wood to build with, and were so poor, that one of them was obliged to borrow a hatchet."[58]

As servants of God, the prophets were pulled from every tribe and every class of men within Israel. Besides other things, these men were the champions of the Lord, sworn to fight against and resist any unfaithfulness unto the living God, became constant witnesses of the Lord God throughout Israel, and upheld the rights, the law, the words, and the will of God during a rebellious and resistant people. Their anger was constantly provoked by the encouragement of pagan worship through the Israelites. The prophets were a better witness to the case of God than the priests were.

One who obtained the prophetic office was considered a minister of the Highest God and of His temple. In essence, whether a prophet came from the line of Levi, he was considered a special priest to God, and at times had access to every part of the house of the Lord, including the Holy Place and the Holy of Holies (Lamentations 2:20; Jeremiah 26:7, 23:11, 28:5–6; Zechariah 7:3).

That a prophet had access on occasions to the sanctified area of the temple which was from the court of the Israelites to the Holy of Holies was commonly known. Why? A prophet of the Lord came in the name and person of God by prophesying. As such, the prophet of the Lord was and is considered the Lord's mouthpiece through whom God can speak.

Moreover, the Lord stood with them, showed people that He favored the prophets by fulfilling their predictions, proved that the prophets were His messengers and retaliated against the enemies of the prophets. Even a little slight against the prophets was enough for the divine anger to be released against someone. The rejection of a prophecy breathed by the Lord God through His prophets was no small slight; it was great in the mind of God and the minds of the prophets. It was a refutation against the will of God and the exaltation of man's will over God's will. Though free will was permitted, the blatant rejection of a prophecy from the prophets was enough for God to retaliate against those standing in the way of the prophecy. Unless there was a good reason for the rejection of the prophecy, free will must bow before the will of God. If not, nothing but terrible consequences will occur. People have the freedom to sin, and they have the freedom to receive its fruits and consequences. For example, Saul sought to destroy David and keep the prophecies of Samuel from being fulfilled in his life. There were twenty-one attempts on the life of David by Saul or his messengers (1 Samuel 18:6–26:25). Such attempts were blatant efforts to reject, stop, or remove the prophecies from being fulfilled in the life of David. Such behavior, being as witchcraft, is a direct defiance against the prophetic ministry and office of a prophet and is direct insolence against the will of God, the sovereignty of God, the authority of God, the power of God, the nature of God, and the omnipotence of God. In truth, such a person who stands against the way of prophecy being fulfilled is doomed regardless of intention and is a wretched person.

The Baal of Phoenicia and Jezebel

Understanding the background of this part of the Old Testament is far more critical than anyone dares think. To understand Jezebel, all must understand the background, the cultures, the societies, and idolatry in its various forms. Since the people of that time were already aware of these facts, the Scriptures do not explicitly state them, as such explanation would have been redundant and unnecessary given their pre-existing knowledge. But modern Christians are incredibly ignorant of many facts about these times. The facts, which some have already mentioned, must be brought forth here in a summary:

1. Both Jezebel and her father hailed from Phoenicia, a land rich in history and culture, making them both Phoenicians by birth and heritage.

2. Tracing their ancestry back to the Canaanites, the Phoenicians shared a common heritage with this ancient group.

3. The same divine condemnation that was visited upon the Canaanites extended to their descendants, the Phoenicians, as a consequence of God's wrath.

4. Originating in a state of reprobation, the Phoenicians were, from their very inception, burdened by a curse that followed them throughout their history.

5. It was widely believed that the Phoenicians were generally and completely under the influence of malevolent spirits.

6. Ethbaal, the father of Jezebel, had a distinguished career, first serving as a high priest in Phoenicia before ascending to the throne and becoming its king. Even while wearing the crown and ruling the kingdom, he continued to fulfill his sacred duties as a high priest.

7. His position as a high priest of the Baalim and the Astartes demanded that he adopt female attire, comportment, and, in certain instances, engage in passive sexual functions.

8. It was a requirement for high priests and priests of this kind to engage in sexual relationships with these spirits.

9. From the moment of her birth, Jezebel was marked by a state of reprobation, a fate that would follow her throughout her life.

10. Born into a life of religious service, Jezebel's early years were spent as a priestess, specifically worshipping the Baalim and the Astartes.

11. Due to her role as a priestess, she was possessed by demons and was obligated to engage in sexual relationships with these spirits as part of her services, known as sex magic.

12. In her role as the priestess of these deities, she was obligated to don men's clothing and adopt masculine behaviors as part of the necessary rituals for this particular service.

13. Given her status as a priestess and a queen of significant power and influence, it was not an ordinary Baal, but one of exceptional power and stature, who claimed her as his vessel. Among the various principalities ruled by the Baalim, this one stood out.

14. The Baalim, particularly the principality, were the driving force behind every thought and action of Jezebel, a reprobate who stood accused before God and was therefore deemed unfit to marry any Israelite, including the demon-possessed and equally reprobate Ahab.

15. The core beliefs and practices of Jezebel's foundation are rooted in her idolatrous worship of the Baalim and the Astartes, with a particular emphasis on the principality that she served.

16. Through the actions of Jezebel, the powerful principality among the Baalim managed to successfully infiltrate the kingdom of

Israel and subsequently subjugated a significant portion of the northern Israelites, as well as establishing dominance over the Baalim that resided within Canaan.

17. Ahab's marriage to Jezebel, a Phoenician princess, represented not only a human union but also a profound spiritual connection, forming an alliance between the Tyrian god Baal and the Israelite people, intertwining the physical and spiritual realms.

18. Through this insidious influence, the worship of Baal, championed by Jezebel, gradually and insidiously began to corrupt and usurp the authentic spiritual life and practices of the Israelite people, supplanting the true worship of Yahweh with its own idolatrous rituals and beliefs.

19. Throughout the land of Israel, Jezebel's appearance at court was viewed as an outrageous and shocking display of impropriety that deeply offended the entire nation's sensibilities.

20. The accusations leveled against Jezebel depicted her as an exceptionally skilled and loyal follower of the Phoenician deity Baal, a portrayal that has endured throughout time.

21. Culminating her wicked ambition, she became the evil genius who, through the agency of the Phoenician god Baal, inflicted divine wrath and devastating calamity upon Ahab, his family, and his kingdom.

22. Jezebel's pre-existing evil nature meant that she did not require Ahab to be evil nor to influence her to become evil; her evil was self-generated. Even before she married him, there was already a darkness in her heart, a malevolence that foreshadowed the cruelties to come.

23. She embodied the pinnacle of self-discovery and self-acceptance, a triumphant culmination of her journey of self-realization.

As seen, the state of Jezebel was hopeless, reprobated, and demon possessed. The spirit coming from Jezebel was a spirit of reprobation and demon possession; this spirit came from the Phoenician Baal of Jezebel. No one can come from the spirit of Jezebel and not be a reprobate and demon possessed. So one who has or operates in the spirit of Jezebel is one who is a reprobate and demon possessed. Many are oppressed by the spirit that was behind Jezebel, but that does not mean that one is a reprobate or demon possessed.

One who submits to the spirit that was behind Jezebel will have the same fate, either similar or exact, as Jezebel, "This is the word of the LORD, which he spake by his servant Elijah the Tishbite, saying, In the portion of Jezreel shall dogs eat the flesh of Jezebel: And the carcass of Jezebel shall be as dung upon the face of the field in the portion of Jezreel; so that they shall not say, This is Jezebel," 2 Kings 9:36–37. In 2 Kings 9:34, Jehu called Jezebel אֶת־הָאֲרוּרָה or τὴν κατηραμένην ταύτην (this accursed woman). Jehu recognized that she was a reprobate, accursed with anathema by God; Jehu saw Jezebel as the source of all that which was evil and corruption in Israel, not Ahab. The person who uses, has, or submits to the spirit behind Jezebel, the spirit of Jezebel, becomes what Jezebel became.

The words of Jehu are very sobering, "What peace, so long as the whoredoms of thy mother Jezebel and her witchcrafts are so many" (2 Kings 9:22)? Just as there could be no peace with Israel if the fornications and sorceries of Jezebel continued, so there cannot be any peace within a Christian's life or a church's life if the spirit behind Jezebel appears in such a life. The Hebrew noun זְנוּנִים (whoredoms), like in Jeremiah 3:2, 9 and Ezekiel 23:27, has a reference to the practices of idolatry themselves. But like before, the practices of idolatry are always tied to sexual immorality. And sexual immorality is always connected to sex magic and the uniting of partners with evil spirits. Thus, in a roundabout way, Jehu allows a reader to see just how depraved Jezebel was. She was so deep into her sins and depravity, that she was having sexual relationships with humans and evil spirits. The Hebrew noun כְשָׁפֶיה (sorceries) has reference both to a general practice of sorcery and the use of spells or incantations for producing several types of outcomes. From what was said by Jehu, Jezebel was believed to be the foundation of idolatry within Israel.

Jehu destroyed the Phoenician Cult of the Baalim in the kingdom of Israel, not any other form. Both the Hebrew and Greek of 2 Kings 10:28 mean not that all cults of the Baalim were destroyed, but the cultic Baal of Jezebel: וַיַּשְׁמֵד יֵהוּא אֶת־הַבַּעַל מִיִּשְׂרָאֵל: (and Jehu made to be wiped out the Baal from Israel) or καὶ ἠφάνισεν Ιου τὸν Βααλ ἐξ Ισραηλ (And Jehu destroyed the Baal out of Israel). The singular form used here is done intentionally. While Ahab followed the Baalim, including the Baalim in Canaan and the Baal of Jezebel, the war of Elijah was directed more against the Baal of Jezebel than the Baalim of Canaan.

From the Egyptian captivity, the Israelites dealt with various forms of the Baalim. The first were all the Egyptian Baalim. The second was the calf Baalim in the wilderness, including the thirteen calves (Exodus 19–24, 24:29, 32:1–33). The third was the Baal-Peor with the Moabite virgins (Numbers 25:1–18). The fourth was the Baalim in Canaan (Judges 2:13, 3:3, 3:7, 6:25, 6:28, 6:30, 10:10; 1 Samuel 7:4, 12:10). The fifth was the calve Baalim appearing as the two calves (1 Kings 12:28, 12:32; 2 Kings 17:16). The sixth was the Baal of Jezebel from Phoenicia, also known as the Tyrian Baal (1 Kings 16:31–32, 18:18–26, 18:40, 19:18, 22:53; 2 Kings 1:2–3, 10:18–28, 11:18). The Baal of Phoenicia came with Jezebel and was more than any ordinary Baal; he alone was a principality over many spirits. Other Baalim of Phoenicia remained in Phoenicia. The Baalim of Canaan were obedient unto him and did his bidding. And all must remember that every time there appears the Baalim, there also appears the Astartes, since both work together.

Comparison between Jezebel and Elijah

1. Elijah demands repentance while Jezebel hates repentance.

2. Elijah demands righteousness while Jezebel fights righteousness.

3. Elijah speaks of freedom while Jezebel wants control.

4. Elijah demands humility while Jezebel desires to be prideful.

5. Elijah speaks of God's ways while Jezebel wants her way.

Jezebel's Spirit Defined

1. The Jezebel spirit is a behavior that operates through an individual to control, using manipulation, intimidation, and domineering actions. It works amid both witchcraft (without a form of godliness) and Christianized witchcraft (with the form of godliness).

2. The Jezebel spirit is a behavior influenced by demonic powers.

3. It is not a demon, but it is a behavior under demonic influence and power.

4. In many respects, a spirit may be a demon. Still, it may also be the way of thinking, frame of mind, attitude, or behavior controlled or influenced by demonic powers. In a good way, it may be the reverse.

5. The Jezebel spirit is a generational behavior of manipulation, intimidation, and domineering actions wrought by demonic powers.

6. It is a generational curse or spirit.

7. It is a product of the flesh that opens the door to an evil spirit.

8. The Jezebel spirit is a kindred spirit to that of the spirit of Antichrist.

9. It may be said that Jezebel is a figurative and spiritual name for us.

10. It is a witch whose spirit endures in the church by taking over the vineyard of the Lord.

11. The Jezebel spirit is a spirit that seeks to deceive, defile, and destroy God's authority, God's prophetic, and God's anointing.

12. The Jezebel spirit is a treacherous impostor within the church. It is a counterfeit to the movement of the Holy Spirit.

13. The Jezebel spirit is that attitude, way of thinking, frame of mind, and way of life, contrary to God's plans.

Characteristics of the Jezebel Spirit

Whenever a combination of several characteristics exists in the lives of persons, there is a strong indication that the person is under the influence of a Jezebel spirit. A person heavily influenced by the Jezebel spirit will have most or all these characteristics. A person with one does not mean that this spirit influences him or her. This would mean that the person is still spiritually immature. One characteristic may be easily seen, but the others may be hidden.

1. Rebellious children.

2. Divorce is prominent.

3. Jezebel is a controlling and manipulative person.

4. Jezebel says, "If you loved me, you would."

5. Jezebel is non-gender specific. It can work through man or woman.

6. Sometimes, it creates an unholy alliance. This may be a saint with a witch.

7. Causes divided loyalties.

8. Selfish ambition.

9. Personal gain.

10. Usurper.

11. A lust for life.

12. Initial efforts typically involve securing the pastor's perspective.

13. Attempts to warn the pastor of others.

14. Tries to give misinformation.

15. Commands attention.

16. Vengeful (ruthless, heartless).

17. Attempts to make you look like you are Jezebel.

18. Demonic entanglement.

19. Control.

20. Manipulation.

21. Intimidation.

22. Rebellion.

23. Pride.

24. Hate.

25. Unsubmitted.

26. Liar.

27. Religious.

28. Clairvoyant.

29. Cannot admit wrong; it is always someone else's fault.

30. Unrepentant.

31. False humility.

32. Fear.

33. Uses deception and deceit.

34. Overemphasizing its importance.

35. Exaggerating to the extreme.

36. Greedy.

37. Projecting one's power.

38. Living in a world of distortions.

39. Presumption.

40. Pushiness.

41. Showoff (upstaging another).

42. Excessive bragging.

43. Self.

44. The yearning to have a clergyman as a spouse if the spirit chooses a woman.

45. Embracing new beliefs, new methods, and new spiritual practices.

46. Courts all false prophets.

47. Tries to steal the microphone. It tries to take over.

48. It uses people to accomplish its agenda.

49. Withholds information.

50. Talks in confusion.

51. Volunteers for everything.

52. Takes credit for everything.

53. Does not pay attention to people.

54. Spiritualizes everything.

55. It seeks to impart its anointing, power, or spirituality.

56. This spirit seeks to gain favor.

57. It seeks intimacy with power.

58. It is bittersweet, dripping with honey.

The Purposes of the Jezebel Spirit

1. It operates in witchcraft.

2. It operates in lawlessness.

3. It operates in dominance.

4. It operates in seduction.

5. It operates in sexual perversion.

6. It operates as a spirit of seduction.

7. It makes all who follow it become eunuchs.

8. It strips men of their manhood and men and women of their free will.

9. It is an anti-prophetic spirit.

10. It is an anti-anointing spirit.

11. It sows discord and sedition.

12. It undermines authority.

13. It is an anti-charisma spirit.

14. It insists on the right to teach and practice licentious indulgence and claims inspiration for its teaching.

15. It works in divination.

16. It works in political idolatry (worshipping the state rather than God).

17. It desires to rule and control the people of God, especially the church's prophetic voice.

18. It appeals to the pride in us.

19. It tries to control the minister or pastor.

20. It tries to brainwash all.

21. It tries to control the teaching and preaching of the pastor.

22. The spirit will try to stop and destroy God's plans.

23. It operates in an exact contrast to the will of God.

24. It will steal authority by lies and distortions.

25. It seeks after the anointing. The anointing will attract the good, the hungry, and the genuine, but also it will attract those who have the Spirit of Jezebel.

26. It despises prophecy, forbids true prophecy and true prophets from having a place in the service, and promotes false prophecy and false prophets to have their way (Revelation 2:22, 19:10).

27. It will proclaim a true prophet's downfall (1 Kings 19:2).

28. It will often cause prophetic people to run from their responsibility.

29. It tries to dismantle a wall of prayer.

30. It brings in occultism and claims to be taught by a voice, an angel, or God.

31. It makes up its theology from these sources and not from studying Scripture.

32. It brings in hearsay.

33. When a person comes with gossip, the pastor must have the accuser, and the accused, confront the other over what was said.

34. Someone with this spirit will have a strange doctrine.

35. It has false dreams and visions.

36. It has false voices.

37. It will carry false burdens and create spiritual dependency on others.

38. It will appear more spiritual than anyone else, including Jesus Christ.

39. Jezebel operated in "spiritual whoredom" when she persuaded Ahab to allow her to usurp authority in the Kingdom and had Naboth killed (1 Kings 21:4–10, 20, 25; 2 Kings 9:22).

40. Jezebel wants to become the center of worship and attention and demands obedience to their every command.

41. The more spiritually minded a church grows, the more dangerous is the operation of the Jezebel spirit. This means that one must hold on entirely to the Bible.

42. Jezebel uses the soulish prophecy (John 16:13–14).

43. It also tries to control the flow of intercession and the flow of the music.

44. It will try to turn people away from Scripture so that they can be controlled through false teachings and the use of occult power (Revelation 2:20). For example, it will take revelation over Scripture.

45. It will always try to paralyze the prophetic flow of God.

46. It tries to confuse the pastor or minister with various revelations, dreams, visions, and other supernatural manifestations presented to him. This is misinformation, so the pastor or minister cannot hear from God.

Other Facts About the Jezebel Spirit

1. The Jezebel spirit is not a demon but a spirit like the spirit of the Antichrist, which has a far-reaching influence (1 John 4:3).

2. The Jezebel spirit will work either openly or secretly. The open spirit can be easily identified; the secret form of this spirit is hard to identify. It will take time.

3. In the secret form, Jezebel is sitting in our churches, secretly undermining and controlling because leaders are afraid of confrontation. It is getting away with it (Revelation 2:20).

4. Such was the might of this spirit that Elijah, fearing Jezebel's vengeance, ran away and sought refuge.

5. When this spirit functions through a woman, the Jezebel spirit seems to serve as Satan's answer to a male-dominated world, giving false protection in a world where a woman seemingly never gets her rights nor has the protective love of a father or husband.

6. The Jezebel spirit tries to get what it wants.

7. The Jezebel spirit destroys families, churches, businesses, and relationships.

8. This spirit can work in both a sinner and a saint.

9. This spirit must not be tolerated within a church.

10. It will corrupt all, as Jezebel was trying to and almost succeeded in doing to Israel.

11. The Jezebel spirit can be found in any church. The greater the church, the greater the chance of an attack by this spirit. And the greater the prophetic works, the greater the chance of attack by this spirit.

12. Those under this spirit's control prefer to pray for people in isolated situations—in a corner or another room. Thus, false prophetic words cannot be challenged quickly. By doing this, they gain credibility.

13. Jezebel uses the excuse of "good motives" to operate in the church. However, this spirit operates through the mind and ego of the person and is carried out by spirits of witchcraft.

14. Mind control spirits work to subject the mind, emotions, will, and body to the control and whims of the Jezebel spirit.

15. If the Jezebel spirit is after a husband, it will try its best to destroy his marriage. It will attack his wife. And if he is not

married, the Jezebel spirit will try to destroy or attack anyone close to him (Revelation 2:22).

16. The Jezebel spirit will try to embarrass the pastor or minister.

17. The Jezebel spirit will try to confront the pastor or minister publicly.

18. The Jezebel spirit will seek out a prophetic ministry that begins with a pastor or minister lacking experience dealing with people, especially the Jezebel spirit. This spirit hopes to infiltrate the church so that it can be destroyed.

19. After exposing the Jezebel spirit, it will try to play the victim.

The Reappearance of the Jezebel Spirit

1. Satan has loosed this spirit to destroy the prophetic. When the prophetic appears, so does this spirit.

2. This spirit has always been in the shadows.

3. It has revealed itself in the last days' battle between God and Satan.

Key Phrases or Sentences to look for

1. I just want to be your friend.

2. I just want to help you get to where God has called you.

3. There are no strings attached to my help.

4. You can trust me. I will always support you.

5. You do not acknowledge my gift.

6. You do not understand me.

7. I do not feel like I can talk to you.

8. The Lord has given me some things I need to share with you.

9. My last pastor did not know how to use me or my gifts.

10. God has sent me to teach you and guide you.

11. God uses me to build churches.

12. You will not be under my spiritual covering if you leave this church. Notice that the Jezebel spirit loves the movement where it is taught that the pastor or minister is the spiritual covering.

13. I want to guide your anointing.

14. I need private counseling.

15. I am unhappy with many things in the church.

16. "Season of our lives." Very dangerous phrase for a pastor/minister. It means that the people who say it cannot be trusted, will soon leave and try their best to take people with them.

17. There are many things wrong with this church.

18. Lose the fear of the Lord.

19. I cannot be helped in this ministry.

20. This church/minister does not meet all my needs.

Ways of Discerning a Jezebel Spirit

1. Look for strange behavior.

2. Look for someone who flies off over nothing.

3. Look for someone who claims to be a great intercessor, but there is no proof.

4. Look for someone who claims to be sent by God to build churches or help build your church.

5. Look for someone who wants to do everything.

6. Look for someone who is exalted and believes that he or she is the answer to all your problems.

7. Look for someone who wants prayer always, though there is no change in behavior.

8. Look for someone who wants to be seen as a hero.

9. Look for someone who exaggerates his accomplishments.

10. Look for someone who proclaims his accomplishments.

11. Look for someone who constantly lies.

12. Look for someone who takes credit for everything.

13. Look for someone who takes credit for the anointing of God coming upon a service.

14. Look for someone very friendly with the other workers.

15. Look for someone who oversteps his or her office or calling.

16. Look for someone who is overcome with grief.

17. Look for someone who is insubordinate.

18. Look for someone who will try to destroy another reputation.

19. Look for someone who loves to generate hype.

20. Look for someone who has great charm, dripping with honey.

21. Look for someone who makes unfounded accusations.

22. Look for someone who will eventually overplay her or his hand. In other words, this spirit will try to expose the pastor or minister, but this spirit will be the one who has been exposed.

23. Look for someone who will gang up with others, and if not getting their way, will finally leave a church, minister, business, or anything else.

Purposes of the Anointing and Prophets

1. In the Old Testament, it was the anointing of God connected to the prophets of God who destroyed Jezebel (1 Kings 16:31,

18:4,13, 19:1, 19, 21:5, 7, 11, 14, 15, 23, 25; 2 Kings 9:7, 10, 22, 9:30–37; Revelation 2:20).

2. Today, it will always be the prophet of God who can discern, defeat, and destroy the Jezebel spirit in connection with the anointing of God.

3. It may be said like this: Ahab and Jezebel are rooted in witchcraft, and only the anointing of God roots these out. It takes God's anointing to destroy Jezebel's spirit: Elijah, Elisha, and Jehu were all anointed by God.

4. God seeks those who will become an Elijah or a Jehu (1 Kings 19; 2 Kings 9).

5. A person (especially a pastor) following the ways of Elijah, Elisha, and Jehu will expose the works and darkness of the Jezebel spirit and finally destroy it within a church.

6. The person may also be a prophet or an apostle.

Humble Intercessors

1. Humble Intercessors must stand as watchmen at the church's gate (2 Samuel 18:24–27; 2 Kings 9:17–20; Ezekiel 22:30; 33:2–7).

2. Trustworthy intercessors or watchmen will have the fruit of the spirit (Galatians 5:22–23).

Jezebel Spirit Fears Real Prayer and Warfare Prayer

1. Prayer through the anointing can also destroy the power of this spirit.

Controlling the Jezebel Spirit

1. All persons influenced by this spirit in a decisive manner should not be allowed any official part of the ministry.

2. Another way to stop the Jezebel spirit is not to use the person or persons who are under its power.

3. Keep personal and confidential information from a Jezebel spirit as much as possible.

When Confronting the Jezebel Spirit

1. Pastors or ministers keep your ground.

2. Stand firm against it, and it will back up.

3. Do not believe it, even if it tells some truth.

4. Have witnesses.

5. There will always be a confrontation with this spirit. This spirit may choose the time and the place, but the pastor or minister will be ready if he or she is following the leading of the Holy Spirit. In cases like these, it will be the Holy Spirit who will take over.

Those who have the Jezebel Spirit

1. They will reap what they have sown (Galatians 6:8; Obadiah 1:5).

2. God will bring recompense upon them (2 Thessalonians 1:6).

3. They may be destroyed (Acts 5:5–10; 2 Thessalonians 1:6; Hebrews 12:8).

4. They may prosper for a time, yet this prosperity will cease, and God's judgment will fall (Acts 5:5–10; Hebrews 12:8).

5. God's justice will, in due time, fall upon them (Deuteronomy 7:10, 12–13; 2 Chronicles 6:15; Job 1:21; Psalm 58:11; Matthew 25:21; Romans 2:7; Hebrews 11:26).

6. The gift of "working of miracles" may bring judgment in cases like this (Acts 13:4–12, 5:5–10).

7. They must be removed from the church (1 Corinthians 5:4–5).

Deliverance and The Jezebel Spirit

1. Most who are oppressed with this spirit will never be delivered.

2. This is not due to the lack of God's power but because those under its power desire not to give up their control, manipulation, and intimidation.

3. By His grace and His power, God can bring people to repentance from the pattern of control and deliver them.

4. Remember that the Jezebel mentioned in the Old Testament and the one mentioned in the New Testament did not give up the Jezebel spirit.

5. They died having this spirit.

6. Their free will can never submit entirely to God's power and sovereignty.

7. The Jezebel spirit is not a demon but a behavior designed by demonic powers or influences. It would be easier if this were a demon. Why? It could be cast out.

Deliverance Does Come If:

1. There is genuine repentance (2 Chronicles 7:14). This is key!

2. All strongholds are broken.

3. All generational curses are broken.

4. All connections with this spirit are broken.

5. The person continues to submit to God, working upon them on the potter's wheel, as mentioned in Jeremiah 18. Changing them, in many respects, layer by layer. This may take days, months, or years.

The Spirit of Fornications

In Hosea 4:12, the Hebrew phrase רוּחַ זְנוּנִים (spirit of fornications) attributes fornications and other sexual immoralities to demoniacal power, which the Israelites could not, in their backslidden state, resist. The Hebrew noun זְנוּנִים (of fornications) includes both spiritual and physical fornications. The demoniacal power described under the Hebrew phrase רוּחַ זְנוּנִים (spirit of fornications) is limited here to just the Baalim and the Astartes; besides the Pythonic demons and the Kundalini demons, both the Baalim and the Astartes also work in fornications, both spiritual and especially sexual. The singular use of the term spirit is expected, since all evil spirits mentioned are united into one group or one force. The Israelites were influenced by an evil spirit, a demoniacal power, which led to an insatiable passion for idolatry. Both idolatry and fornications were united together and became a collective seductive and addictive power against the Israelites, which could not be resisted any longer.

The Hebrew phrase רוּחַ זְנוּנִים (spirit of fornications) should well be interpreted as a collective host of evil spirits that are involved in the practicing of fornications as referring to behaviors, demonically controlled, coming upon men and women, and dominating them. This demonically controlled behavior around the activity of fornications, produces more and more sexual practices done outside of God's law and God's nature, and so brings more and more sexual sin upon the nation.

This Hebrew phrase רוּחַ זְנוּנִים (spirit of fornications) is tied to idolatry. And sex magic or any other type of sexual practice is connected to idolatry. And it is quite clear that evil spirits are involved in such behavior and practices. Every physical act of a sinful sexual act is an act united with evil spirits. In other words, the practices are with humans and demons.[59]

In Hosea 2:5, 7 (9), 10 (12), 2:12 and 2:15, the Greek Septuagint does not recognize the lovers of Israel as just spiritual. The Greek noun ἐραστής (lover) cannot be void of sexual practices and sexual involvement among humans and demons. The lovers represented here are the idols, the demons behind the idols, and other humans. There is a spiritual fornication that is clearly seen here, but there is also a physical (sexual) fornication that is occurring between the Israelites and the demons behind the idols wrought upon by demon possession among the devotees to the many practices of paganistic superstition.

Within the Hebrew phrase רוּחַ זְנוּנִים (spirit of fornications), there is a sexual intoxication and addiction that is tied to sexual sin, regardless of the kind; both this sexual intoxication and addiction are means whereby the demons unite with their human vessels. The union of the demons and their human vessels, besides spiritual, are physical by possession and sexual by that same possession. The possession opens a means by which evil spirits become partakers of sexual sin along with their human vessels and spread their evil to others. The evil spirits, residing in their human vessels, engaged in sexual intercourse simultaneously with both the human vessel and their partner.

Both fornication and prostitution spread demons and sexual diseases across the whole nation.

With such forces released by the רוּחַ זְנוּנִים (spirit of fornications), men and women have no choice, no will, nor any freedom at all. Sexual love is released in force with no restraint. Many who suffer from this spirit have reached the point of no return with God; others are simply its slave. But some, thank God, are removed from its hold only by the power of God. This spirit has become the destruction of many and has never saved anyone.

The Spirit of Religion Defined

1. The Spirit of Religion is groups of evil spirits that inspire loyalty to religious concepts and practices in such a way as to oppose and possibly to counterfeit the proper work of the Holy Spirit (Matthew 9:2–34, 12:8–33, 15:2, 16:1, 21:23–27, 22:15–22, 29–34; Luke 10:19; John 17:15–16; Romans 7:22; Galatians 5:16–18; 1 Thessalonians 5:23). The Baalim, the Astartes, the Kundalini demons, and the Pythonic demons can be used in this method.

2. The Spirit of Religion sets up a wall of opposition against the new movement and directions of the Holy Spirit.

3. The Spirit of Religion tries to prevent the continual movement and direction of the Holy Spirit, especially in the domain of Christianity.

4. The spirit seeks to separate the saints from the power of God and make them lifeless in power by preventing them from following the moving and directions of the Holy Spirit. We become stagnant, with no life-living water flowing from us or to us.

5. The Spirit of Religion always tries to get people to camp in one place. It will hold on to that which is familiar and comfortable rather than moving on from glory to glory. Remember, Peter, under the inspiration of Satan, tried to rebuke Jesus because He was going to the cross to suffer and pay for the sins of mankind. But Jesus turned and rebuked Satan in Peter because Peter was operating with a religious spirit.

6. The Spirit of Religion is an agent of Satan assigned to prevent change and maintain the status quo by using religious devices.

7. The Spirit of Religion seeks to destroy the anointing.

Characteristics of the Spirit of Religion

1. Fear of not being good enough.

2. Fear of people.

3. Performance-based, not grace or faith-based.

4. Doing works to atone for our guilt rather than trusting the blood of Christ.

5. Emphasis on external things.

6. False prophecy.

7. Quenching the moving of the Spirit.

8. Emphasis on the traditions of the elders.

9. Emphasis on ritual, special rules, and regulations.

10. Pride in personal sacrifice (Matthew 6).

11. No Mercy (Matthew 12:7).

12. Lack of concern for the needs of people.

13. Follows the letter of the law rather than the spirit of the law.

14. Hypocrisy—play acting.

15. The love of religious power but the rejection of the power of the Holy Spirit (Matthew 12:44; 2 Timothy 3:5).

16. Jealousy and Envy (1 Corinthians 1:12; 2 Corinthians 10:12).

17. Hating the ungodly instead of hating the sins of the ungodly (Luke 18:9; John 7:49).

18. They emphasize their traditions more than the plan, teachings, commandments, and declarations of Scripture (Mark 16:15).

19. Blindness to the work of God.

20. False accusations (Mark 3:2).

21. Seeks to limit God and define how God will move by pointing to how He moved in the past. This puts God in a box.

22. Put to spiritual death your dreams in God and everything God has promised you.

23. Put people below impossible religious demands and burdens.

24. Make your own relationship with God feel inferior.

25. Make other people appear godlier and superior so that the Spirit of Religion can use them to boss you around and make you feel inferior.

26. Silence your voice and what God wants to say through you (Saul the spear-chucker).

27. Snuff out your gift and what God wants to do through you.

28. Kill the prophetic anointing.

Jesus and the Spirit of Religion

Jesus Christ had little trouble dealing with demons provoking sickness and disease in people. However, the Lord faced more significant opposition from people controlled by religious spirits. These people did not know they had religious spirits. They thought they represented the true religion of God. They did not want to be free of the spirits that made them feel important and more righteous than those around them.

Because of their pride and hardness, even the Son of God could not help them come to the Father. These people were known as the Scribes and Pharisees, the chief priests, and experts in the law.

It was these people who hated Jesus and conspired to crucify Him. They were motivated by pride, envy, and self-righteousness. They refused to humble themselves and believe in the Messiah despite Jesus's various proofs. This remained true even after they were confronted with the fact of the resurrection.

We make a grave mistake if we assume that the spirit that motivated these Jewish religious leaders can in no way influence us. Those who think like that are probably the very ones who are influenced by such spirits. While these religious spirits will not promote the same errors now as they did in those people, there will be similarities in attitude and behavior, which will be seen.

Strategy of the Spirit of Religion

1. The Spirit of Religion is to promote the idea that belonging to a Christian church or doing religious things is what saves you.

2. The Spirit of Religion tries to keep that person without foundation or stability. It does not allow believers to move on to filling the Holy Spirit or freedom in Christ or fulfilling God's destiny for their lives. Paul specifically warns that the devil, by his craftiness, can corrupt minds and keep them from "the simplicity that is in Christ" (2 Corinthians 11:3).

3. The Spirit of Religion also targets a church's religious power and determines the congregation's destiny.

243

Religious Spirits VS. Religious Spirits

While it is true that religious spirits, also known as the spirits of religion, are groups of real demons, there is something more that must be spoken about here. For example, a religious spirit has a double meaning. It can well be a demon, but it can be a religious thought, idea, practice, teaching, and behavior that is perverse and contrary to the divine law, truth, and will. And these thoughts, ideas, practices, teachings, and behaviors come from the communication of men with evil spirits. A religious spirit can be simply a religious system contrary to God's will, divine law, and divine truth. And it is this that controls people, and it is these things coming from real demons.

Demons control the thinking of men and women in religion, setting up their beliefs, tenets, teachings, practices, and behavior. All these things become part of paganism or at least a system that is in direct opposition to Jesus Christ, the Bible, Divine truth, divine law, and divine will.

In Matthew, the religious spirit is seen working in the Pharisees and the Sadducees (Matthew 9:2–34, 12:8–33, 15:2, 16:1, 21:23–27, 22:15–22, 22:29–34). The Pharisees' and Sadducees' thoughts, ideas, practices, and behavior were manifestations of the religious spirits, demons, and their workings.

For example, the attitude of the Pharisees was the opposite of that of John the Baptist. The attitude of the Pharisees led them to have a part in the killing of Jesus Christ. Therefore, this type of resistance is nothing more than the operations of demonic forces that cooperate in forms of religion.

Pride, arrogance, and haughtiness come from religious spirits (Matthew 3:9). This spirit does not come from Jesus Christ (Matthew 9:2–7). It will try to defend a false idea of God's honor and try to destroy the only means of salvation. And the means of going to heaven by good works or other manners rather than Christ is heavily stressed (Matthew 9:10–13). It is an attitude that focuses on the form of godliness and, at the same time, denies the power of God. It misrepresents the law. And it confuses the traditions of men with the holiness of God.

CHAPTER 5

TEACH ME TO PRAY

I was very naive when it came to prayer. Like others, I thought prayer was easy. As I've said, prayer is far from easy; it is a work and a task. And it will take a lifetime to learn how to pray effectively.

To touch the hem of the Lord requires precise and successful prayer. It requires constant, repeated, and persevering prayer. We must continue to pray on a subject until we have prayed through and received assurance that the answer of the Lord God is on its way.

Like the apostles, I sought the Lord to teach me how to pray. We see this in Luke 11:1, where one of the disciples said unto Jesus, "Lord, teach us to pray."

Hard Knocks

Over many years of learning to pray, I went on a journey from hard knocks to common sense. Within the first few years of public ministry, I went crazy praying for every person I could find, taking their burdens to the extreme, draining myself, and almost going to the point of mental and emotional breakdown.

However, I began to notice something in Scripture that caught my attention. I learned that Paul himself ran from a battle, for a time, until God moved (a critical word: moved) him to go into battle. When the time was right, God moved upon Paul, and the fight was won.

I am referring to the incident in Acts 16, where the damsel was possessed with the Pythonic demon, and the demon kept running after Paul, harassing him. Finally, God moved upon him, and Paul stood against the demon.

I realized that if Apostle Paul avoided this battle until God moved upon him to stand his ground and commanded that evil spirit to be exorcised from the damsel, maybe I needed to stop running into battles that God did not want me to get into. Maybe I, too, needed to wait until God moved upon me to become engaged in a battle that He alone commanded me to fight with the authority of Christ and the power of the Holy Spirit.

I learned that not every battle is for me to fight. I also realized that people have their own battles to face, and sometimes, I am not allowed or ordered by God to fight for them or with them.

In 1 Corinthians 6:9–15, Paul, being very honest, after listing various kinds of people who are excluded from eternal life if they do not change, said, "Such were some of you" (1 Corinthians 6:11). What would be the best way to translate this phrase of 1 Corinthians 6:11? There are three ways of translating Greek here that are better than how the King James Version has translated it:

1. "These things are what some of you were."

2. "These dreadful things were some of you."

3. "These detestable sinners were some of you."

The neuter form of the demonstrative pronoun in the Greek text points out a horrifying view about these practices. Paul regards all the vices listed as horrors or monsters. By the simple phrase "such were some of you," Paul is entirely pointing back to the vice list and saying to each sort of former sinner at Corinth, "Some of you were fornicators, some of you were idolaters, some of you were adulterers, and so on; but now you are washed, sanctified, and justified."

John Owen says it quite well. "Hell can scarce, in no more words, yield us a sadder catalogue. Yet some of all these sorts were justified and pardoned."[1] John Calvin, in his commentary on First Corinthians, writes, "The simple meaning, therefore, is this, that prior to their being regenerated by grace, some of the Corinthians were covetous, others adulterers, others extortioners, others effeminate, others revilers, but now, being made free by Christ, they were such no longer."[2] Charles Hodges, in his commentary on First Corinthians, says, "The idea being, 'Some were impure, some drunkards, some violent, etc.'"[3] Calvin, Owen, and Hodge understood "some" as distributive in nature. Repetition is meant.

In the Corinthian congregation, a good variety of such former immoral persons was to be found. Paul points out a contrast between their present state and their past. Their moral condition made an uncompromising demand to leave all the past sins and deeds and never practice them again. Their sinful lives are in the past. So their moral lives are monuments of the power of the blood.

To Paul, such debased sins are so strong that only some can submit to the call of God and receive the redemption wrought by the blood of Christ Jesus. Paul acknowledges the power of these debased sins to create defiance against God within the majority of those who practice them. Few ever want to change.

Paul divides the Corinthian church into ten main categories of former evildoers. Out of each sinful category at Corinth, only some denounced their particular sins, came out of that category, and were changed. The majority of former sinners in the Corinthian church had come from these ten categories.

Paul clearly tailored his vice list of 1 Corinthians 6:9–11 to the needs of the Corinthian community he addressed. In Paul's vice list, the absence of a sin does not give a license to commit it. Any sin not mentioned in this list is still understood as an evil practice. The sins that afflicted Corinth considerably were mentioned. The sins that did not dominate Corinth were understood as still present, but very little problem for that city.

Paul's emphasis here is a warning. Only some who practice a particular abomination will be saved and delivered from it. In such cases, the blood of Christ can only reach a few. Why? It is not because the blood is insufficient; it is not because the power of God is impotent. Instead, the response rests with the majority of these types of sinners never wanting to be saved. So I learned that I must pursue after those sinners who wish to be saved and changed from their sins.

Then, again, I remembered the parable of the sower, and within that parable, the four grounds (Matthew 13:18—23). The seeds were broadcast throughout the ground and landed on four types of ground. Out of the four types of ground, the seeds grew consistently and in a sustained manner in only one type. The other seeds were destroyed, or their plants were destroyed. But the seeds that grew on the good ground significantly produced. I learned for this to happen, people must cultivate their lives. So I learned not to focus on uncultivated land, but on land that has been cultivated by prayer, obedience, faith, consecration, dedication, the fruit of the Holy Spirit, the power of the Holy Spirit, and the authority of Jesus Christ. Some will accept Christ, but others will not. People must have their ground (lives) cultivated (prepared) to receive Christ. But they must also have that ground cultivated to have their prayers answered, and to be healed, delivered, and have prophetic words come to pass.

What is Prayer?

One of the most significant statements about prayer was by Tertullian, a father of the early church in the third century, in his book on prayer:

sola est oratio quae deum uincit; sed christus eam nihil mali uoluit operari, omnem illi uirtutem de bono contulit. Itaque nihil nouit nisi defunctorum animas de ipso mortis itinere reuocare, debiles reformare, aegros remediare, daemoniacos expiare, claustra carceris aperire, uincula innocentium soluere. Eadem diluit delicta, temptationes repellit, persecutiones extinguit, pusillanimos consolatur, magnanimos oblectat, peregrinantes deducit, fluctus mitigat, latrones obstupefacit, alit pauperes, regit diuites, lapsos erigit, cadentes suspendit, stantes continet.

Oratio murus est fidei, arma et tela nostra aduersus hostem, qui nos undique obseruat. Itaque numquam inermes incedamus. Die stationis, nocte uigiliae meminerimus. Sub armis orationis signum nostri imperatoris custodiamus tubam angeli expectemus orantes. Orant etiam angeli omnes, orat omnis creatura, orant pecudes et ferae et genua declinant et egredientes de stabulis ac speluncis ad caelum non otioso ore suspiciunt uibrantes spiritum suo more. Sed et aues tunc exurgentes eriguntur ad caelum et alarum crucem pro manibus expandunt et dicunt aliquid quod oratio uideatur. Quid ergo amplius de officio orationis? etiam ipse dominus orauit, cui sit honor et uirtus in saecula saeculorum

(Only prayer is that which prevails with God, but Christ has willed that it works no evil. He has bestowed on it all the virtue of goodness. Therefore, it knows nothing except how to call back the spirits of the dead from the very path of death, to transform the weak, to heal the sick, to purge those who are demon possessed, to open the doors of prisons and to release the chains of those who are innocent. Also, it washes away faults, repels temptations, quenches persecutions, comforts the fainthearted, delights those who are high spirited, leads travelers, calms the waves, paralyzes robbers, feeds the poor, rules over the rich, raises up the fallen, props up those who are falling, and sustains those who are standing. Prayer is the wall of faith; its arms and missiles are thrown against our enemy who watches over us on all sides. And so, we never walk defenseless. By the day of our station and by the night of our vigil, we must be mindful. Under the arms of prayer, we guard the battle standard of our general; we must wait in praying for the trumpet of an angel. Likewise, all angels pray; every creature prays; cattle and wild beasts pray and bend their knees; and when they come out of their dens and caves, they look up toward heaven with no idle mouth and make their breath vibrate rapidly after their own manner. But then the birds too raise out of the nest, lifting themselves up toward heaven, and instead of hands, they spread out the cross of their wings, and say something that may seem to be like a prayer. What, therefore, is greater

than the office of prayer? Even the Lord Himself prayed;
to whom must be the honor and virtue unto the ages of
the ages)![4]

The first sentence about prayer by Tertullian, "Only prayer is that which prevails with God," refers to the wrestling of Jacob with God through an angel (Genesis 32:24–32) and Matthew 11:12: "And from the days of John the Baptist until now the kingdom of heaven suffereth violence, and the violent take it by force." Further, the prevailing (wrestling) cannot mean that a person can make God do anything against His will. Instead, the idea is that only prayer can move God to change His will and plan about a circumstance if God so wills. For instance, there was a struggle between God and Moses about the Israelites. God had decided to destroy the Israelites and choose another people as His chosen people because they made and worshipped the golden calves. As said before, according to Jewish sources, there was more than one calf; there were thirteen golden calves.[5]

But by intercessory prayer and fasting, Moses tugged on the heart of God and changed the mind of God about the Israelites. Therefore, God did not destroy them (Exodus 32:9–35).

The possibilities of prayer are always found to be in alliance with the purposes and will of God. Prayer can only change the purposes of God if God allows it (Matthew 26:39; John 18:11; Judges 10:13; 2 Kings 20:1; Jonah 3:4).

Accordingly, while the practice of prayer is widespread, there are very few Christians who know how to pray and how to receive results from their prayers. Indeed, we are often unable to grasp the fullness of prayer. We think too little about prayer or that it is just words. We do not know the power of prayer when our words are united with God's will.

Today, the belief that God will answer our requests is almost non-existent. If we pray thinking we will not receive anything back, we should stop praying. We are defeated before we begin. And if people do pray, their prayers easily become a selfish practice, where the self is exalted rather than selflessness. Today, there is very little submission and humility.

It is sad, but our prayer life has become the prayer life of a young granddaughter. For instance, "An elderly gentleman passed his granddaughter's room one night and overheard her repeating the alphabet in an oddly reverent way. 'What on earth are you up to?' he asked. 'I'm saying my prayers,' explained the little girl. 'But I can't think of exactly the right words tonight, so I'm just saying all the letters. God will put them together for me because He knows what I'm thinking.'"[6]

In truth, prayer must have holiness, dedication, determination, perseverance, obedience, integrity, commitment, simplicity, purity, humility, and faith interwoven into it before we even begin to pray.

Sometimes, a prayer might be prayed only once. Other times, a prayer must be repeatedly prayed before an answer is given. And other times, the results of our prayers will be long and drawn out. That requires continual prayer over many hours, days, or years.

For example, George Mueller, a Christian evangelist in the AD 1800s,

> began to pray for a group of five personal friends. After five years one of them came to Christ. In ten years, two more of them found peace in the same Saviour. He prayed on for twenty-five years, and the fourth man was saved. For the fifth he prayed until the time of his death, and this friend, too, came to Christ a few months afterwards. For this latter friend, Mr. Mueller had prayed almost fifty-two years! When we behold such perseverance in prayer, we feel that we have scarcely touched the fringe of real importunity in our intercessions for others.[7]

Prayer may need to go on for decades to see the complete fulfillment of its results.

And a century earlier, in AD 1727, twenty-four men and twenty-four women of the Moravians begin to pray each, one hour a day in scheduled prayer. This prayer vigil continued an astonishing one hundred years; when an intercessor died or became too sick to continue, another one took his or her place. The results of their prayers included the greatest missionary movement in the world until that time, the massive movement of God's Spirit in the First Great Awakening in AD 1734 and the founding of America in AD 1776.[8]

In one special instance of continual prayer, until the Lord moved, Reverend Harry E. Bowley, a Pentecostal revivalist and pioneer, and Reverend Lawrence, another Pentecostal revivalist and pioneer, faced one of the greatest times of their lives. A man named Joe French had died, and they knew to pray for his resurrection. They fell on the floor of their room and stayed there in agony of soul and spirit for at least three or four hours in continual prayer, rebuking death, and speaking life upon Joe French. They did not stop praying intensively until there came a knock at the door, and a woman said, "Hallelujah! Joe's alive." The words of Reverend Harry E. Bowley are worth noting: "God can do things when people pray." The man whom they prayed for was saved and began preaching the gospel and giving his testimony to many people.[9] Most Christians would have allowed the man to die, and God would have been robbed of a great testimony of His grace and power.

For approximately two thousand years, the Spirit and the bride continue to say, "Come" to the Lord Jesus Christ (Revelation 22:17). This simple prayer is the only recorded prayer of the Holy Spirit. And that prayer focuses on the coming of the Lord for His saints (1 Thessalonians 4:15−18). If the Holy Spirit continues to pray in repetition over the coming of the Lord, we should follow His example in certain circumstances.

Prayer has many facets and many means. Many definitions of prayer can well be used to define prayer, and some of them are as follows:

1. Prayer, at its very foundation, is a conversation between God and us, communion and unity between God and us, and a relationship with God.

2. Without prayer in the life of a saint, there cannot be any relationship with God.

3. Therefore, without prayer in the life of a saint, that person cannot be a saint.

4. Prayer is crying out to God from your heart.

5. Prayer is intermingling with God.

6. Prayer that is of God will consist of the prevalence of truth, faith, obedience, purity, simplicity, and the gift of grace at its very simplest forms.

7. Prayer is like a spiritual gun. This holy gun comprises three things: faith, the name of Jesus, and the promise from God. Faith is the barrel of that gun, the name of Jesus is the trigger, and the promise of God is the bullet.

8. Prayer is recognizing the presence of God, talking with God, listening to God, identifying with God, and knowing God.

9. Prayer becomes an act, a practice, and a way of life that will lead those who pray to know Christ. If not, prayer is not true.

10. Prayer is used to express everything that we are in Christ (Matthew 7:7–8; John 16:13).

11. Only by prayer can we experience a relationship with God.

12. Our life of prayer determines or regulates the value, quality, and state of our spiritual life with God.

13. Prayer is entering and enjoying the presence of God.

14. Prayer can unleash the power of God on our behalf.

15. Prayer can open the many passages of God's blessing into our lives.

16. Prayer is the means by which God accomplishes the various things that He wants to see in our lives.

17. Prayer can open many opportunities for God to move and bless our lives.

18. Prayer is the originator and channel of devotion; the spirit of prayer is the spirit of devotion to God.

19. Prayer and devotion are united like body and spirit.

20. Prayer is not repeating void formulas or void repetition of words (Matthew 6:7).

21. Prayer is the work of the Spirit who uses our organs of speech for instruments of the divine praises. In such cases, every stop and pause of those instruments is the conclusion of a prayer.

22. Prayer is a great duty, and the most significant benefit and privilege of a Christian.

23. Prayer is the primary instrument whereby we minister to God.

24. Prayer is the ascension of the mind of God and petitioning for such things as we need for our support and duty.

25. Prayer is a theoretical and practical representation of a Christian's life and dedication unto God.

26. Prayer is an act of religion and divine worship.

27. The presence of prayer differentiates religious events from morally comparable ones.

28. Prayer seeks all that God is, and we give Him all that we have or all that we can give.

29. Prayer confesses the power, grace, and mercy of God.

30. Prayer is an intense emotion and intense aspiration.

31. Prayer is the most perfect and divine action of which a saint is capable.

32. Prayer celebrates the attributes of God.

33. Prayer confesses God's glories, reveres His persons, implores His aid, and gives thanks for His blessing.

34. Prayer is an act of humility, respect, and dependence, expressed in the prostration of our bodies, and the humiliation of our spirits.

35. Prayer is an act of charity when we pray for others.

36. Prayer is an act of repentance when the prayer confesses and begs pardon for our sins.

37. Prayer is an act of grace and mercy.

Necessities of Prayer

1. We pray because we love God and want a relationship with God.

2. We pray because we must depend on God rather than upon ourselves (Colossians 3:4).

3. Only by prayer, do we obtain the comfort, ease, endurance, potency, determination, and other supplies we need for every part of our Christian life.

4. Prayer is as necessary unto our spiritual life as breathing is essential for our natural life.

5. We must pray to stop, hinder, or resist temptation (Matthew 26:41).

6. Without prayer as a weapon in our lives, it is impossible to stop, hinder, or resist temptation.

7. By prayerlessness, we become weaker and weaker in our spiritual life.

8. By prayerlessness, we finally become lukewarm or backslidden.

9. By prayerlessness, Satan can gain an advantage in our lives.

10. We must pray because we need God, and we need salvation from Him.

11. We must request God into our lives so that He will work.

12. If no Christian prays, Satan controls and dominates the affairs of men and the issues of the church, and the judgment of God will eventually come to pass.

13. By prayer, we beseech God to reach down and touch multitudes to be saved, who otherwise may not be saved.

14. The necessity of prayer is grounded upon the commandment of God to pray (Colossians 4:2; 1 Thessalonians 5:17).

15. Prayer is necessary for what God wants to happen in the world of men (Daniel 9:2).

16. We pray to spend time with God.

17. By prayer, we identify with God (Galatians 5:16).

18. By prayer, we gain strength to resist temptation.

19. By prayer, we can get right with God.

20. By prayer, we can find forgiveness, mercy, and grace.

21. By prayer, we learn the will of God.

22. By prayer, we learn the authority of God.

23. By prayer, we offer sacrifices to God.

24. By prayer, we can release the authority and power of God.

25. Without prayer, all our knowledge, our libraries, and our education become useless.

26. Prayer makes a person a saint.

27. Prayer determines the status of a saint.

28. Prayer moves God in the world if He wants to be moved in the direction that is being prayed.

29. To a prayerful man or woman, God is present in realized power.

30. Prayer is the established and singular condition of God to move His Son's kingdom ahead.

People, Please Pray and Pray Right

Christians pray for numerous reasons, and many of these reasons are unbiblical, even selfish. Christians pray because it might work. Or we pray because our mother, father, or grandparents may have prayed. We remember in the back of our minds that, if all else fails, pray. For many, if not most, prayer has become the last choice when there is no hope. Instead, it should be the first hope and first practice.

As Christians, we know that we must pray and should pray, but we may still not understand what prayer is in the first place. Or why God wants us to pray about our needs. Or why God needs our prayers to be fulfilled. Indeed, most Christians have forgotten the task and duty of prayer. And in so doing, we have forgotten the weapon of prayer.

Our Call to Pray

Genuine prayer unlocks the entrance for God to work in our lives and the nations of the world. Without prayer in our lives, there is no submission to God. For prayer and submission are united together. It is impossible to submit to God without prayer; it is impossible to really learn how to pray without submission. And prayer is the means by which Christians submit everything to the Lord God.

Further, genuine prayer calls God to come forth and work for us in our lives and in the things that affect us in our lives. By obedience to His commandments, and placing our cares, troubles, trials, and thoughts on Him, we put those things under His sovereignty and power instead of our own. When we pray and believe in the power of prayer, we reject our independence and learn to submit and depend upon the Lord (1 Peter 5:6–7). By doing this, we learn dependence upon the Lord God.

Many years ago, I personally heard Lester Sumrall saying that he refused to give counseling. He saw that it never helped. Instead, he led people to Jesus Christ, told them to pray, set them there before His feet, and walked away. Lester Sumrall had much success in this way of taking people to Jesus. And this was primarily when the anointing of God was present.

Another example is the case of Daniel. During this time, the condition of the Israelites was awful (Daniel 9:1–2). God had not moved; He promised that the Israelites were to experience only seventy years of captivity. God had not fulfilled that promise for His people; it appeared that the captivity was to continue, or something worse was to occur. It was possible that the Israelites were to be destroyed, if not rescued. But when Daniel stood up in prayer and fasting—he stood and prayed alone—remembering the promise of God and reminding God of that promise, God began to work for Daniel and the Israelites. Though God knew about the promise and what the problem was, He was waiting for someone to pray and care enough about that promise and problem to pray.

Many problems in the world go unsettled because Christians refuse to pray as God directs them to pray. Then we blame God when He is not at fault. We have just not prayed.

What if Christians had become proactive about Hitler or Stalin? The evils done by them might have become non-existent or greatly reduced just by the prayers of the saints. Too many saints focus on themselves and not on the divine plan. When the self-rules prayer, prayer becomes useless to the kingdom of God.

Furthermore, in genuine prayer, we declare and confess that God can take care of us in all our circumstances. In prayer, we must confess our sins and our condition before the Lord as we pray.

In prayer, it is key to come before God with repentance, thanksgiving, and humility. We come before God as repentant men or women, bowing ourselves before the Lord God and His sovereignty. In so doing, our condition is right to receive answered prayer, and our spirits are allowed greater fellowship with the Lord.

Lord, Teach Us to Pray!

After living daily with Jesus and learning so much at His feet, his disciples asked, "Lord, teach us to pray" (Luke 11:1). This petition came from men who had seen the robust results of Christ's praying. They sought after a more in-depth experience in prayer than they had experienced in their own lives. It takes years to learn prayer, its importance, and the various ways of praying.

Beginning to Pray

1. We must begin to talk to God.

2. We must acknowledge God as our Father.

3. We must acknowledge Jesus as our Friend, Helper, Lord, Intercessor, Master, and Savior.

4. We must recognize the Holy Spirit as our Comforter, Helper, Intercessor, and Guide.

5. We must know just who we are in Jesus Christ.

6. We should pray unto the Father in the name of Jesus Christ (John 14:6; Hebrews 10:19).

7. We must confess our unconfessed sins.

8. By confessing our sins, the blood of Jesus Christ cleanses us and allows us entrance into the presence of God.

9. We must "enter into his gates with thanksgiving" (Psalm 100:4).

10. We must thank God for forgiving our sins, for coming into our lives, and for making us His children.

11. We must ask God for whatever we need.

12. We must thank God and praise Him for His answer.

13. We must also spend time asking for His Spirit to help us to pray and to pray for us as an intercessor.

14. We must also pray that Jesus will be our intercessor.

15. We must talk to the Holy Spirit.

16. We must tell the Holy Spirit what we want Him to know (Romans 8:26).

Preparations for Prayer

1. Our inner man must be prepared to have fellowship with the Lord God by confessing our sins (Psalm 24:3–5; Mark 11:25–26; Hebrews 10:19; 1 John 1:6–9, 3:21–22).

2. Without preparing our inner man, it is impossible for a Christian to enter the presence of God and have fellowship with Him.

3. We must be determined in what we are petitioning God.

4. We must have a direction to our prayer.

5. We must focus ourselves on one subject at a time.

6. We should have a specific prayer.

7. Our prayer must proceed from the right perception of God.

8. We must have faith in what we are asking the Lord.

9. We must ask according to the will of God.

10. We must know what the Word of God says.

11. We must renew our minds with the Word of God (Romans 12:1–2).

Common Patterns of Prayer (John 16:23–26)

1. Prayer is addressed to the Father. So the Father hears and answers the prayers.

2. Prayer is sent through Jesus. So Christ permits, acknowledges, accepts, receives the prayer, and sends it to the Father.

3. Prayer is collected, influenced, and sent to Jesus by the Holy Spirit.

4. There are exceptions to this typical pattern of prayer.

Keys to the Prayers of the Ancient Church

1. Prayers were grounded in the Bible itself.

2. Prayers were formed by phrases and words directly from the Bible.

3. Prayers emphasized the holiness of God.

4. Prayers expressed a spirit of reverence to God.

5. Prayers stressed the Trinity.

6. Prayers were more collective than individual, which reduces self in prayer.

The Model Prayer

1. Prayer begins with a statement and a testimony to God and with the reward of faith (Matthew 6:9–13).

   a. We are reminded of our duty to God.
   b. We are reminded to obey, fear, and give reverence to God.

2. "Hallowed be thy name" means that His name is to be holy, sacred, and to be esteemed. It is universally recognized that God is to be blessed by every man and woman in every place and time because of the memory of His benefits falling upon all mankind.

3. "Thy Kingdom come" has reference to petitioning the rule of God over and in our lives.

   a. This also denotes a cry that His reign will be hastened upon the earth.
   b. It is a cry, "How long, O Lord, holy and true, dost thou not judge and avenge our blood on them that dwell on the earth?" (Revelation 6:10).
   c. It is a cry that the long foretold millennial kingdom would soon come.

4. According to this model, the phrase, "Thy will be done in earth as it is in heaven" means that we pray for His will to be done in all the universe.

a. We want God's will to be done on earth the way it is done in heaven.

b. We make a petition.

c. After that, He supplies us with the substance of His will, and the capacity to do it, so that we may be saved.

d. This phrase also denotes that we must perpetually petition in Christ for our whole life and everything we need.

5. "And forgive us our debts as we forgive our debtors." This phrase deals with clemency for sinners.

a. All the sins of infirmity, invasion, sudden surprise, and those great sins that were washed off from our spirits and the stain taken away by the blood of Christ are meant here.

b. It is repentance again of all sins, including past and present.

6. "And lead us not into temptation." He prays that the saints of God will suffer not to be led into temptation.

a. This will be done through spiritual warfare, being watchful, being careful, and ever ready.

b. It also means not to be overcome by temptation.

7. "But deliver us from evil."

a. Deliver us from the assaults or violence of evil, from the wicked one, who not only presents us with temptations, but heightens our concupiscence, makes us imaginative, fantastical and passionate, and makes the lust active coming against us, and our appetite for that lust complete and ready to receive it.

8. "For thine is the kingdom, the power, and the glory, forever."

a. These things we pray for must be for the honor of His kingdom, for the manifestation of His power, and the glory of His name and mercies.

Guidelines of Prayer

1. We must depend on the Holy Spirit.

2. We must meditate on the Lord Jesus Christ, and His Word, and petition in our prayers what we need.

3. We must realize who we are in Christ (John 16:24–26; Colossians 3:17).

4. We must know how God hears us (John 16:24–26; Colossians 3:17).

5. We must remember that we are the saints of God, and His children (John 1:12; Galatians 3:26; Revelation 1:6).

6. We must believe and expect that God will answer our prayers (1 Peter 3:12).

7. When we pray, we must forgive those who have hurt us (Mark 11:25).

8. When we pray, we must ask for forgiveness (Luke 18:9–14).

9. We must remove all hindrances (Matthew 5:23–24).

10. We must accept the answer of God (2 Corinthians 12:7–9).

11. We must do something for God (John 15:16).

12. We must be right with God and right with others (Psalm 139:23–24).

13. We must listen to the Lord (Psalm 46:10).

14. We must trust the Lord (Proverbs 29:25).

15. We must pray and pray again (James 5:13–18).

16. We must fast (Daniel 9:3–4).

17. We must accept correction, chastisement, reproof, and pruning from God (Hebrews 12:5–7).

18. We must live a holy life (1 Peter 1:15–17).

19. We must meet the conditions of God (Isaiah 55:6–7).

20. We must pray in agreement (Matthew 18:19–20).

21. We must recognize the presence of God (Matthew 6:5–6).

22. We must put God first (Matthew 6:10).

23. We must thank God for answers to prayer and for our salvation.

24. We must tell God how great He is.

25. By thanking God, we will increase our faith.

26. We must worship God.

27. We must submit completely to God.

28. We must ask for daily provision.

29. We must pray the Word.

30. According to Romans 10:8, the Word of God must be in our spirits and our mouths when we pray.

31. When we pray, we should notice that God desires to meet, fulfill, and keep His promises.

32. Then, we should use the Word of God, continue reminding God of His promises, and keep asking God to fulfill His promises.

33. We must plead the glory and honor of God's name (Psalm 106:8; 2 Samuel 7:26).

34. We must plead the nature of God, which means His glory, majesty, power, and other divine attributes (Isaiah 16:5).

35. We must plead our sorrows and needs (Psalm 35:11–13).

36. We must remind God of His answers to our past prayers (Psalms 27:9, 78, 85:1–7).

37. We must quote a promise and show our assurance in receiving an answer.

38. We must quote a fulfilled promise as a reason for praise.

39. We must find a particular verse of Scripture to claim for the situation.

40. We must pray the Word of God over our needs.

41. We must pray the Word of God into the lives of people and ourselves.

42. We must pray the Word of God into situations, trials, and other types of troubles.

43. We must be in one accord with the Father, the Lord Jesus Christ, and the Spirit.

44. True prayer begins at the Father; true prayer will always be answered. Why? It is the will of the Father to answer it. It comes from the Father.

45. Unanswered prayers are prayers that do not originate from the Father.

46. We must ask God for definite things that we want (Psalm 37:4).

47. We should pray in such a way that we will know afterward what we prayed for, and we will recognize when the answer to our prayer is manifested.

48. We must allow God to lead us to pray for others rather than praying our wills.

49. We must thank God for the results of prayer, even if we have not seen them (Philippians 4:6−7).

50. We must pray with thanksgiving.

Two Main Rules for Prayer

1. We are bound to pray for all things that concern our duty, and all that we are bound to labor for, such as glory and grace, the necessary assistance of the Spirit, spiritual rewards, heaven, and heavenly things.

2. We are bound to pray for both spiritual and temporal blessings. We may lawfully testify our hope and express our desires by petition.

After We Pray

1. We must stand firm.

2. We must take firm control of our thought life.

3. We must think on positive things (Philippians 4:6−9).

4. By praising God and confessing the applicable truths of the Word, we must cast down every thought and every imagination that is contrary to our prayer.

5. We must use the Word.

6. We must wait on the Lord.

7. We must be confident in mind.

8. We must keep speaking what the Word says on the issue at stake (2 Corinthians 4:13; Hebrews 10:23).

9. We must act in line with our faith and our confession (James 2:17).

10. We must continuously meditate upon the promises and the Word of God.

11. We must emphasize the greatness, majesty, and holiness of God.

12. We must expect the prayer to be answered.

13. We must live in expectancy when we pray.

14. If we expect nothing, we will receive nothing.

General Types of Prayer

1. Worship (1 Chronicles 16:10−12; John 4:23)

    a. In prayer, as we worship the Lord, we must worship Him in spirit and truth (John 4:23).

b. In true worship, we bow down and submit our spirits unto the Lord God.

c. In worship, we express love and admiration to God.

d. As we worship God, we submit to the love, will, and moral law of God.

e. In worship, we should hear the voice of God.

f. We are responding to God's glory.

2. Confession (Romans 10:9; 1 John 1:9)

a. In the confession of sin, with our mouths, we tell God our sins.

b. In the confession of the Word, with our mouths, we tell God what He has said in His Word.

c. We are responding to God's holiness.

3. Thanksgiving (1 Chronicles 16:34; Ephesians 1:15–19a; Colossians 3:15, 4:2)

a. In this type of prayer, we thank God for what He has done for us, both blessings and those blessings not yet seen.

b. It is natural and correct that we should thank God (1 Thessalonian 5:18).

4. Supplication (Matthew 26:42; Acts 1:14)

a. Supplication is pleading concerning sins, in which one who is sorry for his present or past evil deeds asks for pardon (Matthew 26:42).

5. Praise (Psalms 92:1, 100:4; Acts 16:24–26)

a. As we praise God, we declare the good things about God, both about His nature and His actions.

6. Petition (Ephesians 1:15–19a, 6:18–19)

a. As we petition God, we are asking Him for the things we desire.

b. We are commanded to ask God.

7. Intercession (Daniel 9:1–21; Philippians 1:19)

a. The practice of intercession, also known as intercessory prayer, does not focus on self or our desires. Instead, it focuses on the needs and wants of other men and women.

b. Intercession involves all other types of prayers.

c. As intercessors, we stand in proxy or "in the gap" between God and other people seeking God's favor for them.

8. Waiting (Habakkuk 2:1)

a. As we wait on God, our spirits are silent and wait for God to move or speak something by His Spirit.

b. We must wait patiently on God.

c. Through waiting on God, we practically express unto God that the will of God will be done in this world, not our own will.

d. As we pray, we should not always be talking, but we should talk and listen.

9. Warfare (Psalm 149:6−9; James 4:7; 1 John 4:4)

a. This is a prayer directed against the powers of darkness.

b. We announce against Satan and his forces the written judgment by reading the Scriptures of judgment against them (Psalm 149:9).

c. We command Satan and his forces to be bound, to be loosed, or to leave their positions of authority or influence in the name of Jesus Christ (Matthew 16:19; Mark 16:17−20).

d. We rebuke the forces of evil (Zechariah 3:2; Malachi 3:11; Matthew 4:1−10; Luke 4:4−10; Titus 2:1−2; Jude 9).

e. We resist the onslaughts of evil (James 4:7).

f. This is another form of intercessory prayer.

g. Warfare prayer is not for the untested (1 Timothy 3:1−7).

10. Praying in Tongues (Acts 2; 1 Corinthians 14:2, 15; Jude 20)

11. The Prayer of Faith (Matthew 21:21–22; Ephesians 6:18)

    a. The prayer of faith is shades of all these prayers; the prayer of faith is that which gets results; it is the prayer that begins with the Father and ends with the Father.

12. Ministering Prayer (Psalm 40:1; Acts 13:2)

    a. We need times of waiting on God and ministering to the Lord.

    b. We need times when we are not asking for anything, not petitioning, but ministering to Him.

    c. This type of prayer, where we minister to the Lord and wait on Him, is something that can make the impossible possible.

13. Imprecatory Prayer (1 Corinthians 16:22; Galatians 1:8)

    a. There is no more significant example of an imprecatory prayer than 1 Corinthians 16:22: "If any man love not the Lord Jesus Christ, let him be Anathema Maranatha." It is impossible to forget the cries and prayers of the martyred saints mentioned in Revelation 6:10, which shall be done in the future: "How long, O Lord, holy and true, dost thou not judge and avenge our blood on them that dwell on the earth?" In Revelation 6:10, the martyred saints will manifestly make an appeal to the divine court because of the gross miscarriage of justice that will be done against them.

    b. Imprecatory prayers are based upon God hearing the cries of His people and acting to shield and to deliver them for the sake of fulfilling His promises.

    c. In such prayers, we repeat Scripture, reminding God of what He already promised for the sake of His saints, or simply petition God, and it is God Himself who decides.

    d. Further, such prayers mean absolutely nothing, if not done in the inspiration of the Lord. The Lord is the One who breathes it, the One who inspires it, and the One who desires it. The saint simply repeats it.

e.   In the early church, the legitimate imprecatory prayers were uttered fundamentally for blatant violation of the moral order and the moral law, and often in a public forum with appeal unto the Lord God.

f.   Jesus Christ, in life-threatening circumstances, uttered woes and imprecations against the most evil forms of unbelief (Matthew 11:20–24; 23:13–39; Mark 11:12–14, 20–21).

Prayer and Church Tradition

Within church tradition, the variety of orthodox ways to pray is almost limitless. Very few of the ancient authorities denounced such variety. Most held that since very few apostolic forms of prayer existed, Christ, as well as the apostles, only intended to give the saints a starting point, and allow them to change their ways of prayers as the Holy Spirit directed.

What would be most noteworthy today about the variety of prayers that was sanctioned by the church was that the church prayed to Christ, as well as to the Holy Spirit, and not just to the Father through Christ and the Holy Spirit. But the church understood that the Scriptures that stated not to ask Christ anything were dealing with Christ's humanity, and not His deity (John 16:23).

The church understood that since Christ is just as much God as the Father is God, then they have the right to address their prayers to Christ, not as a man, but rather as God. Since all three persons are God, by addressing one, all three persons are addressed. So by addressing Christ as God, the other persons are also addressed. Scripture gives several examples of saints praying to Christ (Acts 1:24, 7:59, 9:10–16; 1 Corinthians 16:22; 2 Corinthians 12:8; Revelation 22:20).

Prayer of Petition

Out of all prayers, I pray the prayer of petition more than any other prayer. It was the prayer that I understood first. The prayer of praise should be the first prayer used by us. And only after that should we petition. Praise causes us to enter the very throne room of God and sets everything in biblical perspective and relationship.

Apostle Paul prays a prayer of petition:

> Wherefore I also, after I heard of your faith in the Lord Jesus, and love unto all the saints, cease not to give thanks for you, making mention of you in my prayers; that the God of our Lord Jesus Christ, the Father of glory, may give unto you the spirit of wisdom and revelation in the knowledge of him: The eyes of your understanding being enlightened; that ye may know what is the hope of his calling, and what the riches of the glory of his inheritance in the saints, and what is the exceeding greatness of his power to us-ward who believe. (Ephesians 1:15–19a)

Besides the prayers of petition, I pray many warfare prayers and prayers of intercession.

Leonard Ravenhill, a well-known minister and author on prayer, once said, "A sinning man will stop praying. A praying man will stop sinning."[10] Ravenhill also said,

> The true man of God is heartsick, grieved at the worldliness of the Church, grieved at the blindness of the Church, grieved at the corruption in the Church, grieved at the toleration of sin in the Church, grieved at the prayerlessness in the Church. He is disturbed that the corporate prayer of the Church no longer pulls down the strongholds of the devil. He is embarrassed that the Church folks no longer cry in their despair before a devil-ridden, sin-mad society, "Why could we not cast him out?" (Matthew 17:19).[11]

And he said, "A man may study because his brain is hungry for knowledge, even Bible knowledge. But he prays because his soul is hungry for God."[12]

Furthermore, Ravenhill nails the main problem with the modern church:

> No man is greater than his prayer life. The pastor who is not praying is playing; the people who are not praying are

straying. We have many organizers, but few agonizers; many players and payers, few prayers; many singers, few clingers; lots of pastors, few wrestlers; many fears, few tears; much fashion, little passion; many interferers, few intercessors; many writers, but few fighters. Failing here, we fail everywhere.[13]

John Wesley once said, "I value all things only by the price they shall gain in eternity."[14]

Charles Finney said as follows:

If Christians were not such cowards, and absolutely disobedient to this plain command of God, one thing would certainly come of it—either they would be murdered in the streets as martyrs, because men could not bear the intolerable presence of truth, or they would be speedily converted to God.[15]

Charles Finney also said as follows:

I have never known a person sweat blood; but I have known a person pray till the blood started from his nose. And I have known persons to pray till they were all wet with perspiration, in the coldest weather in winter. I have known persons pray for hours, till their strength was all exhausted with the agony of their minds. Such prayers prevailed with God.[16]

Matthew Henry said as follows:

The prayers and supplications that Christ offered up were, joined with strong cries and tears, herein setting us example not only to pray but to be fervent and importunate in prayer. How many dry prayers, how few wet ones, do we offer up to God! [17]

Learning About Prayer

From many years, I learned just what our prayers must consist of:

273

1. We must pray in the name of Jesus Christ (John 14:13, 14, 15:16, 16:23–26; Romans 1:8; Ephesians 5:20; Hebrews 4:14–16; 1 Timothy 2:5).

2. We must pray by the will of God (Matthew 26:39; 1 John 5:14–15).

3. We must pray with understanding (Matthew 6:7; 1 Corinthians 14:15–16).

4. We must pray with our whole heart (Jeremiah 29:12–13; Matthew 6:5; Luke 22:44).

5. We must pray in faith and not in doubt (Mark 11:24; James 1:5–8).

6. We must pray concerning God and with great humility (2 Chronicles 7:14; Luke 18:9–14).

7. We must pray with repentance (Genesis 18:27; 2 Chronicles 33:10–13).

8. We must pray and forgive others (Matthew 6:12, 14–15; Mark 11:25).

9. We must pray and live a faithful life (James 5:16; 1 John 3:21–22).

Greatest Prayer Warrior in American History

Sometimes, history is rewritten, and some facts are forgotten. Secular writers and historians love to ignore Christians and their works. In the history of America, there is no more magnificent prayer warrior than Father Daniel Nash, a companion of Charles Finney (AD 1775–1831).

At the age of forty, Nash became a pastor at Stow's Square Congregational-Presbyterian Church, Lowville Township, in upstate New York. During his first year as the pastor, a revival sprang forth, and seventy people were saved.

By AD 1822, his services were no longer needed in the church. The church members believed that Father Nash was too old to be a pastor and fired him. Besides this, there is little more known about him. Nevertheless, his praying has not been forgotten. Nash's prayer ministry makes him a great hero in the ministry of revival.

Through the infirmity of an eye disease, the Lord led Nash to become the personal intercessor of young Charles Finney. In time, the enemies of Finney feared and hated the prayers of Father Nash more than anything else.

Father Nash was known to prophesy and work in the gifts of the Holy Spirit. For example, there remains a prophecy that he gave over several young men who resisted the moving of the Holy Spirit in the Second Great Awakening. From his prophecy, we can see his determination, faith, and strength in God. In Father Nash, there could not be any compromise.

Charles Finney, who was a witness of the incident and the prophecy, wrote,

> The next Sabbath, after preaching morning and afternoon myself—for I did the preaching altogether, and Brother Nash gave himself up almost continually to prayer—we met at five o'clock in the church, for a prayer meeting. The meetinghouse was filled. Near the close of the meeting, Brother Nash arose, and addressed that company of young men who had joined hand in hand to resist the revival. I believe they were all there, and they sat braced up against the Spirit of God. It was too solemn for them really to make ridicule of what they heard and saw; and yet their brazen-facedness and stiff-neckedness were apparent to everybody.
>
> Brother Nash addressed them very earnestly and pointed out the guilt and danger of the course they were taking. Toward the close of his address, he waxed exceeding warm, and said to them, "Now, mark me, young men! God will break your ranks in less than one week, either by converting some of you, or by sending some of you to hell. He will do this as certainly as the Lord is my God."

He was standing where he brought his hand down on the top of the pew before him, so as to make it thoroughly jar. He sat immediately down, dropped his head, and groaned with pain.

The house was as still as death, and most of the people held down their heads. I could see that the young men were agitated. For myself, I regretted that Brother Nash had gone so far. He had committed himself, that God would either take the life of some of them, and send them to hell, or convert some of them, within a week. However, on Tuesday morning of the same week, the leader of these young men came to me, in the greatest distress of mind. He was all prepared to submit; and as soon as I came to press him he broke down like a child, confessed, and manifestly gave himself to Christ. Then he said, "What shall I do, Mr. Finney?" I replied "Go immediately to all your young companions, and pray with them, and exhort them, at once to turn to the Lord." He did so; and before the week was out, nearly if not all of that class of young men, were hoping in Christ.[18]

In addition to this, Father Nash had great faith in God and determination. He refused to give up. When he prayed, he believed that God would hear his prayers and finally answer them, one way or another. Father Nash did not stop praying on a particular subject until God answered his prayer. After that, he only reminded God of His promise.

Father Nash prayed daily. His prayers were prayed with great struggling and weakened health. Throughout his intercessory ministry, he paid many prices that God would move in His power during the Second Great Awakening. There were many results of such a type of prayer. The power of God was highly manifested in the revival and the cities; men and women were saved, people glorified God, and there was a continual opening heaven.

Following Paul

In my journey, I have learned much from Paul when it comes to prayer. I learned to pray as Paul did; I learned to commune with God as Paul did; I sought to seek the Holy Spirit as Paul did. Following what Paul did will cost a person everything. As I heard many times, a prayer that costs nothing will get us nothing.

In Acts 9:11 and Acts 16:13, we learn how to pray in the very school of prayer as founded for the church by Paul. We owe much to Paul, and that includes how to pray to get results.

Paul and Barnabas established every church with prayer and fasting. Both made a habit, a business, and a life out of prayer. Paul's greatest spiritual trait was a strong tendency to pray, regardless of the circumstances, and regardless of the cost.

Paul knew quite well that a Christian who did not pray did not live for God. And a praying saint was a praising saint (Acts 20:36–37).

In Colossians 2, we see Paul was so burdened down and in a spiritual conflict that he wrestled in prayer against Satan, who was seeking to lead these believers astray. Paul knew how to overcome Satan—through prayer and the Word of God (Ephesians 6:17–18). This is also true of the ancient church. He longed to see the saints united in Christ and enjoy the riches of blessing in Him.

According to ancient Christian sources, the prayers of the ancient saints rallied against all the forms of magic, witchcraft, and all the forces of evil; nothing evil could stand against their prayers. There is no comparison between the church of today—at least in modern, wealthy nations—to that of the ancient church.

According to the early church, a person can arise in their prayers to a life of perfection of prayer in their lives.

It is possible today for the saints of God to work in such a perfect form and method of prayer that nothing can stand in their way, nor withhold from them the blessings of God. And this journey of prayer should start with Jesus, or at least Paul.

Paul and Silas

Acts 16:24–26 reads,

> Who, having received such a charge, thrust them into the inner prison, and made their feet fast in the stocks. And at midnight Paul and Silas prayed, and sang praises unto God: and the prisoners heard them. And suddenly there was a great earthquake, so that the foundations of the prison were shaken: and immediately all the doors were opened, and every one's bands were loosed.

For the sake of Christ, and the preaching of the gospel, both Paul and Silas were arrested at Philippi (Acts 16:24). The imprisonment of Paul and Silas was because Paul cast out the spirit of Python from a damsel (Acts 16:16–18). By Paul's casting out that Pythonic demon, various consequences took place. For example, besides being imprisoned, they were beaten.

Despite being in an awful state, they could still sing a song of victory. From Paul and Silas came a song of victory, which issued out of the blackness of a dark dungeon. Such a song of victory went through the walls of the prison, beyond the roof, into the clouds, and finally entered heaven itself and the throne room of God.

The song of victory was unto God. Paul and Silas were ministering to God, not asking for deliverance, but worshipping Him because of who He is.

All Christians must have the right attitude, behavior, and motive when dealing with terrible circumstances. Both Paul and Silas had the right frame of mind. They held that they were living in victory, regardless of their circumstances. Why? Because of their relationship with the Lord and having knowing-faith—knowing that God would move. There was no positive mental attitude here, no positive confession. Both Paul and Silas were not living in disobedience— they were right in God's will. And still, they were imprisoned.

The earthquake that shook the foundations of the prison at Philippi was in answer to the power of intensified prayer. This earthquake saved Paul and Silas and showed the pagans just who God is.

Paul and Silas understood the road to victory. In this case, the way to victory must begin and end with devotion. Paul and Silas saw that devotion is a necessity when one is in difficulties. To Paul and Silas, devotion is the deathblow to challenges and problems of all kinds.

We do not need counseling, but we need to release the power of God within a situation. This is done by entering the presence of God, and that is done through devotion.

From Acts 16:16–26, we learn that circumstances are no criteria of character. And doing good does not necessarily produce equal results. Further, the righteous are non-resistant in their method of meeting persecution. The ungodly are permitted great freedom.

God moved at the last minute only when Paul and Silas were lifting prayers and praises. God will not act unless we act first. And we must act first with prayer. The results are manifold.

Smith Wigglesworth said, "First thing every morning when I get out of bed, I jump out; I don't just drag out, but I jump out. And when my feet hit the floor, I say, 'Praise the Lord,' and I praise God every morning."[19]

Limits on Prayers

Prayer begins to decay before us, and the perfection of prayer begins to be lost when we interject our wills, passions, and desires above the mind and will of God. Therefore, prayer has limits and can well be undone due to our attitude and our volition entering such a holy place of God's presence.

It is clear that this also happened to Paul when he prayed that the angel of Satan, who had been allowed by the Lord to buffet Paul for his own good, might be removed, saying, "And lest I should be exalted above measure through the abundance of the revelations, there was given to me a thorn in the flesh, the messenger of Satan to buffet me, lest I should be exalted above measure. For this thing I besought the Lord thrice, that it might depart from me. And he said unto me, My grace is sufficient for thee: for my strength is made perfect in weakness. Most gladly therefore will I rather glory in my infirmities, that the power of Christ may rest upon me" (2 Corinthians 12:7–9).

Paul was praying contrary to God's mind and will. And he was praying beyond the ability for God to move. For God will not move against His will, His character, and His advantages. He bids us that we must have the full and undoubting confidence of the answer, only in those things which are not for our benefit or temporal comforts but are in conformity to the Lord's will.

When we sometimes ask for things opposed to our salvation, we are most providentially refused.

Looking also to Jesus, we see a limit on prayer. Scripture reads, "And Jesus said unto them, Because of your unbelief: for verily I say unto you, If ye have faith as a grain of mustard seed, ye shall say unto this mountain, Remove hence to yonder place; and it shall remove; and nothing shall be impossible unto you" (Matthew 17:20).

If there are four persons praying that the mountain be removed, one on each side of the mountain, just whose prayers will be answered? The person whose prayers follow God's sovereignty, His will, His omnipotence, and His nature. And this is also true for our faith as well. Faith, which has no power, must line up with the object of that faith: God Himself.

Praying beyond God's ability to answer is praying a prayer that draws from God the answer, "I am sorry, but I cannot or will not do what you ask." Many teach that there is nothing that God cannot do, but this is wrong since He cannot lie or sin. If there were no limit to what we can pray about, then we would be God and God would be our servant.

In studying prayer, we forget that prayer works in the best interest of everyone concerned. The ability of God to answer us should not be a worry or concern but a blessing. For by this, we know that God will answer according to His will and not ours, as John says in 1 John 5:14. These boundaries have been determined by God's grace, God's sovereignty, God's will, God's power, time, and especially free will.

God gives man the choice to obey or not obey (Deuteronomy 11:26; 1 Samuel 15:22).

Godly Restrictions on Prayer

Like all spiritual weapons, prayer can never be used as a weapon against God. All the weapons are to be used against the powers of Satan and his forces (Matthew 10:1; Mark 3:15, 16:17; Luke 9:1, 10:19; John 16:8–11; 2 Corinthians 10:5–7; Ephesians 2:6–7, 6:10– 18; Colossians 1:13, 2:14–17; Hebrews 2:8–9, 14; 1 Peter 2:9, 14– 15, 5:7–8; James 4:7; 1 John 3:8).

In prayer, God is the Master while the saint is the servant. Prayer cannot make us the master of God (1 Samuel 23:10; 2 Samuel 7:20–26; Isaiah 42:1, 49:3–6, 52:13, 53:11; Ezekiel 34:23– 24; Zechariah 3:8; Matthew 8:19, 9:11, 10:24–25, 12:38, 19:16, 22:16, 20:28, 22:36, 23:8, 23:10, 26:18; Luke 22:27; John 13:13–14; Galatians 4:7; Ephesians 2:6–7; 6:9; Colossians 4:1; Titus 1:1; Jude 1:1; Revelation 15:3). This is clearly seen from the Greek.

Prayers cannot make God act for our benefit and in the way we wish. If that were the case, then the saints would be able to manipulate God. God would subsequently and invariably be dethroned, and the universe would have many gods. As such, prayers cannot be universal laws or formulas that even God must obey. The heathen believes prayers are like that.

If God moves when we pray, it is because we are praying according to His will in a situation, and God wants to move in that situation before we even prayed; He is only waiting to see if we will join in the battle. Remember, God will not fight in spiritual warfare for us until we enter the fight. For example, God did not move for Daniel until Daniel began praying and fasting (Daniel 9–10).

Conditions of Prayer

In Mark 11:20–26, Jesus uses the fig tree to teach us that there are conditions of prayer.

The first condition of prayer is that we must have faith in God, even if God is silent. A Jewish Holocaust victim said, "I believe in the sun even when it is not shining. I believe in love even when I am not feeling it. I believe in God even when He is silent."[20] Smith Wigglesworth said about faith, "I am not moved by what I see. I am not moved by what I feel. I am moved only by what I believe."[21]

The second condition of prayer is expectancy. A person must believe and expect the answer to his prayers.

The third condition of prayer is forgiveness. This is a critical condition of prayer; a condition that is stressed time and again by Jesus (Matthew 5:23–24, 6:14–15, 18:32–33). It does no good to pray unless one forgives.

The fourth condition of prayer is that prayer must be in the dominion of Christ—abiding in Christ (John 16:7). We can ask what we will, and it shall be done unto us only if we abide in Christ, and His words abide in us.

One of the principles of the kingdom is "draw nigh to God, and he will draw nigh to you" (James 4:8). God always hears Christ, and if we abide in Christ, He will always hear us. Conversely, we have the right to be heard if we abide continually in Him. We must admit that thousands of prayers go up to God that are not answered. Why? Either God does not fulfill His promises, or else those who pray are not fully abiding in Christ Jesus.

Matthews 7:7–8 says, "Ask, and it shall be given you; seek, and ye shall find; knock, and it shall be opened unto you: For every one that asketh receiveth; and he that seeketh findeth; and to him that knocketh it shall be opened." Asking, seeking, and knocking are all continual and progressive. Not one time, but repeatedly. We must keep the mind fixed, as much as possible, at the end of life and on that which follows it.

Prayer is Not Mindless Prayer

Christianity is not a mindless and reasonless faith that must be followed blindly. Christianity demands that the minds, understandings, reasons, and judgments of men and women play a part in their Christian faith, prayer life, and life. God has not made men and women some mindless machines, but rational beings with reasoning, understanding, and other faculties. When people become Christians, they do not lose their faculties and check their minds at the door.

Genuine prayer is not a mindless act, process, or state. It is united with the mind of God, and God forms in our mind the words of prayer to be spoken. God does not empty our minds of thoughts, nor does He demand that we use some sort of mental meditation. Instead, it is demons who want this. They seek to empty our minds to put their thoughts, directions, and desires into them.

In Matthew 6:7, Jesus said that we must not regard genuine prayer as a magical incantation where phrases or words are repeated like mantras. Mindless chants have no place in the Christian life.

Genuine prayer is speaking to God with His will in mind (1 John 5:14). One of the goals of genuine prayer is not a mindless prayer, but a prayer that reasonably conveys our needs and our concerns unto a merciful God. Paul points out that sincere prayer is not a mindless prayer. Paul pleads with his readers to "continue in prayer and watch in the same with thanksgiving" (Colossians 4:2). In the Greek language, the idea of Colossians 4:2 is a mental state of continual alertness or watchfulness when we vocally pray (see also Matthew 26:41; Mark 14:38; 1 Corinthians 16:13; Ephesians 6:18; 1 Thessalonians 5:6; 1 Peter 5:8). The watching is "to give strict attention to, to be active, to take heed lest through remissness and indolence some destructive calamity suddenly overtake one."[22] Alertness or watchfulness is part of genuine prayer. If not, prayer has no value. No method of prayer that supports the techniques of the New Age has any value for Christian life. On the other hand, passive receptibility does not mean a mindless state, but a state that is passive unto the movements of the Holy Spirit. For example, the prophets were not robbed of their self-consciousness, or their self-control, but were in a state of passive receptibility (Numbers 11:25, 12:6–8; 1 Samuel 10:5–6, 19:20–21; 2 Kings 9:11; 1 Corinthians 14:32).

What would be the best way to translate Colossians 4:2? It must be translated like, "Continue steadfastly in the occupation of prayer, and be mentally alert in it with an attitude of thanksgiving." The Greek concludes that a mental state of alertness (watchfulness) is required for a prayer to be a genuine prayer. Further, the Greek word Paul uses for prayer here in Colossians 4:2 is rarely without the article. The emphasis means that the term prayer is not a general term, but a separative term that separates words, requests, intercessions, and petitions of the saints from the prayers of the pagans. Just by this alone, the prayers of the saints must be separate from the prayers of the heathens. Therefore, the prayers of the saints must not follow the practices or techniques of the pagans.

However, a considerable portion of prayer today is nothing more or less than mysticism. Mysticism, a pagan practice, focuses on extended mental meditation, abstracts from the phenomenal world, and generally rejects vocal prayer. In these methods, mental prayer is used to make the minds of men and women lose their consciousness. In such a state, the minds become ready to be controlled and manipulated by demons.

Practices like these, being a part of the realm of the demonic, also incorporate into themselves hypnotism and the power of suggestion. Neither of these is part of genuine prayer.

Further, these practices open people up to instability, fanaticism, heresies, and above all, demon possession. Since these practices make the mind thoughtless (or mindless) in nature, this explains the rampant phenomenon today of Christians who are mentally unstable after trying these techniques. Only deliverance can help undo the damage done by such practices.

In such cases, people lose their minds, become irrational and lifeless in their faces, and accept the demonic spirits of the ancient world. These evil spirits take over the minds of men and women; in essence, they are mind snatchers.

A Few More Facts on Faith

Faith is a gift, a fruit, an act, a process, and a state. The Bible speaks of the importance of faith when it says that without faith, it is impossible to please God (Hebrews 11:6).

Faith is always tied to what God has already promised. Faith will never work with something that God has not promised.

Faith is something that a person has already: "God hath dealt to every man the measure of faith" (Romans 12:3).

Faith can be increased from glory unto glory. The Bible says that saints must "grow in grace, and in the knowledge of our Lord and Saviour Jesus Christ" (2 Peter 3:18).

Faith can only be increased by the Word of God, fasting, praying, and answered prayer (Matthew 17:20–21; Romans 10:17; Jude 20).

When we exercise our faith, if we have a proper motive, attitude, and behavior, God is obligated to answer our prayer as long as it is in God's will.

CHAPTER 6
PRAYER AND TRIALS

Prayer without some type of trials following it or at least being associated with it is foreign to the ancient church and the ancient Jews. Daniel prayed amid tribulation (Daniel 2–12). This is true for all the apostles and early Christians.

When facing a wall of opposition, men and women have found prayer to be the key to their survival and success. Jeremiah prayed regardless of the opposition; he had no real success from his prayers. He had no actual results, yet he prayed. Jeremiah's success came after his death—by the miracles God performed through Daniel (see Daniel 9).

We must pray, regardless of any visible success. Noah faced great odds alone. The Bible says that "Noah walked with God" (Genesis 6:9), which implies that he was a man of prayer. Noah sought prayer as a relief from the evil and sins of the world, and as a means of comfort and power. Noah heard the voice of God; God spoke to him as a friend (Genesis 6:13–7:1).

Abraham talked with God and had a visitation from God (Genesis 17–19). Abraham genuinely enforced the practice of praying in the history of the Hebrew patriarchs. The significance of the altar is that prayers must accompany it (Genesis 12:7–8, 13:3–4).

The three Hebrew children mentioned in Daniel 3 were men who did not bow, give in, or compromise their faith, despite tribulation. Their strength came from their lives of prayer, their relationship with God, and their knowledge that God was able. We must remember where our strength in God originates.

Jesus, the apostles, and the saints sought help through prayer against the opposition (Matthew 4:4−10; Acts 16:25).

2 Corinthians 11:23−30 reads:

διάκονοι Χριστοῦ εἰσι; παραφρονῶν λαλῶ ὑπὲρ ἐγώ· ἐν κόποις περισσοτέρως, ἐν πληγαῖς ὑπερβαλλόντως, ἐν φυλακαῖς περισσοτέρως, ἐν θανάτοις πολλάκις. ὑπὸ Ἰουδαίων πεντάκις τεσσαράκοντα παρὰ μίαν ἔλαβον. τρὶς ἐρραβδίσθην, ἅπαξ ἐλιθάσθην, τρὶς ἐναυάγησα, νυχθήμερον ἐν τῷ βυθῷ πεποίηκα· ὁδοιπορίαις πολλάκις, κινδύνοις ποταμῶν, κινδύνοις λῃστῶν, κινδύνοις ἐκ γένους, κινδύνοις ἐξ ἐθνῶν, κινδύνοις ἐν πόλει, κινδύνοις ἐν ἐρημίᾳ, κινδύνοις ἐν θαλάσσῃ, κινδύνοις ἐν ψευδαδέλφοις· ἐν κόπῳ καὶ μόχθῳ, ἐν ἀγρυπνίαις πολλάκις, ἐν λιμῷ καὶ δίψει, ἐν νηστείαις πολλάκις, ἐν ψύχει καὶ γυμνότητι. χωρὶς τῶν παρεκτός, ἡ ἐπισύστασίς μου ἡ καθ᾽ ἡμέραν, ἡ μέριμνα πασῶν τῶν ἐκκλησιῶν. τίς ἀσθενεῖ, καὶ οὐκ ἀσθενῶ; τίς σκανδαλίζεται, καὶ οὐκ ἐγὼ πυροῦμαι; εἰ καυχᾶσθαι δεῖ, τὰ τῆς ἀσθενείας μου καυχήσομαι (Ministers of Christ, are they? I am speaking as if I was quite irrational−I am also more than them, in labors even more abundantly, in stripes much greater degree, in imprisonments much greater, in the dangers of deaths repeatedly. From the hands of the Jews, I received five times forty stripes, except one. Three times I was beaten with rods, once I received a stoning, three times I was shipwrecked, both a night and a day I have spent time in the deep sea; by journeyings frequently, by dangers within rivers, by dangers with robbers, by dangers with my own race, by dangers from the Gentiles, by dangers within the city, by dangers within the wilderness, by dangers in the sea, by dangers among false brethren; by toil and hardship, by sleepless nights frequently, by hunger and thirst, by fastings frequently, by cold and poorly clothed. Apart from those external things that are the regular routine of my office and my labors, there is the pressure that is on me daily, the anxiety about all the churches. Who is weak, and I am not weak? Who is led to commit sin, and I do not burn with indignation)?

Jesus and the Wilderness

When Jesus was led out in the wilderness to be tempted by Satan, He used the written word as His main weapon.

One of the key phrases that I repeatedly used in my fights and battles against evil was, "It is written." Jesus used that critical phrase, "It is written," when He was tempted by Satan (Matthew 4:4–10). I told the devil and his evil spirits, "It is written, devil, if I stand against you, you must flee in the name of Jesus Christ." I have also used "it is written" in many other ways like, "It is written, devil, that God is the God of healing, and I stand upon that word. Therefore, I stand to be healed in the name of Jesus Christ."

Furthermore, the battle starts with the Word of God and ends with the Word of God. We must get God's Word into our spirits, souls, and minds if we ever want to be able to stand in faith and hold on to His promises when the adversary rises against us.

As we learn to battle in spiritual warfare, we must always remember who we are in Jesus Christ. We are nothing outside of Jesus Christ, but we are kings and priests in training with the Lord Jesus Christ.

Key Phrases to use in Spiritual Warfare

There are seven key phrases that need to be used in spiritual warfare and battle, which never fail:

1. "It is written. . . in the name of Jesus Christ."

2. "If I resist you, devil, you must flee in the name of Jesus Christ."

3. "Greater is He that is in me, than He that is in the world."

4. "We are more than conquerors in the name of Jesus Christ."

5. "I plead the blood of the Lamb in the name of Jesus Christ."

6. "I plead the bloodline in the name of Jesus Christ."

7. "I plead the blood over my mind, sub-conscious mind, spirit, body, soul, and brain in the name of Jesus Christ."

In warfare, there is always both offense and defense. Too many Christians always take the defensive when it comes to the devil and his demons. They never take the offensive against them. As I have heard many times that the best defense is a good offense. So we, as Christians, must learn how to attack the forces of evil, and after that, how to live.

For example, offensive warfare can be tearing down the stronghold, which Satan has whispered into our minds. Ephesians 6:12–13 reads,

> For we wrestle not against flesh and blood, but against principalities, against powers, against the rulers of the darkness of this world, against spiritual wickedness in high places. Wherefore take unto you the whole armour of God, that ye may be able to withstand in the evil day, and having done all, to stand.

Within the kingdom of evil, there is a preoccupation with offense. Witches, warlocks, and other occultists seek to take the high ground, strike first, and keep all others from ever striking back. They care little about defense. And that is their weakness. We, as Christians, should fight fire with fire and become proactive. Offense should be first in our strategy. But unlike the occultists, we must have a good defense before we become proactive in our warfare.

Pleading the Blood of the Lamb

Few people truly know the significance or the power of pleading the blood of Jesus. The word "pleading" is not found in the Bible in this connection. Its meaning deals with legal rights associated with the blood of the Lamb.

The practice of pleading the blood of the Lamb is traced back to the revivalists, men like John Wesley, and C. H. Spurgeon, the reformers—including the Puritans, and the liturgies of the ancient church. So it is not something foreign to Christianity.

Additionally, every time Christians practice the Lord's Supper (the Eucharist), they are practicing the pleading of the blood, regardless of what they may think (1 Corinthians 11:23–26). Each time we practice the Lord's Supper, we are to remember the body and blood of Christ, and what both have done, including conquering Satan, his forces, sin, and evil.

By pleading the blood, the saints of God are pleading their cause and their case before God according to the power of the blood (Revelation 12:11). And the blood of Christ is pleading our blood-brought rights before God.

In the Old Testament, it was common to plead someone's case before the Lord (1 Samuel 24:15; Job 16:21).

Here are three main benefits of pleading the blood of the Lamb:

1. Forgiveness (Matthew 26:28; Ephesians 1:7, 2:13)

2. Deliverance (Colossians 1:13, 2:15; Hebrews 2:14; 1 John 3:8)

3. Protection (Exodus 12:22–23)

Requirements for Pleading the Blood

1. Salvation

2. Full surrender

3. Faith

4. Purity

5. Simplicity

6. Obedience

The Basics of Pleading the Blood

1. Plead the blood over the object that needs to be protected.

2. Plead the blood against whatever type of evil could come against that object.

3. End the prayer in the name of Jesus Christ.

Offensive Prayers Used

Over the years of public ministry, both my mother and I have found many prayers that repeatedly work. They may not work the first time, but they will work progressively. Sometimes, it is not the first time we say a prayer that it will work; sometimes, we must say a prayer numerous times before we receive results. We must keep on knocking. Here are some examples of offensive prayers:

1. Father, I repent of all my sins of thought, word, and deed. I repent of my sins of omission and commission. Father, I ask for your forgiveness in the mighty name of Jesus and receive it by the precious blood of Jesus Christ.

2. I bind my calling, my election, my healing, my wealth, my ministry, my gifts, and my promises of God to me. I will not allow anyone to take them from me—they are mine!

3. I loose all ungodly prayers against me, and I send them back to the one who sent them, for their instruction and correction. Now, I apply the blood of Jesus over my mind, my subconscious mind, my spirit, my soul, my body, and my brain.

4. I break all curses, hexes, spells, and all prayers over me that are contrary to the will of God for my life.

5. In the name of Jesus Christ, by the power of His cross, His blood, and His Word, I bind the evil spirits, the evil powers, the evil forces of the earth, the underground, the air, the water, the fire, the netherworld, and all other satanic forces of nature. I rebuke any curses, spells, or hexes sent against me, and send them directly to Jesus for Him to deal with as He will. Lord, I ask you to bless our enemies by sending your Holy Spirit to lead them to repentance. I bind all interplay, interaction, and communication of evil spirits. I claim the protection of the shed blood of Jesus Christ over any evil forces.

6. O Satan, O Satan, I openly and publicly announce that I have won the victory over you in the name of Jesus Christ. In the name of Jesus Christ, I have put my foot upon your neck, O Satan. I proclaim victory over my finances, over my wealth, over my health, over my job, over my children, over my mother,

over my father, over my sister, over my brother, over my wife or husband, and everything in my life. I have put my foot upon your neck, O Satan, and I proclaim victory in the name of Jesus Christ. You shall not take from me any longer. I have put my foot upon your neck, and I say that enough is enough, devil, in the name of Jesus Christ. Now, I take authority over my life, over my ministry, and everything in the mighty name of Jesus Christ.

Praying the Psalms

Modern Christians, time and again, overlook or forget the power released by praying the Psalms. One of the reasons for the success of the ancient Christians' prayers rests in the fact that they repeatedly prayed the Psalms. Psalms cover every circumstance possible:

1. Psalm 1 emphasizes the flourishing of the righteous, while the wicked are destroyed. It is also the most important way to see blessings and prosperity.

2. Psalm 4 is a prayer of faith.

3. Psalm 9 is praise to God for deliverance so far, and a plea that the deliverance may continue: "When my enemies are turned back, they shall fall and perish at thy presence. ... Thou hast rebuked the heathen, thou hast destroyed the wicked ... O thou enemy, destructions are come to a perpetual end: and thou hast destroyed cities; their memorial is perished with them" (vv. 3, 5–6).

4. Psalm 12 is a prayer to God to rescue the godly from the wicked. Important: this Psalm is good to remember when the whole world seems to be against you or seems to be out of control.

5. Psalm 15 is a prayer for a life pleasing to God.

6. Psalm 22 is a prayer of deliverance from enemies.

7. Psalm 23 is a prayer of deliverance from evil and from enemies.

8. Psalm 29 is a prayer of the power of the voice of God to shake.

9. Psalm 34 is a prayer of deliverance from evil and evildoers.

10. Psalm 54 is a prayer of deliverance from trouble, evil, and evildoers.

11. Psalm 70 is a prayer of deliverance from trouble, evil, and evildoers. David emphasizes that he is poor and needy.

12. Psalm 73 is a prayer about the rich and wealthy being destroyed in a moment, but the righteous have the happiness that lasts forever.

13. Psalm 78 shows that when Israel was obedient, God sent prosperity. When Israel was disobedient, God sent judgment.

14. Psalm 82 is a prayer of deliverance.

15. Psalm 85 is a prayer of mercy.

16. Psalm 94 is a prayer of judgment against evil and the wicked and a prayer of deliverance against evil and the wicked.

17. Psalm 102 is a prayer of mercy and help from distress.

18. Psalm 118 is a prayer over distress.

19. Psalm 121 is a prayer of protection.

20. Psalm 141 is a prayer of deliverance from evil and enemies.

A Psalter for Prayer

1. If you need deliverance, pray Psalms 77, 104, and 113.

2. If you need prosperity, pray Psalms 1 and 106.

3. If you need protection, pray Psalm 19.

4. Psalms 10 and 11 are used by the saints to express faith and prayer.

5. If you are in distress, pray Psalms 53, 55, 56, and 141.

6. If you need to be blessed, pray Psalms 1, 31, 40, 111, 118, and 127.

7. If you are persecuted by your own family and opposed by many, pray Psalm 3.

8. At your affliction's end, pray Psalms 4, 74, 114, and 115.

9. In great times of trouble, pray Psalm 5, especially when the wicked are ready to ensnare you.

10. If you feel yourself under the Lord's displeasure, pray Psalms 6 and 37.

11. If someone is plotting against you, pray Psalm 7.

12. For victory over your enemy, pray Psalm 9.

13. Under great distress, especially when the wicked and the backslidden are surrounding you, pray Psalm 11.

14. If someone blasphemes the Lord, pray Psalms 13 and 52.

15. If you are in warfare against the enemies of God, pray Psalms 16, 85, 87, and 139.

16. If you want to know how Moses prayed, pray Psalm 89.

17. When you have been delivered from these enemies and oppressors, pray Psalm 17.

18. If enemies are surrounding you, pray Psalm 24.

19. If the enemies of God persist, pray Psalms 25, 34, and 42.

20. If your foes press yet harder, pray Psalms 26 and 30.

21. If your safety is in question, pray Psalm 38.

22. If you wish to learn the value of endurance, pray Psalm 39.

23. Trust God and how He will deal with your enemies by praying Psalm 41.

24. If you have been slandered, pray Psalms 51, 53, 55, and 54.

25. If still, the persecution follows hard on you, and he who seeks your life enters, pray Psalms 56 and 141.

26. If you need deliverance from God's enemies, pray Psalms 63, 64, 69, and 70.

The Tools of Satan

While there are several tools of Satan, the main three tools are deception, temptation, and accusation. When we learn these three main tools and how to rebuke them by using Scripture, and my seven keys of warfare, we can win almost every time. Of course, not every battle is ours. We will win the battles that God has called us to fight, but not necessarily every struggle before us.

The deceptions used against the believers are based upon carnal reason, the guilt of conscience, jealousies, and fears (2 Corinthians 2:11, 11:3; Ephesians 4:14, 6:11; Revelation 12:9). Satan uses deception, accusation, temptation, false reasoning, and arguments in an effort to overthrow our faith.

Because of this, evil spirits study an individual and contrive the best plan of deception, temptation, and accusation to destroy that person. The whole business of evil spirits is to examine men, women, and children to terminate them. It is this reason that the demons go up and down upon the earth. Though they are not omniscient, demons know all the ranks and classes of men, women, and children in the state of grace and holiness. By studying us, they understand what deceptions, temptations, or accusations need to be used against each one of us (1 Peter 1:6).

Evil spirits are diverse and are capable of a diversity of suggestions and reasonings. But God's workings and with His saints are also various, and He desires to move upon His believers and teach them how to defend themselves.

The ignorance of the meaning of the Scriptures has become the downfall of many saints. And it is wise to remember that demons manipulate legalities, through which people cede illegitimate rights to them.

Satan and his evil spirits first put their false suggestions and solicitations of sexual and worldly objects into our hearts (John 13:2; 1 Corinthians 7:5; Ephesians 6:12; Hebrews 8:5). These false suggestions and solicitations do not come from sinners or saints. Rather, they come from outside the sinners and the saints. As long as people do not commit or fulfill these false suggestions and solicitations, no sin is committed.

Satan and his evil spirits have six main advantages over us when it comes to deception, temptation, and accusation:

1. They frequently convey false reasonings and suggestions unto us.

2. They can send us a multitude of false reasonings and considerations together at once.

3. They can hold the attention of our minds.

4. They add weight to their false reasonings and accusations by a powerful affirmation that it is so.

5. They back their false conclusions with warnings and terrors.

6. They try to make us think that their false reasonings and suggestions are from us.

No sinner or saint can avoid the false reasonings and suggestions of Satan and his spirits. They come to all of us. And no person can take the false reasonings and suggestions of Satan and his spirits off any other person; only God can do this. We can pray, but it is only God who can remove these darts of Satan (1 Corinthians 12; Ephesians 6:16).

Luther, in his sermon on the Gospel of John, adds another kind of advantage that Satan has over us. He says, "For the devil goes to work with might and main to impede and obstruct the Gospel, he uses every obstacle at his disposal. Besides, he enjoys the advantage of having as an ally within our own hearts that great piece of Adam, who is too lazy by nature, too sluggish, and too tired to engage in a battle like this and always draws us back, thus making it especially hard and unpleasant to keep on contending with opposition and obstacles of so many kinds and to fight to the finish."[1]

Lord's Prayer and Satan

In the Large Catechism, Luther, speaking about the Lord's Prayer, says, "The entire substance of all our prayer is directed against our chief enemy."[2] Why? Satan is proactively and offensively working against everything Jesus teaches us to pray for in His prayer. By the Lord's Prayer, we see the areas of conflict in the cosmic-earthly rebellion presented before us. No one describes this better than Luther in the Large Catechism.

> For no one believes how the devil opposes and resists them, and cannot suffer that any one teach or believe aright. And it hurts him beyond measure to suffer his lies and abominations, that have been honored under the most specious pretexts of the divine name, to be exposed, and to be disgraced himself, and, besides, be driven out of the heart, and suffer such a breach to be made in his kingdom. Therefore he chafes and rages as a fierce enemy with all his power and might, and marshals all his subjects, and, in addition, enlists the world and our own flesh as his allies. For our flesh is in itself indolent and inclined to evil, even though we have accepted and believe the Word of God. The world, however, is perverse and wicked; this he incites against us, fans and stirs the fire, that he may hinder and drive us back, cause us to fall, and again bring us under his power. Such is all his will, mind, and thought, for which he strives day and night, and never rests a moment, employing all arts, wiles, ways, and means whichever he can invent.

> If we would be Christians, therefore, we must surely expect and reckon upon having the devil with all his angels and the world as our enemies who will bring every possible misfortune and grief upon us. For where the Word of God

is preached, accepted, or believed, and produces fruit, there the holy cross cannot be wanting. And let no one think that he shall have peace; but he must risk whatever he has upon earth—possessions, honor, house and estate, wife and children, body and life.[3]

The Main Strategies of Satan

Like a physical enemy, Satan has strategies that he continues to use against mankind, and especially the saints of God. Every sinner who goes to hell and every saint who fails God are proof that the strategies of Satan are quite successful. These strategies are older than humanity, and it is impossible for any man, woman, or child to defeat these strategies on their own terms and in their own strength.

A strategy is a plan of action devised, by Satan and his evil spirits, to attain a certain objective. The main strategies are as follows:

1. Deception (2 Samuel 24:1–8; 2 Corinthians 2:11, 11:3, 11:14; Ephesians 4:27).

2. Blinding the minds of men (Colossians 1:9; 1 John 5:20).

3. Working in men without the men knowing it (Ephesians 2:2).

4. Working to snatch away the truth from men (Matthew 13:19).

5. Giving men a false peace (Luke 11:21).

6. Inciting opposition to the truth (2 Timothy 2:25–26).

7. Counterfeiting the real work of God (Matthew 13:25–39).

8. Targeting the leaders of the church for disgrace and destruction (2 Corinthians 12:7).

9. Dishonoring the purpose of God with a person, nation, or church (2 Samuel 24:1–8).

10. Stealing, killing, and destroying (John 10:10).

11. Resisting the removal of the filthy garments spotted by sin (Zechariah 3:1).

12. Using others to tempt a saint to sin (Matthew 16:22–23).

13. Inflaming the life of nature into chaos, confusion, and strife (James 3:14–15).

14. Weakening the authority of the Scriptures (Galatians 1:8; 1 John 5:5–10).

15. Distorting the teaching of the Scriptures (Galatians 1:8; 1 John 5:5–10).

16. Adding to the Scriptures (Galatians 1:8; Revelation 22:18).

17. Putting the Scriptures entirely aside (Galatians 1:8; Revelation 22:18).

This is noteworthy here: While many have crazy dreams, visions, and other experiences that pull people away from Scripture, my experiences with the Lord have always pulled or pushed me more toward the Word of God. Any experience that pulls a person away from the Word of God cannot be of God. Both the Word of God and these experiences must line up together. If the experiences are of God, they will always agree with the Word of God and draw a person closer to God.

And always remember that the Word of God is superior to experiences. Spiritual experiences coming from the Holy Spirit are always subservient to the Word of God.

I dealt with a woman who held that her experiences superseded the Word of God. With no authorized anchor, she went from one extreme to another and finally ended up in occultism. Nothing could be done to help her.

Generally, after a saint receives revelation from studying the Word of God, the fight will be on, and the saint will be engaged in spiritual warfare. For the sake of the saint, God is a deliverer and not a destroyer.

Immediately after the fight is on, the saint will be tempted by the devil, mainly to stop the fight and turn back to the old ways. This is the reason James said, "My brethren, count it all joy when ye fall into divers temptations; Knowing this, that the trying of your faith worketh patience" (James 1:2–3).

CHAPTER 7

WARFARE AND INTERCESSION

The call of Jesus Christ is a call to warfare. And accepting Christ is being enlisted into His army.

In AD 1845, Christian authors Gurnall and Campbell wrote about the power of Christian prayers, especially imprecatory prayers.

> A word to the wicked. Take heed, that by your unmerciful hatred to the truth and church of God, you do not engage her prayers against you. The imprecatory prayers of the saints, when shot at the right mark, are murdering pieces, and strike dead where they light. "Shall not God avenge his own elect, which cry day and night unto him, though he bears long with them? I tell you he will avenge them speedily," Luke 18:7, 8. They are not empty words, as the imprecations of the wicked poured into the air, and vanish with their breath, but are received into heaven, and shall be sent back with thunder and lightning upon the wicked. David's prayer unravelled Ahithophel's fine-spun policy and twisted his halter for him. The prayers of the saints are more to be feared than an army of twenty thousand men in the field. Esther's fast hastened Haman's ruin, and Hezekiah's prayer against Sennacherib, brought his huge host to the slaughter.[1]

If we, as saints, could understand the power of prayer, nations could be changed for the good, and the powers of darkness could be pushed back. If only we understood the power of prayer, we could have a different life—a life where the powers of darkness are dethroned, and where we do not submit to anyone but God.

Moses and Possessing the Promised Land

God informed Moses at the burning bush,

> I am come down to deliver them out of the hand of the Egyptians, and to bring them up out of that land unto a good land and a large, unto a land flowing with milk and honey; unto the place of the Canaanites, and the Hittites, and the Amorites, and the Perizzites, and the Hivites, and the Jebusites. (Exodus 3:8)

In other words, God told Moses that the Promised Land was occupied with strange and demonic powers that had to be dispossessed.

When the Israelites came out of Egypt, the words of the Lord were again noteworthy.

> And it came to pass, when Pharaoh had let the people go, that God led them not through the way of the land of the Philistines, although that was near; for God said, Lest peradventure the people repent when they see war, and they return to Egypt: But God led the people about, through the way of the wilderness of the Red sea: and the children of Israel went up harnessed out of the land of Egypt. (Exodus 13:17–18)

The Israelites needed absolute discipline and faith in God to prepare themselves for the coming conflict with the nations of Canaan. Therefore, God demanded unconditional obedience and no compromise among His people. The demands of God were extreme, but the reasons were severe.

At Kadesh Barnea, Moses sent spies into the Promised Land. Out of the twelve spies, only two spies believed that the Promised Land could be taken. The remaining spies brought fear and doubt into the midst of the Israelites (Numbers 13:1–33). The two spies who took a strong stand against the unbelief and negative report of the other ten spies were Joshua and Caleb (Numbers 14:1–45). Despite their efforts, the Israelites became fearful and alarmed. Numbers 14:3–9 expresses their fear:

> And wherefore hath the LORD brought us unto this land, to fall by the sword, that our wives and our children should

> be a prey? were it not better for us to return into Egypt? And they said one to another, Let us make a captain, and let us return into Egypt. Then Moses and Aaron fell on their faces before all the assembly of the congregation of the children of Israel. And Joshua the son of Nun, and Caleb the son of Jephunneh, which were of them that searched the land, rent their clothes: And they spake unto all the company of the children of Israel, saying, The land, which we passed through to search it, is an exceeding good land. If the LORD delight in us, then he will bring us into this land, and give it us; a land which floweth with milk and honey. Only rebel not ye against the LORD, neither fear ye the people of the land; for they are bread for us: their defence is departed from them, and the LORD is with us: fear them not.

Once again, the Israelites retreated in fear at the very thought of war against the nations of Canaan, which were steeped in demonism. Because of this sign of doubt, God led the Israelites around until almost all the old generation died off. The wilderness became their graves. And a new generation arose, with Joshua and Caleb still living, and was able to enter the Promised Land.

The Israelites had repeatedly witnessed the supernatural intervention of God in their deliverance from Egypt, and throughout their years in the desert. Israelites were shown a supernatural lifestyle, which many may hope for within their lives and never receive.

Paul speaks to the Corinthians about the Israelites who left Egypt.

> All our fathers were under the cloud, and all passed through the sea; And were all baptized unto Moses in the cloud and in the sea, And did all eat the same spiritual meat; And did all drink the same spiritual drink: for they drank of that spiritual Rock that followed them: and that Rock was Christ.
> (1 Corinthians 10:1–4)

Experiencing the good pleasure of God, the Israelites saw bread come down from heaven, and their clothes never wore out in all those years of wandering in the wilderness (Deuteronomy 29:5). The pillar of the cloud over the tabernacle led them from one oasis to another.

Aaron repeatedly prayed this prayer over the Israelites in the wilderness:

> The LORD bless thee, and keep thee: The LORD make his face shine upon thee, and be gracious unto thee: The LORD lift up his countenance upon thee, and give thee peace. And they shall put my name upon the children of Israel; and I will bless them. (Numbers 6:24–27)

The Israelites never took possession of their whole inheritance. While they went far and experienced so much, they never wholly experienced the heritage of God. Nor did they ever completely remove the nations of Canaan from the Promised Land.

The failure of the complete conquest of the land of Canaan is well documented in Judges 1:27–36:

> Neither did Manasseh drive out the inhabitants of Beth-shean and her towns, nor Taanach and her towns, nor the inhabitants of Dor and her towns, nor the inhabitants of Ibleam and her towns, nor the inhabitants of Megiddo and her towns: but the Canaanites would dwell in that land. And it came to pass, when Israel was strong, that they put the Canaanites to tribute, and did not utterly drive them out. Neither did Ephraim drive out the Canaanites that dwelt in Gezer; but the Canaanites dwelt in Gezer among them. Neither did Zebulun drive out the inhabitants of Kitron, nor the inhabitants of Nahalol; but the Canaanites dwelt among them and became tributaries. Neither did Asher drive out the inhabitants of Accho, nor the inhabitants of Zidon, nor of Ahlab, nor of Achzib, nor of Helbah, nor of Aphik, nor of Rehob: But the Asherites dwelt among the Canaanites, the inhabitants of the land: for they did not drive them out. Neither did Naphtali drive out the inhabitants of Beth-shemesh, nor the inhabitants of Beth-anath; but he dwelt among the Canaanites, the inhabitants of the land: nevertheless the inhabitants of Beth-shemesh and of Beth-anath became tributaries unto them. And the Amorites forced the children of Dan into the mountain: for they would not suffer them to come down to the valley: But the Amorites would dwell in mount Heres in Aijalon, and in Shaalbim:

> yet the hand of the house of Joseph prevailed, so that they
> became tributaries. And the coast of the Amorites was from
> the going up to Akrabbim, from the rock, and upward.

Judges 1 says quite well that the tribe of Asher did not drive out the Canaanites but dwelled among them. What does that mean? They merged their customs, habits, behavior, and religion with that of the Canaanites. The Asherites who did not destroy or capture Tyre or Sidon but cultivated friendly relations with the Phoenician inhabitants utterly disobeyed the mandate of God. The Asherites may have, at first, made some hostile demonstrations against their pagan neighbors, but they were so thoroughly checked by the superior power and skill of their opponents that they soon settled down side by side with them, and made no further attempts at conquest or taking hold of their inheritance. Deborah, the judge of Israel, said it the best. "Asher continued on the sea shore, and abode in his breaches" (Judges 5:17).

The general estimate of the conquest here in Joshua 10:38−43 is the same time period of the conquest of Southern Palestine. With the exemption of the Gibeonites, the sons of Anak continued to live until the times of David, along with the Philistines and several groups of Canaanites. This shows that the Israelites never carried the mandate from God, through Moses, to its completion in both Southern and Northern Palestine. Not until the reign of David was the Philistine power entirely broken.

God's Battle or Our Battle

As soon as the Israelites left Egypt, they were attacked by the Amalekites. The battle lasted one day. The Israelites ebbed and flowed but finally ended in victory (Exodus 17). The victory, however, was not due to the talent of the Jewish warriors. It occurred as a result of the deeds of Moses, Aaron, and Hur on the hilltop.

As Moses, supported by Aaron and Hur, held the rod of God in the air, the battle finally turned in favor of the Israelites. The lesson here is that the victory is first won in the spiritual world, and that the real enemy of the Israelites was not the Amalekites, but Satan and his evil spirits who were using the Amalekites.

The conflict with the Amalekites was a dress rehearsal for what was to take place in the Promised Land. And it was a warning of what else would come upon the Israelites when they entered the Promised Land.

As the Israelites stood in their faith, they could and would experience nothing but victory. In this conflict with the Amalekites, the Israelites were taught the principle of faith. It was to be by this principle alone that they could defeat all their enemies.

If the Israelites unreservedly believed in God, they would experience maximum success. But if they only partly believed in God, they would only obtain some success in their endeavors. As they believed in God, so God would move for them. God Himself was to drive their enemies out before them, not they themselves. It came down to this fact: if they wanted complete success, they had to attain it by unconditional obedience and faith.

After the trouble with the Amalekites, the Israelites did not encounter any other enemy nation throughout their wilderness experience, until they reached the land of Canaan.

In all the superseding years, there were plenty of conflicts, but the main conflicts that faced the Israelites were of an internal nature. The Israelites had to fight themselves to gain success. And many times, they lost that fight because of sin.

What is Spiritual Warfare?

To Israel, spiritual warfare came in the outward form of physical, brutal, bloody battle. And victory or loss resulted from obedience or disobedience, rather than strength, skill, or numbers—as Moses declares in Deuteronomy 11:22–25:

> For if ye shall diligently keep all these commandments which I command you, to do them, to love the Lord your God, to walk in all his ways, and to cleave unto him; Then will the Lord drive out all these nations from before you, and ye shall possess greater nations and mightier than yourselves. Every place whereon the soles of your feet shall tread shall be yours: from the wilderness and Lebanon, from the river, the river Euphrates, even unto the uttermost sea shall your

coast be. There shall no man be able to stand before you: for the Lord your God shall lay the fear of you and the dread of you upon all the land that ye shall tread upon. as he hath said unto you.

To the apostles, spiritual warfare is based on the sacrificial love of Christ that exemplified by His earthly ministry. It is empowered by Christ's work of the cross and the power of the resurrection. The physical war transitions into a spiritual war of invading the darkness and setting people free from demonic bondage and oppression. The purposes of the spiritual holy war are as follows:

1. To spread the gospel of the cross throughout the world.

2. To defeat Satan in his own area and arena.

3. To set the captives free.

4. To heal the brokenhearted.

5. To restore life as God intended it to be.

6. To preach deliverance to the captives.

7. To recover sight for the blind.

8. To set at liberty them that are bruised.

9. To expose and overthrow the kingdom of darkness.

10. To significantly advance the kingdom of light.

11. To move out under the authority of the Word of God, the name of Jesus, the power of the blood, and the power of the cross.

To Jesus, spiritual warfare is an armed struggle between the forces of good and the forces of evil (Matthew 4:4–10, 8:1–3, 8:28–31, 9:1–7, 9:18–35, 14:21, 14:34–36, 15:29–31, 17:14–18, 21:19–20).

Spiritual warfare denotes spiritual resistance against all the evil works and operations of Satan through spiritual weapons of war.

To Paul, this part of the call of Christ is a call to arms. At the new birth, the person is (often unbeknown to him or her) enlisted in the army of God. Christian life means warfare.

307

According to Paul, our warfare is controlled and restricted under the domain of faith, the domain of a good conscience, and the domain of the Spirit (Romans 4:12; 1 Corinthians 8:7; 2 Corinthians 5:7; Galatians 5:16–17). It is impossible for a saint to be victorious in spiritual warfare without being in the domain of faith, the domain of a good conscience, and the domain of the Holy Spirit. The word domain is a term that originates in Greek grammar, as understood in the New Testament. For example, our faith has a domain, an influence, or an area of dominance. We must remain in that domain.

Furthermore, spiritual warfare is using our godly weapons and attacking spiritual strongholds of Satan and his evil spirits, which are against the gospel of Christ (Matthew 18:18–20). Spiritual warfare is possessing the authority of the believer in the name of Jesus Christ, and the power of the Holy Spirit by the baptism of the Holy Spirit (Luke 10:17; Acts 1:8).

The Modern Church

Today, most of us are like scared children hiding in the bedroom or lost in a dark forest with no light. Most of the church has become useless and pathetic, especially in the realm of prayer and spiritual warfare. Few are fighting, while the rest are on the sidelines. On the other hand, Paul told Timothy and the rest of the Christians at Ephesus to fight the good fight of faith (1 Timothy 6:12). And Paul asked the Corinthians a question in 1 Corinthians 14:8, "For if the trumpet give an uncertain sound, who shall prepare himself to the battle?" Paul understood the life of a Christian is war. Walter Martin, a minister and an expert on cults and the occult, once said, "The methodology and the philosophy governing the Christians today, in many areas, is that there is no battle."[2] Walter Martin did not believe that there is no battle. He said, "The moment you enlist in the army of God, you personally become a target. You need to remember that if you're living for and walking with Jesus Christ, the powers of darkness are aligned against you."[3] And lastly, he said, "Christ imparts the capacity of conquest to our lives every single day that we are willing to believe Him."[4]

Some say that it is easy to pray against the forces of evil. Really?

We are in many ways defenseless, hopeless, and helpless against an evil that we cannot defeat on our own. We have refused to understand our enemy. We have denounced the weapons of warfare and laid down our sword and shield, hoping that the devil will not see us or come near our home or our families.

Denying the devil's existence will not save us. Lowering our weapons and refusing to take up our armor will not save us. Paul, the apostles, and the ancient church knew how to overcome Satan: through prayer and the Word of God (Ephesians 6:17–18). Paul longed to see the saints united in Christ, enjoying the riches of blessing in Him.

We all need to pick up our weapons and fight.

Weapons of our Warfare

Within the Bible, we can draw up a list of weapons to be used by the saints in our never-ending battle against Satan and his evil spirits.

I have never used extra-biblical weapons. These have no reference in Scripture and should never be used. They are not weapons authorized by God or by His Word. These supposed weapons are tied to the occult, and I have never seen them be successful. For example, some Christians use salt or holy water as a weapon. I have never seen salt or holy water work, nor have I ever used them to fight a spiritual battle. There is a biblical limit on weapons that should be used by Christians.

"Holy water" was officially used in AD 850 as a weapon by the Roman Catholic Church. Before that date, holy water was never used as a weapon; it was purely for Catholic rituals. As a weapon, it should not be used. Other conventional modern methods of spiritual weapons were never used by the ancient church. Such modern armaments hinder or destroy our attempt to stop Satan and his evil spirits. We should go back to the earliest times of the church.

Luther taught that we should not depend on holy water, sacred salt, and other sacraments as weapons, but we must now fight by the Word of God and the prayer of faith.[5]

Here is a general list of these weapons:

1. Word of God (Matthew 4:4–10; Luke 4:4–10).

2. Blood of Christ (Exodus 12:7; Acts 20:28; Romans 3:25, 5:9; 1 Corinthians 10:16, 11:27; 1 Peter 1:2, 1:19; 1 John 1:7; 5:6).

3. Name of Jesus (Matthew 18:19–20, 28:18; John 14:12–15; Acts 2:21–38, 3:6, 4:18, 5:40, 9:27, 16:18).

4. Power of praise (Luke 19:28–43; Revelation 5:11–12).

5. Power of the cross (John 19:30; Hebrews 2:2, 9:9).

6. Power of prayer (Mark 11:24; Acts 4:24–32; Romans 8:26).

7. Word of wisdom (1 Corinthians 12–13).

8. Word of knowledge (1 Corinthians 12–13).

9. Gifts of healing (1 Corinthians 12–13).

10. Working of miracles (1 Corinthians 12–13).

11. Gift of discerning of spirits (1 Corinthians 12–13).

12. Gift of faith (1 Corinthians 12–13).

13. Gift of tongues (1 Corinthians 12–13).

14. Gift of prophecy (1 Corinthians 12–13).

15. Gift of interpretation of tongues (1 Corinthians 12–13).

16. Power of love (1 Corinthians 13:13).

17. Power of hope (1 Corinthians 13:13).

18. Fruit of the Holy Spirit (Galatians 5:22–23).

19. Power of fasting (Psalms 35:13, 69:10; Daniel 10:1–21; Matthew 4:1–2; 1 Corinthians 7:5).

20. Gospel music (1 Samuel 16:15–23).

21. Repentance (Matthew 18:22, 3:11, 9:13; Luke 17:4; Acts 17:30; 2 Corinthians 7:8; Revelation 3:19, 3:3, 2:16).

22. Communion (Matthew 26:26; Mark 14:22–26; Luke 22:19; John 13:1–14:31; 1 Corinthians 11:23–34).

23. Walking in holiness (Luke 1:75; Romans 6:19–22, 8:4, 12:2, 13:8–10; 1 Corinthians 7:19; 2 Corinthians 7:1; Ephesians 4:24; Hebrews 12:10–14; 1 Timothy 2:15; 1 Peter 4:6).

24. Anointing with oil (Exodus 28:41, 29:7, 29:36, 30:22–27, 40:9–13; Mark 6:13; James 5:14).

25. Faith (Matthew 17:20; Hebrews 11:1–39, 12:2).

26. Suffering for Christ (Matthew 5:11; 1 Corinthians 4:9, 10:13; 2 Corinthians 4:8, 6:3; Hebrews 2:10, 11:25; 2 Peter 2:9).

27. Girt of truth (Ephesians 6:11–19).

28. Breastplate of righteousness (Ephesians 6:11–19).

29. Feet shod with the preparation of the gospel of peace (Ephesians 6:11–19).

30. Shield of faith (Ephesians 6:11–19).

31. The helmet of salvation (Ephesians 6:11–19).

32. Shield of protection (Job 1:10, 3:23).

33. Exorcism and prayers of exorcism (Matthew 8:16, 12:28; Acts 16:18).

34. Baptism in water (Matthew 3:6–16, 28:14–18; Mark 1:4; Acts 2:38).

How to Begin to Fight

The Bible teaches us how to fight Satan and his evil spirits. A general list of how to fight in spiritual warfare is as follows:

1. We must submit to God (James 4:7).

2. We must resist the devil (James 4:7).

3. We must draw near to God (James 4:8).

4. He will draw near to you (James 4:8).

5. We must keep our eyes on Christ.

6. We must take a public stand for Christ.

7. We must keep a balanced status in our faith.

8. We must not become fanatical in our faith.

9. We should join a balanced church.

10. We must begin a regular prayer life (Matthew 7:7–8).

11. We must read the Bible daily.

12. We must be faithful in giving to God (Genesis 28:20–22).

13. We must know the Bible.

14. We must know Christ, not know about Him.

15. We must know the authority of the Bible.

16. We must know that Christ is the Victor over Satan.

17. We must remain in the presence of God.

18. We must be ready to receive divine authority for a battle.

19. We must step out of our safety zones.

20. We must know how to pray.

21. We must know our enemy.

22. We must focus on what we are spiritually attacking.

23. We must know our place and position in Christ.

24. We must know who we are in Jesus Christ.

25. We must know who is backing us up.

26. We must know our spiritual authority.

27. We must be righteous and holy.

28. We must be obedient.

29. We must keep our relationship with Christ in good standing.

30. We must not go into spiritual warfare over a situation unless we are ready to pay the cost and are ready to be attacked by Satan.

31. We must know our limits.

32. We must know the ploys and strategies of Satan.

33. We must know that Satan will use anyone to try to detour us from our goal of victory.

34. We must know the limits of the weapons used.

35. We must be certain that God is leading us into spiritual warfare for a situation.

36. We must make sure that we have repented.

37. We must have on the armor of God.

38. In spiritual warfare, we must fight by the name of Jesus, the power of the blood, and the power of the cross through prayer.

39. In prayer, we must tell Satan and all his forces that they are rebuked and rejected by these weapons.

40. We must denounce the works of Satan.

41. We must loose and bind the forces of Satan.

42. We must use other weapons and other means, as God so directs.

43. We must focus on what Satan is doing and attack or counterattack that and all his strongholds.

44. In spiritual warfare, the saints of God must have determination, direction, specific prayer, and faith.

Seven Prayers of a Spiritual Warrior

These prayers are beyond what many know. Every spiritual warrior (intercessor) should recognize these prayers:

1. O Lord, open my eyes, like Elijah's servant, so that I may see the spiritual battles that are going on in my life in the name of Jesus Christ (2 Kings 6:17).

2. Teach, O Lord, my prayerful hands to war, and my prayerful fingers to fight in the name of Jesus Christ (Psalm 144:1).

3. O Lord, give unto me one heart and one way so that I may fear You always in the name of Jesus Christ (Jeremiah 32:39).

4. Uphold me, O Lord, with Your directing Spirit, in the name of Jesus Christ (Psalm 51:12).

5. O Lord, grant me Your divine authority and power so that I may fight against the forces of evil in the name of Jesus Christ (Colossians 1:29).

6. O Lord, give me heroic friends whose hearts You have touched in the name of Jesus Christ (1 Samuel 10:26).

7. O Lord, teach me to guard my words so that my words can be used as weapons against the forces of evil in the name of Jesus Christ (Psalm 141:3).

Battles in Biblical History

The Apostle Paul explained one critical purpose for Old Testament battles. He said, "Now all these things happened unto them for ensamples: and they are written for our admonition, upon whom the ends of the world are come. Wherefore let him that thinketh he standeth take heed lest he fall" (1 Corinthians 10:11–12).

In Origen's commentary on the Book of Joshua, he speaks of the reason for the historical mentioning of all the Old Testament battles.

> Unless those physical wars can bear the likeness of spiritual wars, I do not ever suppose that the Books of Jewish History would have been delivered from the apostles to the disciples of Christ, who came to teach peace, so that they could be read in the churches. For instance, what can the description of these physical wars achieve unto those followers to whom it is said by Jesus, "My peace I bestow unto you; My peace

I leave behind unto you," and unto whom it is being commanded and being spoken by the apostle, "Not avenging your own selves," and, "Rather, you receive injustice," and, "Rather, You suffer wrongdoing"? From that, in summary, knowing that now we do not have to conduct wars physically, but the struggles of the soul have to be performed with exertion against spiritual adversaries, the apostle, just as if a military commander, gives a command unto the soldiers of Christ, saying, "You put on the armor of God, in order that you may be able to stand stable against the cunning strategies of the devil." And so that we may have examples of these spiritual wars from the militaristic exploits of old, he wished such narratives of these militaristic exploits to be recounted aloud unto us in church, in order that, if we are spiritual, hearing that the law is spiritual, we may compare spiritual things with spiritual in those things that we may hear. And we may consider very carefully, by the aid of those nations that battled against physical Israel, how mighty can the groups of opposing armies be from among the spiritual races that are being called "spiritual wickedness in the heavenlies," and how they can wage wars against even the church of the Lord, which is the true Israel. Both the Moabites and the Ammonites come, and all those kings and invisible races that we have already mentioned. They come against us, planning to give us battle, so that they may make us sin.[6]

Since the Greek text of Origen has not survived, this translation is from the Latin text (version). The remarkable thing, besides others, is the words, Moabitae veniunt et Ammonitae, et omnes illi reges, et gentes invisibiles, quas superius memoravimus, adversum nos veniunt pugnaturae, ad hoc ut peccare nos faaciant (Both the Moabites and the Ammonites come, and all those kings and invisible races that we have already mentioned. They come against us, planning to give us battle, so that they may make us sin). Origen identifies the demons—gods of the Moabites, the Ammonites, and other races of the Canaanites as coming against us. In other words, the main demons that attack us come from the region of Canaan and thereabouts, the area of Canaan connected to Egypt, Babylonia, Assyria, and Phoenicia, all point to one common source or grouping of evil spirits, though different names may be given, behind all those names, they are the same groupings. Next, he understands that behind the Canaanites were evil princes and evil demonic creatures. And he calls the invisible demons races, which could not be said of fallen angels.

If the Israelites had done what God completely wanted, the world would not have been affected by the rites of the Canaanites and their Baalim and Astartes. Even the Egyptians and the Babylonians, for example, were affected by the rites of the Canaanites and their Baalim and Astartes. The religion of Greece and that of Rome have as their source the Canaanites, and their Baalim and Astartes.

Moreover, Origen discusses the condition of the world before the coming forth of Joshua and the Israelites:

> Vides quanta adversum Jesum et Israeliticum exercitum, contrariarum virtutum et pessimorum daemontum examina concitentur. Isti omnes daemones ante adventum Domini et Salvatoris nostril, quieti et securi humanas animas possidentes, in earum mentibus corporibusque regnabant. Sed ut in terris apparuit gratia et Misericordia Salvatoris nostril Dei, edocens nos ut pie et sancta in hoc mundo, et segregati ab omni contagione peccat vivamus, ut libertatem suam atque imaginem Deit, in qua ex initio creata est anima unaquaeque recipiat, ista de causea ab illis iniquis veteribus possessoribus earm pugnae exoriuntur et proelia. Et si opprimantur primi, multo plures exsurgunt postmodum atque in unum coeunt, et conspirant in malum, qui semper dissident, a bono. Et si secundo victi fuerint, iterum tertio aliae virtutes nequiores exsurgunt. Et fortassis quanto magis augetur populus Dei, et multo plus crescit et multipilicatur, tanto illi plures ad oppugnandum conspirant (You see how many swarms of hostile hosts and of the vilest demons may be stirred up against Joshua and the Israelite army. Before the advent of our Lord and Savior, all those demons, who were at peace and secure, possessed the human spirits and ruled in their minds and bodies. But so, grace appeared in the world and the mercy of God our Savior instructs us thoroughly in order that we may live righteously and morally in this world and be separated from every contagion of sin, that each spirit of a human may take back its freedom and

the image of God also in which it was created from the beginning. Because of this reason, battles and fights arise from their wicked old possessors. And if the first ones can be defeated, much more arise subsequently, and they also gather together into one force and collaborate in evil that are always separated from the good. And if they may be defeated for a second time, again a third time other more wicked hosts will rise up. And so, possibly the more people of God are being increased, and the more they both prosper and are multiplied, there are so much more evil hosts who collaborate to attack).[7]

When we read the Old Testament, we will find many records of battles fought in the physical world. The significance of these battles goes beyond their physical and immediate outcomes. These battles give us spiritual principles and strategies in the spiritual world to defeat our enemies, both Satan and his evil spirits.

From studying the physical battles recorded in the Old Testament, we can develop abilities, principles, and strategies to use in our battles against Satan and his evil spirits. Paul and the rest of the early church saints followed suit and developed their means of conflict based upon the natural battles of the Old Testament.

The physical battles of the Old Testament were fought for seven spiritual reasons:

1. So that the people of God could defeat their enemies.

2. So that the people of God would not be enslaved by their enemies.

3. So that the people of God would fulfill the promises of God in occupying the Promised Land and in other promises.

4. So that the people of God could take the territory of their enemies.

5. So that the people of God could chastise their enemies, which are also the enemies of God.

6. So that the people of God would be punished by their enemies when they are in a state of disobedience.

7. So that the people of God would obtain their inheritance and defend that inheritance once obtained.

General Principles of Old Testament Warfare

1. A battle must be ordered and endorsed by God (Deuteronomy 20:1–4).

2. We cannot be afraid of our enemies (Deuteronomy 20:1–4).

3. The Lord God will be with His people and will go before His people (Deuteronomy 20:1–4).

4. The battle is the Lord's (Deuteronomy 20:1–4).

5. We must prepare ourselves for the battle (Deuteronomy 20:1–4).

6. Our enemies must be utterly destroyed (Deuteronomy 20:1–4).

7. We must not run after the abominations of the Gentiles (Deuteronomy 20:1–4).

8. God promises protection to His soldiers (Deuteronomy 20:1–4).

9. The enemies of God's people are the enemies of God (Exodus 17:16; Judges 5:31).

10. We are to trust in God for victory (Exodus 17:16; Judges 5:31).

11. We are never to trust in our strength (Exodus 17:16; Judges 5:31).

12. The Lord makes war with the enemies of God's people (Exodus 17:16; Judges 5:31).

13. The presence of God must go before us in battle (Exodus 25:21–22, 30:6).

14. Without the presence of God, there can be no victory (Exodus 25:21–22, 30:6).

15. The presence of God must be in our camp; the Ark of the Covenant symbolized the presence of God with the Israelites during a battle (Exodus 25:21–22, 30:6).

16. We have to be a holy people for God to fight for us against our enemies. No holiness = no victory, but inevitable defeat (Deuteronomy 23:9–14).

17. Holiness is key for the saints of God in battle (Deuteronomy 23:9–14).

18. We must be and remain a holy people so that the battle can be won (Deuteronomy 23:9–14).

19. We must separate ourselves from anything sinful (Deuteronomy 23:9–14).

20. Repentance must go before a battle (Deuteronomy 23:9–14).

21. Those who live in fear cannot fight or win any battle (Deuteronomy 20:8; Judges 7:1–6). No cross, no crown.

22. Those who focus more on the affairs of life than the issues of the Lord are not permitted to fight for God or the people of God (Deuteronomy 20:5–8).

23. We are supposed to fight against our enemies until they are destroyed. So we cannot give up or retire until we attain total victory (Numbers 31:10–11).

24. Both offensive and defensive warfare are found in the lives of the saints.

25. We must become submissive to the command of God either to fight or to cease fighting (Judges 7:18; 2 Samuel 2:28, 18:16).

26. We must have spiritual walls around our lives by the pleading of the blood of the Lamb.

Strategies of Warfare

The Old Testament battles provide clear warfare strategies for the modern saint. These strategies can be brought beyond the natural world into the spiritual world. These strategies should be used daily by all the saints of God. Such a strategy can only be used in each battle if the strategy can be used in that case. Using all the strategies in each battle is impossible. Some battles may only need a few strategies. Other battles may require almost all strategies.

As pertaining to different strategies and their uses, Ignatius, an apostolic father, said it best in medical terms unto Polycarp, another apostolic father, οὐ πᾶν τραῦμα τῇ αὐτῇ ἐμπλάστρῳ θεραπεύεται (Not every wound is healed with the same salve).[8] The Greek noun ἔμπλαστρος may be translated *treatment* or *remedy,* but it is better translated as *salve,* which follows the full thought of the Greek.

Edward Longstreth summarized the strategies of warfare in the Old Testament times.

> Yahweh stated His relationship with men very positively and very explicitly to Moses, saying: I am the Lord your God, you shall have no other gods before me. You shall not make for yourself any graven image of anything that is in the heavens, on the earth, or in the water. For I am a jealous God and you shall worship Me only, and with all your heart and soul and mind.

> That was it! There was to be no compromise, no extenuation, no equivocation. There had never before been such a concept of a God. The impact of this unique idea shook the world. It could not be exterminated. It took root in the empty places in man, possessed him, fulfilled his unfulfillment. Death and disaster only made it grow. The point all the major prophets made was that any repudiation of, or lapse from, these two basic commandments would be punished. Any backsliding generation would wish it had never been born.

> In the decisive battles of ancient Israel, more was involved than the clash of arms. It was not his body the Israelite feared to have pierced, it was not his life he feared to lose; the loss he dreaded most was the loss of the favor of His God because he had broken his covenant with Him.[9]

The following three phrases describe the strategies extracted from the battles of the Old Testament better than any other: "No compromise, no extenuation, no equivocation."[10]

Here is a list of the overall strategies extracted from the battles of the Old Testament and from several books about the battles in the Old Testament:[11]

1. When a saint goes into the territory of the enemy, he or she must expect a battle (Genesis 14).

2. Victory in a battle rests upon implementation of the plan of God, and the involvement of God in the battle (Genesis 14).

3. The battle plan is not ours, but it is our Lord's (Genesis 14).

4. Without God, everything can stand against the saint of God (Genesis 14).

5. With God, everything, sooner or later, will crumble before His power (Genesis 14).

6. With God, sooner or later, we will be able to conquer what stands against us (Genesis 14).

7. In battle, we should fight only the portion that we can handle (Genesis 14).

8. We must refuse to give any help to the enemy (Genesis 14).

9. We must enter a battle with the right motive, behavior, and attitude (Genesis 14).

10. The credit of victory rests upon God (Genesis 14).

11. We must not look at the enemies or the evil circumstances with fear (Exodus 14:10–11).

12. We must not go back into captivity (Exodus 14:12).

13. Sometimes we must stand still or become unmovable (Exodus 14:13).

14. We must allow the Lord to fight since it is His battle (Exodus 14:14).

15. Despite our circumstances, we must keep our peace (Exodus 14:14).

16. We must go forward and rarely retreat (Exodus 14:15–16).

17. God moves for His saints in supernatural means (Exodus 14:19–31).

18. God will orchestrate events for our benefit in our conflicts (Exodus 14:19–31).

19. In prayer, we must call upon the Lord and learn to wait and minister unto the Lord (Exodus 14).

20. We must wait in faith and patience (Exodus 14).

21. We can only overcome or conquer the enemies of God through prayer (Exodus 17:9–11).

22. We must hold to the authority and power of God, regardless of our circumstances (Exodus 17:9).

23. We must follow spiritual leadership, as long as that leadership follows the leading of God (Exodus 17:9–10).

24. We must go out from our safety zone and fight in plain sight (Exodus 17:9).

25. We need to seek help from the Lord (Exodus 17).

26. We must remember the victories and conquests that took place in the past (Exodus 17).

27. We should not grumble (Number 14:2–3).

28. We must never rebel against God in or outside a battle (Numbers 14:9).

29. We must not accept evil or slanderous reports (Numbers 14:36–38).

30. We must never do the reverse of what God has spoken (Numbers 14:25).

31. We must never go up when the Lord is not with the people of God (Numbers 14:28–29).

32. We must not be overoptimistic or arrogant, regardless of the circumstances (Numbers 14:42–44).

33. We must not make any decision in fear but always make decisions according to the principles of faith (Numbers 14).

34. We must not be forced into a battle (Numbers 21:1–3).

35. Any failure experienced by the people of God is temporary and never permanent (Numbers 21:1–3).

36. We do suffer failures, but any failure of God's people is beneficial (Numbers 21:1–3).

37. Conflict in life, especially if a person is a saint of God, is inescapable (Numbers 21:21–32).

38. If we are to have the promises of God, spiritual warfare is unavoidable (Numbers 21:21–32).

39. Enemies will never allow the people of God safe passage through their territory (Numbers 21:21–32).

40. We must repent and purify ourselves before the battles (Numbers 31).

41. In battle, the interests of God's people are foremost (Numbers 31).

42. We must claim the promises of God (Deuteronomy 2:24–37).

43. We must allow God to fight for us (Deuteronomy 2:24–37).

44. We must possess the promises of God (Deuteronomy 2:24–37).

45. We must contend with the enemies in battle (Deuteronomy 2:24–27).

46. We must see that nothing is hard for the Lord (Deuteronomy 2:24–37).

47. The enemies of God's people will be delivered into our hands by the Lord (Deuteronomy 3:1–11).

48. We must overcome all obstacles by the power of God (Deuteronomy 3:1–11).

49. We must claim victory and its consequences (Deuteronomy 3:1–11).

50. We must follow the ways of God and not our ways (Joshua 6).

51. Sometimes we must divide and conquer the forces of evil (Joshua 6). In such cases, we should fight one evil spirit, or one group of evil spirits at a time rather than take on many evil spirits.

52. We must trust God, regardless of our circumstances (Joshua 6).

53. We must fight the battle God's way (Joshua 6).

54. We should seek assurance from God (Joshua 6).

55. We should practice silence on occasion (Joshua 6).

56. We should never go against the directions of God (Joshua 7).

57. We must never underestimate our enemies (Joshua 7).

58. We should understand the reasons for defeat or failure (Joshua 7).

59. We must not compromise with the world (Joshua 7).

60. We must not accept any accursed thing nor violate the warnings of God (Joshua 7).

61. We must always be prepared and ready to do battle (Joshua 8).

62. We must use the sword of the Lord, which is the Word of God (Joshua 8).

63. We must turn toward the enemies and face them (Joshua 8).

64. We should not run from our enemies unless God demands us to retreat for some reason (Joshua 8).

65. We must face our enemies in the strength of God (Joshua 8).

66. We must focus on the Lord God, nothing else (Joshua 8).

67. We must put our enemies under our feet (Joshua 10:1–27).

68. We must be stable and of good courage (Joshua 10:1–27).

69. We must learn to attack key strongholds (Joshua 10:28–43).

70. We must persevere and remain faithful in battle (Joshua 11).

71. We must never fear the type or the size of any enemy (Joshua 11).

72. We should always heed the warnings from the Lord God (Judges 6:1–8:35).

73. God must restore us (Judges 6:1–8:35).

74. We must learn to be alone with the Lord God (Judges 6:1–8:35).

75. We must destroy all our altars of idolatry (Judges 6:1–8:35).

76. We must persevere by the Spirit of God (Judges 6:1–8:35).

77. We must seek greater and more powerful levels of faith (Judges 6:1–8:35).

78. We must learn to depend upon the Lord (Judges 6:1–8:35).

79. We must learn to move and not hesitate when God commands us to move (Judges 6:1–8:35).

80. We must not fear our enemies (Judges 6:1–8:35).

81. We must call down and invoke the authority and power of God (Judges 6:1–8:35).

82. We must learn that God can turn a defeat into a victory (Judges 15).

83. We should acknowledge God as our provision and support (Judges 15).

84. We must be refreshed by the Lord (Judges 15).

85. We must ask the counsel of God (Judges 20).

86. We must accept corporate discipline (Judges 20).

87. We must not stop fighting (Judges 20).

88. We must be patient in the day and hour of crisis (1 Samuel 13–14).

89. We must stress commitment, but never highlight numbers (1 Samuel 13–14).

90. We must draw strength from past victories (1 Samuel 17).

91. We must have faith that is strengthened in the difficulties of the past, which always yields faith for new challenges (1 Samuel 17).

92. We must see obstacles and other trials as opportunities of God (1 Samuel 17).

93. We must use a proven armor and not a new armor (1 Samuel 17).

94. We must face the enemies in the name of the Lord (1 Samuel 17).

95. We must not be limited by our capabilities (1 Samuel 17).

96. We must confess our victories (1 Samuel 17).

97. We must recognize the purposes and reasons for spiritual warfare (1 Samuel 17).

98. We must not give in to despair (1 Samuel 30).

99. We must claim restoration of all things that have been taken by our enemies (1 Samuel 30).

100. We must realize that victories, whether personal or corporate, are for all (1 Samuel 30).

101. We must not be intimidated by the mockeries of our enemies (2 Samuel 5:1–16).

102. We must fight offensively (2 Samuel 5:17–25).

103. We must attack our enemies in the Lord's timing (2 Samuel 5:17–25).

104. We must overcome the giants in the land (2 Samuel 21:15–22).

105. We must know that God uses different methods in battles (2 Samuel 21:15–22).

106. We must remember that our enemies will return (1 Kings 20).

107. We must not be deceived by flattery (1 Kings 20).

108. We must set appropriate priorities (1 Kings 20).

109. We must praise God for revelation (2 Kings 3).

110. We must repeatedly pray, especially in battles (2 Kings 6:8–23).

111. We must develop spiritual perception (2 Kings 6:8–23).

112. We must allow the power of God to be manifested (2 Kings 6:8–23).

113. We must move toward the realm of the impossible (2 Kings 6:24–7:20).

114. We must not be critical or untrusting of God's power (2 Kings 6:24–7:20).

115. We must worship God (2 Kings 17).

116. We must understand the consequences of sins in our lives (2 Kings 24:1–25:30).

117. We must hold on for victories (1 Chronicles 14:8–17).

118. We must humble ourselves before the battle (2 Chronicles 12).

119. We must learn to submit to the service and tasks of God (2 Chronicles 12).

120. We must not make any unholy alliances (2 Chronicles 18).

121. In a battle, we must use discernment (2 Chronicles 18).

122. In a battle, we must use fasting as a means of defeating our enemies (2 Chronicles 20).

123. We must always keep our eyes upon the Lord God (2 Chronicles 20).

124. We must believe and trust in God rather than ourselves (2 Chronicles 20).

125. We should rejoice during the occurrence of a battle (2 Chronicles 20).

126. We should follow good and godly advice if it agrees with the will of God (2 Chronicles 25:5–16).

127. We must rebuke pride in our lives (2 Chronicles 25:17–24).

128. We must not allow corruption to come into our lives because it will bring destruction (2 Chronicles 28).

129. We must cut the supply line of our enemies (2 Chronicles 32:1–23).

130. We must reject all types and forms of deceptions (2 Chronicles 35:20–24).

131. We must always listen when God speaks (2 Chronicles 35:20–24).

Jesus and His Prayer Life

Prayer was the priority in the life of Jesus. To Jesus Christ, prayer was communication with His Father. He teaches us that we must talk to our heavenly Father.[12]

Prayer and Intercession

While intercession is a form of prayer, there is a difference between general prayer and intercession.

Intercession is a prayer for others, while general prayer does not necessarily follow that pattern.

Definitions and Nature of Intercession

Intercession means "to intercede for," "stand in the gap for," "to stand in proxy for," "to mediate," "to intervene," and "to desire to be part of what God is doing." Intercessory prayer is standing in for a person.

The foundation of intercession is to have the mind of Christ. By having the mind of Christ, we join with Christ to fulfill the will of God and to intercede for the fulfillment of His will.

Intercessory prayer is for all the saints. All the saints are priests (Revelation 1:6). All saints of God have been given the ministry of reconciliation (2 Corinthians 5:17–18).

At its heart, intercession is standing in the gap or proxy for another person. When a person stands in the gap, he is so concerned about a person, that he will intercede for him or her and stand in his or her place for a point of contact or so all other people can have a visible representation before their eyes for which to pray (Isaiah 53:12, 59:16; Jeremiah 7:16, 27:18, 36:25; Romans 7:25, 8:26–27, 8:34, 11:2; 1 Timothy 2:1).

In intercession, the ultimate criterion remains not the worthiness of the pleader, but God's will and those for whom the person is pleading (Ezekiel 14:14–20).

Intercession originates in a revelation from God. Such prayer is praying God's will into the world. Intercession is making a demand upon the abilities of God. If we pray right, intercession begets wealth, power, and rewards.

Intercession takes upon itself two aspects: warfare and travail (taking on a burden). The warfare aspect is facing Satan on behalf of a person, while the travail aspect is beseeching God for an answer to a situation for a person.

One powerful intercessor that the church has forgotten was Pandita Ramabai, a Pentecostal revivalist, missionary, and pioneer. Speaking of the burden of young intercessors, she said, "The burden of their prayer is intercession, that all the mission and all India may be converted, may experience a great revival and receive the Pentecostal baptism."[13]

Lastly, intercessors repeatedly pester God with prayer until He does something. Whether He punishes them or moves and brings forth a manifestation of His power, they continue to pray. The idea of pestering God through prayer has its origin in Old Testament times. Abraham and the other intercessors of the Old Testament pestered God repeatedly.

Intercessors and Fanaticism

Most Christians do not understand intercession. They do not understand the ministry of reconciliation, which is a form of intercession. And intercession is a closet ministry—away from the public eye.

Intercessors receive no recognition. If the spirit of intercession should come to a person, that person should find someplace to pray. The intercessor will do nothing that brings confusion into the church.

An intercessor is in a ministry of love. We cannot do spiritual warfare over someone if we do not have love in our hearts. It is impossible for a person to be an intercessor without the love of the Lord God. As an intercessor, one can and does stand between an individual or nation and the wrath of God. That is the essence of love.

To be an intercessor requires a lot of self-discipline and a continual crucifying of the flesh. This has been hard for me.

We, as intercessors, become the cutting edge of the Lord's sword. We pull down strongholds of darkness and prepare the way for others. We are birthing the will of God upon the earth. We are posted as watchmen on the walls. Isaiah 62:6–7 reads, "I have set watchmen upon thy walls, O Jerusalem, which shall never hold their peace day nor night: ye that make mention of the LORD, keep not silence, And give him no rest, till he establish, and till he make Jerusalem a praise in the earth."

During the Great Awakenings of the past, the ministers spoke of the "sword of the Lord." This was a manifestation of the power of the Lord. When it was used, hundreds and more would experience a great conviction of sin. The meetingplace would resemble a battlefield full of people slain in the Spirit. Some of the ministers of these revivals spoke of the spirit of revival and the spirit of prayer. The spirit of prayer was a supernatural ability to pray for revival and to pray for God's moving. The spirit of revival was groaning for revival, a groaning for change in the church, and groaning over the sinners. No wonder the Lord wanted someone to stand in the gap (Ezekiel 22:30–31).

Today, we need intercessors like Moses and Daniel. Daniel prayed three times a day and received remarkable revelations of present and future events. His example inspired me to make an appointment with the Lord God three times a day in prayer.

The Prayer of Agreement

Matthew 18:19–20 reads, "Again I say unto you, That if two of you shall agree on earth as touching anything that they shall ask, it shall be done for them of my Father which is in heaven. For where two or three are gathered together in my name, there am I in the midst of them."

We must be in one accord. If one does not agree with our prayers, it can hinder or block those prayers from being answered. We must agree in prayer and leave our feelings at the door.

Prayer of Binding and Loosing

Matthew 16:19 reads, "And I will give unto thee the keys of the kingdom of heaven: and whatsoever thou shalt bind on earth shall be bound in heaven: and whatsoever thou shalt loose on earth shall be loosed in heaven."

Violent Intercession

Intercession can become violent. Psalm 48:6, "Fear took hold upon them there, and pain, as of a woman in travail."

Tertullian viewed the prayers of the saints as violence going up to the Lord God. Tertullian wrote,

> Edam iam nunc ego ipse negotia Christianae factionis, ut qui mala refutaverim, bona ostendam. Corpus sumus de conscientia religionis et disciplinae unitate et spei foedere. Coimus in coetum et congregationem, ut ad deum quasi manu facta precationibus ambiamus orantes. Haec vis deo grata est. Oramus etiam pro imperatoribus, pro ministris eorum et potestatibus, pro statu saeculi, pro rerum quiete, pro mora finis (I will proceed and display at once the duties of the Christian society, that, as I may refute the evil things charged against it, I might also draw attention to its good things. We are a body united together as such by a common conscience of religion, by unity of discipline, and by the bond of a common hope. We assemble in a meeting-place

and congregation, that, approaching God in prayer, as if massing into a united force, we might struggle with Him in our prayers. This violence is pleasing unto God. Further, we pray for emperors, for their ministers, and their magistrates, for the state of the world, for peace on the earth and the delay of the final consummation).[14]

William T. Ellis, a writer for the Heritage Magazine, described his experience with Pandita Ramabai, and other intercessors in Kedgaon, India, on July 24, AD 1907. His description of the intercessors and how they were praying is utterly remarkable. The intercessors were practicing violent intercession. Ellis describes what was before his eyes, and then Pandita Ramabai speaks about testing the spirits.

> For half an hour I had been hearing strange sounds, now of one person shouting in a high voice, then of the mingled utterance of a crowd, and later of song. At last, it settled down into a steady roar. "What is that?" I asked. "It is the girls' prayer meeting," was the answer. "Could I visit it?" I pointedly asked my guide, after hints had proved unavailing. "Why—I—suppose—so, I'll see." In a few minutes I found myself witnessing a scene utterly without parallel in all my wide experience of religious gatherings.

> In a large, bare room with cement floor, were gathered between 30 and 40 girls, ranging in age from 12 to 20. By a table sat a sweet-faced, refined native young woman, watching soberly and without disapproval the scene before her. After a few minutes she too knelt on the floor in silent prayer.

> The other occupants of the room were all praying aloud. Some were crying at the top of their lungs. The tumult was so great that it was with difficulty that any one voice could be distinguished. Some of the girls were bent over with heads touching on the floor. Others were sitting on their feet, with shoulders and bodies twitching and jerking in convulsions. A few were swaying to and fro, from side to side or back and forth. Two or three were kneeling upright, with arms and bodies moving.

One young woman, the loudest, moved on her knees, all unconsciously, two or three yards during the time I watched. She had a motion of her body that must have been exhausting. She also swung her arms violently. And often the gestures of the praying figures showed one or both hands outstretched, in dramatic supplication. Several girls would clap hands at the same time, though each seemed unconscious of the others. The contortions of the faces bespoke extreme agony, and perspiration streamed over them. One girl fell over sideways, asleep, or fainting from sheer exhaustion.

All had their eyes tightly closed, oblivious to surroundings. Such intense, such concentrated devotion I had never witnessed before. It was a full of 15 minutes before one of the girls, who had quieted somewhat, saw me. And thereafter she sat silent praying or reading her Bible in comparative tranquility ...

"We do not make a special point of the gift of tongues," Ramabai insisted gently; "our emphasis is always put-upon love and life. And undoubtedly the lives of the girls have been changed. About 700 of them have come into this blessing. We do not exhibit the girls that have been gifted with other tongues, nor do we in any wise call special attention to them."

"We try to weed out the false from the true; for there are other spirits than the Holy Spirit and when a girl begins to try to speak in another tongue, apparently imitating her sisters without mentioning the name or blood of Jesus, I go up to her and speak to her or touch her on the shoulder, and she stops at once. On the other hand, if a girl is praying in the Spirit I cannot stop her, no matter how sharply I speak to her or shake her. My own hearing is peculiar," continued Ramabia, "in that I can understand most clearly when there is a loud noise (a well-known characteristic of the partially deaf) and I move among the girls, listening to them in awed wonder. I have heard girls who know no English at all utter beautiful prayers in your tongue. I have heard others pray in Greek and Hebrew and Sanskrit, and others again in languages that none of us understood. One of my girls was praying in this very room a few nights ago and although in her studies she has not gone beyond the second book she prayed so clearly and beautifully in English that the other teachers marveled who could be praying, since they did not distinguish the voice."[15]

Levels of Spiritual Warfare

Spiritual warfare is a battle. The Bible says, "For in death there is no remembrance of thee: in the grave who shall give thee thanks? I am weary with my groaning; all the night make I my bed to swim; I water my couch with my tears. Mine eye is consumed because of grief; it waxeth old because of all mine enemies" (Psalm 6:5–7).

The Book of Ephesians is all about spiritual warfare. And we must remember that Satan does not have the last moment or the final say. Our God has the final say: "Weeping may endure for a night, but joy cometh in the morning" (Psalm 30:5).

Baby Christians should go easy on spiritual warfare. It is very dangerous for baby Christians or unstable Christians to cast out demons. They need to grow and mature in faith and their identity in Christ. If not, they may be able to have success for a time, but a time will come when they will face a principality, and they will be destroyed.

Spiritual warfare has levels, and baby Christians cannot go to the highest level of spiritual warfare first.

John Cassian was an apologist and theologian during the fourth century. He wrote a considerable portion of work on spiritual warfare based upon the lives of the monks. He showed that every aspect of their life had been patterned to spiritually combat Satan and his forces.

With words, John Cassian painted the life of the saint as a spiritual contest with victors and losers. He said that in this spiritual contest, for one to obtain the greatest rewards, he or she must enter the highest contest where there is no quarter given. In this type of contest, Satan pushes forth extremely hard against the saint, but the saint attacks and counterattacks extremely hard against the forces of evil.

Cassian discussed four levels of spiritual warfare between the saints and the forces of evil.

1. The level of babies in Christ. Baby Christians receive the least attacks by Satan and the least rewards.

2. The level of immature youth. More attacks, and more rewards; power to combat; few crowns and prizes seen by Satan upon these Christians in the spiritual world.

3. The level of maturity. For the saints to reach this level, they must have carefully been tested and have passed all tests; more attacks, and more rewards; power to combat; more crowns and prizes seen by Satan upon these Christians in the spiritual world.

4. The level of victors (overcomers). These are saints who have already become victors many times against Satan and are decked out with many crowns and prizes already seen by Satan in the spiritual world. Those saints who reach the level of victors can do the most damage against Satan, the power of Satan, and all the forces of evil.[16]

Exorcisms

According to the ancient church, removing exorcism from the public removes its primary purpose. According to the ancient church, the main use of exorcism is to show the power of God over the power of Satan.

Bill Bean, a well-known deliverance minister, taught an associate about exorcism. The associate took on a case, which he should have left alone. He faced an Egyptian Baal, a principality, that was possessing a young man. The evil spirit faced the associate with little fear. The spirit threw him back to a couch, and the man ran away from the house. He called Bill Bean, and Bean came to the house and did the exorcism. This time—with the mature, seasoned minister— the Egyptian Baal was cast out of the young man.

We should remember that the purpose of the coming of Jesus Christ was so that "he might destroy the works of the devil" (1 John 3:8).

Historian Ramsay MacMullen wrote in his book on the church's history,

> The manhandling of demons through exorcisms—humiliating them, making them howl, beg for mercy, tell their secrets, and depart in a hurry—served a purpose quite essential to the Christian definition of monotheism: it made physically (or dramatically) visible the superiority of the Christian's patron power over all others. One and only one was God.[17]

Formalism, Fanaticism, and Necromancy

An anonymous minister once said, "If you have the Bible only, you have formalism, but if you have the Holy Spirit only, you have fanaticism." If a church has formalism, it is dead and has no life. If a church has fanaticism, there is no balance, stability, nor consistency with the Lord. In fact, fanaticism will lead to movements and manifestations that are not of God. Commonly, it will lead to necromancy and blending occultism with Christianity.

There was disagreement among both reformers and revivalists. They sought not to be in formalism, fanaticism, or necromancy. They warred to stay balanced in the Word of God and in experiences. They did not want to be pulled into extremes.

Princeton theologian and scholar Dr. Charles Hodge rightly warned,

> No amount of learning, no superiority of talent, nor even the pretension to inspiration, can justify a departure from the . . . truths taught by men to whose inspiration God has borne witness. All teachers must be brought to this standard; and even if an angel from heaven should teach anything contrary to the Scriptures, he should be regarded as anathema, Gal. 1:8. It is a matter of constant gratitude that we have such a standard whereby to try the spirits whether they be of God.[18]

A balanced Christian will want the ministry of the Bible and the ministry of the Holy Spirit to have a place in their lives and church services. The movements and manifestations of the Holy Spirit never supersede the Word of God. Instead, they confirm the Word of God.

Many of the revivalists throughout history have followed this view about the ministry of the Bible and the ministry of the Holy Spirit. Almost all ancient Christians also accepted this concept.

Peter Cartwright, a Methodist revivalist in the Second Great Awakening, held the Word of God as the only infallible guide in trying the spirits. He judged all movements and experiences by the Word of God.

Cartwright faced many types of fanatics in the Second Great Awakening. Fanaticism unrestrained will lead to deception and finally to death. One fanatic believed that he became immortal in this life. Regardless of arguments to the contrary by his friends, he still believed that he had become immortal. He refused to eat and drink. Within sixteen days, he died. His death helped restrain much fanaticism.[19]

Peter Cartwright wrote about one class of fanatics that he faced and his view about the Word of God.

> First, there are many that are truly awakened and soundly converted to God, and are pious, but instead of taking the word of God for their only infallible guide, and trying the spirits, and their impressions, or feelings, by that as a standard, they take all their impressions and sudden impulses of mind as inspirations from God, and act accordingly. If you oppose them, they say and believe you are fighting against God. If you try to reason them out of their visionary flights, and settle them down on the sure foundation, the word of God, they construe it all into the want of religion and cry out persecution.[20]

In another part of his autobiography, Peter Cartwright mentions a woman who received a wrong Jesus Christ and a wrong doctrine over the Word of God. He stood against this woman with the Word of God and prayer. He was proven right in his views on Jesus Christ and his opinions on the Word of God. He wrote,

> There was a very confirmed Arian lady in the congregation who denied the supreme divinity of Jesus Christ. Late on Monday, she professed to get very happy, and shouted out aloud; but said, while shouting, among other things, she knew I was wrong in my views of Jesus Christ, but she

desired someone to go and bring me to her, for she wanted to show me, that though I was in error, she could love her enemies and do good for evil. At first, I refused to go; but she sent again. I then thought of the unjust judge, and less by her continual coming she might weary me, I went. She told me she knew I was wrong, and that she was right, and that God had blessed her and made her happy. Said I, "Sister, while I was preaching, did you not get mad?"

She answered, "Yes, very mad; I could have cut your throat. But I am not mad now, and love you, and God has blessed me." Said I, "I fear you are not happy; you have only got in a little better humor and think this is happiness. But we will test the matter. Let us kneel down here and pray to God to make it manifest who is wrong." "But," said she, "I don't want to pray; I want to talk." "Well," said I, "I have no desire to talk; I always go to God in prayer; and I now believe God, in answer to prayer, will recover you out of the snare of the devil, for you certainly are not happy at all."

So, I called upon all around—and they were many—to kneel down and help me to pray God to dislodge the lingering Arian devil that still claimed a residence in this woman's heart. We knelt, and by the score united in wrestling, mighty prayer; and while we prayed it seemed that the bending heavens came near; and if the power of God was ever felt among mortals, it was felt then and there. The woman lost her assumed good feelings, and sunk down into sullen, dumb silence, and so she remained during the meeting; and for weeks afterward many of her friends feared she would totally lose her balance of mind.

She became incapable of her business till one night she had a dream or vision, in which she afterward declared she saw her Savior, apparently in all his supreme glory, and he told her she was wrong, but he frankly forgave her; and when she came to herself, or awoke, she was unspeakably happy, and never afterward, for one moment, doubted the supreme divinity of Jesus Christ. She joined the Methodists and lived and died a shining and shouting Christian.[21]

338

The counsel of John Wesley about manifestations is quite wise, even today,

> Do not hastily ascribe things to God. Do not easily suppose dreams, voices, impressions, visions, or revelations to be from God. They may be from him. They may be from nature. They may be from the devil. Therefore, "believe not every spirit, but try the spirits whether they be of God." Try all things by the written word and let all bow down before it.[22]

Smith Wigglesworth, a Pentecostal revivalist, seeing all the movements and manifestations of the Holy Spirit most of his life, was a man of the Word. He had a "consuming love for the Word of God," and "he had an overwhelming confidence in the God of the Word,"[23] which settled any matter for Wigglesworth.

Having learned the secret of God's power, which is His Word, Wigglesworth said,

> I understand God by His Word. I cannot understand God by impressions or feelings. I cannot get to know God by sentiment. I can only know Him by His Word. . . It is a dangerous practice to be governed by feelings. We are saved not by feelings, but by the Word of God. Salvation does not fluctuate as do feelings.[24]

Wigglesworth, with all his movements and experiences of the Holy Spirit, condemned any experience that excluded the Word of God.[25]

Lastly, Wigglesworth held the Word of God supreme and said, "Nothing substitutes for the Word of God."[26]

It is common to hear today about experiences that do not agree with the Word of God. And there has become a fascination with seeing the dead, or necromancy (Leviticus 20:6; Deuteronomy 18:11; 1 Samuel 28:7, 25; 2 Kings 21:6, 23:24; 1 Chronicles 10:13; 2 Chronicles 33:6; Isaiah 8:19, 19:3, 29:4).

There is a popular minister who claims to have gone to heaven and communicated with the dead apostles. This is an abomination before God.

Another strange manifestation on the rise is the appearance of Jesus Christ as a woman. Run! If that Jesus Christ prophesies ten prophecies to a person and all are fulfilled, that person must still run away from that experience. Jesus Christ must be the same Jesus Christ who ascended. If not, rebuke that false Christ. Jesus Christ will not appear as a woman.

I believe in the movements and manifestations of the Holy Spirit, but they will agree with the Word of God. And they will not be part of the abominations mentioned in Scripture.

Many forget that God is bound to His Word. He will never do anything contrary to His Word.

False Visitations of the Dead

One thing the modern church needs is a proper theology of the dead. Today, some Christians claim that they are having visitations of the dead saints. Apostle Paul, David, Abraham, Ezra, and a host of other dead saints are proclaimed to be seen and heard. It is said that these dead saints are speaking to people and giving them insight into biblical interpretation, their faith, and their lives. Those who are experiencing these visitations claim that all these visitations are within the bounds of Christian experience. But this experience is spiritualism and necromancy. As already stated, communication with the dead is forbidden. It is not the dead speaking, but it is demonic forces (Deuteronomy 18:11; Isaiah 8:19; 1 Samuel 28; 1 Chronicles 10:13).

We must never allow a vision or other experience to interpret Scripture. Such experiences are very dangerous, and they do not follow the rules of interpretation for Scripture. The more we enter the spiritual world, the closer we must be to the Word of God. We must judge an experience by the Word of God, not the Word of God by the experience.

Consequently, I only accept the experiences ordained by the Holy Spirit and authorized in the Bible, especially in the New Testament.

Moving our authority from Scripture to spiritual experience changes the end zone from that which is certain to that which may not be certain. Such changes allow us not only to be deceived but also to become fanatical. And if that is not enough, we will become devotees to mysticism and other forms of paganism.

Scripture has boundaries. And such boundaries give Christians security from false and demonic experiences. Second Peter 1:3 reads, "According as his divine power hath given unto us all things that pertain unto life and godliness, through the knowledge of him that hath called us to glory and virtue." Moving away from the authority of Scripture means the destruction of Christians.

Counterfeit Christians and True Believers

Paul warns that Satan will certainly disguise himself as an angel of light (2 Corinthians 11:14) and that demonic manifestations may behave like the manifestations of the Holy Spirit in order to deceive and destroy people.

Paul states that people may depart from sound doctrine and adhere to the doctrines of demons (1 Timothy 4:1). He warns us to never fall into the snare of the devil nor end up ruined by the devil's wiles (Ephesians 6:11; 1 Timothy 3:7; 2 Timothy 2:26).

It is interesting to note that Paul never worried about genuine Christians being influenced by counterfeit gifts. This fact is seen in the pagan city of Corinth (1 Corinthians 10:20, 14:2). To Paul, it was impossible for genuine Christians, who have the Holy Spirit working through them and abiding in their life, to receive anything counterfeit.

He utilizes 1 Corinthians 12:3 as reassurance that demonic and pagan worship, medieval (Oriental) mysticism, as well as other contrary (alien) or occultic practices, cannot influence, nor corrupt the genuine spiritual gifts of the Spirit. The verse reads, "No man speaking by the Spirit of God calleth Jesus accursed: and that no man can say that Jesus is the Lord, but by the Holy Ghost." This passage sets forth a clear understanding that the genuine gifts of the Holy Spirit are not used by mediums or other occultists. Their gifts come from Satan and his evil spirits.

It is quite clear that Satan can counterfeit the gifts of the Holy Spirit for unbelievers (Matthew 7:22–24; John 10:10; Ephesians 5:11). On the contrary, it is impossible for Satan to counterfeit the gifts of the Holy Spirit for genuine believers who do not fall into a state of lukewarmness and continue to manifest positive fruits in their lives from the Holy Spirit (Matthew 7:16–20; 1 Corinthians 12:3; 1 John 4:4).

Appropriately, genuine Christians do not manifest counterfeit gifts, regardless of what people may think. Those who do manifest counterfeit gifts are deceived, have become lukewarm or backslidden, and may even be demon possessed unbelievers. When Christians accept counterfeit gifts and their demonic origin and do not heed the strong warnings from the Bible, they become deceived, lukewarm, or backslidden, and become the property of the devil again. If Christians manifest such counterfeit gifts, it is impossible for them to remain saved and still be in a state of holiness, grace, and faith. A principle should be noted here: "A good tree cannot bring forth evil fruit, neither can a corrupt tree bring forth good fruit" (Matthew 7:18). A person using counterfeit gifts, or producing evil fruit, points to the fact that the person has become an evil tree.

The Danger of Mediumistic Abilities and Powers

The Bible consistently links occultism and sorcery with mediumistic abilities and powers (Leviticus 20:6, 27; Deuteronomy 18:1–12). In Acts 16, Paul calls the mediumistic power of the damsel demonic. These abilities emerge in a person through generational inheritance, transference by the laying on of hands in occultic prayer, or through occultic experimentation. There are some ten to twenty types of mediumistic (occultic) gifts, which are all demonic in origin.

The effects of occultic practices are various and never good. Here is a short list of the negative effects upon the lives of people:

1. The faith of a Christian is greatly affected.

2. The person who is under occultic influence or infestation is unable to practice his or her faith.

3. The person is unable to keep a stable and living relationship with Christ.

4. The person often falls victim to damning sects and heresies.

5. The person is plagued with doubts.

342

6. The rational mind of a person is wounded, and rational thought is almost entirely gone in that person's life.

7. In such a state, the person is unable to concentrate on the Word of God or to pray with a rational mind.

8. In such a state, the person regularly becomes immune to the working and movements of the Holy Spirit and does not know the difference between genuine manifestations of the Holy Spirit and those that are counterfeit.

9. The character of the person is greatly changed.

10. Mental and emotional illnesses will regularly be present.

11. Involvement in magical practices and sorcery will affect the whole family, even to the third and fourth generations.

Beware of Voices

We should be cautious of several types of Christians. For example, beware of Christians who are quitting their fifth or sixth church because a voice or a feeling directed them somewhere else. Beware of Christians who keep hearing a voice telling them not to work. Beware of those who every time they change their husband, wife, underwear, or their business plan it is because they say God's voice told them so. Beware of a voice if,

1. It is always telling you to say "no" (especially to reading and studying the Bible).

2. The voice keeps telling you to say "yes" to every request for help.

3. The voice tells you to go where the money is.

4. The voice tells you what other people should do and never what you should do.

5. The voice tells you something different from the last instruction.

6. The voice assures you that you are always right.

7. The voice tells you that you are an exception to the rule.

8. The voice leads you away from the Bible, Jesus Christ as the only means of salvation, the power of the cross, and the power of the blood.

Determining a True Manifestation

Again and again, we must face the fact that as long as God endures, His Spirit will work and continue to work. We cannot say that all manifestations are coming from Satan. We cannot say that all manifestations are coming from God, either. Every time all manifestations are said to be of Satan, we understand that we are dealing with ignorance or jealousy.

Many years ago, Augustine, dealing with the miraculous in his midst and its variety, wrote, siue alia istis, alia illis modis, qui nullo modo conprehendi a mortalibus possunt: ei tamen adtestantur haec fidei, in qua carnis in aeternum resurrectio praedicatur (Whether finally by these or by those means so that they are unable in any means to be understood by mortals; nevertheless—these miracles bear witness to this faith, which does preach the resurrection of the flesh to eternal life).[27]

Jonathan Edwards, in *Marks of a Work of the True Spirit*, discussed the manifestations of the Spirit during the Great Awakening. Edwards writes as follows:

> He has brought to pass new things, strange works; and has wrought in such a manner as to surmise both men and angels. And as God has done thus in times past, so we have no reason to think but that he will do so still. The prophecies of Scripture give us reason to think that God has things to accomplish, which have never yet been seen. No deviation from what has hitherto been usual, let it be never so great, is an argument that a work is not from the Spirit of God if it be no deviation from his prescribed rule. The Holy Spirit is sovereign in his operation; and we know that he uses a great variety; and we cannot tell how great a variety he may use, within the compass of the rules he himself has fixed. We ought not to limit God where he has not limited himself.[28]

In the days of Azusa Street Revival, there was a prophecy of warning toward the coming generations of believers: "In the last days three things will happen in the great Pentecostal Movement: 1) There will be an overemphasis on power, rather than on righteousness. 2) There will be an overemphasis on praise, to a God they no longer pray to. 3) There will be an overemphasis on the Gifts of the Spirit – rather than on the Lordship of Christ."[29]

Understanding Signs and Wonders

We must be careful to understand that. If not, we will be fooled.

Signs and wonders do not determine truth, either. Truth is already determined and established, and it is the Word of God. In John 17:17, Jesus is praying to the Father, and He says, "Your word is truth." In Psalm 119:89, the psalmist said, "Forever, O LORD, thy word is settled in heaven."

In 2 Thessalonians 2:9, Paul says there are such things as lying signs and wonders here. There are genuine signs, and there are lying signs. True signs attest to the truth. Lying signs attest to lies. Satan is fully capable of supernatural signs and wonders. Unfortunately, many have the attitude that if something is supernatural, it must be from God.

There is no scriptural basis for that assumption. Satan can perfectly produce powerful signs and wonders to attest his lies, and such people are deceived because they did not receive the love of the truth. On such people, God will send strong delusion.

In 2 Thessalonians 2:11, there is one of the most frightening statements in the Bible. If God sends people strong delusions, they will be deluded. This statement is one of the most severe judgments of God recorded in Scripture. They will be condemned because they did not believe the truth but took pleasure in unrighteousness.

Therefore, signs and wonders do not guarantee that something is the truth. There is only one sure way to know the truth. It is in the Word of God. Jesus said in John 8:32, "You shall know the truth, and the truth shall make you free." There is no other way to be sure that we can escape deception these days except that we know and apply the truth of God's Word, the Scripture.

Mixture of Manifestations

Today, there is a mixture of manifestations, and this causes confusion. The confusion does not come from God but from Satan and men and women. Further, there is a mixture of spirits, a blending of the smoke and few have any discernment. Those who genuinely have discernment will be crucified and seen as evil by those who have no discernment at all.

Jonathan Edwards made it clear that satanic and fleshly manifestations will try to appear among the genuine manifestations. Satan and flesh will always try to discredit the true manifestations. Satanic and fleshly manifestations generally began to appear at the middle or last stage of any true revival and Great Awakening.[30]

Also, he writes as follows:

> A work is not to be judged of by any effects on the bodies of men; such as tears, trembling, groans, loud outcries, agonies of body, or the failing of bodily strength. The influence persons are under, is not to be judged of one way or other, by such effects on the body; and the reason is, because the Scripture nowhere gives us any such rule. We cannot conclude that persons are under the influence of the true Spirit because we see such effects upon their bodies, because this is not given as a mark of the true Spirit; nor on the other hand, have we any reason to conclude, from any such outward appearances, that persons are not under the influence of the Spirit of God, because there is no rule of Scripture given us to judge of spirits by, that does either expressly or indirectly exclude such effects on the body, nor does reason exclude them.[31]

The total acceptance of manifestations is very dangerous, to say the least. Still, the total rejection of physical manifestations can destroy the refreshing of the Holy Spirit in our lives.

When we study the history of the church, particularly the evangelical and holiness movements of the eighteenth to early twentieth centuries, we see that many of these manifestations have occurred in these movements. Still, such phenomena were neither accepted out of hand nor dismissed summarily.

We need a bridge and a buffer that will help us understand and identify the manifestations themselves, whether they are from God, and how to stop them if they are not of God.

We do not want people to throw out any genuine manifestation of the Holy Spirit, which may include angelic appearances permitted by the Holy Spirit. Many hold that we must reject all manifestations due to this. I beg to differ. It is more dangerous to say that an incident or manifestation of power is from Satan, only to find out later that it was indeed from God, than to say nothing at all. If you are uncertain or ignorant about a supernatural occurrence, it is better not to judge and say something foolish. God judged the people who denied that the Great Awakening was of God and blessed Jonathan Edwards for believing that the movement was of God.

Someone once wrote something like this, "Men plan, and God laughs." It must be understood that His Spirit has His own rules and patterns. The Spirit will move as He sees fit, not as men so believe or think. God's people must stop judging with their physical eyes and finite minds the supernatural manifestations that have either been seen or merely heard and begin judging these occurrences by the Spirit in accordance with the Holy Word of God (Galatians 1:8; 1 John 5:5–10).

None of us must ever place God in a box. Christians must follow the leadership of Edwards when Edwards says that no saint should limit the Holy Spirit in His moving. If a person limits God the Holy Spirit so much, then he is grieving the Holy Spirit. If he is grieving the Holy Spirit, it will come to pass that the Holy Spirit may leave him. He will become lukewarm, having the form of godliness but denying the power thereof and never tasting the Holy Spirit's refreshing upon his soul and life again. All must remember that if there are counterfeit manifestations of the Spirit, there must also be genuine manifestations.

How to Identify the Source of Manifestations

1.   The intention of the manifestation.

2.   The fruit of the manifestation.

3. What does the manifestation point to?

4. What does the manifestation do for the person?

5. Why did it come?

6. When did it come?

7. What are the aftereffects of the manifestation?

8. Does it draw us away from Christ, or does it draw us toward Christ?

9. Does the manifestation manifest with no godly purpose or intention?

10. Are people drawn to seek after more signs and wonders, or are they drawn to seek after Jesus Christ more?

11. Does the manifestation lift up another instead of Jesus?

12. Does the manifestation point back to itself?

13. Does the manifestation point to an angel rather than Jesus?

Any manifestation that takes us away from Jesus Christ and the Word of God cannot be from God. Results must include a hunger for the closest to the Lord Jesus Christ and a hunger for the Word of God. When people become entangled in a manifestation or experience that causes them not to be able to read, study, or hunger after the Word of God, it cannot be of God.

1 John 5:5–10 demands the Holy Spirit, and the Word must agree. The Holy Spirit testifies of Jesus, and He will ever confirm the Written Word of God and desire people to study it, where the light is found.

The Word of God is the light for the saint. Remove that light, and the saint will have no light to find his way through the darkness (Psalm 119:105). The saints of God must have a love for the Word of God (Psalm 119:47; Jeremiah 15:16). The Word of God is the final authority, test, or measuring stick in such manners as life, godliness, and practice (Luke 11:29; Acts 17:2–3, 17:17; 2 Timothy 3:16, 4:2; 2 Peter 2:7–8, 3:15–16; 1 John 2:7–8). The Word gives food (1 Peter

2:1–2). The Word of God must be written in the hearts of the saints (Deuteronomy 6:6; Psalm 119:11).

Testing the Spirits

Every believer has the indwelling presence of the Holy Spirit. In 1 John 2:27, John calls the presence of the Spirit "the anointing which ye have received of him." God has given us His indwelling Spirit, but John now points out that other "spirits" are loose in the world. If we have the Spirit, we should "test the spirits."

Christians often test teaching by how it sounds, the words used, the inflection of the voice, and the stories told, and whether it moves them or makes them feel good. None of these are appropriate tests.

John writes, "Beloved, believe not every spirit, but try the spirits whether they are of God: because many false prophets are gone out into the world" (1 John 4:1–4). The term "try" means "to approve" or "to examine." The term was used for gold being put into the fire to test its purity.

Paul wrote in 1 Thessalonians 5:20–21, "Do not despise prophecies. Test all things; hold fast what is good." Jesus warned in Matthew 7:15–17, "Beware of false prophets, which come to you in sheep's clothing, but inwardly they are ravening wolves. Ye shall know them by their fruits. Do men gather grapes of thorns, or figs of thistles? Even so, every good tree bringeth forth good fruit; but a corrupt tree bringeth forth evil fruit." Peter also offered this warning in 2 Peter 2:1, "But there were also false prophets among the people, even as there will be false teachers among you, who will secretly bring in destructive heresies, even denying the Lord who bought them, and bring on themselves swift destruction."

Today, there is still a great need for biblical discernment and discrimination. Many believers remain biblically illiterate and spiritually gullible. They naively accept any teaching as truth.

In Ephesians 4:14, Paul says that a sure sign of spiritual immaturity is "tossed to and fro, and carried about with every wind of doctrine, by the trickery of men, in the cunning craftiness of deceitful plotting."

Failing to Test the Spirits

If a person follows the wrong spirit, that person will pay a price. The famous circus entrepreneur, P.T. Barnum, is thought to have said, "There's a sucker born every minute." Satan has many slick sideshows that sidetrack God's children and rob them of their spiritual riches.

There are "many" false teachers (antichrists) in the world today. The spiritual candy store is full. Satan has all flavors of teachers and preachers ready to fill your spiritual appetite with a sugarcoated experience that will leave you with a bellyache.

The reformers insisted that even the humblest believers have "the right of private judgment."

The Criteria for Testing the Spirits

The first test is the acknowledgment of the historical incarnation of Jesus, that "Jesus Christ has come in the flesh." Believers are to test for truth based on a teacher's attitude concerning the person and the work of Jesus.

Christ must be seen to have come in the flesh and be seen as remaining in the flesh. If any man poses as an apostle or Christian teacher and does not teach the true doctrine of Christ—the Deity, the incarnation, the death, burial, and bodily resurrection of Jesus Christ—do not receive him or give him entertainment in your home. Do not even bid him Godspeed. If a person does, that person is a partaker of the teacher's evil deeds and will be punished with him for the same sins (2 John 1:10–11).

The first test is simple: any spirit (or person) who denies the facts revealed in the New Testament regarding the life of Christ is under satanic influence and is the Antichrist. This would include those who reject the details of His birth to the Virgin Mary, His miraculous ministry, His innocence, His death, burial, bodily resurrection, and ascension to the right hand of God.

The test of orthodoxy is the incarnation of Christ. Orthodoxy means adhering to the established faith-based on God's Word.

If it's wrong when compared to God's Word, it does not matter if it is right anywhere else.

Other Tests

1. There must be a harmony with the Word of God (1 John 5:5–10).

2. Judge the fruits (Matthew 7:16–20).

3. Test the lives of those pretending to be sent by God.

4. Are there inconsistencies in their lives?

5. Are their lives in agreement with the Word of God?

6. Are they receiving glory from God for what they do?

7. Are they relying on God only for direction?

8. Are they basing their teachings only on writings from men?

9. The Spirit and Word will always agree (2 Peter 3:3–7; 1 John 5:5–10).

10. The Spirit of God always speaks according to God's Word, the Bible. He acknowledges its authority.

11. Anyone putting anything above the Bible or anyone degrading the Bible is not from God!

Breaking the Confusion over Manifestations

There must be a focus on the strong preaching of God's Word. True manifestations hardly appear apart from the preaching of God's Word.

True Manifestations will be connected to a strong call for repentance. Any refreshing that bypasses repentance is not scriptural and, therefore, is suspect. That was primary demand of the apostles on the people to whom they ministered. Some people call what we are seeing today "a refreshing." Still, in Acts 3:19, Peter says that repentance must precede refreshing.

Clues in Discernment

1. If the spirit tells a person it is the spirit of a dead relative or friend, it is not from God.

2. Does this spirit socialize and spend undue time with a person—it is not a Spirit of God.

3. Does this spirit use physical things to impress a person; it is not a Spirit of God. God's angels deliver messages to God's people and then vanish. They do not "hang out" with humans.

4. Does the spirit flatter a person and build up that person's pride? This is not coming from God.

5. Does the spirit try to force a person to do something against his will? This is not from God.

6. Did the spiritual encounter bear spiritual and godly fruit?

Look at the Sequence of the Great Awakenings

1. Powerful Prayer.

2. Powerful singing of songs or hymns (sometimes, this part was omitted).

3. A kind of preaching where the power of God was released as the minister spoke throughout the congregation. Jesus was focused on; He was their center. It is all about Jesus from the beginning to the end. A few times, preaching in a service was omitted or shortened, but this was not the rule.

4. People especially experienced the power of God through preaching.

5. The power brought on hard conviction, repentance, healings, miracles, and other godly manifestations.

6. Salvation was not easy; the people experienced salvation in a groaning way so that they would keep it, and most did keep it.

7. No preaching like this, very little moving of God.

8. When they focused on signs and wonders, the revivals fell into trouble.

Signs and wonders were the end results of the movement of the Holy Spirit in said revivals, not the beginning. One key thing in the Great Awakenings of the past was the fact that the revivals were birthed by powerful preaching endowed with the power of the Holy Spirit going forth first as a convicting force to shine a light on the sins of the sinners and the state or condition of the saints.

The Holy Spirit will never degrade a church, a ministry, or a saint with such manifestations.

Degrading the Holy Spirit

The Holy Spirit is precious. He is awesome, and He is God. Equating the movement and the manifestations of the Holy Spirit to animal behavior, smoking marijuana, taking heroin, and sexual behavior is blasphemy, or it is downright hysteria and fanaticism. I cannot see how equating the Holy Spirit with the things mentioned can also not be blasphemy. The questions that must be asked are, "Are we tempting God?" and "Are we not only blaspheming, but also are we committing the Blasphemy of the Holy Spirit?"

In many revivals, such manifestations have appeared. Their purpose has always been to destroy genuine revival and to take our focus off Jesus. Real revival is birthed into by the fear of God and prayer, reaps genuine repentance that is confirmed by signs and wonders, tempered by persecution, and witnessed by many genuine conversions. We are choosing counterfeit manifestations, which are degrading and lowering the Holy Spirit to a level that will bring judgment upon the church.

True Manifestations Will Come

True Manifestations will come with or without laying on hands. Suppose good things or benefits alone are the very criteria by which something is judged to be of God. In that case, we may have well been brought into deception. There is something more important than benefits, something more important than being released from depression; it is the holiness of God, it is His name, it is His honor, it is He Himself.

Receiving a benefit of a dubious kind is too high a price to pay if it is going to throw any shadow upon His great name. We have lost everything for the sake of benefit when the desire for benefit is suspect.

Remarkably, though we are explicitly warned about end-time lying signs and wonders, we somehow imagine that it is the future and mindlessly trust ourselves in our greed for experiences, empowerments, or releases to dubious personalities who have caught the public fancy in incredible overnight popularity (Matthew 24:24; 2 Thessalonians 2:9). I profoundly respect God's use of the weak and the foolish thing. Still, for that reason, I cannot endorse what is garish, cheap, and coarse as being that weak and foolish thing of which Paul speaks.

"Holiness unto the Lord" is still the standard of God's House, even when it is unspectacular and unassuming in the eyes of the world and our own.

Waiting is a priestly function, and we must wait to see if our spirits are hospitable to what is being mediated from church platforms. Is it compatible with our already existing knowledge of God? They can stand on their heads, run all over the platform, and do every other kind of madness if it is incompatible. We are not to mindlessly give ourselves to it at all. Our integrity in God needs to be guarded, and we should not allow ourselves to be influenced, taken up, and affected by the current trends, or else we will never have anything significant to give.

The teaching of the Scripture is to seek out, through the word and prayer, the root of the problems that come in life. One usually finds that unacknowledged disobediences are at their root, and the correction is accomplished primarily through that part of the body to whom one is accountable and authentically joined.

But speaking the truth in love, we are to grow up in all aspects into Him, who is the head, even Christ, from whom the whole body, being fitted and held together by that which every joint supplies, according to the proper working of each part, causes the growth of the body for the building up of itself in love (Ephesians 4:15–16).

The Holy Spirit is Holy

The Holy Spirit is Holy. This is His primary title: the Holy Spirit. He is the Spirit of Holiness (Romans 1:4). He has many other titles: for instance, the Spirit of Grace, the Spirit of Truth, the Spirit of Power, and so on, but they are all subsidiary. His name and His primary title is the Holy Spirit.

The Scripture also speaks of the beauty of holiness. There is beauty in holiness when it proceeds from the Holy Spirit. It is not necessarily external. It may be internal beauty. For instance, in 1 Peter 3:4, Peter speaks about the hidden person of the heart and the adornment of a meek and quiet spirit, which, in the sight of God, is of great price. This is not external beauty. It is internal beauty that comes from the Holy Spirit.

In the Christian life, holiness is not optional. Many Christians seem to think about holiness as if it is like something added to a car, such as fancy leather upholstery, instead of the normal kind of plastic. But that is not true.

Holiness is an essential part of salvation. In Hebrews 12:14, the writer says, "Pursue peace with all people, and holiness, without which no man will see the Lord." Anything unholy or ugly cannot proceed from the Holy Spirit.

Derek Prince gave a list of twelve words that cannot ever belong to the Holy Spirit.

1. Self-exalting

2. Self-assertive

3. Flippant

4. Rude

5. Sham

6. Vulgar

7. Indecent

8. Insensitive

9. Stupid

10. Silly

11. Degraded

12. Degrading[32]

True Manifestations Glorify Jesus

The Holy Spirit glorifies Christ (John 15:26). The Spirit glorifies Christ by revealing His Majesty and glory in Scripture and producing Christ-centered lives in believers.

A life focused on knowing, loving, obeying, and serving Christ brings honor to Him by placing His characteristics on display to the watching world (Matthew 5:16).

In the church, as in the ministry, the Holy Spirit bears this testimony in numerous persons and in various ways in the same people. He testifies to men's need for Christ by convincing them of sin. He reveals Christ as a Savior and enables the penitent to receive and rest on Him for salvation. The spirit of adoption is a testimony of Christ. When we cry, "Abba, Father," it is by the Spirit of God's Son. The spirit of adoption is also the Spirit of Holiness, and growth in holiness is inseparably connected with the knowledge of Christ.

According to John 15:26, the Holy Spirit bears witness to Christ also by revealing His glory. The Holy Spirit testifies of Christ, not Himself. We are forced to face facts. Any time a work, a minister, a ministry, a movement, or a church exalts the Holy Spirit or His gifts above Jesus Christ, we are in trouble.

This type of thinking will result in fanaticism, heresy, error, or blasphemy. Any revival that focuses on the Holy Spirit and His gifts and forgets Christ will fail. The manifestations of the Holy Spirit confirm Christ and the Word.

The failure of Christians from time to time has been mainly due to focusing more on the gifts of the Holy Spirit and the Holy Spirit Himself rather than staying focused on Christ. The Holy Spirit points back to Christ. We can welcome the Holy Spirit into our services, which we should, but the reason is so that Christ will be exalted. The

Holy Spirit moves amid His people; He works according to His manners and ways but has banks and boundaries.

One of the leading banks and boundaries He has set upon Himself is that He will only point to Christ. Where the Holy Spirit is in control, Jesus is proclaimed the Head, not forgotten. Jesus is the Head, the Holy Spirit, His executive. Therefore, the Holy Spirit glorifies Christ, not His movements or manifestations (Matthew 5:16).

There seems to be a great danger of losing sight of the fact that Jesus was "all in all." The work of Calvary, the atonement, must be the center for our consideration.

The Holy Ghost will never draw our attention from Christ to Himself but reveal Christ in a fuller way. We are in danger of slighting Jesus—getting Him "lost in the temple" by the Holy Ghost's exaltation and the gifts of the Spirit. Jesus must be the center of everything, "And he is the head of the body, the church: who is the beginning, the firstborn from the dead; that in all things he might have the preeminence" (Colossians 1:18–19).

We make Christ a stranger by giving the Holy Spirit preeminence over Him. Christ is made a stranger when people praise Him but will not pray to Him.

In 1 Corinthians 12:3, Paul said, "I make known to you, that no one speaking by the Spirit of God, says, 'Jesus is accursed.'" Some Corinthians had called Jesus accursed while speaking prophetically or in a false tongue that they thought was prompted by the Holy Spirit. But the spirit would never do that. Such practices were reflective of the spiritual abuses taking place in the Corinthian church at that time.

Just as God alone grants faith and repentance, He also grants the ability to confess Jesus as Lord, which He does through His Spirit.

The Spirit exalts and affirms the Lordship of Christ for three reasons:

1. He enables believers to see Christ's glory, majesty, and authority so they might submit to His will.

2. He enables believers to see Christ's purity and righteousness so they will pattern their lives after His.

3. The Spirit exalts and affirms the Lordship of Christ and confirms His deity, messiahship, humanity, and work.

The Holy Spirit glorifies Christ to believers. In a practical sense, Christ becomes increasingly significant and precious to us as we walk in the Spirit and are filled by Him.

Conversely, if we walk in the flesh, we will short-circuit the Spirit's ministry, and Christ will seem less precious. Just how precious Christ is to you shows where you are spiritually.

Further, the Holy Spirit glorifies Christ by displaying His glory through the word and transforming believers into His image. The more we meditate on Christ's beauty and majesty, the more we become like Him. Paul longed to see Christ's glory reflected in every believer (Galatians 4:19). But for that to happen, they had to forsake their attempts to be sanctified by human efforts and return to depending on the Holy Spirit. It is the same for us.

Tests of Jonathan Edwards

In response to the criticisms against the moving of the Holy Spirit in the First Great Awakening, Jonathan Edwards developed tests to determine the genuine movements of the Holy Spirit. Such movements or manifestations are of the Holy Spirit when:

1. an activity is such as to raise the very esteem of Jesus Christ who was born of the Virgin and was crucified (Matthew 10:32; Romans 15:9; 1 Corinthians 12:3; Philippians 2:11; 1 John 4:1–3, 15);

2. such operation is used to shine a light upon the gospel of Christ (Matthew 10:32; Romans 15:9; 1 Corinthians 12:3; Philippians 2:11; 1 John 4:1–3, 15);

3. such operation seems more than anything else to confirm and establish in the minds of people the truth of what the gospel declares to all that Christ is the Son of God and the Savior of men (Matthew 10:32; Romans 15:9; 1 Corinthians 12:3; Philippians 2:11; 1 John 4:1–3, 15);

4. a spirit operates against the interests of Satan's kingdom (1 John 3:8, 4:4−5);

5. a spirit operates in such a manner as to cause in men a greater reward for the Holy Scriptures and establishes these men more soundly in their truth and divinity (Ephesians 2:20; 1 John 4:6);

6. a spirit operates in such a manner as to lead people into the full truth of the fundamentals (1 John 4:1−6);

7. a spirit operates in such a manner as to promote a spirit of love for God and man (1 John 4:6−7);

8. a spirit operates in such a manner as to promote agreement with the Holy Scriptures (1 John 5:5−10);

9. a spirit operates in such a manner as to promote the holiness, greatness, and majesty of God (Luke 1:75; Romans 6:19−22, 8:4, 12:2, 13:8−10; 1 Corinthians 1:8, 7:19, 34; 2 Corinthians 7:1; Galatians 5:14, 6:2; Ephesians 4:24; Philippians 1:11; 1 Thessalonians 3:13, 4:3−7, 5:23; 1 Timothy 2:15; Titus 2:5; Hebrews 12:10−14; 1 Peter 4:6; 1 John 4:1−7, 5:5−10);

10. a spirit causes unusual and extraordinary events and effects upon the lives, minds, and bodies of persons that emphasize the holiness of God, His greatness, and His Majesty (Luke 1:75; Romans 6:19−22, 8:4, 12:2, 13:8−10; 1 Corinthians 1:8, 7:19, 34; 2 Corinthians 7:1; Galatians 5:14, 6:2; Ephesians 4:24; Philippians 1:11; 1 Thessalonians 3:13, 4:3−7, 5:23; 1 Timothy 2:15; Titus 2:5; Hebrews 12:10−14; 1 Peter 4:6; 1 John 4:1−7, 5:5−10). In such cases as these manifestations, people will have an extraordinary conviction of the dreadful nature of sin, a very uncommon sense of the Christian life, extraordinary views of the certainty, and glory of divine things, will be proportionally moved with extraordinary affections of fear, sorrow, desire, love, or joy, and will be changed suddenly with no infringing upon Scripture. Reactions include tears, trembling, groans, loud outcries,

agonies of body, the failing of bodily strength, and what has been known as being "slain in the Spirit." All of this will always be in the realm of God's holiness, His greatness, and His Majesty. [33]

THE END NOTES

Preface

1. John Foxe, *The Acts and Monuments of John Foxem* (London: Pub. by R.B. Seeley, and W. Burnside, sold by L. & G. Seele, 1837–41),7.421.
2. *TBS Quarterly Record*, No. 475, April-June 1981, 3.
3. Johann Griesbach, *Novum Testamentum Graece,* (London: Impensis J. Mackinlay, et Cuthell et Martin, 1806), 3, 561–563.
4. Ibid., pages 428–432.
5. Johann Wettstein, *Novum Testamentum Graecum,* (editionis receptae cum lectionibus variantibus codicum manuscriptis. Amsterdam: Ex Officina Dommeriana, 1752) 2, 330–335 and 721–727.
6. Joseph Thayer, *Thayer's Greek English Lexicon of the New Testament (Grand Rapids, MI: Baker Books, 1977), vii.*
7. Ibid., 287.
8. Gregory Nazianzus, *Oration XXXII: Fifth Theological Oration: On the Holy Spirit.*
9. Theordore Beza, *Novum Testamentum Graecum (Published by Henricus Stephanus,* 1589), 328.
10. Ibid, 466.
11. Brian Waltson, *The Considerator Considered (London: Printed by Tho: Roycroft, and are to be sold at most book sellers shops,* 1659), 88–89.
12. Ibid., 90–94.
13. Arthur Fenton Hort, *Life and Letters of Fenton John Anthony Hort* (London: Macmillan and co., ltd.; New York, Macmillan & co, 1896), 1, 211.
14. Ibid., 1, 117.
15. Ibid., 1, 421.
16. Ibid., 1, 117–121.
17. Ibid., 1, 430.
18. Ibid., 1, 275.
19. Ibid., 1, 400.
20. Ibid., I, 77; Brooke Foss Westcott, *Life and Letters of Brooke Foss Westcott (*London: Macmillan, 1903) 1, 251.
21. Ibid., 2, 69.
22. Ibid., 1, 207.
23. Brooke Foss Westcott, The New Testament in the original Greek: introduction and appendix [to] the text revised by Brooke Foss Westcott and Fenton John Anthony Hort (New York: Harper, 1908), 2, 131.

24. Brooke Foss Westcott, *The Gospel According to St. John* (London: John Murry, Albemarle Street, 1896), 297.

25. Ibid., 16.

26. Ibid., 2, 132, 159.

27. Irenaeus, *Adversus Haereses*, 1. Pro.1.1.

28. Samuel Lee, *A Lexicon, Hebrew, Chaldee, and English: compiled from the most approved sources, Oriental and European, Jewish and Christian: containing all the words with their usual inflexion, idiomatic usages, &c as found in the Hebrew and Chaldee texts of the Old Testament* (London: Duncan and Malcolm, 1840), 90–91.

29. Francis Brown, S. R. Driver, and Charles A Briggs, *The New Brown, Driver, and Briggs Hebrew and English Lexicon* (Baker Book House, 1907), 135.

30. William Gesenius, *Gesenius's Hebrew and Chaldee Lexicon* (Baker Book House, 1979), 138.

31. William Gesenius, *Gesenii Lexicon Manuale Hebraico-Latinum Ordine Alphabetico Digestum (Published by J.-P. Migne,* 1848), 100.

32. E. F. Leopold, *Lexicon Hebraicum Et Chaldaicum: in libros Veteris Testamenti ordine etymologico compositum in usum scholarum (Lipsiae: Sumtibus et typis Caroli Tauchnitii,* 1878), 55.

33. George Benedict Winer, *Lexicon Hebraicum et Chaldacum,* in veteris testamenti libros ordine etymologico descriptum (Publisher Leipzig, Fleischer, 1828), 150.

34. Pagnius (Santes), *Thesaurus Linguae Sanctae ex R. David Kimchi (Ed.* Robert Estienne. Paris: Robert Estienne, 1548).135.

35. Edmund Castell, *Lexicon Heptaglotton, Hebraicum, Chaldaicum, Syriacum, Samaritanum, Aethiopicum, Arabicum, conjunctim; et Persicum, Separatim. Cui accessit Brevis, & Harmonica. quantum fieri potuit Grammaticae, Omnium praecedentium Linguarum Delineatio. Castell, Edmund; Jacobus Golius (Londini [London]: Thomas Roycroft,* 1669. First Edition), 424.

36. Johann Habermann, *Liber Radicum Seu Lexicon Ebraicum* (Published by Wittenberg, Johann Krafft, 1589), 97.

37. Valentin Schinder, *Lexicon pentaglotton, Hebraicum, Chaldaicum, Syriacum, Talmudico-Rabbinicum, & Arabicum (Londini : Excudebat Gulielmus Iones, Prostant apud Cornelium Bee et Laurentium Sadler in vico vulg dicto Little Britaine,* 1612), 239.

38. Johannes Buxtorf, *Lexicon Hebraicum et Chaldaicum* complectens omnes voces ... quae in Sacris Bibliia, hebrae& ex parte caldae lingu scriptis, extant. Interpretationis fide, exemplorum biblicorum copi , locorum plurimorum difficilium ex variis Hebraeorum commentariis explicatione, auctum & illustratum (Londini, typis Jacobi Junii, & Mosis Bell, sumptibus Richardi Whitakeri & Samuelis Cartwright, 1646), 82.

362

39. Pagnius (Santes), *Thesaurus Linguae Sanctae ex R. David Kimchi* (Ed., Robert Estienne. Paris: Robert Estienne, 1548), 977.

40. Edmund Castell, *Lexicon Heptaglotton, Hebraicum, Chaldaicum, Syriacum, Samaritanum, Aethiopicum, Arabicum, conjunctim; et Persicum, Separatim. Cui accessit Brevis, & Harmonica. quantum fieri potuit Grammaticae, Omnium praecedentium Linguarum Delineatio. Castell, Edmund; Jacobus Golius (Londini [London]: Thomas Roycroft, 1669. First Edition)*, 2927–2928.

41. Johann Habermann, *Liber Radicum Seu Lexicon Ebraicum* (Published by Wittenberg, Johann Krafft 1589), 605.

42. Valentin Schinder, *Lexicon Pentaglotton*, Hebraicum, Chaldaicum, Syriacum, Talmudico-Rabbinicum, & Arabicum (Londini: Excudebat Gulielmus Iones, Prostant apud Cornelium Bee et Laurentium Sadler in vico vulg dicto Little Britaine 1612), 1399–1400.

43. Petevius, *Theologicalis Dogmatirus, De Angelis,* (1653) 3:2.

44. Basil, *Hexaemeron,* 2.3.13–23.

45. Samuel Lee, *A Lexicon, Hebrew, Chaldee, and English: compiled from the most approved sources, Oriental and European, Jewish and Christian: containing all the words with their usual inflexion. idiomatic usages, &c as found in the Hebrew and Chaldee texts of the Old Testament* (London: Duncan and Malcolm, 1840). 546.

46. William Gesenius, Gesenius's *Hebrew and Chaldee Lexicon* (Baker Book House, 1979), 752.

47. Francis Brown, S. R. Driver, and Charles A Briggs, *The New Brown, Driver, and Briggs Hebrew and English Lexicon* (Baker Book House, 1907), 912.

48. Johann Habermann, *Liber Radicum* Seu Lexicon Ebraicum (Published by Wittenberg, Johann Krafft, 1589), 722.

49. Edmund Castell, *Lexicon Heptaglotton, Hebraicum, Chaldaicum, Syriacum, Samaritanum, Aethiopicum, Arabicum, conjunctim; et Persicum, Separatim. Cui accessit Brevis, & Harmonica. quantum fieri potuit Grammaticae, Omnium praecedentium Linguarum Delineatio. Castell, Edmund; Jacobus Golius (Londini [London]: Thomas Roycroft, 1669. First Edition)*, 3490.

50. Valentin Schinder, *Lexicon Pentaglotton*, Hebraicum, Chaldaicum, Syriacum, Talmudico-Rabbinicum, & Arabicum (,Londini: Excudebat Gulielmus Iones, Prostant apud Cornelium Bee et Laurentium Sadler in vico vulg dicto Little Britaine, 1612), 1680.

51. Ibid., 1680.

52. William Gesenius, Gesenius's *Hebrew and Chaldee Lexicon* (Baker Book House, 1979), 634.

53. Pagnius (Santes), *Thesaurus Linguae Sanctae ex R. David Kimchi* (Ed. Robert Estienne. Paris: Robert Estienne, 1548), 924.

363

54. Johann Habermann, *Liber Radicum* Seu Lexicon Ebraicum (Published by Wittenberg, Johann Krafft, 1589), 579.

55. Valentin Schinder, *Lexicon Pentaglotton*, Hebraicum, Chaldaicum, Syriacum, Talmudico-Rabbinicum, & Arabicum (Londini: Excudebat Gulielmus Iones, Prostant apud Cornelium Bee et Laurentium Sadler in vico vulg dicto Little Britaine, 1612), 1329.

56. Edmund Castell, Lexicon *Heptaglotton, Hebraicum, Chaldaicum, Syriacum, Samaritanum, Aethiopicum, Arabicum, conjunctim; et Persicum, Separatim. Cui accessit Brevis, & Harmonica. quantum fieri potuit Grammaticae, Omnium praecedentium Linguarum Delineatio. Castell, Edmund; Jacobus Golius (Londini [London]: Thomas Roycroft, 1669. First Edition),* 2774.

57. Johannes Buxtorf, *Lexicon Hebraicum et Chaldaicum complectens omnes voces ... quae in Sacris Bibliia, hebrae& ex parte caldae lingu scriptis, extant. Interpretationis fide, exemplorum biblicorum copi , locorum plurimorum difficilium ex variis Hebraeorum commentariis explicatione, auctum & illustratum* (Londini: typis Jacobi Junii, & Mosis Bell, sumptibus Richardi Whitakeri & Samuelis Cartwright, 1646), 527–528.

58. Bailey, *Homosexuality, and the Western Christian Tradition* (Hamden, Conn.: Archon Books, 1975), 193.

59. Boswell, *Christianity, Social Tolerance and Homosexuality (Chicago; London: University of Chicago Press,* 1980), 341–53.

60. Scroggs, *The New Testament and Homosexuality* (Philadelphia: Fortress Press 1983),109.

61. Martin, *Arsenokoites and Malakos: Meanings and Consequences',* in *Brawley (ed.), Biblical Ethics and Homosexuality: Listening to Scripture* (Louisville, Ky.: Westminster John Knox Press, 1996), 119–120.

62. Scobie, *The Ways of Our God: An approach to biblical theology (Wm. B. Eerdmans Publishing Co,* 2003), 838; Campbell, *Marriage, and Family in the Biblical World (InterVarsity Press,* 2003), 243.

63. Liddell, Scott, Jones, & McKenzie, *A Greek-English Lexicon* (Oxford: Clarendon Press, 1996), 246.

64. Arndt, Danker, & Bauer (eds.), *A Greek-English Lexicon of the New Testament and Other Early Christian Literature (University of Chicago Press.* 2000), 135.

65. Joseph Thayer, *Thayer's Greek English Lexicon of the New Testament,* (Grand Rapids, MI: Baker Books, 1977), 75.

66. Arndt, Danker, & Bauer (eds.), *A Greek-English Lexicon of the New Testament and Other Early Christian Literature* (University of Chicago Press, 2000), 613.

67. Joseph Thayer, *Thayer's Greek English Lexicon of the New Testament,* (Grand Rapids, MI: Baker Books, 1977), 387.

68. J.P. Lange, C.F. Schaff, & D.W. Poor, *A Commentary on the Holy Scriptures (New York: C. Scribner & Co: 1 Corinthians,* 1976) 126.

69. Josephus, *Against Apion,* 2:215.

70. Ps–Lucian, *Forms of Love,* 20.

71. Dio Cassius, *Historiae Romanae,* 79.13.1.

72. Pasor, *Lexicon Graeco-Latinum in Novum Domni Nostri Jesu Christi Testamentum,* (excudebat Edw. Griffin, sumptibus J.K. & S.T. & prostant venales apud Abelem Roper sub signo folis in vico vulgo dicto Fleetstreet, 1644), 455.

73. Edward Leigh, *The Critica Sacra, (London: Printed by James Young for Thomas Underhill.* 1639), 357.

74. Parkhurst, *A Greek and English Lexicon to the New Testament, (London, F.C. & J. Rivington,* 1769), 358.

75. Pasor, *Lexicon Graeco-Latinum in Novum Domni Nostri Jesu Christi Testamentum,* (excudebat Edw. Griffin, sumptibus J.K. & S.T. & prostant venales apud Abelem Roper sub signo folis in vico vulgo dicto Fleetstreet, 1644), 403.

76. Guillaume Bude, *Lexicon Graeco-Latinum* (Venetiis: Aldus Manutius, Romanus, 1532), no page number.

77. Petrus Giles, *Lexicon Graecolatinum (Basileae: ex officina Valentini Curionis,* 1532), no page number.

78. Junius Hadrianus, *Lexicon sive dictionarium Graecolatinum Dictionum, explicationum & allegationum copia uberriumum, omniaca quae alia habent, et multo plura, corrplectens (Basileae: Ex officina Hieronymi Cvrionis ; impensis Heinrichi Petri,* 1532), no page number.

79. Robert Constantinus, *Lexicon Graecolatinum by Robert Constantini* (1592), V. 1, 248.

80. Guillaume Bude, *Lexicon Graeco-Latinum* (Venetii: Aldus Manutius, Romanus, 1532), no page number.

81. Petrus Giles, *Lexicon Graecolatinum (Basileae: ex officina Valentini Curionis,* 1532), no page number.

82. Junius Hadrianus, *Lexicon sive dictionarium Graecolatinum Dictionum, explicationum & allegationum copia uberriumum, omniaca quae alia habent, et multo plura, corrplectens* (Basileae: Ex officina Hieronymi Cvrionis ; impensis Heinrichi Petri, 1532), no page number.

83. Henry Stephanus, *Thesaurus Graecae Linguae,* in quo ... (auctor) vocabula in certas classes distribuit, multipliciderivatorum serie ad primigenia, tanquam ad radices unde pullulant revocata (etc. Cum appendicibus, Stephanus, 1572) 2, 293.

84. Ibid., 2, 799–800.

85. Buxtorf or Joannes Dawson *Lexicon Novi testament Graeci Alphabeticum (Impensis J. F. & C. Rivington, B. Law, G. & T. Wilkie, G. G. J. & J. Robinson, R. Baldwin; et T. Pote, Eton* 1700), 62.

86. Cornelius Schrevelius, *Thesaurus Graecae Linguae,* (Cantabrigiab, Excudebat Johnannes Hayes, Celeberrimae Academiae Typographus, Impensis Geogii Sawbridge, apud quam prostant Venales Londini, Vico, Vulgo Vocato, 1676), no page number.

87. George Babiniotis., *Dictionary of Modern Greek, The Dictionary of Modern Greek (Greek: Λεξικό της Νέας Ελληνικής Γλώσσας, ΛΝΕΓ), more commonly known as Babiniotis Dictionary (Λεξικό Μπαμπινιώτη), is a well-known dictionary of Modern Greek published in Greece by Lexicology Centre and supervised by Greek linguist Georgios Babiniotis,* 338.

88. Ibid., 1165.

89. *The Institute for Modern Greek Studies of the Artistotle University of Thessaloniki, the Dictionary of Standard Modern Greek* (2013), 207.

90. Ibid., 816.

91. Caelius Aurelianus, *On Acute Diseases, and on Chronic Disease, On Chronic Disorders,* 4.9.

92. John Chrysostom, *Homily on Romans 1:24–27 (In epistulam ad Romanos 60.416–422),* AD 400.

93. Ibid, 60.417.

94. Cyprian of Carthage, *Treatises 1.7–9.*

95. St. Epiphanius, *Against Heresies, 26.3, 4, 5, 9.6 and 11.*

96. Seneca the Younger, *Natural Questons,* 1.16.

97. Justin Martyr, *2 Apology 12.*

98. Basil, *Epistulae* 160.3.47–57.

99. Josephus, *Against Apion,* 2:215.

100. Ps–Lucian, *Forms of Love,* 20.

101. Dio Cassius, Historiae *Romanae,* 79.13.1.

102. Seneca the Younger, *Moral Epistles. 95.21.*

Introduction

1. Charles G. Finney, *Decay of Conscience* (The Independent, New York 1873).

2. Winston Churchill, *Speech on War Prospects,* (New York Times, Text of Churchill's Speech on War Prospects, 1940, January 21), 30, column 4.

3. General William Booth, *Founder of The Salvation Army, What is the chief danger, social or political, confronting the new century?* (Christian Budget).

4. Catherine Booth, *Aggressive Christianity (Boston: McDonald & Gill, Office of the Christian Witness,* 1883), 31–32.

5. Zephaniah Swift, *A System of the Laws of the State of Connecticut (Windham: Printed by John Byrne, for the author,* 1796) 2, 309–310, 347–360.

6. Frank Bartleman, *Azusa Street* (Whitaker House, 1973), 43.

7. John Foxe, *Acts and Monuments, The Acts and Monuments of John Foxem* (London: Pub. by R.B. Seeley and W. Burnside, sold by L. & G. Seele, 1837–41), 7. 550.

8. Gregory R. Reid, *Stray Cats and Other Stories* (CreateSpace Independent Publishing Platform, 2017), 37.

Chapter One
The Spirit Of Leviathan

1. Joseph Barber Lightfoot, *Saint Paul's Epistles to the Colossians and to Philemon*, 8th ed., Classic Commentaries on the Greek New Testament (London; New York: Macmillan and Co., 1886), 186.

2. Ibid., 188–189.

3. Ibid., 188–189.

4. Origen, *Contra Celsum*, 1.55.

5. Chrysostom, *In epistulam ad Colossenses*, homily 6; 62.341.1– 62.341.27.

6. Athanasius, *On the Incarnation of the Word*, 25.6.

7. J. Peirce, *A Paraphrase and Notes on Colossians 2* (Printed for J. Noon at the White Hart near Mercers Chapel Cheapside, 1733), 32.

8. Hippolytus in *Matt. 16.8, 12.28; in John 6.53.*

9. Justin Martyr, *Dialogue with Trypho*, 41.

10. Justin Martyr, *Dialogue with Trypho*, 44; *The Second Apology of Justin*, 13.

11. Jerome, *Jerome's Apology for Himself Against the Books of Rufinus*, 2.

12. Athanasius, *Festal Letters, Letter 19.*

13. Gregory Nazianzen, *Orations*, 39.

14. Cyril, *Catechetical Lectures*, 7; Ambrose, *Exposition of the Christian Faith*, 5.2.

15. Gregory the Great, *The Book of Pastoral Rule of Saint Gregory the Great Roman Pontiff to John, Bishop of the City of Ravenna,*

16. Augustine, *On the Psalms 104.*

Chapter Two
The Pythonic Demons

1. Sulpitius Severus, *The Sacred History of Sulpitius Severus*, 1.2–3.

2. Louis Ginzberg, Henrietta Szold, and Paul Radin, *Legends of the Jews*, 2nd ed., (Philadelphia: Jewish Publication Society, 2003), 139.

3. Sarna, Nahum M, *The JPS Torah Commentary*, Genesis (Philadelphia: Jewish Publication Society, 1989), 49.

4. Clement of Alexandria, *Paedagogus* 2.1.15.

5. Philochorus of Athens, *Fragmenta* 3b,328,F.78.5–79.

6. Hesychius of Alexandria, *Lexicon* pi.4315.1; Suidas, *Lexicon*, pi.3140.

7. Tertullian, *De anima*, 28.45.

8. Ibid., 28.57.

9. *Recognitions of Clement*, 4.20.

10. *The Clementine Homilies*, 9.16.

11. *Erotianus grammaticus Fr.*, 21 (ed. E. Nachmann [1918], 105, 19 f.).

12. Plutarch, *De Defectu Oraculorum*, 9.

13. *Linguarum seu dictionum exoletarum Hippocratis explicatio* 19.94.10–11.

14. Clement of Alexandira, *Protrepticus, Exhortation to the Greeks, 2.11.1–3.5.*

15. Jacob Neusner, *The Mishnah: A New Translation* (New Haven, CT: Yale University Press, 1988), 598; Jerusalem Talmud, 7:10G–I.

16. Cicero, *De Divinatione* 1.37.

17. Charles S. Bowen, Delphi, *Considered Locally, Morally, and Politically, The Arnold Prize Essay for 1859*, 12.

18. Ibid., 13–15.

19. Virgil, *Aeneid*, 6.900; John Conington, P. Vergili Maronis Opera. P. Vergili Maronis Opera. *The Works of Virgil, with a Commentary by John Conington*, M.A. Late Corpus Professor of Latin in the University of Oxford, Commentary on Vergil's Aeneid (Medford, MA: Whittaker and Co., Ave Maria Lane, 1876), 538–539; Charles S., Bowen, Delphi, Considered Locally, Morally, and Politically, The Arnold Prize Essay for 1859, 13–15.

20. Diodorus, 16.6–27.

21. Pausanias, *Description of Greece, 10.5.7;* Plutarch, *De Pythiae Oraculis*, 17.

22. Herodotus, *Histories*, 1.46–61.

23. G.H. Pember, *Earth's Earliest Ages, and their Lessons for us: Including a Treatise on Spiritualism* (London: Samuel Bagster and Sons, 16, Paternoster Row, 1854), 238–240.

24. *Received by a Lady, An Angel's Message, Being A Series of Angelic and Holy Communications* (London: John Wesley and Co., 54 Paternoster Row, B.C., 1858).

25. Theodore J. Lewis, *"Ancestor Worship,"* ed. *David Noel Freedman, The Anchor Yale Bible Dictionary* (New York: Doubleday, 1992), 240; Charles A. Kennedy, "Dead, Cult of the," ed. David Noel Freedman, *The Anchor Yale Bible Dictionary* (New York: Doubleday, 1992), 105; Victor Harold Matthews, Mark W. Chavalas, and John H. Walton, *The IVP Bible Background Commentary: Old Testament*, (Downers Grove, IL: InterVarsity Press, 2000), 1 Sa 28:7–11.

26. Homer, *Odyssey*, 11.23–56.

27. Origen, *De Engastrimytho* 6.1–46.

28. Gregory of Nyssa, *Ad Eustathium de sancta Trinitate* 3,1.9.15−16.

29. William Hazlitt, *Martin Luther, the Table Talk*, (London: Bel. &Daldy, York Street, Covent Garden 1872), 250.

30. John Glanvil, *Evidence Concerning Witches and Apparitions* (London, England: Printed for A. L., 1678). 1−60

31. Ibid., 1−60.

32. Ibid., 111.

33. James M. Gray, *Spiritism, and the Fallen angels in the light of the Old and New Testaments* (New York, Chicago, London, and Edinburgh: Fleming H. Revell Company), 1920, 23.

34. Origen, *Contra Celsum*, 7.3.

35. Virgil, *Aeneid*, 6.45−51 (62−67).

36. Vaudeville: *From the Honkytonks to the Palace*, by Joe Laurie, Jr. (Henry Holt and Company, 1953) 321.

37. *Ventriloquism for Fun and Profit by P. Winchell* (Pringle Press, 1751), 30−34, 43.

38. Clement of Alexandria, *Paedagogus*, 2.1.15.

39. Tertullian, *De anima*, 28.45; *De anima*, 28.57.

40. Origen, *Contra Celsum* 1.36.15−26.

41. Gregory Nazianzen, *Apologetica* 35.453−456.

Chapter Three
The Kundalini Demons

1. Jeevartnam, *The Pentecostal Evangel* (Springfield, Missouri: October 20, 1934) 2; Number 1070.

2. Jerone, *Epistulae (letters)*, 108.13.

3. Boyd Seevers and Rachel Korhonen, *"Seals in Ancient Israel and the near East: Their Manufacture, Use, and Apparent Paradox of Pagan Symbolism,"* (The Near East Archaeological Society Bulletin 61 (2016), 10.

4. Josephus, *The Antiquities of the Jews*, 2.12.3.

5. Gideon R Kotz, *"Daughters and Dragons in LXX Lamentations 4:3,"* Journal of Northwest Semitic Languages (Published by the Department of Semitic Languages and Cultures, University of Stellenbosch), 89.40, no. 2 (2014): 160−161.

6. James Henry Breasted, ed., *Ancient Records of Egypt: The Nineteenth Dynasty*, (Chicago: University of Chicago Press, 1906), 3.9.

7. Martin G. Klingbeil, *"Syro-Palestinian Stamp Seals from the Persian Period:* The Iconographic Evidence," Journal of Northwest Semitic Languages 18 (1992): 115.

8. William W. Hallo and K. Lawson Younger, *Context of Scripture* (Leiden; Boston: Brill, 2000), 14−15, 37; Miriam Lichtheim, *Ancient Egyptian*

Literature. Volume II: *The New Kingdom* (Berkeley: University of California Press, 1973–), 14.

9. Florentino García Martínez and Eibert J. C. Tigchelaar, *"The Dead Sea Scrolls Study Edition (translations)"* (Leiden; New York: Brill, 1997–1998), 153.

10. Origen, *De Principiis*, 3.3.3.

11. Janice Hartley & Michael Daniels, *A Grounded Theory investigation into negative Paranormal or Spiritual Experience, based on the 'diabolical mysticism of William James*, Transpersonal Psychology Review, Vol. 12, No. 1, 51–72. (April 2008) [Preprint Version].

12. Amma, Swami Muktananda Paramhansa, *The Saint, and His Mission* (Shree Gurudev Ashram, Ganeshpuri, 1969), 32.

13. Ibid., 33.

14. Ibid., 35.

15. Ibid., 42.

16. Ibid., 55.

17. William James, *The Varieties of Religious Experience: a Study in Human Nature, Being the Gifford Lectures on Natural Religion, Delivered at Edinburgh in 1901–1902* (Longmans, Green, And Co, New York, London, Bombay, Calcutta, and Madras, 1917), 421.

18. Ibid., 421.

19. Romain Rolland, *The Life of Ramakrishna* (Calcutta, India: Advaita Ashrama, trans, from the original French by E.F Malcolm-Smith, 1979), 41.

20. Amma, Swami Muktananda Paramhansa, *The Saint, and His mission* (Shree Gurudev Ashram, Ganeshpuri, 1969), 55.

21. Walter Martin, *The New Age Cult*, (Minneapolis: Bethany House Publishers, 1989), 13.

22. Fritz Ridenour, *So What's the Difference?* (Ventura, Calif.: Regal Books, revised edition, 2001), 91.

23. John Ankerberg and John Weldon, *The Facts on Hinduism in America* (Chattanooga, TN: ATRI Publishing, 2011), 7.

Chapter Four
The Baalim And Astartes

1. George Stanley Faber, *The Origin of Pagan Idolatry* (London: Printed by A.J. Valpy for F. and C. Rivingtons, 1816), 1.25–26; 3.73, 93.

2. Ibid., 1.25–26; 3.73, 93.

3. Sir Walter Raleigh, *The History of the World in Five Books* (Printed for Tho. Basset, Ric. Chiswell, Benj. Tooke, Tho. Passenger, Geo Dawes, Tho. Sambridge, M Wotton, and G Conyers, London, 1687), 115.

4. Augustine, *On Christian Doctrine* 2.20.

5. Saint Thomas Aquinas, *Summa Theologica, Editio altera Romana.* (Romae: Forzani et Sodalis, 1894), II-II q.178 a.2 ad 3.

6. Willem Berends, *"The Biblical Criteria for Demon-Possession,"* in *The Westminister Theological Journal*, 37, no. 3 (spring 1975): 342; R. H. Robbins, *The Encyclopedia of Witchcraft and Demonology* (New York: Crown Publishers, 1959), 395.

7. Augustine, *De Ciutate Dei*, 15.23.

8. Tertullian, *Scorpiace*, 3.

9. Eusebius Pamphius, *The Church History of Eusebius*, 8.12.4.

10. Jerome, *The Life of St. Hilary, Vita Sancti Hilarionis*, 80.

11. Francessco Maria Guaxzzo, *Compendium Maleficarum*, (Mediolani, Apud Haeredes August. Tradati, 1608, London) 34.

12. Edward F. Murphy, *Handbook for Spiritual Warfare* (Nashville: Thomas Nelson, 1996), 225.

13. R. W. L. Moberly, *At the Mountain of God: Story and Theology in Exodus 32–34, vol. 22, Journal for the Study of the Old Testament Supplement Series (Sheffield: JSOT Press, 1983)*, 46.

14. Louis Ginzberg, Henrietta Szold, and Paul Radin, *Legends of the Jews*, 2nd ed. (Philadelphia: Jewish Publication Society, 2003), 621.

15. *Constitutions of the Holy Apostles*, 6.4.

16. Louis Ginzberg, Henrietta Szold, and Paul Radin, *Legends of the Jews*, 2nd ed. (Philadelphia: Jewish Publication Society, 2003), 621.

17. J. Neusner (2008). *The Jerusalem Talmud: A Translation and Commentary, (Hendrickson Publishers), Sanhedrin 10:28b.*

18. Louis Ginzberg, Henrietta Szold, and Paul Radin, *Legends of the Jews*, 2nd ed. (Philadelphia: Jewish Publication Society, 2003), 620–621.

19. Clement of Alexandria, *Stromata*, 3.4.27.5.–28.1.

20. Tertullian, *De Idololatria* 1.

21. Ibid., *Idololatria* 1.

22. George Stanley Faber, *The Origin of Pagan Idolatry* (London: Printed by A.J. Valpy for F. and C. Rivingtons, 1816), 1.25.

23. Irenaeus, *Irenaeus Against Heresies, 4.26.*

24. Tertullian, Scorpiace, 3.

25. Ibid., *De Jejunio*, 6.

26. *Gerald* Friedlander, *Pirke De Rabbi Eliezer, The Chapters of Rabbi Eliezer the Great*, (London: Kegan Paul, Trench, Trubner & Co. LTD. New York: The Bloch Publishing Company, 1916), 356; Louis Ginzberg, Henrietta Szold, and Paul Radin, Legends of the Jews, 2nd ed. (Philadelphia: Jewish Publication Society, 2003), 621.

27. *Wisdom of Solomon, 12:3–7.*

28. Philo, *On the Life of Moses. 1* 295–305.

29. Tertullian, *Scorpiace*, 3.

30. Cyril of Alexandria, *Commentaries on Hosea*, 4:12—14.

31. Strabo, *Geography*, 17.1.46.43—48.

32. Oriphica, *Hymni*, 55.2.

33. Homer, *Hymn* 10.

34. Strabo, *The Geography of Strabo*, 8.6.20.

35. Herodotus, *Histories*, 2.64.

36. Clement of Alexandria, *Stromateis*, 1.16.74.1—3.2.

37. Quintus Curtius Rufus, Historiarum Alexandri Magni Macedonis Libri Qui Supersunt, 5.1.36—39.

38. Strabo, *The Geography of Strabo*, 11.14.16—9.

39. Athenagoras, *Adv. Graecos*, 27.

40. Marcus Junianus Justinus Frontinus, *Epitome of the Philippic History of Pompeius Trogus*, 18.5.

41. Herodotus, *Histories*, 1.199.

42. Ibid., 1.196.

43. Marcus Junianus Justinus Frontinus, *Epitome of the Philippic History of Pompeius Trogus*, 21.3.

44. Strabo, *The Geography of Strabo*, 11.16.

45. Herodotus, *Histories*, 4.172; Diodorus Siculus, 5.18.

46. Athanasius, *Against the Gentiles*, 26.

47. Eusebius, *Vita Constantini*, 3.55.

48. Caelius Aurelianus, *On Acute Diseases, and on Chronic Disease* 4.9; John Chrysostom, *Homily on Romans 1:24—27 (In epistulam ad Romanos)*, *60.416—422;* 60.417; Cyprian of Carthage, *Treatises 1.7—9; Epiphanius, Against Heresies, 26.3, 4, 5, 9.6 and 11; Seneca the Younger, Natural Questions, 1.16.*

49. *The Epistle of Maria the Proselyte to Ignatius*, 4.

50. Maimonides, *Laws of the Foundations of the Torah 7:6 (Principles of Faith 13).*

51. Thomas Reverend Stackhouse, *A New History of the Holy Bible* (Glasgow: J. Galbraith, 1718), 1.xxxvii.

52. Claude Fleury, *The Manners of the Ancient Israelites* (N. Bangs and J. Emory 1809), 155.

53. Origen, *Contra Celsum*, 7.7.1—18.

54. Claude Fleury, *The Manners of the Ancient Israelites* (N. Bangs and J. Emory 1809), 154.

55. *Lives of the Prophets*, 2.1.

56. Claude Fleury, The Manners of the Ancient Israelites, (N. Bangs and J. Emory 1809), 154.

57. Ibid., 153.

58. Ibid., 153.

59. Cyril of Alexandria, *Commentaries on Hosea*, 4:12—14.

Chapter Five
Teach Me To Pray

1. John Owen, *The Works of John Owen* (London, England: W. H. Goold, Ed. Edinburgh: T&T Clark, 1862), 6.446.
2. J. Calvin & J. Pringle, *Commentaries on the Epistles of Paul the Apostle to the Corinthians* (Wheaton, Illinois: Crossway Books, 1999), 1.210–211.
3. Charles Hodge, *Commentary on the Epistle to the First Corinthians* (Wheaton, Illinois: Crossway Books, 1995), 104.
4. Tertullian, On Prayer 29.
5. L. Ginzberg, H. Szold, & P. Radin, *Legends of the Jews* (Philadelphia, Pennsylvania: Jewish Publication Society, 2003), 621; Sanhedrin 10:28b.
6. Roy B. Zuck, *The Speaker's Quote Book* (Grand Rapids, Michigan: Kregel Publications Inc., 1997), 298.
7. P. L. Tan, *Encyclopedia of 7700 Illustrations: Signs of the Times* (Garland, Texas: Bible Communications, Inc., 1997), 1052.
8. Leslie K. Tarr, *Christian History Magazine—Issue 1*: "A Prayer Meeting that lasted 100 Years."
9. Harry E. Bowley, *Assemblies of God Heritage*, Volume 2, No. 2, Summer (Springfield, Missouri: 1982), 1 and 3.
10. Mark Water, *The New Encyclopedia of Christian Quotations* (Alresford, Hampshire: John Hunt Publishing Ltd., 2000), 766.
11. Leonard Ravenhill, *"Have we no Tears for Revival?"* Sermon.
12. Mark Water, *The New Encyclopedia of Christian Quotations* (Alresford, Hampshire: John Hunt Publishing Ltd., 2000), 519.
13. Leonard Ravenhill, *Why Revival Tarries* (Eastbourne, England: Kingsway Publications, 1959), 7.
14. Randy C Alcon, *The Law of Rewards: Giving What You Can't Keep to Gain What You Can't Lose* (Carol Stream, Illinois: Tyndale Momentum, 2003), 18.
15. Charles Finney, *Lectures to Professing Christians* (New York, New York: Fleming H. Revell Company, 1837), 75.
16. Mark Water, *The New Encyclopedia of Christian Quotations* (Alresford, Hampshire: John Hunt Publishing Ltd, 2000), 777.
17. Ibid., 1032.
18. Charles Finney, *Memoirs of Rev. Charles G. Finney* (New York, New York: Fleming H. Revell Company, 1876), 122–123.
19. Kenneth E. Hagin, *Praying to Get Results* (Tulsa, Oklahoma: Kenneth Hagin Ministries, Inc., 1990), 14.
20. Mark Water, *The New Encyclopedia of Christian Quotations* (Alresford, Hampshire: John Hunt Publishing Ltd., 2000), 104.
21. Ibid., 107.

22. Kenneth S Wuest, *Word Studies in the Greek New Testament* (Grand Rapids, Michigan: Eerdmans, 1953), 6.233.

Chapter Six
Prayer And Trials

1. Luther, M., *Luther's works* (Saint Louis, Missouri: Concordia Publishing House, 1972), 24.383.

2. Luther, *Large Catechism, The Lord's Prayer, Book of Concord* (Saint Louis, Missouri: Concordia Publishing House, 2005), 422–423.

3. Ibid., 415–416.

Chapter Seven
Warfare And Intercession

1. W. Gurnall, & J. Campbell, *The Christian in Complete Armour* (London, England: Thomas Tegg, 1845), 731.

2. Walter Martin, "*Curtains for Walter Martin and Doug Clark at TBN,*" 1985, YouTube video, 24:50 https://youtu.be/wYviYC5f_6Q.

3. Walter Martin Quotes. BrainyQuote.com, Brainy Media Inc, 2020. ttps://www.brainyquote.com/quotes/walter_martin_306426, accessed June 3, 2020.

4. Walter Martin Quotes. BrainyQuote.com, Brainy Media Inc, 2020. https://www.brainyquote.com/quotes/walter_martin_306412, accessed June 3, 2020.

5. Marc R. Forster, *Piety and Family in Early Modern Europe*: Essays in Honour of Steven Ozment (Milton Park, Abingdon-on-Thames, Oxfordshire, United Kingdom: Routledge, 2005), 90–91.

6. Origen, *Homilies on Joshua*, 15.1–2.

7. Origen, *Homilies on Joshua*, 14.1.

8. Ignatius, *Ignatius to Polycarp*, 2.

9. Edward Longstreth, *Decisive Battles of the Bible* (Philadelphia, Pennsylvania: J.P. Lippincott, 1962), 16–17.

10. Ibid., 7.

11. Edward Longstreth, *Decisive Battles of the Bible* (Philadelphia, Pennsylvania: J.P. Lippincott, 1962); Boyd Seevers, *Warfare in the Old Testament* (Grand Rapids, Michigan: Kregel Academic, 2013); Stephen Leston, *Illustrated Guide to Bible Battles* (Uhrichsville, Ohio: Barbour Publishing Inc., 2014); Brenda Lewis, *Battles of the Bible* (New York, New York: Chartwell Books, Inc., 2009).

12. Elizabeth Alves, *Becoming a Prayer Warrior* (Ventura, California: Regal Books, 1998), 23.

13. William T. Ellis, *Assemblies of God Heritage*, Volume 2, No 4, Winter (Springfield, Missouri: 1982–1983), 1.

14. Tertullian, *Apology*, 39.

15. William T. Ellis, *Assemblies of God Heritage*, Volume 2, No 4, Winter (Springfield, Missouri: 1982–1983), 1 and 5.

16. John Cassian, *The Institutes of the Coenobia*, 5:12–18.

17. Ramsay Macmullen, *Christianizing the Roman Empire* (New Haven, Connecticut: Yale University Press, 1984), 28.

18. Charles Hodge, *Commentary on the Epistle to the Romans* (Wheaton, Illinois: Crossway Books, 1995), 395.

19. Peter Cartwright, *The Autobiography of Peter Cartwright*, The Backwoods Preacher (Cincinnati, Ohio: Swormstedt & A. Foe, 1859), 102.

20. Ibid., 275.

21. Ibid., 221–223.

22. John Wesley, *The Works of John Wesley* (London, England: Wesleyan Methodist Book Room, 1872), 11:429.

23. Smith Wigglesworth, *The Secret of His Power* (Tulsa, Oklahoma: Harrison House Inc., 1982), 29–30.

24. Ibid., 32.

25. Ibid., 33.

26. Ibid., 33.

27. Augustine, *The City of God*, 22.9.

28. Jonathan Edwards, *The Works of Jonathan Edwards* (Carlisle, Pennsylvania: Banner of Truth Trust, 1834), 2.261.

29. Dave Hunt, *"Beyond Seduction: A Return to Biblical Christianity"*, (Eugene, Oregon: Harvest House, 1987), 260.

30. Jonathan Edwards, *The Works of Jonathan Edwards* (Carlisle, Pennsylvania: Banner of Truth Trust, 1834), 2.261.

31. Ibid., 2.261.

32. Derek Prince, *Protection from Deception* (Whitaker House, New Kennington, 2009), 39.

33. Jonathan Edwards, *The Works of Jonathan Edwards* (Carlisle, Pennsylvania: Banner of Truth Trust,1834), 2:261.

www.ingramcontent.com/pod-product-compliance
Lightning Source LLC
Chambersburg PA
CBHW061548120626
46550CB00004B/1404